How the Russians Read the French

How the Russians Read the French

Lermontov, Dostoevsky, Tolstoy

Priscilla Meyer

THE UNIVERSITY OF WISCONSIN PRESS

This book was originally published with
the support of a publication assistance grant from
Wesleyan University.

The University of Wisconsin Press
1930 Monroe Street, 3rd Floor
Madison, Wisconsin 53711-2059
uwpress.wisc.edu

3 Henrietta Street
London WC2E 8LU, England
eurospanbookstore.com

5 4 3 2

Printed in the United States of America

Library of Congress Cataloging-in-Publication Data
Meyer, Priscilla.
How the Russians read the French : Lermontov, Dostoevsky, Tolstoy /
Priscilla Meyer.
p. cm.
Includes bibliographical references and index.
ISBN 978-0-299-22930-6 (cloth: alk. paper)
1. Russian literature—19th century—French influences. 2. Lermontov, Mikhail IUr'evich, 1814–1841—Criticism and interpretation. 3. Dostoyevsky, Fyodor, 1821–1881—Criticism and interpretation. 4. Tolstoy, Leo, graf, 1828–1910—Criticism and interpretation. I. Title.
PG2981.F5M49 2008
891.73′3—dc22
2008012316

ISBN 978-0-299-22934-4 (pbk.: alk. paper)

FOR

BILL

. . . a (scholarly!) study of how writers (Schiller, George Sand) influenced Russia and to what extent would be an extraordinary and serious undertaking . . . the history of the reincarnation of an idea into another idea.

Fyodor Dostoevsky, 1876

Contents

Illustrations

Acknowledgments

This book was inspired decades ago by my then-colleague in the Romance languages department, Michael Danahy. We cotaught a course on the French and Russian novel, which has continued to develop over the years with the help of Wesleyan students. Several wonderful colleagues who have written on related subjects generously read my drafts and led me to new insights. I am particularly grateful to Michael Armstrong Roche, Vladimir Golstein, Gary Kern, Robin Feuer Miller, and David Powelstock for their knowledge, thoughtfulness, and careful commentary. Many others have helped me in a variety of invaluable ways—Yaron Aronowicz, Evgenii Belodubrovsky, Nicholas Beauchamp, Ron Cameron, Jenefer Coates, Marianna Tax Choldin, Robert Conn, Neil Cornwell, Andrew Curran, June Pachuta Farris, James Gubbins, Reverend John Hall, Vera Milchina, Maria Nankova, Tatyana Nikiforova, Donald Rayfield, Ashraf Rushdy, Ralph Savarese, Alexander Schenker, Bronwyn Wallace, Kate Wolfe, and Andrei Zorin have read drafts, contributed insights, provided technical assistance, and/or given bibliographic aid. Sheila Moermond was an attentive and punctilious editor. Liza Knapp's astute and learned reader's report was an excellent guide to the revision process. My biggest debt is to my treasured colleague Susanne Fusso, who read the entire manuscript, much of it more than once, with her usual care, precision, and insight.

Wesleyan University's liberal sabbatical policy and research grants have been an essential boon, allowing me to spend months on end exploring the British Library's marvelous collection of French and Russian literature. Wesleyan's remarkable students of several generations have lent me their enthusiasm and given me their insights.

My husband and daughter, William and Rachel Trousdale, provided years of invaluable editorial and culinary aid.

I am grateful to the following publications for permission to publish segments of this book that have appeared in earlier versions:

"Lermontov's Reading of Pushkin: *The Tales of Belkin* and *A Hero of Our Time*," in *The Golden Age of Russian Literature and Thought*, ed. Derek Offord (Basingstoke: Macmillan, 1992), 58–75. Reproduced by permission of Palgrave Macmillan.

"*Anna Karenina*: Tolstoy's Polemic with Flaubert's *Madame Bovary*," *Russian Review* 54, no. 2 (April 1995): 243–59; in Russian, *Znanie—sila* 11 (1994): 98–102.

"Dostoevsky's Modern Gospel: *Crime and Punishment* and the Gospel of John," *Dostoevsky Studies* 2, no. 1 (1998): 69–79.

"*Crime and Punishment* and Jules Janin's *La Confession*," *Russian Review* 58 (April 1999): 234–43.

"An Author of His Time: Lermontov Rewrites George Sand," *Festschrift to Honor Arnold J. McMillin*, ed. Irene Zohrab, *New Zealand Slavonic Journal* 36 (2002): 173–82.

"Petersburg's Vasisdas: The *Revue étrangère*," *Zapiski russkoi akademicheskoi gruppy v SShA / Transactions of the Association of Russian-American Scholars* 33 (2004): 67–80.

"*Anna Karenina*, Rousseau, and the Gospels," *Russian Review* 66, no. 2 (April 2007): 204–19.

A Note on Transliteration and Translation

I have followed the custom of using the nonspecialist transliteration in the text and the Library of Congress system in the footnotes (e.g., Dostoevsky and Dostoevskii, respectively). All unattributed translations are mine.

How the Russians Read the French

Introduction

The Russians and the French

A nation is a soul, a spiritual principle.
Ernest Renan, *Discours et conferences*

The heroes of French literature create the formulas for the Russian reader's self-expression.
Yury Lotman, "Russkaia literatura na frantsuzskom iazyke"

We can't blindly imitate the French.
P. A. Plavil'shchikov, "Teatr"

Europe and her destiny *will be completed by Russia.*
Fyodor Dostoevsky, letter to Apollon Maikov

The nineteenth-century Russian novel has a philosophical depth and moral power that distinguishes it from its European peers. Where does this come from and can it be located? Russian censorship constrained the discussion of political and philosophical questions in expository prose, so that the issues had to appear in disguised form in fiction, but that is only part of the answer; Russian authors eluded these restrictions by emphasizing the universal in their novels and doing so at an earlier stage of the desacralization of literature than their Western counterparts. They did this in dialogue with Europe.

Nineteenth-century Russian writers, like many others of the period, were quite consciously creating a new national literature. Literate Russians who lived in an imitation European subculture were painfully aware that the level of Russian culture was far lower than that of

Western Europe and saw themselves self-consciously through Western European eyes, at once admiring Europe and feeling inferior to it; they suffered from the disease of "France," whose language and culture had shaped the world of the Russian aristocracy from the time of Catherine the Great.[1] Germany was going through a similar process at the same time; the Germans, too, strove to surpass French culture, to attain "a release from the hegemony of French literature," in order to construct their own national identity.[2]

The Russian arts had openly imitated the European throughout the eighteenth century, a rich subject that will go unexamined here. Perhaps because Russian critics have wanted to see their tradition as having finally achieved independence from Europe by the middle of the nineteenth century, few have investigated the effects of French literature on the great Russian novel.[3] Since the two monumental volumes of *Literaturnoe nasledstvo* published in 1937–39, Yury Lotman has contributed the most important theoretical and historical studies of the effects of the French tradition in Russia.[4] He has discussed Russian literature written in French from 1730 to 1830, reaffirming that "until the middle of the nineteenth century, the French language was the bridge for the movement of ideas and cultural values from Europe into Russia."[5] As we shall see, it continued to bridge the two cultures well into the 1870s, in *Anna Karenina*.

Lotman's theory of interacting cultures explores how a foreign text becomes essential for the creative growth of one's own: Russians view the foreign cultural world through the lens of their own national self-image and create a construct of the West in contrast with Russia's own dominant codes, a process that is inevitably dialectical.[6] When in 1778 Denis Fonvizin writes of the French that "money is their divinity" and "amusement the sole object of their desires," he is implicitly opposing their "inexpressible moral degradation" to Russia's high religious morality.[7] This cultural self-perception underlies the method of composition I propose to analyze.

National consciousness is notoriously difficult to define, yet, as Hugh Seton-Watson says, it nonetheless exists.[8] In Russia the sudden importation of Western European culture and technology under Peter the Great was the impetus for a growing national self-awareness in which admiration of Western Europe conflicted with the desire to feel pride in Russia. The replacement of things Russian by things European penetrated the countryside; Peter's 1722 decree that houses face outward along a linear street altered the traditional circular settlement.[9] The continued presence of privileged German advisers under subsequent tsars led to a reaction against all things foreign—"German" dress, coffee, tea, tobacco—and to the identification of foreignness with deceit and corruption.[10] The German Tsarina Catherine, in attempting to avoid the reaction to her predecessor, the German Tsarina Anna, fostered the emergence of an official nationalism, praising the Russian national character in order to create loyalty to herself.

The period of German regents, ministers, and officers appointed by Tsarina Elizabeth was followed by one of French fashions, books, manners, and language. To be distinguished at court or society, one had to speak French and master French manners; dancing, drawing, and fencing became as important as knowledge of mathematics, history, and military affairs had been. The importation of French luxuries—wines, perfumes, clothing, furniture—and French purveyors of style—dancing masters, hairdressers—meant that French culture pervaded the life of the gentry. This soon begot a reaction. As one contemporary put it, "The way people walk has improved since they learned how to dance from the damn foreigners. . . . But that imparts neither morality nor convictions. The one comes from the heart and the understanding, and the other from the legs."[11] The playwrights of the second half of the eighteenth century satirized the superficiality of French manners and their adoption by the Russian gentry. Hans Rogger details how Francomania was the focus of the plays of Sumarokov, Khemnitser, Kantemir, Kniazhnin (*Misfortune from a Carriage,* 1779), Khvostov (*The Russian Parisian,* 1783), Novikov, Fonvizin, and others.[12] In the letter quoted above, Fonvizin, who spent 1777–78 in France, contributed to the formulation of Russia's vision of the French by characterizing them as a product of the cold rationalism of the Enlightenment, with a brilliant exterior but no content; the intelligentsia was selfish, haughty, greedy, and had replaced religion with materialism. He contrasts the vanity and pomp of French sophisticated cosmopolitan society with its opposite, to be found in provincial Russia, and concludes—ironically, in French: "Nous commençons et ils finissent."[13] The eighteenth century began by assimilating French culture into Russian manners and literature and, with the help of European Romantic quests for national identity, ended by asserting the value of Russian culture: the publication of the six-volume Academy dictionary from 1789–94, books of Russian folk songs and mythology, and Nikolai Karamzin's *Pantheon of Russian Writers* (1800) and *History of Russia* (1811) set out Russia's native resources and became the basis for the call to make Western elements truly national, with

Russian content; as Admiral Shishkov put it, "If we don't stop thinking in French, then we shall always lie, and lie in our own language."[14]

In his edition to Karamzin's *Letters of a Russian Traveler*, Andrew Kahn describes the Enlightenment of Catherine's Russia as "poised between the incomplete conversion from a culture dominated by religion to secular values," a product of "the erratic telescoping of generations of Western literature and aesthetic change into several decades."[15] His characterization can be extended throughout the nineteenth century. Russia recognized that it was behind Western European development in every way. Linguistically: Russia, not being Latin-based, had missed the humanist revival of antiquity, so that it was only in the 1830s, when Pushkin, with the help of French and Italian, created a flexible modern language close to spoken Russian and devoid of Old Church Slavonic diction and syntax, that the language became suitable for literary prose. Culturally: Lermontov published the first Russian modern novel in 1840, a hundred years later than the genre appeared in England and France. Politically: Russia remained monarchical, dynastic, after the French and English had created parliaments. And historically: it was feudal, until the liberation of the serfs in 1861, and relatively unindustrialized. While, in Benedict Anderson's terminology, Western Europe was becoming increasingly a modern, legal, lateral society, Russia remained high-centered. At its apex it had a tsar whose authority derived from divinity, not from the population, a system that had been in decline in Europe since the seventeenth century.[16] Russian thinkers consequently saw themselves as marginalized, spurned by Europe and indeed by their own intelligentsia. The conflict between loyalty to their motherland and awareness of their own belatedness led Russians to defend the values of the old system by defining the new Western European ones as decadent. The essential virtue of Russian otherness was its Orthodox Christianity, held to be best embodied in the peasantry that had not been corrupted by exposure to Western Europe.

The readings here suggest that the depth we sense in the greatest Russian novels is the result of this intense, ambivalent dialogue with the European tradition. This dialectical process demands a self-definition that Russians base, especially after the end of the Romantic period, in biblical texts whose images and intonations they had been imbibing in visual, written, and oral form for hundreds of years. Adrian Hastings calls the Bible "Europe's primary textbook," the mirror through which the ideal of a nation state was originally imagined.[17] But by the mid-nineteenth century, the serious (non-ironic) use of biblical imagery was rare in Western European fiction, while in Russia the New Testament provided a mythic dimension to the novel that conveys an eternal aspect beneath the illusion of immediate reality.[18] Biblical texts became the locus of Russia's specialness because of her Orthodoxy; from the Russian point of view, the West had lost its spirituality because it was Roman Catholic, a religion Russians considered legalistic in the Roman tradition, an unduly secular, rational approach to the divine. To this the Slavophils in particular, but others as well, opposed the more mystical, intuitive faith of Eastern Christianity.

Lermontov, Dostoevsky, and Tolstoy grew up reading French literature in the original. In their novels, they pit works of French literature against countertexts that refute the value system of the French texts. Lermontov elects Pushkin, both his life and his art, as the embodiment of his ideal; for both Dostoevsky and Tolstoy Pushkin's art provides the aesthetic ideal, whereas the moral aspect of the ideal is contained chiefly in the Gospels. The Russian authors establish the opposition between French values and the ideal in order to arrive at a genuinely Russian synthesis. Their contemporaries define genuineness negatively: as *not* an imitation of European literary models or mores.[19] The three novels discussed in this book at once create and are created out of a deeply national culture, using its language (Slavic roots and words, not Gallicisms), genres (folk poetic forms, not alexandrines), places (Petersburg, not Paris) and subject matter (a moral-philosophical quest, not sensational entertainment).

A Hero of Our Time, Crime and Punishment, and *Anna Karenina* use French subtexts according to a dialectical pattern. The thesis (French texts) is countered by an antithesis (text[s] containing cherished values), and this opposition is suspended in a synthesis, in the Schellingian sense: only in a work of art can an opposition remain in tension without being resolved.[20] That synthesis is the Russian work of art that gains a kind of moiré shimmer from the tension between the French material and the Russian author's refutation of it: you can look at the work from either angle but can never entirely dissolve one pattern in the other; the movement between oppositions prevents a static vision of the whole.

Subtext studies (a way of examining "what goes into and what comes out of a . . . creative mind," as Robert Belknap puts it) have the virtue of providing a verifiable point of access to both the creative process and its reception.[21] The French texts underlying the great Russian novels form a coherent body of subtexts we can know to have been shared by writers and readers; by identifying them we may better participate in the conversation about French prose among the Russian novelists and their contemporaries. At the same time as the earlier (French) text reveals and explicates the later (Russian) text's argument, it gains a coherent reading that projects it into a new meaningfulness. The new reading provided by refraction through these novels allows the earlier text to take part in a dialogue, despite its priority: we understand the French work differently after reading it through the Russian writer's eyes.

To discuss this process of cultural synthesis, we need to define the term "subtext" as it will be used here. It is to be distinguished from a "source," which implies a borrowing that remains intact, undisputed by the text it inspires, as was often the case with the more imitative work of the Russian eighteenth century. An author may transfer a plot to Russia from France, but may do so without the intent of commenting on the French text, only changing the names, as parodied by Pushkin in *Eugene Onegin* when Monsieur Triquet transposes "Tatyana" for "la belle Nina." An author uses a source intending no tension between the French original and its Russian transposition.

The term "subtext" is also to be distinguished from "intertext." While there is a clear intersection between the two concepts, inasmuch as both involve the creative response of a later text to an earlier one, studies of intertextuality in the tradition of Julia Kristeva have emphasized the indeterminacy of the text, all texts, due to the degree to which they are, largely unconsciously, made up of and determined by a wealth of other texts. Thus a great range of interpretation of the text is opened up quite independently of authorial intent, demonstrating the intentional fallacy. The analysis in this book demonstrates clear authorial purpose by using precise verbal details in relation to plot, characterization, structure, and theme that support an argument for the use of a given prose subtext in the same way as the Russian scholar Kiril Taranovsky argues for the presence of poetic subtexts in the work of Osip Mandel'stam. Verbal echoes occur in prose as readily as in poetry.[22] The word "intertext" has been used to designate what I am calling subtext ("the intertextual attitude is . . . a critical attitude, and that is what defines it"), but will here be used only in the sense identified by Michael Riffaterre, to designate the entire complex of a real world, physical and cultural—"France" and "the French"—to distinguish an author's invocation of a shared cultural reference from references to specific texts.[23] Of course a French subtext will invoke the whole general intertext of France, and this intertext encompasses French literary texts, but the distinction is clear, just as a subtext is in some sense a source, but a source that has been fully analyzed, commentated, and parodied by the author.

As T. S. Eliot wrote, "every nation has not only its own creative, but its own critical turn of mind."[24] Eliot was among the first to discuss the presence of past texts in present ones and their role in the creation of a national tradition. Because the modern Russian novel developed much later than the Western European one, its growth was extraordinarily condensed—a mere forty-nine years separate Pushkin's completion of *Eugene Onegin* (1831) from Dostoevsky's publication of *The Brothers Karamazov* (1880). This compression led to an unusually explicit dialogue between generations of Russian writers, whose underlying subject is the nature of literary creation: Pushkin discusses prosody, diction, genre, and stylistics with his contemporaries in *Onegin*; Lermontov imitates and responds to Pushkin in his poetry and prose; Dostoevsky answers Gogol's poor-clerk tales in the 1840s and the socialist thought of Turgenev and Chernyshevsky in his later novels. Perhaps conditioned by this tightly interrelated tradition, Taranovsky made this kind of dialogue among texts the focus of his study of Mandelstam's densely allusive poetry. He calls the past texts that create meanings in the poems "subtexts," texts that underlie the present one he examines. The parallels between Mandelstam's poems and the subtexts he uses are so explicit that there is little question that they are conscious references. In this book, too, we will consider the highly intentional choice of subtexts; the reference points to the French subtexts are subtle but clear and the Russian polemic with each consistent, leading to a coherent reading of both parts of the dialogue. We will interpret this process in three landmark novels of the nineteenth century, *A Hero of Our Time, Crime and Punishment*, and *Anna Karenina*.

Taranovsky defines a subtext as "an already existing text (or texts) reflected in a new one," of which he identifies four kinds:

1. That which serves as a simple impulse for the creation of an image.
2. Borrowing of a rhythmic feature and the sounds contained therein.
3. The text which supports or reveals the poetic message of a later text.
4. The text which is treated polemically by the poet.[25]

He points out that types 3 and 4 may be blended, and possibly combined with 2. All four aspects play a role in our analysis of the three novels.

Taranovsky also speaks of context, which he defines as "a set of texts containing the same or a similar image." The definition can include a shared theme, here, for example, a set of texts about adultery. Within these sets of subtexts, we can identify what Omry Ronen calls a dominant subtext, one that "subordinates and organizes thematically the rest of a poem's subtexts," one whose relationship is frequently thematic, and "not represented in the poem by an actual, readily identifiable quotation."[26] In each of the three novels discussed here, two sets of subtexts are set in opposition; a dominant one can sometimes be identified within the French set. For example, in *Anna Karenina* the dominant subtext among several that describe an adulteress is *Madame Bovary*.

The French subtexts, drawn from written sources, further function as a metonymy for France itself, its language, culture, and moeurs. The Russian novels conduct an implicit dialogue with French cultural reality as well as with its literature. An example of Michael Riffaterre's (and the Tartu structuralist school's) use of the word "intertext" to refer to the reality implied by the literal (mimetic) level of the fictional work is Toporov's treatment of the Petersburg myth, and the numerous allusions to Russian literature that represent it, as an intertext in his analysis of *Crime and Punishment*.[27] We can speak not only of literary texts but also of France itself, particularly but not exclusively France of the nineteenth century, as an important intertext for the small group of literate Russians in the nineteenth century.

France functions as an intertext for Russian writers both as cultural context and as literary tradition, two overlapping categories. As cultural intertext, the French material serves several purposes. It provides the reality of aspects of life—prostitution, homosexuality, criminality, divorce, the loss of religious faith, the "woman question"—that, due to censorship, could not be described in detail even in a fictional work in Russian, but that writers could count on their readers to be familiar with through their reading of French journals and novels. Thus the very thematics of the realist novels are the "ungrammaticalities," the "trace" of an intertext, the telltale bump under the carpet that are the connectives pointing the reader to the French intertext, in life and in art.[28] Lermontov's *A Hero of Our Time* is about the theme of the Romantic hero, framed in dialogue with a long line of French (as well as English and German, inasmuch as Romanticism is a European phenomenon) embodiments. Dostoevsky's depiction of the Petersburg poor in *Crime and Punishment* goes far beyond the conventional Russian naturalist tales of the 1830s and 1840s in rendering the horrors that can be visualized through association with more sensational French serial novels and the life of the Paris poor they portray. By contrast, Gogol's tales of the poor clerk generally do not send us to French subtexts, drawing more from a fanciful German supernatural tradition and treating poverty in a comico-tragic grotesque style learned from E. T. A. Hoffmann.[29] Tolstoy can create one special adulteress in *Anna Karenina,* confident that his audience will be familiar with the French sexual mores with which Anna's behavior is contrasted. Here we will examine only French subtexts, although the three novels discussed also drew importantly from English and German sources.

The subject of this book, distinct from source studies, or the idea of influence, is the dialogue between the earlier (French) and later authors, the Russian writer's interpretation of his subtexts. This book gives "an account of the work performed upon intertextual material and its functional integration into the later text."[30] The three novels discussed here follow a similar pattern: the Russian writer views the French texts he selects as outmoded, harmful, or decadent and rewrites them in the direction of purported Russian aesthetic vigor and moral integrity. Depending on the French text in question, the interpretation of the subtextual dialogue shows the Russian author to be parodying a well-known type of text, correcting a revered text, or rejecting a despised one. The Russians take their subtexts from high and low culture, from fiction, and from essays. Lermontov has his hero parody the Romantic hero as embodied in an array of works. Among the positive reactions, Lermontov values Diderot's deliberation on fatalism but wants to dramatize it; Dostoevsky reveres Balzac as an artist but wants to supply the missing spiritual dimension to his novels; Tolstoy is pleased that a Frenchman—Alexandre Dumas fils—can take marriage seriously and so wants to correct his version of it. Among the negative responses, Lermontov parodies George Sand's elevated treatment of the Romantic fairy tale by lowering it; Dostoevsky elevates the prostitute's spirituality in contrast to the French emphasis on her sensuality; Tolstoy is revolted by Zola and even by the aestheticism of Flaubert, whose art he esteems. The Russian authors use their subtexts in highly specific ways: each of the five chapters of *A Hero of Our Time* and each of the principal characters in *Crime and Punishment* and *Anna Karenina* has its own particular set of subtexts, since each is related to a distinct genre.

The French subtexts addressed by Lermontov, Dostoevsky, and Tolstoy are drawn from the best French writers (de Vigny, Diderot, Balzac, Flaubert, Sand), popular writers (Janin, Sue, Zola, Dumas fils) and forgotten writers (Charles de Bernard, Philarète Chasles, Abbé Tiberge). The subtexts represent France at transitional historical moments from the late 1820s to the 1870s. Dostoevsky and Tolstoy incorporate the French material to highlight the decadence of France from the Russian point of view: the triumph of bourgeois culture and increased loss of religious faith from the time of the "citizen king" Louis Philippe onward should be taken as a warning to Russia, where the materialism of the 1860s was replacing the idealism of the 1840s.

The French cultural intertext represents a negative model for Russia, while the texts counterposed to it contain the Russian writers' ideals for Russia and its literary tradition. Lermontov wrote the first Russian (prose) novel, one that transcended mere imitation of European models, at the end of the Romantic period, and is concerned with Russia's literacy. For him, Russian literature and its readers must become sophisticated interpreters aware of the dialogic nature of literary works; he finds that idea to be the theme and texture of Pushkin's creation. This awareness would then enable Russians to take control of their own fate, to become active creators of their lives. Pushkin himself transcended all his models, avoided provincialism, and represented independence and sophistication in his art; Lermontov selects Pushkin's prose as the counterforce to Russian imitation of French models. Writing twenty and thirty years later, well after the end of the Romantic period, Dostoevsky and Tolstoy are concerned with a more religiously defined spiritual truth; they take as antithesis to Western decadence a countertext that can outweigh, universalize, transcend, and unite the conflicting elements established in their novels: the Gospels. These writers are so successful at creating synthesis that the binary opposition underlying the novels' construction is barely visible, but without awareness of it, the novels lose their shimmer and might be misread as representations of simpler polemical positions dressed up as tales of murder, prostitution and adultery.

Mikhail Bakhtin finds Dostoevsky's novels polyphonic and dialogic and Tolstoy's epic, monologic.[31] The subtext analyses here do not support that view. Both writers set their subtexts into tension, between ideal and real, spirit and reason, faith and unbelief. The tension is unresolved for the characters within their novels; their heroes need faith but have only tentatively moved to attain it while the forces drawing them away from it continue to have power over them. But the subtexts suggest that for both authors there is an ideal resolution to be found in a form of Christianity, whose attainment is hampered by the pride of reason, earthly pleasures, the force of ego. The interplay of the subtexts counters Bakhtin's opposition between Dostoevsky's dialogicity and

Tolstoy's monologicity and modifies the sense in which Dostoevsky's novels can be called polyphonic, inasmuch as a clear, strong argument is made for the authorial position, one none of his characters is capable of refuting.[32] The analysis in this book finds the potential for a multi-voiced reading in the implicit bicultural argument carried on between the author and his subtext rather than in the ambiguity of the author's position. Each of these geniuses is caught in an uncomfortable dual allegiance, to a high level of cultural attainment in France, on the one hand, and to his national culture with its Orthodoxy on the other.

During the transition from eighteenth-century imitations of Europe to the next stage of intertextual dialogue with it, the Russian struggle with the distinction between imitation and true cultural adaptation of an original became the explicit topic of literary discussions. In *Archaists and Innovators,* Yury Tynyanov describes the debates between those who deplored foreign influence and the poets who allegedly imported it in undigested form.[33] He describes the furor over Zhukovsky's three translations of Gottfried August Bürger's "Lenore" (1808, 1812, 1831), which were accused of being insufficiently Russian because of their use of Gallicisms and periphrasis. In 1816, as part of the debate, the poet Katenin translated "Lenore" (not a Russian name) as "Olga" in the manner and the meter of the Russian fabulist Krylov, whose style was based on the oral tradition of the Russian peasantry. Not only form and lexicon but also Romanticism itself were markers of Western culture; to thoroughly assimilate the tale into Russian, these had to be recast into local reality in language and genre appropriate to it. Russian writers were acutely aware that they were, as Ashraf Rushdy puts it, setting the "fictional text in complex dialogic negotiation with various spheres that together form the cultural moment of its production."[34] Lexicon and stylistics, not to mention the texts themselves, were a matter of national identity, as Pushkin playfully points out in *Eugene Onegin*:

With toilette in the latest taste
Having engaged your curious glance,
I might before the learned world
Describe here [Eugene's] attire;
This would, no doubt, be daring;
But "dress coat, "waistcoat," "pantaloons"—
In Russian all these words are not;
In fact, I see (my guilt I lay before you)
That my poor idiom as it is
Might be diversified much less

> With words of foreign stock,
> Though I did erstwhile dip
> Into the Academic Dictionary.[35]

In *Onegin,* Pushkin suggests that he will descend to humble prose; to do so he is again compelled to diversify his "poor idiom" with "words of foreign stock." After an age of poetry, new materials were needed to transpose into prose the overcoming of Romanticism that Pushkin had achieved in his novel in verse. The year after Pushkin finished *Onegin* (1831), a new French journal began to appear in Petersburg, the *Revue étrangère.* The realist fiction it published helped Pushkin to invert the technique of writing a prose genre in poetry—the novel-in-verse *Onegin*—and write prose-in-poetry in *The Bronze Horseman.*

Gogol too, whose first work was a narrative poem in the German Romantic tradition, was helped by the *Revue étrangère* to move beyond Romanticism. The eruption of French realist prose in the 1830s provided material for constructing a modern Russian prose language and repertoire of genres that could treat urban life. Pushkin's poetry and prose and Gogol's short stories made possible Lermontov's novel; indeed, all three Russian authors found material in the *Revue étrangère* to move from poetry to prose, Romanticism to realism and short story to novel. We begin with two case studies of adaptation of French prose techniques by Pushkin and Gogol in chapter 1 and continue with Lermontov's use of their insights in chapter 2. These first two chapters address the Russian overcoming of European Romanticism up to the 1840s; the second two show the Russian dialogue with French realism of the 1860s and 1870s.

1

From Poetry to Prose

Pushkin, Gogol, and the *Revue étrangère*

The Russian novel, beginning with Gogol, poses the problem not of a change in the situation of the hero, but of a transformation of his inner essence.

Yury Lotman, "Siuzhetnoe prostranstvo russkogo romana XIX veka"

The *Revue étrangère*

The *Revue étrangère de la littérature, des sciences et des arts* is an unusual literary journal in that it was published in French in Petersburg for Russian consumption.[1] In 1832 the booksellers Ferdinand Bellizard and his associate in Paris, S. Dufour, began publishing it every ten days in installments that made up four volumes yearly. In 1834 they increased its size and in 1846 added a monthly supplement on the sciences, continuing to issue the journal until 1864.[2] Despite its significant role in the history of Russo-European literary relations, there are few references to it even in the criticism dealing with Russian writers' reading of French literature. In Paris, Dufour either clipped articles from current publications and sent them by courier to Petersburg or had agreements with journals that gave him items even before their publication, as with the *Revue de Paris* and the *Revue des deux mondes*. The *Revue étrangère* could then label the articles "unpublished" (*inédit*) and they often appeared in Petersburg before they did in Paris.[3]

In the 1830s, literary circles were following everything that happened in France with particular interest, and the *Revue étrangère* successfully competed in Russia with the major French journals, like the

REVUE

ÉTRANGÈRE

DE LA

LITTERATURE, DES SCIENCES ET DES ARTS.

TOME HUITIÈME.

SAINT-PÉTERSBOURG.

CHEZ Fd. BELLIZARD ET Co. LIBRAIRES DE LA COUR,
ÉDITEURS.

1833.

Revue étrangère 8 (1833)

Revue des deux mondes and the *Revue de Paris* that Russians subscribed to through their bookstores. It followed the usual format of French journals: each issue contained articles on popular science (life vests, lighting agents, the instincts of spiders), current socio-historical topics (penal colonies in England, the financial situation in the United States), theater reviews, travel notes, sketches of mores (*The Physiology of the Cigar, Gastritis*), anecdotes, and works of French literature. The *Revue* published stories, poems, and novels, sometimes in installments, by the foremost French authors—Alfred de Vigny, Victor Hugo, Honoré de Balzac, Alexandre Dumas fils, Eugène Sue, Jules Janin—as well as by lesser-known writers. The *Revue*'s first ten volumes each contained something by Balzac, including "The Arrangement" (1832), *Ferragus* (1833), *Eugénie Grandet* (1834), and part of *Séraphita* (1834); by 1837 the list included *The Lily of the Valley* and *Lost Illusions*. The journal, like all French journals entering Russia, was subject to the Russian censorship, which demanded some changes and seems not to have allowed *Père Goriot*. Works published in French were generally allowed greater freedom because only an elite could read them, but in 1832 the censorship, noticing the public hunger for new French novels, decided to increase its vigilance toward novels translated from French.[4] In their prospectus, the *Revue étrangère* pledges that it will not publish any political articles, a condition required for permission to publish the journal.[5]

The appeal of the *Revue étrangère* was its lively evocation of the Parisian scene; for writers, moreover, some of the lesser literary works provided refreshing stimulus. The *Revue* appears to have had greater impact in the first few years of its existence, during which time Pushkin, Gogol, and Lermontov drew material from it. Pushkin's *Bronze Horseman* is an example of this cross-fertilization.

Pushkin bought many books from Bellizard, and his library contained the first eight volumes of the *Revue étrangère*; in the issues that appeared during his lifetime the pages are cut, suggesting that Pushkin had read them.[6] The very first volume contains Madame Aimée Harelle's tale, "The Flood at Nantes" (*Inondation à Nantes*). The obscure French work contributed to the conception of Pushkin's *Bronze Horseman* that has become an emblem of the mythology of Saint Petersburg.

The Bronze Horseman

Pushkin's letters; diaries; articles; notebooks; epigrams; his friends' letters and memoirs; and the huge literature in Italian, French, Russian, and English he is known to have read make us think that it must be possible to penetrate his creative process. But *The Bronze Horseman* has posed an exceptional problem because the manuscripts provide little insight into the poem's genesis.[7] Some of the finest critical literature identifies sources for particular themes: Waclaw Lednicki examines Pushkin's ambivalent assessment of Peter the Great and his implied dialogue with Mickiewicz about Peter in *The Bronze Horseman*; Roman Jakobson reveals the continuity from the Boldino autumn of 1830 to the next one in 1833.[8] "The Flood at Nantes" (1832) provides new insight into the genesis of Pushkin's poem.

We know the history of Pushkin's involvement with many of the components that went into *The Bronze Horseman*: Peter the Great; the Decembrist uprising; the flood of 1824; the sources he himself cites in his notes to the poem; his own characters Evgeny and Parasha. Commissioned by Nikolas I, Pushkin started research in the State Archives for a history of Peter the Great in 1831 but was also covertly researching the Pugachev rebellion in the summer of 1833, a juxtaposition of Pushkin's circumstances and the two histories he was writing that is suggestive of the *Horseman*'s drama between Peter and Evgeny.[9]

The salient elements incorporated into *The Bronze Horseman* have been discussed by a battalion of Pushkin scholars. These include:

1. Pushkin's complex understanding of the role of Peter the Great in Russian history as both bearer of enlightenment and destroyer of the old boyar nobility. His discussions with Mickiewicz of both the historical Peter and his mythic representation in Falconet's monument led to a dialogue between the Polish poet's *Digression*—especially *The Day Preceding the Inundation of St. Petersburg in 1824: Oleszkiewicz and The Monument of Peter the Great* in which Mickiewicz calls Peter a "bronze tsar"—and "The Bronze Horseman." Pushkin copied Mickiewicz's poems into his notebook sometime after the end of 1832.[10]
2. The Decembrist uprising of 1825, which is encoded in *The Bronze Horseman*.[11] Evgeny sits astride the lion in front of the house from which they fired on the Decembrists on what is now Decembrists' Square, and Pushkin gives the names of the generals sent out by the tsar to help the drowning (Count Miloradovich and Adjutant-General Benkendorf) because of their role in the suppression of the revolt the following year.[12] Even Pushkin's particular use of the Neva shore (*"vzmore"*), as Anna Akhmatova has shown, refers to the unidentified burial place of the five executed Decembrists.[13] Pushkin's notes to his poem themselves hint at the Decembrist theme.[14]

Pushkin's characters Evgeny and Parasha evolve out of his earlier work. The hero of the unfinished poem *Ezersky* (1832), a fragment of which became *My Hero's Pedigree* (1836), has been taken to be a first draft of the character that will become Evgeny, stripped of Ezersky's aristocratic trappings and defiance.[15] Evgeny's musings on his humble future resemble some of Pushkin's own that he had given to Evgeny Onegin in chapter 8 (later destroyed), but in *The Bronze Horseman,* Pushkin omits them to emphasize Evgeny's ordinariness and initial humility.[16] Pushkin's implied identification with Ezersky is instead taken up by the figure of the poor poet in *The Bronze Horseman* who inherits Evgeny's abandoned apartment. Perhaps he will tell Evgeny's tale and, in so doing, somehow reconcile the poem's conflicts between nature and culture, citizen and state, thereby redeeming Evgeny and Parasha from oblivion.

Parasha is clearly connected to the Parasha of "The Little House in Kolomna" (*Domik v Kolomne* [1830]). The earlier Parasha and her widowed mother live in a little house that the narrator tells us has disappeared.[17] In *The Bronze Horseman* it is Evgeny who lives in Kolomna (as Pushkin had until his exile in 1820), while the widow and her daughter live on an island in the Neva. The action of "The Little House" takes place "*tomu let vosem*'" (eight years ago), writes the narrator of the tale written in 1830, therefore in 1822. This is two years before the beginning of the action of *The Bronze Horseman.* If we connect the two poems, as it appears Pushkin must have done, the house could have vanished by 1830 because it was swept away in the flood of 1824, but there is no hint of this in the poem; the narrator asks at the opening of the poem, "Are they alive?" but Parasha's story in "Little House" is a playful farce. Pushkin appears to have chosen only to hint at the flood but not to address it. Another tale, "A Solitary Little House on Vasiliev Island," is said to have been taken by V. P. Titov from an anecdote Pushkin told in 1828 about a poor Petersburg clerk who lost his fiancée during a flood. Even if the later "Little House" is the germ of the tale of Evgeny and Parasha, Pushkin still waited five years to incorporate it into the constellation of features that comprise *The Bronze Horseman.*

But *The Bronze Horseman* is the tale of the conflict among three agents, Peter, Evgeny, and the Petersburg flood of 1824, and so far we have only accounted for the first two.[18] How did Pushkin's deep interest in Peter, in uprisings from Pugachev to the Decembrists, and his earlier characters Evgeny and Parasha all occupying him in the early 1830s, become connected to and merge in the fact of the flood of 1824?

Was the flood the missing element that united all the aforementioned components for the first time to produce "the greatest work ever penned in Russian verse," as Mirsky calls it?[19] Mickiewicz's poem, *Olieszkiewicz*, treats the day preceding the inundation, which contains only a four-line description of the ocean.[20] In a variant of the Introduction of *The Bronze Horseman*, Pushkin says he had felt it an obligation to the "mournful hearts" of his contemporaries to describe the flood since 1824; Andrew Kahn, on the other hand, says there is nothing else to link the theme of the flood to an early version of the work, nor was it an event Pushkin dwelled upon.[21] No one has suggested how this historical event, connected neither to Peter nor Catherine, whose reigns Pushkin had been studying so exhaustively, came to be the subject of his "Petersburg tale." Why, then, at the end of a six-week trip researching the Pugachev rebellion in Uralsk and Berdy, did Pushkin, having reached Boldino on October 1, 1833, start writing *The Bronze Horseman* on October 6, completing it October 30?

Jakobson mentions an implied connection between Catherine's monument to Peter and the flood of Catherine's time: in Pushkin's lyceum poem *Vospominania v Tsarskom sele* (1814) he describes a monument in Tsarskoe selo to the Battle of Chesma as "surrounded by waves" with "grey billows lapping its base with shining foam."[22] Although the elements of statue, waves, and foam do link the description of the Chesma monument to that of the "Bronze Horseman," the connection to the flood of Catherine's time is only indirect. In any case, this conjunction of statue, monarch and water and/or flood did not inspire a poem until a full nineteen years later.

In the absence of clues to the stages of the poem's development, I propose that Pushkin read Madame Harelle's "The Flood at Nantes" sometime between its publication in January 1832 and September 1833, and that this may have precipitated the conjoining of the compositional elements of *The Bronze Horseman*, many of which Pushkin had been actively assembling in 1832. As Lednicki suggests, the poem is so rich in (other) precise citations that Pushkin must have brought materials for it with him from Petersburg.[23] "The Flood at Nantes" could have been among them.

"The Flood at Nantes" appeared in the very first issue of the journal *La Revue étrangère* in January 1832. Given Pushkin's life-long avid interest in everything French, especially literature, and even more so French prose of the 1830s, as Vera Milchina has shown, as well as his active participation in the world of Petersburg journalism both as contributor and as publisher, it is not surprising that his library contains the first eight volumes of the *Revue étrangère*.[24] He is likely to have read right away the first issue of this new journal that appeared in Petersburg, where he was in residence that year until mid-September, as his letters attest. His last letter from Petersburg in 1832 in fact contains a critique of French critics, journals, and poetry of the period: "Their prose barely manages to redeem the vileness (*podlost'*) of what they call poetry," he writes Pogodin, in a letter discussing his program for the contents of his "own" newspaper, *Literaturnaia gazeta*.[25]

What would Pushkin have found in "Inondation à Nantes" that would inspire his own "Inondation à Petersbourg"? Madame Harelle's tale is a chapter from her novel, *The Accursed, or an Episode from the Wars of the Vendée*, of which the editors say: "the main characters are marked with a seal of verisimilitude that raises the suspicion that they are far from fictitious." "The Flood at Nantes" opens with a realistic description of the Nantes harbor, where the Loire flows into the Atlantic (see appendix). Of course, flood conditions have general similarities, but these are reasonably specific; the setting of a river delta with its islands, the everyday detail, and Harelle's descriptions of the effects of the flood are close to Pushkin's:

> The river . . . *roils its troubled waters impetuously*. It overflows everywhere.[26]

Neva vsiu noch'	All night the Neva
Rvalasia k moriu protiv buri,	Surged toward the sea against the storm,
Ne odolevshikh burnoi duri	Not taming its stormy folly
. . . .	. . . .
Tesnilsia kuchami narod	People crowd in heaps
Liubuias' bryzgami, gorami	Admiring the splashes, the mountains
I penoi *raziarionnykh vod*	And foam of the *infuriated waters*.[27]

Naturally the islands at the conjunction of rivers and oceans are most vulnerable:

> *Charming islands*, rich plains, which, just yesterday, covered with numerous flocks, offered on its left bank gracious scenes, today are no more than *a surging sea from which stick out here the tops of trees filled with tufts of foam, there a group of houses against which the waves surge and break.*

No siloi vetrov ot zaliva	But by the force of the winds from the gulf
Peregrazhdionnaia Neva	Fenced off, the Neva
Obratno shla, gnevna, burliva,	Angry, stormy, went backward
I zatopliala ostrova.	*And flooded the islands.*

And naturally the lowest places are the first to flood:

> From moment to moment the flood makes frightening progress: it has already *penetrated several low quarters of the city . . .*

Vody vdrug	The waters suddenly
Vtekli v *podzemnye podvaly*	Flowed into the *underground cellars*

Both writers describe the people's desperation at the loss of all they've labored for and depend upon:

> However much a crowd of arms hastens to remove from riverside houses *objects that the water could take off or destroy,* the river mounts so rapidly that it seems impossible to save everything. *And every owner is distressed thinking about the ruinous damage that he tries in vain to prevent.*

Pushkin uses a metaphor of theft on the one hand and God's anger on the other to paint the same picture:

Osada! Pristup! Zlye volny	Siege! Attack! The angry waves
Kak vory, lezut v okna. . . .	Like thieves crawl in the windows. . . .
Lotki pod mokroi pelenoi,	Boats under soaked canvas,
Oblomki khizhin, brevna, krovli,	Pieces of huts, wood, roofs.
Tovar zapaslivoi torgovli,	*The wares of thrifty trade,*
Pozhitki blednoi nishchety,	*The chattels of pale poverty,*
Grozoi snesennnye mosty,	Bridges swept away by the storm,
Groba s razmytogo kladbishcha	Coffins from the swamped graveyard
Plyvut po ulitsam. Narod	Float along the streets. The people
Zrit bozhyi gnev i kazni zhdet.	Sees God's anger and awaits punishment.
Uvy! Vse gibnet; krov i pishcha!	*Alas! All's ruined, roof and food!*
Gde budet vziat'?	*How will we get them?*

As Vernadsky has noted, the waves of the Neva "attacking the lofty buildings of Petersburg, were for Pushkin symbolic of human crowds in revolt against peace and order," close to his own description of the Pugachev uprising.[28] "The Flood at Nantes" also contains a hidden political commentary.

The description of the flooded Nantes harbor introduces the tale of a sixteen year-old girl, Hélène, who is trapped in a collapsing house. Workers are trying to save her under the direction of a Marquis and his son the Vicomte, who is apparently in love with Hélène. He is "pale and agitated," "trembling with emotion" and experiencing "extreme anxiety" as she sits on a beam over a large hole. "Her feet, deprived of a point of support, are bathed by the steadily rising water."

Hélène is saved, as Parasha is not, but several elements of her story relate to *The Bronze Horseman*: the beloved girl drowned (or not) in a house destroyed by a flood, her anxiety-filled lover, and the detail of the waves mounting beneath dangling feet, which in *The Bronze Horseman* describes the "terrifyingly pale" Evgeny as he sits astride the stone lion:

On strashilsia, bednyi,	He feared, poor man,
Ne za sebia. On ne slykhal,	Not for himself. He did not hear
Kak podymalsia strashnyi val,	*How the terrifying billow rose,*
Emu podoshvy podmyvaia.	*Washing his soles.*

In the connection of "The Little House in Kolomna" and "Ezersky" to *The Bronze Horseman* Pushkin turns from classicism and Romanticism toward "the poetry of everyday life and of the little man."[29] The juxtaposition to the Vicomte in "The Flood at Nantes" heightens our appreciation of Pushkin's choice of the "little man" as the one to suffer the tragic loss of his beloved. Pushkin presumably demoted Ezersky to Evgeny, lowering his social status, in order to have him represent everyman. This concern must be somehow connected to the Decembrist material in the poem. "The Flood at Nantes" provides insight into this question.

From the opening paragraph, we learn that "The Flood at Nantes" takes place in 1789. At the quai we meet the young captain of an American ship, *L'independence,* who becomes the heroic rescuer of Hélène. He "has undergone more than one combat to assure America's liberty"[30] and now his former warship has been converted to commerce. On an errand, the captain arrives at the scene of the collapsed building, where someone has proposed that the only way to rescue Hélène is to swim under the building and take her out through the raging river. The Vicomte offers 10,000 francs to anyone who will make this dangerous attempt. A pale, thin man dressed in miserable clothing offers to try, although he is clearly too weak to succeed. He is willing to die in the attempt if the money will go to his starving wife and children. Overhearing this, the captain hands him his own purse and volunteers to undertake the rescue himself.

> "You?" replies the Marquis . . ."No, monsieur, I won't permit it."
>
> "My life is not any more precious than that of this unfortunate man," the sailor interrupts with some severity.[31]

The implied discourse on the equality of man is further underscored when the Marquis regrets that he is "only the useless witness of your generous action!" and the captain responds, "You or me, what's the difference?"[32] "The Flood at Nantes" thus hints at both the French and the American revolutions and the ideals they represent.

Pushkin's political views, as Eidelman emphasizes, cannot be neatly classified, which has given rise to debate among a variety of scholars.[33] Semen Frank distorts the evidence in demonstrating Pushkin's profound conservativism when he quotes only the second paragraph of *John Tanner,* which gives a negative view of American democracy, and which was in any case written in 1836, at the end of Pushkin's life.[34] Presumably the first paragraph of Pushkin's essay reflects his earlier views: "For some time the North American States have been attracting the attention of the most thoughtful people in Europe. This is not the result of political events: America peacefully goes about its business, up to now harmless and blooming, strong in its peace, assisted by its geographic position, proud in its institutions."[35] This is not to say that Pushkin was not "firmly convinced of the futility of revolutions," afraid of a repetition of the French terror in Russia.[36] But while Pushkin cherished the Russian aristocracy and was ambivalent about tsardom, he was also a Decembrist sympathizer who opposed serfdom and despotism, and whose poetry continued to inspire liberal thought after 1825.[37] He attributed the failure of the Decembrist uprising to the absence of a third estate in Russia, that is, as is clear in "André Chénier" (1825), he drew a parallel between the Russian uprising and the French revolution which he studied in the 1820s, getting books from Eliza Khitrovo in order to write a (never completed) history of it.[38] In "André Chénier," *ravenstvo* (equality) is twice rhymed with *blazhenstvo* (blessedness), even if Pushkin then deplores the absence of law that leads to regicide. "Holy freedom" is nonetheless a "pure goddess," not to be blamed for the madness of the people, who "in the shade of equality / In your embrace will rest sweetly."[39] The egalitarian sentiments of "The Flood at Nantes," the 1789 (not 1792) setting, and the glowing treatment of the American revolution with its heroic, victorious representative, would provide *The Bronze Horseman* a hidden positive variant of the events of 1825, a happier resolution than is achieved in Russia or by Evgeny and Parasha. That Evgeny's humble rank resonates with Pushkin's thoughts about the French revolution is clear from a line of the eighth stanza of Ezersky: *"iz bar my lezem v tiers etat"* (from gentry we crawl into the third estate), even though in this line Pushkin is regretting the decline of the Russian aristocracy.[40] "The Flood at Nantes" can be read at least as the basis for a bitter comparison to the situation in Russia, in which the American captain embodies individual freedom and the self-respect that Pushkin considered attributes of an ideal member of the Russian aristocracy.

Besides the thematic points of contact between the two poems—the flood, the love story, the revolution—there are two suggestive stylistic correspondences. The American captain passes through the humble and chaotic dwellings of the poor part of Nantes—a "sad, miserable scene"—and reaches the Stock Exchange: "This was not the beautiful building of which Nantes is proud today, but a wooden barracks of pitiful aspect."[41] Past poverty and disorder is replaced by present beauty, as in Pushkin's Introduction.

What of the essential aspect of *The Bronze Horseman,* the statue's pursuit of Evgeny? Pushkin's sources for the animated statue have been found in Molière's Commendatore, Washington Irving and even Lemercier.[42] But Evgeny is clearly not Don Juan; his madness does not derive from those sources. There has been some disagreement over what precisely drives Evgeny mad—the loss of Parasha, the flood itself, or his helplessness before the all-powerful Peter, but clearly it is when he discovers that Parasha's house has been swept away that he goes mad: *zakhokhotal* ("he burst out laughing").[43] His traumatic experience leads him to hallucinate his pursuit by the statue. There is a parallel moment at the end of "The Flood at Nantes." Although it is used simply for a kind of lyrical closure rather than as a thematic line, the hero reexperiences his adventure in a brief hallucination:

The Captain is hastening back to his ship in order to set sail at high tide after rescuing Hélène. "Arriving before the place of the ruin, he stops, his heart beats violently. . . . A trick of his imagination presents to him the young girl still placed on that wobbling beam whence he had removed her. This vague airy form, this pale and gracious face that he had only managed to glimpse, seemed at this moment to lean towards him, to implore his help. He extends his arms, crosses them on his chest, as if he were again clasping the charming being he thinks he sees."[44] But the captain is sane, and the adventure was successful; he comes to himself. "Sweet and cruel mirage, he says, should I fear or desire to see you reappear?" The mirage contains several elements of Evgeny's madness: Evgeny's challenge to the Horseman relates to the captain's role in the American Revolution. The captain hallucinates Hélène imperiled by the flood shortly after rescuing her, but Evgeny's hallucination comes a year after Parasha's disappearance in the flood, 1825, which clearly relates Evgeny's challenge to the Decembrist uprising.[45] Pushkin endows the events of December as well as of the flood with a Shakespearean historical perspective by having Evgeny trace Parasha's fate to its source in Peter and implicitly comparing that conflict with those of other countries.

With so many points of contact between "The Flood at Nantes" and *The Bronze Horseman,* the realistic descriptions of the flood; the indirect allusions to revolutionary ideas; a girl in a house that is swept away by the flood; the city setting that emphasizes the gulf between rich and poor; and the hero's hallucination, we can hypothesize that the French tale served as a catalyst for Pushkin, bringing together elements he had not hitherto combined: his archival work on Peter the Great, the bitter experience of his Decembrist friends, the poems of Batiushkov, Mickiewicz, Vyazemsky, his own work from the "freedom poems" such as "Freedom" and "André Chénier" to the less obviously civic works "Ezersky" and "A Little House in Kolomna," and an array of other intertexts (*Genesis, The Aeneid, The Tempest, Don Juan*). The shift from the odic Introduction to the prosaic part of the poem may have been triggered by French prose; Pushkin's poem becomes a "Petersburg *tale*" when he introduces the story of Evgeny and Parasha into the scene of the flood.[46] The story of Hélène's plight may have allowed Pushkin's rich materials to crystallize, causing him to recreate the Petersburg flood of 1824 in the Boldino autumn of 1833.

Many literate Petersburgers would have recently read the first issue of the *Revue étrangère*, so that Pushkin could expect them to be familiar with "The Flood at Nantes." Reading *The Bronze Horseman* so soon after Madame Harelle's rendition of something like what they themselves may have witnessed, they would have connected the two, at least thematically. The more literarily sophisticated might have seen that Pushkin uses bits and pieces from Madame Harelle's description as part of the self-conscious movement away from Romantic stylistics toward a new realism. Pushkin's Petersburg contemporaries might have even more readily understood his Aesopian hint at the theme of revolution.

The relationship between the two works shows how the *Revue étrangère* was a source of French realist prose for Russian writers in the 1830s. It helped Pushkin, and later Gogol and Lermontov, replace Romantic genres and stylistics with "low" everyday subject matter and its attendant physical detail.

"The Overcoat"

It is perhaps more surprising that the non-Francophile Gogol was reading the first issues of the *Revue étrangère*. Balzac's story "The Arrangement" (*La Transaction*) appeared in two successive installments of the *Review*'s second volume, at about the same time as it appeared in France in the journal *L'Artiste*, also in two installments, in February and

Honoré de Balzac (*Revue étrangère* 17 [1836])

March of 1832.[47] An expanded and edited version became first "Count Chabert" (1832), then "The Countess with Two Husbands" (1835), and finally the novel *Colonel Chabert,* its definitive form, in the novel sequence *Human Comedy* (1844), among "Scenes from Parisian Life."[48] The changes Balzac made in expanding "The Arrangement" suggest that Gogol read it in its earliest version.

Balzac's tale provided Gogol material for the then new genre of poor clerk tales. After the supernatural tales set in the Ukraine—the second part of the *Dikanka* cycle appeared in 1832—Gogol's first comic realist tale, "The Tale of How Ivan Ivanovich Quarreled with Ivan Nikiforovich," was published in the *Mirgorod* cycle in 1835; he had read it to Pushkin (who said, "very original and very funny") as early as December 1833.[49] When he moved to Petersburg, Gogol first responded to the popularity of Ukrainian tales there and then took up the newly popular genres of city sketches and poor clerk tales.

Nils Åke Nilsson showed that Victor-Joseph Jouy's feuilletons describing scenes from life in Paris, collected in *L'Hermite de la Chaussée d'Antin,* were an important source for the numerous Russian treatments of life in Petersburg and in particular of Gogol's *Petersburg Stories.*[50] For example, Gogol imitates Jouy's device of describing a part of the city at different times of day in the opening of "Nevsky Prospect." But for the fantastic element in "Nevsky Prospect" Nilsson credits Balzac, whose *Wild Ass's Skin* (*La Peau de chagrin*) itself combines the realism of Jouy with Hoffmann's fantastic. In another article, on "The Overcoat," Nilsson identifies a character from Balzac's *The Civil Servants* (*Les Employés*) (1847) as a source for Akaky Akakievich: the clerk Poiret has "bluish moles," has worn the same hat for nine years, and is depicted as too stupid to understand the jokes his fellow clerks play on him.[51] The *Revue étrangère* contains an earlier source.

"The Arrangement," a tale involving Parisian poor clerks, also provided material for the Russian genre of the poor clerk tale. It appeared five years earlier than *The Civil Servants,* in time to help Gogol develop a new manner with which to create his Petersburg universe. As was his habit, Gogol cannibalized Balzac's story for scenes and images that he distributed among his Petersburg tales.

Balzac's "Arrangement" tells the story of a colonel in the Napoleonic wars, Chabert. He has been reported dead at Eylau but returns after many years to try to reclaim his wife and his fortune. He arrives in Paris utterly destitute and goes to a lawyer, where he learns that his wife has taken a second husband. She will not even answer his letters, continuing to pretend he is dead. The lawyer aids him in his attempt to exact revenge and arranges a meeting with his wife after ten years of separation. She plays on Chabert's love for her and outsmarts him, so that he loses both his wife and his fortune, ending his days in a public institution for the aged. The colonel's return from the Napoleonic wars, his desperate destitution, his resurrection from the dead, his unavailing appeal to the "authorities" and his desire for revenge can be found in the "Tale of Captain Kopeikin" from *Dead Souls* and (without the military aspect) in Akaky Akakievich's tale in "The Overcoat." Both represent a lowering of the tale of the rebel soldier who becomes a brigand, a type identified by Yury Lotman in his discussion of "Captain Kopeikin."[52] The variant in "The Overcoat" omits the return from the Napoleonic wars but includes all the remaining elements of Captain

Kopeikin's story. Characteristically, Gogol apparently omits Balzac's love story between the colonel and his wife, but Akaky and his "life's companion," the new overcoat, act out Balzac's tale of the beloved gained and lost and its connection to the money that is the difference between abject poverty and normal human existence.

The opening of "The Arrangement" promises a tale about poor clerks of the Dickensian sort.[53] Its connection to "The Overcoat" is made by an oddity in the first sentence of Balzac's story: the English word "carrick," a word rare in French, whose use is first noted in 1805.[54] It is the word Vladimir Nabokov uses to translate "*Shinel'*" in his book on Gogol.[55] "Carrick" originally denoted a coachman's overcoat in English; in French it connoted a redingote with several collars. Balzac's father wore one, and the fact that Chabert is characterized by this coat suggests that he belongs to an earlier age. Balzac uses the word metonymically the same way Gogol often did, where an article of clothing stands for the person wearing it. The clerks see the carrick and not the man:

> "Look! Here's the old carrick coming back up here again!" [*Allons! Voilà encore le vieux carrick qui monte ici!*]
>
> Having said this, the junior clerk made a little ball out of the inside of the piece of bread he had been chewing on, and threw it, through a vasisdas, onto the hat of a stranger who was crossing the courtyard of a house situated in the Rue Vivenne, where Monsieur Derville the lawyer lived.
>
> "The boss has just gone to bed, he's not seeing anyone!" answered the first clerk as he finished adding up a memorandum of expenses.
>
> "What trick can we play on this chinaman?" said the third clerk in a bass voice. . . .
>
> "Let's tell him that the boss can't talk to his clients except between two and three o'clock in the morning. . . . We'll see if he comes, the old brigand!"[56]

In Gogol's "Diary of a Madman," the little ball of bread gets fed to the disgusted dog Madgie: "Some gentleman or other sitting at the table who's held all sorts of trash in his hands will start mashing bread with these hands, call you over and shove a little ball in your teeth."[57] The food falling on the hat brim is given to Akaky Akakievich: "He possessed the rare talent, walking along the street, of arriving under a window precisely at the very time when someone was throwing all sorts of rubbish out of it, and therefore he perpetually carried away watermelon and cantaloupe rinds and similar trash on his hat" (71).[58] The clerk's instructions to arrive between two and three in the morning may explain the puzzling advertisement for old shoe soles that Major Kovalev of

"The Nose" reads in the newspaper office containing "the invitation to appear at the bidding every day from eight to three o'clock in the morning" (35). This supposition is reinforced by the parallelism between the two scenes. Balzac's "carrick" is maltreated by the clerks and tries to get the attention of a clerk who is busy making calculations:

> The poor petitioner remained unperturbed. He began to look modestly around him, like a dog that has slipped into the kitchen fearing blows; but the clerks . . . left him to look around the place and look for a chair, since the old man was horribly tired.
>
> "Monsieur," he said, finding neither a place to sit nor a friendly face to console him, . . . I will wait until [M. Derville] awakens. . . ."
>
> The principal clerk, having finished his tally . . . looked at the carrick, made an indescribable grimace; and thinking probably that if one were to wring the petitioner one wouldn't get a cent out of him, intervened with a brief speech:
>
> "They're telling you the truth, monsieur! The boss only works at night. . . . I advise you to return at one in the morning. . . ."
>
> The petitioner looked vacantly at the master clerk and remained immobile for a moment. (152)

Gogol's Major Kovalev encounters a similar scene in the newspaper office:

> Kovalyov, gasping for breath, ran into a small reception room where a gray-haired old clerk in an old tailcoat and glasses sat at a table and, holding a pen in his teeth, was counting the small change that had been brought in.
>
> "Who here takes notices? shouted Kovalyov. "Oh, hello!"
>
> "My respects, said the gray-haired clerk, raising his eyes for a minute and lowering them again to the distributed piles of money. (34–35)

Kovalyov is made to wait, the clerk refuses his request although Kovalyov suggests he is willing to offer a bribe, and he is given useless advice—"to print a little article in the *Northern Bee* . . . for the edification of youth" about the loss of his nose.

Balzac's description of the merciless reception of the poor petitioner has elements of Gogol's presentation of Akaky petitioning Petrovich for repairs. Here is the scene of the "carrick" entering the establishment:

> The petitioner in the old carrick, having closed the door with the attention of an unfortunate man, looked for some symptoms of politeness on the inexorable and indifferent faces of the six clerks . . . he addressed himself very humbly to the lowest clerk, *hoping that this victim would have some pity.*

> "What do you want, Monsieur?" asked the fourth clerk, swallowing a piece of bread with which one could have loaded a cannon, while brandishing his knife and crossing his legs, *placing the lower foot at eye's height.* (151, emphasis mine)

At Petrovich's,

> Akaky Akakievich . . . saw Petrovich sitting on a broad wooden unpainted table and crossing his legs under him like a Turkish pasha. His feet, as is the custom of tailors sitting at their work, were bare. And *the first thing to strike the eye was his big toe,* very well known to Akaky Akakievich, with a sort of deformed nail, thick and strong as the shell of a tortoise . . . *Akaky was distressed that he had come precisely at a moment when Petrovich was angry . . .* (74, emphasis mine)

Balzac uses an animal simile that compares Chabert to a dog in the kitchen; Gogol compares Petrovich's toenail to a tortoise shell; the pitiful insignificance of the petitioner facing the mocking clerks is matched by Akaky's fear of Petrovich.

Part 2 of "The Arrangement" is entitled "The Resurrection," a title Balzac removed in later variants. The first full description of Chabert emphasizes his deathlike appearance:

> The colonel Chabert was as perfectly immobile as *a wax figure* in Curtius's exhibit can be . . . The man was dry and thin; his eyes, instead of having a spark or shining, seemed covered with a transparent film . . . The pale face, white, and like a knife blade, . . . seemed *dead* . . . The borders of his hat which covered the old man's face projected a black trough on his upper face, and this effect . . . by the brusqueness of the contrast made white wrinkles stand out, cold sinuosities, the colorless sentiments of this *cadaverous* physiognomy. The absence of all movement in the body, of all warmth in the gaze, accorded with a certain expression of sad dementia, with the degrading symptoms characterizing the *idiot* that covered this face. (155–56, emphasis mine)

Chabert is depicted as an inanimate figure, as dead, as an idiot. In later editions Balzac, who appears to have wanted to mitigate Chabert's idiocy to correspond better with his noble character, softened the word "idiot," and removed Chabert's words, "I looked more like a match salesman than a count of the Empire."[59] But idiocy is the effect of Gogol's famous description of Akaky, and in life he is depicted as similarly inert: "He was always seen at one and the same place, in the same position, in the same spot, the same copying clerk, so that later they were convinced that he, evidently, was born into this world already finished, in a uniform with a bald spot on his head. In the department he was shown no respect whatsoever. The porters . . . did not even glance at him, as if a *simple fly* had flown through the reception hall" (68–69, emphasis mine). One of Balzac's clerks says of Chabert, "He looks like someone *disinterred*!" (152, emphasis mine), which turns out to be the case, figuratively: he returns "from the dead" to wreak vengeance on his wife. Akaky comes back after his actual death, as a "*clerk-corpse*" "breathing the terrible smell of the *grave*" (62, emphasis mine), to reclaim what is his (his "life-companion"/overcoat, his dignity) from the Very Important Personage.[60]

Gogol's redeployment of the fragments of Balzac's rather overwritten early variant of *Colonel Chabert* highlights the nature of his peculiar genius. Balzac's trick is located in Chabert's introduction to Derville, who asks, "With whom have I the honor of speaking?" "With Colonel Chabert . . . the one who died at Eylau, . . . answered the old man" (156). By turning Colonel Chabert's figurative "resurrection" into Akaky's naturalist-supernatural one, Gogol casts the customary parodic treatment of clerkdom into an apocalyptic light. The trivial venality of Chabert's wife is recast as the Petersburgers' misplaced passion for the concerns of daily life. Nilsson traces this idea of *zador* to Jouy, who writes: "Everyone has his *califourchon,* his hobby-horse, as the English say. . . . Some ruin themselves buying books, others with paintings, statues, still others in objects [*enchantillons*] made of minerals, shells, medals, engraved stones, etc."[61] For Jouy, this is merely a sociological observation. Gogol takes the idea to its extreme, the question of the meaning of human existence, which for Akaky becomes embodied in—an overcoat.

Gogol has made only fragmentary use of Balzac's tale; signs of its incorporation in "The Overcoat" are far less visible than the traces of Hoffmann's "Mlle de Scudery" and "The Golden Pot." But Gogol needed to splice Hoffmann's supernatural with some other style to render the everyday Petersburg he knew, and Balzac supplied a congenial descriptive manner. "The Overcoat" merges the German fantastic with the French physiological sketch, and Gogol had the genius to pick out their leading proponents. Petersburg was the window and the *Revue étrangère* a *vasisdas* that let in a brisk gust of French realist prose. The important authors published by the *Revue* in the early 1830s accelerated the growth of Russian fiction, furnishing plots, genres, and stylistics that helped Pushkin and Gogol prepare the ground for Lermontov to create a genuinely Russian novel that both uses the new French prose genres and comments on their recent incorporation by Pushkin and Gogol.

Lermontov, Dostoevsky, and Tolstoy

In the next three chapters we will examine how Lermontov, Dostoevsky, and Tolstoy engage in polemics with their French subtexts in order to define Russian cultural identity in opposition to the West. *A Hero of Our Time, Crime and Punishment,* and *Anna Karenina* mark successive periods in the development of Russian literature as it made the transition from poetry to prose: late Romanticism, romantic realism, and realism.[62] Each novel is the most remarkable work of its decade, whose thematics themselves—the Romantic hero, prostitution, adultery—demand a dialogue with French literature and culture to a degree that other Russian realist novels of the period do not. The three novels follow the line of realist prose established by Pushkin: Lermontov, Dostoevsky, and Tolstoy are inspired by *The Tales of Belkin,* Dostoevsky also by "The Queen of Spades," and Tolstoy's first draft of *Anna Karenina* was triggered by the fragment "The Guests were Arriving at the Dacha."[63] Together the three masterpieces describe the development of the Russian novel from the 1840s to the 1870s.

A Hero of Our Time, Crime and Punishment, and *Anna Karenina* of course contain complex social and political arguments connected to Russian affairs, and other literatures (principally German and English) contribute in their own particular ways. There is a vast and valuable body of criticism on these important topics; it coexists with the findings of this book, whose focus is on only one aspect of three Russian authors' process of generation and construction of their work. My method differs in this respect from, for example, Robert Belknap's in his analysis of *The Brothers Karamazov,* which discusses a multiplicity of sources.[64] And while it is understood that Dostoevsky often uses multiple sources for a given image, scene, or word, here the focus is on analyzing the authors' uses of individual French subtexts, which are far from being the sole determinants of the novels they appear in. Because French culture played such a central and clearly defined role in Russian literary development, isolating the dialogue between the two cultures adds a new and coherent dimension to our understanding of why and how the three great novels examined here became important representatives of world literature.

2

Lermontov, *A Hero of Our Time*

Lermontov created, almost alone, a Russian novel in which the psychology of the hero played a major role.
William Harkins

A Hero of Our Time effects a remarkable synthesis of Western European and Russian literature of the first third of the nineteenth century. Lermontov set himself the task of inventing modern Russian prose and founded a tradition of psychological realism, drawing from Pushkin to go beyond the themes and heroes that Russian Romanticism had learned from Western Europe, in particular from France. Lermontov counters the thesis, French literature, with its antithesis, which for him, a Russian poet starting to write prose in the 1830s, is represented by the new, spare realism of Pushkin's prose.

By 1840 Russia had not yet produced a modern novel; in April of that year, Lermontov published the completed *A Hero of Our Time.* He was only twenty-five and had left two earlier prose works unfinished. The novel is far more accomplished than his first attempt, *Vadim* (1832–34), which echoes the elevated melodrama of Marlinsky.[1] Lermontov's next effort at a novel, *Princess Ligovskaya* (1836), interweaves the account of the hero's romantic life with the tale of an impoverished civil servant, rendered in the naturalist tradition.[2] It appears that Lermontov was attempting to do what Dostoevsky managed a few years later in *Poor Folk* (1846): to merge the two principal lines of contemporary Russian literature by uniting the world of the poor clerk with the sophisticated society novel. But the elements of each are undigested in *Princess Ligovskaya,* the two modes jarringly juxtaposed.[3] Perhaps, as Eikhenbaum conjectures, Lermontov understood this. In June of 1838 Lermontov wrote to

Raevsky that he was abandoning *Princess Ligovskaya*: "I'm not writing, publishing's a lot of nuisance, and I tried it, but unsuccessfully. . . . The novel you and I began dragged on and will probably not be finished, since the circumstances that comprised its basis have changed."[4] In that novel Lermontov had failed to unite the Romantic and the realist schools; in *Hero* he succeeds.

What precipitated this abrupt maturation in Lermontov's prose? He had had Pushkin's prose to draw on since the early 1830s, as well as the abundant new French literature of that period. A few influential works appeared closer in time to the composition of *Hero*: Alfred de Musset's *Confession of a Child of the Century* (1836) suggested the title of Lermontov's draft: *One of the Heroes of the Beginning of the Century,* and Charles de Bernard's *Gerfaut* (1838) provides a few details for "Princess Mary."[5] The appearance of George Sand's "L'Orco" in March 1838 inspired the structure of "Taman" and may have helped crystallize the combination of life experience with earlier reading of Pushkin that allowed Lermontov to begin writing *Hero* that year; together they provided material for elaboration of Pechorin's character, some plot elements, and models for the structure of a novel made up of separate stories.

Each one of the stories comprising Lermontov's novel has its own particular French sources; the form and genres of the five chapters are inspired principally by Pushkin's *Tales of Belkin* but also by de Vigny, Balzac, and possibly Diderot. In the synthesis of these opposed sets of tales, Lermontov achieves a completely new genre of Russian prose, the first Russian psychological novel, answering French Romanticism with Russian "simplicity"; he replaces philosophical, stylistic, and generic clichés of the French and Russian Romantic and naturalist traditions with a spare realism learned from Pushkin and thematizes this achievement by creating a hero who is aware of his literary sources. Lermontov does this self-consciously, even didactically; he deliberately uses French works that would be fresh in his readers' minds, showing them how these models can be renovated to become the basis of a nonimitative Russian tradition, of which Pushkin is the exemplar.

Lemontov's sophistication escaped some of his contemporaries: "It is *simply* the unsuccessful experiment of a youthful writer, one who did not yet know how to write books, who was learning to write: the weak, flimsy essay of a young artist with promise. . . . He took up the novel too soon," wrote Osip Senkovsky of *A Hero of Our Time.*[6] This view of the novel as an "immature sketch," in Senkovsky's words, has caused it to be read as a naive adventure tale. Even Nabokov took the novel's repetitions and clichés as signs of Lermontov's ineptitude rather than as clues to his intentions, his mode of characterizing his multiple narrators.[7] But Lermontov was an attentive reader of both Western European and Russian literature, and the study of his intertexts reveals the subtlety of his creative process.

In France in the late 1830s, when Lermontov wrote *A Hero of Our Time,* Romanticism was being replaced by a new realist movement. In a burst of activity from 1829 through the 1830s the group of writers known as Jeune France began publishing in journals that were read in Russia. The novels of Victor Hugo, Eugène Sue, Jules Janin, Honoré de Balzac, Alexandre Dumas fils, and others, first published serially and later in separate volumes, were widely read both in French and in Russian translation. The naturalism of this new generation contrasted with the Romantic works of Rousseau, Senancourt, Chateaubriand, and Constant, on which the Russians as well as the French had grown up. French literature turned toward a detailed depiction of the everyday that took the form first of the horrors of the *école frénétique,* and subsequently of the realism of Balzac, which replaced the earlier Romantic confessional form of soul-searching with a psychological intimacy rooted in a social-historical setting.

In Russia, the Golden Age of poetry was giving way to prose. The French shift in schools contributed to the emergence of Russian physiological sketches, short naturalist tales, and story cycles. As in France, the Russian transition from poetry to prose was also a movement from Romanticism to realism.[8] But Gogol's tales of the Ukraine, his Hoffmannesque Petersburg stories, the naturalist school's grotesque depictions of poor clerks, and Marlinsky's adventure tales in the Walter Scott manner were not helpful models for writing about contemporary Russia or the Petersburg society that Lermontov frequented.[9] In the second part of this chapter we will see how *The Tales of Belkin* helped Lermontov move from the story cycle to the novel; first we will examine what he learned from two distinct generations of French prose.

Some outstanding critics have studied the subject of French sources for *Hero,* starting with Emile Haumant, M. E. Duchesne, and Sergei Rodzevich in the 1910s and culminating with Boris Tomashevsky and V. V. Vinogradov in the 1930s; little has been added to the topic since then.[10] These critics pay particular attention to the alienated Romantic heroes of whom Pechorin is a distillation: Chateaubriand's René, who affected Constant's Adolphe and Senancourt's Obermann, and Musset's next generation hero, Octave, who learned his type from all of them. The earlier French authors had entered Lermontov's creative consciousness well before 1838, and Pushkin had parodied them in *Eugene Onegin* (1823–31). While the criticism unhesitatingly identifies these French *hommes fatales* as forerunners of Pechorin, they generally do not address Lermontov's purpose in associating his hero with them.

In 1913 the Russian scholar Rodzevich updated the work of the French scholar Duchesne, outlining five French sources for *Hero*: Senancourt's *Obermann,* Chateaubriand's *René, Atala,* and *The Natchez,* Constant's *Adolphe,* and Musset's *The Confession of a Child of the Century.* Tomashevsky, discussing the evolution of Lermontov's prose in relation to Western European models, adducing parallel themes and borrowed images, adds two works of the next generation of French prose to this list, Jules Janin's "The Pedestal" and Charles de Bernard's *Gerfaut.*[11] The relevance of Alfred de Vigny's *Servitude and Grandeur of Arms* (containing "Laurette, or the Red Seal"), mentioned by all these critics, has been further explored by Alexander Woronzoff.[12] This criticism is sometimes forgotten, and later analysts have taken up Pechorin's social position and his psychology, rather than the degree to which Lermontov's protagonist, indeed his entire novel, is the product of an argument with a literary tradition.[13]

None of the critics interpret the "borrowings" as purposeful. Rodzevich, despite his thoroughly documented catalogue of the echoes of French works in *Hero,* sees only "reminiscences" of the French authors rather than prototypes or a deliberate pattern of adaptation, and in most cases Tomashevsky denies "influence," considering the French parallels as providing only general background, the atmosphere of the age, rather than carrying intertextual weight.[14] The allusions to the French *homme fatale* do not function as subtexts; rather they identify a tradition, the intertext of the Romantic hero in literature and life. Lermontov creates a hero who is himself aware of these predecessors as well as of the fact that he is inheriting them from Pushkin, predigested by Onegin.[15] Pechorin knows the outworn type of which his own rendition of himself forms a montage; this criticism has simply identified the material Lermontov points to in order to have his readers recognize that Pechorin is as self-aware literarily as he is psychologically, so that they can draw conclusions about the failure of the type. The review of the already established parallels below will suggest this.

There are other important little-known works embedded in *Hero* that helped Lermontov solve structural and thematic problems. In addition to the Romantic tales of his parents' generation, Lermontov conspicuously used recently published French prose, in at least two cases incorporating tales that had appeared in the *Revue étrangère* within the five years before he wrote *Hero.* Since, as we have seen, the *Revue* was being read closely by literary circles in the first years of its publication, the undisguised presence of the borrowings suggests that Lermontov deliberately drew on tales that he knew his readers would have fresh in their minds. By pointing out his own raw materials this way, he deliberately highlights how he has made a truly Russian novel out of a set of well-known French stories.

Lermontov and the French

While the overall theme of the Romantic hero in *A Hero of Our Time* relies on one group of subtexts, a variety of compositional motives governs the selection of the French subtexts for each chapter of the novel; identifying them helps us appreciate Lermontov's impressive synthesis of French sources with Pushkin's prose. The five stories comprising Lermontov's novel require individual analysis and will be examined in this order:

1. Pechorin's type
   - Chateaubriand, *René* (1805)
   - Benjamin de Constant, *Adolphe* (1815)
   - Etienne Pivert de Senancourt, *Obermann* (1804; second edition 1833)
   - Alfred de Musset, *La Confession d'un enfant du siècle* (1836)
2. "Bela" and "Maksim Maksimych"
   - Chateaubriand, *Atala* (1805); *The Natchez* (1826)
   - Balzac, *Scenes from Private Life* (May 1832)
   - Balzac, *A Woman of Thirty* (*Revue de Paris,* April 1832; as a book, 1891)
   - Alfred de Vigny, *Servitude and Grandeur of Arms* (*Revue des deux mondes,* 1833–35; as a book, 1835)
   - de Vigny, "Laurette, or The Red Seal" (*Revue des deux mondes* and *Revue étrangère,* 1833)
3. "Taman"
   - George Sand, "L'Orco" (*Revue des deux mondes,* March 1838)
4. "Princess Mary"
   - Philarète Chasles, "Eglantine" (*Revue étrangère,* June 1833)
   - Charles de Bernard, *Gerfaut* (*Revue de Paris,* June 1838; as a book, 1889)

5. "The Fatalist"
Diderot, *Jacques the Fatalist* (1796)

PECHORIN'S TYPE

In the *roman personnel* of the Romantic period, the French provide the stereotype of the *homme fatale* that governs Pechorin's life.

The lineage descends from Chateaubriand's René (of *The Natchez*) through Constant's Adolphe to Musset's Octave of *Confession of a Child of the Century.* As Sainte-Beuve put it, "All the contradictions encountered in the character of René are found equally in some close variants in many young men later, especially when reading *René* has warned them of it."[16] *René* and *Atala* were first published as part of *The Genius of Christianity* in 1802 and then appeared separately in 1805. They were originally intended to be part of a longer work, *The Natchez,* set in 1730, which was finally published in 1826. Other descendents of René's, tragic Romantic heroes who have also been suggested as ancestors of Pechorin and express some similarly alienated ideas, are passive characters that suffer in isolation, for example, Senancourt's Obermann and de Vigny's Chatterton. While they are less relevant to Pechorin, they are part of the same typological system and show the omnipresence of variations on the theme.

In *The Natchez,* René, bored with society, goes to America where his inability to love the Indian Celuta leads to her death. "Love and suffering were the double lot of everyone who became close to him. Thrown into the world as a great misfortune, his pernicious influence extended to those who surrounded him." He suffers from a "restlessness . . . that pursues him everywhere," and a sense of "moral solitude" as a "higher nature" with an "unbounded and stormy soul."[17]

Adolphe, devoid of a moral sense and buried in self-analysis, is incapable of deep feeling but, to allay his ennui, courts and wins Ellenore, which leads to her death.

Octave is also a suffering hero who makes others suffer and is involved in constant self-analysis. "Not wanting to admit myself an imitator, I lost myself in exaggeration in order to appear original." He torments his lover Brigitte: "To do harm! That was the role that Providence had imposed on me!"[18]

Lermontov creates a composite of these three egocentric characters in Pechorin, who in turn models himself on their confessions (the traveling narrator alludes to another style of confession in his introduction to Pechorin's journal when he compares Pechorin's diary to

Rousseau's *Confessions,* which the narrator considers relevant for Rousseau's account of his own misdeeds). Like his author, Pechorin is well-read in European literature; he refers to Byron and Goethe as well as to the French Romantics and mentions Jeune France and Balzac. As Pushkin does in *Eugene Onegin,* a novel that Pechorin refers to four times, Pechorin identifies his acquaintances in terms of the Western literary tradition: Princess Mary reads Byron in the original; Dr Werner is a materialist version of a German Mephistopheles who limps like Byron; Pechorin reads Walter Scott's *Old Mortality* before dueling with Grushnitsky; and Goethe's Mignon is part of the stereotype that leads him astray in his story "Taman."[19] Finally, "Princess Mary," as Robert Reid says, "represents Pechorin's attempt to write a society tale."[20] The aristocratic circle of spa society is the perfect theater for him to act out his own version of the type of the *homme fatale.*[21] Pechorin has assimilated the literary stereotype, uses it to plan his actions, and incorporates recognizable fragments of it into his script.

In "Princess Mary," Pechorin himself deliberately evokes *Adolphe* and *The Confession of a Child of the Century* in several prominent places. Constant's novel was published in 1816 and translated into Russian three times, once in 1818 and twice in 1831. Prince Vyazemsky's translation of the separate edition was reviewed in the *Moscow Telegraph* in 1831, so that *Adolphe* was well known to Russian readers of the time.[22] Musset's book had just appeared in 1836, and in France, as Emile Haumant says, was to be found in every self-respecting boudoir by 1840.[23]

When Pechorin makes his pathos-filled confession to Mary about his childhood, he is giving a (rather more efficient) paraphrase of Adolphe's and Octave's words to their mistresses. Pechorin says:

> Yes, such has been my lot since my very childhood! Everyone read in my face the signs of bad inclinations, which were not there, but they were supposed to be there—and so they came into existence. I was modest—they accused me of being crafty: I became secretive. I deeply experienced good and evil—nobody caressed me, everybody offended me: I became rancorous. I was gloomy—other children were merry and talkative. I felt myself superior to them—but was considered inferior: I became envious. I was ready to love the whole world—none understood me: and I learned to hate. My colorless youth was spent in a struggle with myself and the world. Fearing mockery, I buried my best feelings at the bottom of my heart. . . . When I got to know well the fashionable world and the mechanism of society, I became skilled in the science of life, and saw how others were happy without that skill.[24]

Adolphe says:

> The constraint I felt with [my father] had a great influence on my character. I was as reserved as he. . . . I accustomed myself to keep all my experiences and plans to myself, relying on myself alone for carrying them out, considering the opinions, interest, help and even the very presence of others as an embarrassment and an obstacle.
>
> I nursed in the depths of my being a longing for emotional experience, but as this found no satisfaction it alienated me from all the things which one by one aroused my curiosity. . . .
>
> I took refuge in stony silence, but this silence was taken for disdain. . . .
>
> I had . . . an insuperable aversion for all the commonplaces and dogmatic formulae. So when I heard stupid people holding forth complacently about established and incontrovertible principles. . . . I felt moved to contradict them . . . by this conduct I soon gave myself a great reputation for shallowness, sarcastic wit and malice. My bitter words were considered the proof of a spiteful disposition, my jokes as attacks on all the most respectable things.[25]

Similarly, Octave confesses to Brigitte in order to win her love:

> God is my witness that I am not as you believe me; I was never in my life suspicious or defiant. I have been ruined, my heart has been broken . . . If you knew what horrors and monstrous perfidies the child who is before you has seen, how they laughed at everything good that was in him, how they took the trouble to teach him everything that leads to doubt, jealousy, to despair! (192–93)

Adolphe and Octave base their claims for sympathy on Rousseau's view that society corrupts the virtuous man. Lermontov emphasizes the degree to which these characters try to manipulate the women they court using what were by then clichés. When Pechorin warns Grushnitsky of the scenario he may replay, he is giving a thumbnail sketch of the plot of *Adolphe*: "Beware, Grushnitsky! Your silence must excite her curiosity, your talk should never entirely satisfy it; you must disturb her every minute. She will disregard convention, publicly, a dozen times for your sake, and will call it a sacrifice, and, in order to reward herself for it, she will begin to torment you, and after that she will simply say that she cannot stand you" (101–2).

Pechorin's manipulative use of his reading is the reverse of Tatyana's in *Onegin*. While, as Olga Hasty has shown, Tatyana "successfully interrelates what she reads with what she experiences," Pechorin is unable to do this.[26] He is as good a reader as she, but, as a man, has to operate within a public sphere, not a private one. And be it said, whatever imaginative integration Tatyana achieves, she is still married to her fat general, just as Pechorin is subject to the usual constraints of a writer and an army officer in tsarist Russia under Nicholas I. He can only manipulate well-known literary gambits, because there are no real life possibilities: he can become the husband of Princess Mary, and enter society dependent on her wealth and position, constrained by its narrow demands; he can remain an army officer trying to subdue the native Caucasian tribes that he identifies with in the name of an Empire he is alienated from; or he can suffer Pushkin's fate as a censored writer exiled from the capital to the South and eventually murdered in some trumped-up duel, as Lermontov did. Pechorin's despair is well founded; he expresses it through the clichés of the alienated Romantic hero. Only in his writing can he transcend his readings, and then not by "rectifying their failed quests" but by highlighting the failure of the Romantic vision to provide a way out of the real constraints he faces.[27]

Lermontov, however, makes structural use of the literary clichés in taking elements from *Adolphe* and *The Confession.* From *Adolphe* he adopts the time-worn structural device of the found documents: the manuscript of Adolphe's account of his affair with Ellenore is acquired by a traveling "Editor" who publishes it as an instructive lesson, "a reasonably true story of the misery of the human heart" (124–25).[28] The found manuscript is accompanied by a letter to the editor that characterizes the hero in a way that Pechorin could have used as a model. Adolphe is "always the victim of this mixture of egotism and sensibility which worked together in him for his own undoing and that of others; foreseeing the evil consequences of an act and yet doing it; and shrinking back in despair after having done it; punished for his qualities even more than for his defects, because his qualities had their origin in his emotions and not in his principles; showing himself in turn the most affectionate and the most cruel of men, but he always ended with cruelty" (124).

Lermontov takes another structural element from Constant (which overlaps with Pushkin's version of this device in *Onegin*): he places Vera's letter to Pechorin at the end of "Princess Mary." Like Ellenore's letter to Adolphe, it contains an analysis of her lover's personality, her own weakness, and her willing sacrifices for him.

Musset's character, Octave's doctor friend, Desgenais, contributes to Lermontov's characterization of (and Pechorin's fondness for) Doctor Werner. Desgenais is "a man full of heart, but dry as pumice stone. A precocious experience rendered him bald prematurely; he knew life and had cried in his time; but his grief wore armor: he was a materialist, and was waiting for death" (40). This description oddly (and conveniently) fits Lermontov's friend, Doctor Nikolay Vasilievich Maier. While Vladimir Golstein considers Maier too limited a character for Lermontov to base Werner on, some superficial features coincide.[29] Lermontov met Maier in Kislovodsk. Lame, short, thin, nervous, sarcastic, Maier is, according to contemporaries who knew him, described accurately in *Hero*: "He had a caustic tongue . . . he made unobtrusive fun of his patients" but "he would cry over a dying soldier" (91). Possibly with Musset's Desgenais in mind, Lermontov made one important change in turning his friend into a literary character: Maier was religious—Werner is a "materialist."[30] Werner visits Pechorin, whom he finds lying on his divan; Desgenais visits his friend Octave when he is sick in bed. Both pairs discuss love. Desgenais says, "I see you believe in love such as romantics and poets represent it. . . . Wanting to find in real life loves like that, eternal and absolute, is the same as looking for women like Venus in the public square," a reasonable assessment of Pechorin's dilemma (41). Werner, true to his characterization as a materialist, gives Pechorin an account of the Princess's medical condition. Musset points explicitly to the relationship of the ideal to the real; Lermontov parodies the issue in Werner's purely physical approach to the "Venus in the public square," where indeed Pechorin first sees Princess Mary.

Werner and Desgenais attempt to temper their friends' despair with these metaphysical considerations. Octave's meditation at the end of his confession on the futility of existence resembles Pechorin's meditation on the stars at the end of the last tale in *Hero,* "The Fatalist":

> Octave: "And we, poor dreamers without a name, pale and sad semblances, imperceptible ephemerals, we who are animated by a breath for one second so that death can exist, we wear ourselves out with fatigue to prove to ourselves that we play a role and that something I don't know perceives us." (311)

> Pechorin: "It amused me to recall that, once upon a time, there were sages who thought that the heavenly bodies took part in our trivial conflicts. . . . These lampads, lit, in the opinion of these sages, merely to illumine their battles and festivals, were burning as brightly as ever, while their passions and hopes had long been extinguished with them." (188)

Pechorin could have learned to blame Providence for his destructive acts from Octave, who says: "To do evil! Such was the sweet role that Providence had imposed on me! I, do evil! I, whom my conscience, even in the middle of my furors, told me that I was good! I whom a pitiless destiny dragged ever forward to an abyss" (299).

Pechorin has no illusions that he is good, though his evil deeds may be involuntary: "I am the indispensable character in the fifth act; involuntarily I play the miserable part of the executioner or traitor. What could be fate's purpose in this?" (133).

Both blame fate/providence for their own misdeeds, but Musset simply accepts Rousseau's "Man is born good," while Lermontov points to the problem of will and moral responsibility.

In "Taman" Pechorin, who himself provoked the attempt on his life by threatening to report the smugglers to the authorities, wonders, "What business did fate have to land me into the peaceful midst of *honest smugglers*?" (79). Pechorin, though blaming fate, is aware of the consequences of his actions, as Octave is not.

There are many more points of overlap between Pechorin and his three models. Pechorin discards the elevated tone of the French confessions but considers some of the same eternal questions. The irony of his self-awareness lies in his being unable to escape the models that have determined the terms of the argument for his generation. Like Octave—who says, "In me there are almost constantly two men: one who laughs, the other who cries"—Pechorin is trapped by the terms of Romanticism that set head against heart: "Within me there are two persons: one of them lives in the full sense of the word, the other thinks and judges him" (163). The false either/or keeps Pechorin from constructing a satisfying existence; he has no model, literary or otherwise, that could provide an alternative to this destructive conception.

What then does Belinsky's famous statement mean, that Pechorin is "an Onegin of our time"?[31] Pushkin had parodied the same composite of the two generations of Romantic heroes and their readers in the character of Onegin, but neither Onegin nor Tatyana becomes an intelligent reader until it is too late to change the outcome of their relationship; Lermontov gives Pechorin the literary self-awareness to both recognize and deploy his models. But although Pechorin, like the French heroes, sees the dilemma of solipsism that this awareness engenders, he cannot escape its terms. In this Pechorin is an emblem of the dilemma Lermontov faces as a writer: how to move beyond the French literary models of the age to create a truly Russian novel. Pechorin fails to free himself from the models he manipulates, but Lermontov succeeds.

"BELA" AND "MAKSIM MAKSIMYCH"

As Boris Eikhenbaum put it, "you had to be very brave to write a tale set in the Caucasus in 1838."[32] By the 1830s the setting had become a cliché, and contemporaries were bound to compare Lermontov's subject with Pushkin's poem "A Prisoner of the Caucasus" (*Kavkazskii plennik*) (as well as Lermontov's imitation of it) and to Marlinsky's Caucasian tales *Ammalat-Bek* and *Mulla Nur,* which had recently been republished in his collected works.[33] As E. N. Mikhaylova points out, "Bela" contains two abductions, one theft, one attempted murder, and two murders, running the risk of sounding like Marlinsky's overwrought exoticism. She sees Lermontov's antidote to this in "Bela's" narrative strategy: these adventures are recounted by the simple officer, Maksim Maksimych, to the traveling narrator. Mikhaylova thinks Pushkin's *Journey to Arzrum* was the inspiration for this device.[34]

Lermontov pointedly adopts Pushkin's realist reversal of Romantic renditions of the Caucasian tribes.[35] Pushkin's practical differentiation among the Caucasian groups is repeated by Maksim Maksimych. In *Arzrum,* Pushkin tells us:

> The Cherkess hate us. We've pushed them out of their untrammeled pasture lands; their auls [villages] are ruined, whole tribes are destroyed. . . .
>
> The Ossetians are the poorest tribe of the peoples inhabiting the Caucasus; their women are beautiful and, it is said, very well disposed to travelers. (6:647, 649)

Maksim tells the narrator of "Bela":

> "What a people! [The Ossetians] can't even say 'bread' in Russian, but they've managed to learn 'officer, give me a tip!' In my opinion, even the Tatars are better: at least they don't drink." . . .
>
> "An extremely foolish people! They don't know how to do anything and are incapable of any kind of education! Our Kabardans or our Chechens, though they may be robbers and paupers, are at least reckless daredevils; but these people aren't even interested in weapons; you won't see a decent dagger on a single one of them. These are real Ossetians for you!" (6, 8)

Maksim differentiates among the Caucasian tribes in practical terms as Pushkin had; Lermontov juxtaposes Maksim's "realist" manner to the traveling narrator's pseudo-Rousseauian one.[36] For Maksim as for Pushkin, the precise detail of immediate experience renders reality, not someone else's ideas about noble savagery. This is one of the ways *Hero* challenges Romanticism and its clichés. Lermontov sets Maksim's first-hand opinions into a network of points of view, from Rousseau's idealization of a state of nature to the traveling narrator's over-simple understanding of Rousseau to Maksim, who reads nothing at all but speaks from his own experience; the author clearly values the last of these most. For this method Lermontov had another source: Alfred de Vigny's "Laurette, or the Red Seal."

De Vigny's tale consists of three parts, which form the second half of the first book of his *Servitude and Grandeur of Arms.*[37] Published in installments from 1833 to 1835 in the *Revue des deux mondes,* the plot and narrative devices of "Laurette" are the closest models for "Bela" of the many works discussed by critics. The two tales are so very close that Lermontov must have expected his readers to recognize his source, particularly because "Laurette" was published not only in France but also in Petersburg, in the *Revue étrangère,* only five years before Lermontov wrote "Bela." The narrator of "Bela" tells us in "Maksim Maksimych" that he wrote down Maksim's tale of Bela to divert himself, "not imagining that it would become the first link of a long chain of stories" (50). Although we can't be sure of the order in which Lermontov wrote *Hero,* the closeness with which Lermontov patterned "Bela" on "Laurette" suggests de Vigny's *Servitude* as the likely stimulus for his beginning "Bela."

In "Laurette," the narrator encounters an old soldier on the road to Flanders who tells him a tragic tale of two lovers, Laurette and her husband. Woronzoff noted the similarity between this and the way the narrator of "Bela" meets Maksim Maksimych on the Georgian Military Road, where he hears from him the tragic tale of Bela and Pechorin. Woronzoff does not go into the details discussed below, but does quote the descriptions of the two officers. De Vigny's "was a man of about fifty, big and strong, with white mustaches, his back bowed in the manner of infantry officers who have carried a pack. He was in uniform, and one could glimpse a battalion major's epaulette under his threadbare short blue cloak. He had a hard but kindly face, of which there are so many in the army."[38]

Maksim Maksimych "wore an officer's frock-coat, without epaulettes, and a shaggy Circassian cap. He seemed about fifty years old; his tanned complexion indicated that his face had long been acquainted with the Trans-Caucasian sun and his prematurely grayed mustache did not harmonize with his firm gait and vigorous appearance" (4).

Woronzoff's parallel can be supported by comparing the description of Maksim to a sketch Lermontov wrote in 1841, "The Caucasian Veteran" (*Kavkazets*). Lermontov wrote it for Bashutsky's collection of physiological sketches, *Russians, Described by Themselves* (*Nashi, spisannye s natury russkimi*), but it was prohibited by censorship. It begins: "First of all, what exactly is a Caucasian veteran and what are Caucasian veterans like? A Caucasian is a being half Russian, half Asian. . . . He is

Alfred de Vigny (*Revue étrangère* 7 [1833])

usually from thirty to forty-five years old; his face is tanned and a little pock-marked; if he's not a staff-captain, then he's probably a major."[39] After five or six years of repetitious and boring duty, "he has become gloomy and silent; he sits and smokes his little pipe; he also reads Marlinsky and says it's very good" (476).

The sketch is a collective portrait of a type that Lermontov would have distilled from his experience in the Caucasus, and it clearly overlaps with the portrait of Maksim Maksimych. But Maksim lacks the pockmarks and is, importantly for Lermontov's purposes, not a reader, while the "Caucasian veteran" lacks the mustaches, the age, and the contrasting firm tread that echo de Vigny's description. Furthermore, correcting the *Fatherland Notes* version of "Bela" for separate publication, Lermontov changed Maksim's age from "around forty, not more" to fifty, possibly to make the parallel with "Laurette" more precise.[40]

The similarities to de Vigny's tale do not end there. The old major and the captain are important participants in the love stories they recount to the narrators. De Vigny's major was formerly a sea captain. He had taken a young couple onto his ship bound for Cayenne in French Guiana in 1797. The young man has been ordered into deportation by the Directoire; the major is entrusted with a red-sealed letter to be read only upon reaching the Equator. During the trip he develops great fondness for his charges: "I ended up, after a month, looking upon them as my own little children." He even proposes quitting his ship and settling down with them in Cayenne: "Myself, I haven't any more family than a stray dog, which grieves me" (25). Maxim Maksimych regards Bela similarly: "Eventually I got so used to her, she might have been my daughter; and she was fond of me too. I should tell you I don't have a family; it's already been twelve years or so since I have had news of my father and mother, and I never thought of providing myself with a wife" (35). This involvement leads both lonely men to eavesdrop on their charges. The Captain tells the narrator: "I'd only to bend forwards a little to see through the big hatch, into their little room, so I peered in. The young woman was on her knees, saying her prayers, lit by a little lamp. She was in her shift, and from above I could see her bare shoulders, her bare little feet, and her long blonde hair all disheveled. I thought to leave, but then I said to myself: 'Dammit! An old soldier, what's it matter?' So I stayed to watch. . . . What a little love she was!" (28–29).

He watches a long scene between Laurette and her husband in which the young man regrets having married her only to take her into deportation. The Captain, instead of considering the situation, comments only on Laurette's words about himself: "She had put this so sweetly!—calling me that good man of a Captain, that I was much touched. . . . [T]hey began to embrace again; I stamped briskly on the deck to make them stop" (31).

Similarly, Maksim manages to observe Bela and Pechorin through a window: "Never shall I forget one scene: I was going past her window and glanced in; Bela was sitting on the stove ledge with her head bent low, and Pechorin was standing before her" (25). Maksim then relates a dialogue between the two involving Bela's resistance to Pechorin's attempts to win her affection, and another when Pechorin brings her presents and succeeds, which Maksim this time observes "standing on the other side of the door." Maksim too reacts in terms of his own interest: "I must admit . . . it vexed me to think that no woman ever loved me like that" (27). The love story is secondary to the characterization of the old officers.

Both characters, on the verge of tears, relate tragic love stories through the prism of their own hurt and loss; they quell their tears by admitting their own insignificance. The captain, though telling about the execution of the husband and the subsequent madness of the wife, is equally sorry for himself. Horrified when he finds that the letter orders him to execute the young man, but devoted to his duty, he informs the young man of his fate and promises to take care of Laurette. "Oh! It was hard for me, all of it." He describes the couple's leave-taking, asking, "Don't you find my situation appalling?" (35). He rages against the Directoire: "I'd like to have shot all five of them—the cowards! Much I care! A life like mine" (36). Maksim tells of Bela's days of death agony, concluding, "It saddened me: before her death she did not remember me once, and yet, it seems, I had loved her like a father. Well, God forgive her! And in truth, who am I to be remembered by anybody before death?" (47).

The narrators of the stories, however, both of whom belong to a higher class than their companions the traveling soldiers, are less interested in the feelings of the storytellers than in hearing the ending of the tales. De Vigny's narrator recounts: "The Major's voice faltered little by little . . . on he marched, biting his lips and knitting his brows in fierce and terrible abstraction. . . . I realized that he was not going to say any more of his own accord and that I must make up my mind to question him" (36). Lermontov's narrator expects a tale from Maksim ("I wanted dreadfully to get some story or other from him") and constantly prompts him to continue: "Now you will finish your story about Bela. I'm sure it didn't end there." Maksim twice tries to hide his emotions, when telling of Bela's death and in "Maksim Maksimych," after Pechorin rides off without dining with him, which leaves Maksim "trying to assume an indifferent air, although a tear of vexation would still sparkle from time to time on his eyelashes" (60). Unlike de Vigny, Lermontov shows his narrator to be exploitative and insensitive, representing one of a range of faulty narrators whose unreliability is essential to both Pechorin's and Lermontov's realism.

The unnamed young husband of "Laurette" bears some resemblance to the narrator's description of the twenty-three-year-old Pechorin: "he was nineteen; a handsome lad, though rather pale, and too fair for a man" (24). Pechorin's "skin had a kind of feminine tenderness of texture"; he has "fair hair" and a "pale, noble brow" (56). That de Vigny's hero has been condemned to be shot at sea by the Directoire seems to have nothing to do with *Hero.* But the young husband is being punished for having written "three satirical couplets on the Directory . . . I was arrested . . . and at first condemned to death, but then to deportation as an act of clemency" (33). He wails, "Why did I ever learn to write! To write—it's the occupation of a madman! I believed in their liberty of the press! Where were my wits? Oh! And why do it at all? To print five or six little mediocre ideas, read only by those who already agree with them, thrown into the fire by those that hate them, and effective only in getting us persecuted!" (30).

Whether Lermontov read these words before or after he himself was arrested, deported, and sent to the Caucasus for writing "Death of a Poet" in 1837, the substitution of the tsar for the Directoire is an obvious one. The circumstances of censorship in Russia, especially under Nicholas I, as emphasized by the circumstances surrounding "Death of a Poet," were enough to make Lermontov react strongly to the words of de Vigny's young husband even if he first read "Laurette" before 1837. By the time he was writing "Bela" in 1838, the situation would have had particular poignancy for him. His use of "Laurette" in "Bela" not only underscores his literary method but also smuggles an image of his own martyrdom into print.[41] The very closeness with which Lermontov follows de Vigny's story asks the reader to make this connection.

"Laurette" comprises the second half of the first book of *Servitude and Grandeur of Arms,* containing parts 4 through 6: part 4, "Of an Encounter I Had One Day on the High Road"; part 5, "The Story of the Red Seal"; and part 6, "How I Continued on My Way." Parts 4 and 5 correspond to "Bela": In part 4, the narrator recounts his meeting with the old soldier and introduces the tale: "So the good major prepared to talk, solemnly, with a childlike pleasure" (22). Part 5 contains the major's story of the tragic sea voyage that culminates in his executing the young husband. The young widow goes mad, and the major transfers to the land forces in order to keep her with him until the end of his life. The narrator suddenly realizes that Laurette is in the mule-drawn wagon the major has been leading throughout their progress along the road.

Part 6 corresponds to "Maksim Maksimych." In it we are finally introduced to Laurette. The narrator is moved:

> I worked out that from 1797 to 1815, where we now were, eighteen years had gone by in this way for this man. . . ."You're an admirable man," I said to him. . . .
>
> During the fourteen years I have lived in the army, it was in it alone, and above all in the ranks of the poor and despised infantry, that I found again men of this antique character, men pushing the sentiment of duty to its final consequences, having no compunction about their obedience nor shame for their poverty, simple of manners and language. (42–43)

De Vigny's narrator is closely autobiographical, and his closing words quoted above are meant to be taken at face value. Lermontov's narrator asks his readers at the end of "Bela," "You must admit, though, that Maksim Maksimych is a man worthy of respect, isn't he? If you admit that, I shall be fully rewarded for my story, which perhaps has been too long" (49). Unbeknownst to himself, the narrator is as much a character in his own narration as Maskim; revealed to be a narrowly glory-seeking would-be author of exotic travel notes in the course of "Bela," the narrator represents the naive and exploitative "exotic" tradition of Marlinsky and others that Lermontov, following Pushkin in *A Journey to Arzrum,* rejects in *Hero.*[42] By the end of "Maksim Maksimych," Lermontov's author of travel notes has become disillusioned in his hero and concludes, "My good Maksim Maksimych had turned into a stubborn and grumpy junior captain!" (62). De Vigny's narrator is not put to any polemical use, whereas Lermontov's narrator is shown to be in search of literary stereotypes and therefore disappointed by reality.

De Vigny's simple officer tells his tragic tale to a more sophisticated young narrator, who then writes it down for the reading public. De Vigny reproduces the old officer's speech with its colloquialisms, admiring him even while revealing his limitations. *Servitude* is made up of narratives within his narrative throughout. In part 3, "The Malacca Cane," three successive characters within the narrated tale take over the narration, as is the case in "Bela" when Maksim reports Kazbich's tale of his stolen horse. The series of tales in *Servitude* is unified structurally by the principal narrator and thematically by his exploration of how the thinking individual should act.

In Lermontov's hands, de Vigny's structural device takes on complex meaning; the nature of the narration of the tale is as much the subject of the story as the tale told. As Robin Aizelwood puts it, "the theme of multiplicity or variety of voice, language, and viewpoint, and derived motifs such as relativism, contradiction, and the combination of the alternation of opposites can be seen to inform the novel at every level, acting as the constructive principle as well as the character portrait."[43]

Lermontov replaces the secondary theme of the major's (misguided) adherence to duty with the implicit commentary on the condescending traveling narrator; he rewrites de Vigny's tale of the persecuted French exile and his young doomed bride as the tale of the (exiled) Russian man in love with the native woman ("*dikarka*") who loses her life for him, familiar from Pushkin's *A Prisoner of the Caucasus.* By thematizing the narrator, transposing the tragic love tale and setting "Bela" into dialogue with the other four parts of his novel, Lermontov shows his audience how to renovate a Russian cliché with the aid of a French model.

Lermontov could find examples of the genre of the tale of the "*dikarka*" or "*sauvageresse*" in both the Russian and the French traditions from which the Russians had learned it in the first place. Interest in the theme had reappeared in France in the 1830s with the publication of Amedée Pichot's *Pocahontas* in the *Revue de Paris.* There Pichot returns to the American Indians made popular in France by Chateaubriand in 1802 with the publication of *The Genius of Christianity,* containing *René.* Pichot takes up an historical tale that adheres to the pattern of both Pushkin's and Lermontov's *A Prisoner of the Caucasus,* in which the *sauvageresse* kills herself for love of a European. Rodzevich, summarizing the similarities between the tales of a European young man's love for a native maiden, sees *The Natchez* as a predecessor of "Bela."[44] Lermontov wrote his imitation of Pushkin's *A Prisoner of the Caucasus* in 1828, at age fourteen; the theme of the beautiful black-eyed native girl appears to have been as powerful for him as Pushkin's poetry was, and may have merged with his reading of Chateaubriand's prose treatment, which is closer to Bela's tale. The details suggest that Lermontov remembered *The Natchez* clearly.

René marries the lovely Indian maiden Celuta, who is already in love with him, out of gratitude to her brother, who has saved his life.

> The sacrifice was severe: all ties were irksome to [him]; his heart was unsusceptible to passion. . . . [René] had wished for a desert, a wife and liberty; he possessed them all, and yet something poisoned this possession . . . when he pressed his young spouse to his bosom amidst precipices . . . he found not the pleasures of which he had dreamt. The void formed at the bottom of his soul could no longer be filled. . . . René carried trouble with him wherever he went; he was a weight to the earth which he trod with impatience and which bore him with regret" (2:123, 126).

Chateaubriand (*Revue étrangère* 19 [1836])

Celuta is aware that René's love has cooled:

> The alarm of Celuta and the kind of fear which her husband incited in her grows. To her René was inexplicable; she had nevertheless perceived something mysterious lurking at the bottom of the heart of the man to whom she was united. . . . After his return to the hut, René seemed to become more gloomy and less fond: the timid Celuta durst not question him, and she began to take for satiety and inconstancy what was but the effect of an impenetrable character. (2:131).

René's melancholy increases: "He passed whole days in the recesses of the forests" (2:149). "He delighted only in strolling about at random;

he never told what he did, or whither he was going, nay, he did not even know that himself. . . . Seated at the door of her hut, Celuta waited whole days for her husband . . . she reproached herself for having neither beauty nor fondness enough" (2:158). When René is killed, Celuta drowns herself, in grief over the loss of her beloved. Like Pushkin's, Lermontov's Cherkessian maiden in *A Prisoner of the Caucasus* drowns herself when her beloved tells her he loves another; in *Atala* the (half) Indian maid poisons herself to resolve the conflict between her vows of chastity to her mother and her desire for her beloved. In *Pocahontas* the Indian maid poisons herself and takes three days to die because of love for Captain John Smith. But only *The Natchez* contains this description of the native woman's grief at the gradual cooling of the hero's love.

Pechorin too takes to the woods after winning Bela. Maksim tells of trying to console Bela in her grief over the cooling of Pechorin's love:

> "Yesterday I thought and thought all day," she answered through her tears, "I imagined various accidents. . . . And today I'm beginning to think that he does not love me . . .
>
> She started to cry . . .
>
> I began to reason with her . . ."he can't be expected to stay here, as if sewn to your skirt; he is a young man, he likes to chase game; he'll roam for a while, and then come back, but if you're going to mope, you'll bore him all the sooner." (36)

René's history of life among the Indians spans years; Lermontov condenses the adventure aspect of Chateaubriand's long tale (war/torture/near death/rescues/death) into Kazbich and Azamat's reported actions, and the story of Pechorin's failed love for Bela into a few weeks' (and far fewer pages') duration. He parodies Chateaubriand's Indians' high-flown rhetoric by having his traveling narrator relate Kazbich's tale about his lost horse in Romantic style, while claiming to repeat Kazbich's words. Kazbich's love for his horse is the only ideal love in *Hero;* in an ironic commentary on the genre, Kazbich has named his horse "Karagyoz," black eyes, the epithet routinely applied to the "*dikarka,*" a "black-eyed maid" (*chernookaia deva*), and used by Lermontov to describe his "young Cherkesh maid" (*cherkeshen'ka mladaia*) in his *A Prisoner of the Caucasus.*[45] Thus in "Bela," while the actions belong to the natives, the stylistics are those of the author of travel notes who has embellished whatever report-in-translation of Kazbich's oral tale Maksim has given him, using then-popular models. Like many other things in the novel, it is impossible to know the two earlier versions, each of which is eclipsed in turn until all we have is the unnatural language of

Lermontov's self-absorbed narrator.[46] But we can identify both the original material and its parody—the love story of a native maiden for a European man told in elevated style, and Lermontov's resetting of it into a subtly implied rich context that calls into question both the literary (high-flown diction, clichéd plot) and the social conventions (Saidian orientalism, imperial conquest) that created it.

Different genres inform "Maksim Maksimych." When the narrator finally meets Pechorin, he is predisposed by Maksim's account to find him to be a bored Romantic hero, but on seeing him in the flesh, uses a more realist genre to describe him physically, depicting him as a "thirty year-old coquette of Balzac's." He has in mind Madame de Vieumesnil[47] in Balzac's *A Woman of Thirty*:

> Like almost all women who have very long hair, she was pale and perfectly white. Her skin, of a prodigious fineness, a symptom that rarely deceives, announced a true sensibility. . . .
>
> The bend of her neck, the carelessness of her body, tired but supple, that seemed broken in two equal parts in the armchair, the abandon of her legs, the insouciance of her pose, her movements full of lassitude, everything revealed a woman without interest in life.[48]

Compare Pechorin:

> In contrast to the light shade of his hair, his mustaches and eyebrows were black—a sign of breeding in man. . . .
>
> When he settled upon the bench, his straight figure flexed in such a way that you would think there was not a single bone in his spine; the attitude of his whole body expressed a kind of nervous debility. (56–57)

Madame de Vieumesnil's future lover first sees her "sitting in a corner by the chimney in her favorite attitude, an attitude full of melancholy"; the narrator describes Pechorin as he is sitting on a bench at the inn, associating him with her melancholy.[49]

With this allusion to Balzac, Lermontov tells us about the narrator, who concludes his description by emphasizing, "these are my own remarks based on my own observations, and I don't want to force you to believe in them blindly." We are urged to consider how the narrator mediates his experience through literature, and hence to appreciate Lermontov's recasting of the works evoked, directly as here, or indirectly in other cases, in *Hero.* The comparison between a "strongly built" twenty-three-year-old Russian officer in the Caucasus and a thirty-year-old disillusioned woman in a drawing room armchair is funny, parodying both of them by radical juxtaposition.

Balzac's story was first published in a journal and then became part of *Scenes from Private Life.* The book is made up of six associated stories that are *almost* united by their heroine; while they follow a chronology and general plot system that suggests that the heroine is the same throughout, Balzac refused to give her a single name: "The character who traverses, so to speak, these six tableaux of which [this book] is composed is not one figure; it is one thought."[50] Balzac's book, like de Vigny's, shows how resonances can be built up through the juxtaposition of several more or less independent stories. Lermontov does more with this model than either de Vigny or Balzac attempted: while maintaining the independence of each narrative (except for "Maksim Maksimych," the tales may be read separately), Lermontov's tales accrue increasing layers of meaning as they gain the perspectives of different narrators and those narrators' frames of reference.[51]

Lermontov's achievement in "Bela" and "Maksim Maksimych" is to have taken the overblown adventure stories of Scott via Marlinsky, the forthright serial stories of de Vigny, and the high-flown Romantic prose inappropriate to its subject of Chateaubriand, purified them through the pared-down poetry of Pushkin's *A Prisoner of the Caucasus,* and created the rich dialogicity of several elements: the languages of native tribes, simple spoken Russian, and Russian Romantic prose. The reader is forced to consider the personality as well as the literary frame of reference of each narrator, become aware of the collision of several cultural tendencies and thus become a sophisticated interpreter.[52] Lermontov creates for the reader the experience Tatyana had in Onegin's library, when she realizes not only what Onegin read but how he responded by noting his markings in the margins.

While we have some understanding of Onegin's behavior, in *Hero* the multiple filters of clashing narrators make Pechorin's actions, motives, and reactions unknowable. In the first two tales, they have acquired two sets of interpretations: Maksim thinks Pechorin selfish and unfeeling, while the narrator takes him for the embodiment of several literary types; although he has compared Pechorin to a woman out of Balzac, he tells Maksim that the fashion of being bored comes not from the French, as Maksim suggests, but from the English. Presumably he is thinking of Byron, while Maksim may have picked up distant echoes of *René;* Lermontov builds the novel's ambiguity, dialogicity, and parody on the interplay of Russian literature and reality with the whole European, predominantly but not exclusively French, tradition of the first third of the century.

"TAMAN"

Pechorin demonstrates his self-awareness, both as character and as author, in his story "Taman." Lermontov creates this tale from his own experience in Taman, although it is not known just what that experience was; the setting and mysterious characters are based on reality, as suggested by his friend M. Tseidler's description of them, if we can believe his memoir.[53] Tseidler lived in the same house in Taman that Lermontov had stayed in, and wrote an account of its inhabitants—the blind boy, the Tatar, and the girl with the "slender waist" and "antique profile."[54] Lermontov passes these realia through the prism of two fairy tales, George Sand's "L'Orco" and Zhukovsky's "Undine," to provide a double reading of events. On a first reading, "Taman" hints at the uncanny; the second reading reduces the initial ambiguity to mundanity.

"Taman" is clearly a crafted story written by Pechorin, who recreates for the reader his own adventure as he initially experienced it, while at the same time incorporating his later understanding of events that becomes accessible only on a second reading. Because Pechorin wants his reader initially to experience the events of "Taman" in the same supernatural light he had, he invokes German Romanticism in writing his tale; he compares his "mermaid" to Goethe's Mignon from *Wilhelm Meister,* as well as to the German writer La Motte-Fouqué's *Undine* (1811), which Zhukovsky had translated into Russian verse in 1837.[55] The allusions to the German works, like the supernatural atmosphere of the tale, turn out to be false leads; we will return to them after we examine the most determining model for "Taman," which is French.

George Sand's story "L'Orco" was published in the *Revue des deux mondes* in March 1838, just before Lermontov began writing *Hero,* soon after his stay in Taman in 1837. Leonid Zurov discovered the relationship and published a three-page note listing some plot similarities between "Taman" and "L'Orco" in *Novyi zhurnal* in 1961, setting out six brief textual parallels, but he omits the frame tale and offers no interpretation, which leaves it to us to examine what Lermontov made of it.[56]

Sand's story takes place in Venice, then under Austrian power. A masked Venetian beauty has been taking Austrian officers onto her gondola at night; they disappear, never to be seen again. "The customs officers of the coast guard had often seen a black shadow glide over the canals and, taking it for the boat of a smuggler [*contrebandier*], had chased it," but after a police spy drowns, they all develop a superstitious terror of it (586).[57] A young Austrian officer, Franz Lichtenstein,

George Sand (*Revue étrangère* 21 [1837])

encounters the masked lady in front of a church late at night. He loves Venice, and the warnings he has been given about the gondola excite his curiosity about it. He is a free spirit, described in a way Lermontov could identify with: "Despite his nobleman's bad education, he had been able to keep his spirit from all prejudice, and to keep in his heart a place for liberty. His position forced him to conceal his ideas and his tastes in public, but as soon as he had performed his work, he hastened to take off his uniform which seemed to him indissolubly linked to all the vices of the government he served" (587).

By using "L'Orco" as subtext, Lermontov draws an implicit parallel between Austria's imperial domination of Venice and Russia's colonization of the Caucasus.[58] Aware, like Franz, of "all the vices of the government he served," Lermontov sympathizes with the Caucasians, yet, also like Franz, finds himself in the role of Russian officer attempting to impose an oppressive foreign rule on them.

Standing near the veiled lady in front of the church, Franz hears her sigh and "recognize[s] a verse of patois and a popular refrain that he had already heard on the squares" (588). Similarly, when Pechorin first meets his undine, she is singing a mysterious song using a folk language.

The masked lady takes charge: "Follow me," she says and leads Franz to an unknown destination. "The moon had hidden itself. Franz could hardly see where he put his foot, and could distinguish nothing in the deep shadows that enveloped him from every side. At random he followed his guide who seemed on the contrary to know the way very well. From time to time some gleams gliding across the clouds showed Franz the edge of a canal, a door, a vault. . . . Franz quickly realized that he was at the mercy of his guide" (589).

Compare this scene with Pechorin's rendezvous with his undine, when "the moon had not yet risen," and she leads Pechorin to her boat: "'Follow me,' she said, taking me by the hand, and we began to descend. I wonder that I did not break my neck" (76).[59]

The mysterious lady gives Franz a series of rendezvous at night. During one of these at a church, he is "always subjugated by a mysterious power. Although she spoke for several hours, never sitting down, neither her voice nor her body betrayed any fatigue" (590). Their night meetings continue for several days; he never sees her face or asks her name. "Although no single word of love had passed between them, Franz had reason to believe she recognized his passion and felt disposed to share it" (593). Eros motivates Pechorin's involvement with his, also nameless, undine, who lures him to their night meeting with a passionate kiss.

Franz's final encounter with his lady takes place at a ball at a palazzo. There she takes a guitar and sings: "Dance, laugh, sing, gay children of Venice! You are the happy ones of the world, and Venice is the queen of nations. . . . Be on your guard! The eyes see, the ears hear, the tongues speak. . . . Midnight! and the choir of the dead will come to scream in our ears: Servitude! Servitude!" (595). Pechorin uses a similarly declamatory style as he follows the blind boy to the shore, thinking (quoting

Isaiah 35:5–6): "On that day the dumb shall cry out and the blind shall see" (68).

At the ball in "L'Orco," Franz is wearing his uniform so that his lady finally realizes he is Austrian. Lermontov echoes this in "Princess Mary," where Grushnitsky's real status is revealed when he wears his epaulettes to the ball. Leaving the Venetian ball, the masked lady takes Franz to her gondola, which she rows "with a strong arm." "'Where are we going?' he said, after a moment of reflection. 'Where destiny wants us to go,' she replied in a somber voice . . . the gondola seemed to fly over the waters" (596). This resembles the undine's evasive answer: "'What's your name, my songstress?' 'He who christened me knows'" (75). "[Franz] no longer saw anything around him but shadow and before him the great white form of his companion. Standing at the poop, her hands on the oar, her hair loose on her shoulders, and her long white garments in disorder abandoned to the wind, she resembled less a woman than the spirit of shipwrecks playing on the stormy waves. 'Where are we?' Franz cried in an agitated voice. 'The Captain is afraid,' responded the unknown woman with a disdainful laugh" (597). He approaches her but she stamps so forcefully that he loses balance and falls senseless on the deck. He awakes to find her at his feet, and she avows her love for him. Suddenly she exclaims over the stars but adds, "But what does it matter? The stars have no power over our destinies" (597).

In the parallel scene in *Hero,* his undine has made an assignation with him to meet on the shore at night. As the undine leads Pechorin through the moonless night to her boat, he sees "only two little stars, like two rescue beacons, glittering on the dark-blue vault . . . 'Let's get into the boat,' said my companion; I hesitated—I am no amateur of sentimental promenades on the sea—but this was not the moment to retreat. She jumped into the boat, I followed, and had barely recovered my senses when I noticed that we were adrift. 'What does this mean?' I said crossly. 'It means,' she said, seating me on the thwart and winding her arms around my waist, 'it means that I love you'" (77).

The undine throws Pechorin's pistol into the water. "Oh, here a terrible suspicion stole into my soul, the blood rushed to my head. I look around—we're about a hundred yards from the shore and I can't swim!" After a desperate struggle in which the girl tries to throw Pechorin into the water, she confesses, "You saw . . . you'll tell the authorities." In Sand's story, the masked woman confesses to Franz that she has drowned the Austrian officers, just as she is about to determine whether he lives or dies. Having chosen to love Franz rather than to destroy him, the masked lady sacrifices her life; as in "Taman," against her expectations, it is the woman who falls into the sea first instead of her terrified prey.

However fantastical, the story has so far remained within the realm of realism. At this point in "L'Orco," a ship looms on the horizon. It is the Bucentaur, the state barge that, according to ancient Venetian custom, the doge would take out on Ascension Day to wed Venice and the Adriatic by dropping a ring into it. "A red light emanated from its flanks and surrounded it on all sides; great phantoms stood immobile on the bridge, and a quantity of oars rose and fell in cadence, striking the wave with a sinister noise, and cavernous voices sang the *Dies irae,* accompanying themselves with the noises of a chain" (599).

From the ship comes a voice: "Do you love?" The masked lady explains that she has been seeking her beloved among Austrian officers; if she hates him, *he* will die, but if she loves him, *she* will die. She answers, "I love," and is immediately claimed by the Bucentaur. Franz falls into the waves. "Coming to the surface, he saw nothing more, neither the gondola, nor the Bucentaur, nor his beloved. Only little lights gleaming on the horizon. It was the lanterns of the Murano fishermen. He swam in the direction of their island" (599).

In "Taman" the parallels Lermontov draws to "L'Orco" are concentrated in the plot elements of the undine's seduction of Pechorin: the adventurous traveling officer in a foreign place falls prey to a mysterious woman who leads him to the shore in the dark over unknown terrain, takes him into her boat in order to drown him; her defiant song about her hidden motives; the surprising denouement in which the officer is thrown into the water but swims to safety. But the contrast between the elegant masked Venetian lady in a gondola and a poor girl in a dinghy living in a miserable little town on the Black Sea could not be more extreme. Lermontov translates magnificent Venice into grubby Taman and compares the lady at a masked ball to a Ukrainian smuggler girl. Perhaps he was inspired by the exotic dress of the Tatar woman he met at Taman, as described by Tseidler: "Her luxurious braids fell on her shoulders from under a little velvet hat; a silk *beshmet* gathered by a belt outlined her slender waist, and her little feet in yellow *meshty* peeped from under the broad folds of her sharovars."[60] But Lermontov forgoes this eroticized exotic elegance to emphasize the poverty of Taman.

More importantly, Sand's story also inspired the structure of the tale. Sand's plot of the mysterious lady is presented by a framing tale. Similar to the way Pechorin introduces us to Taman, arousing our expectations of a supernatural tale, Sand's introduction sets an ominous scene: "The evening was stormy, the air heavy and the sky filled with black clouds which were furrowed with frequent lightning. We all maintained a melancholy silence. One would have said that the sadness of the atmosphere had entered our hearts, and we felt involuntarily disposed to tears" (584).

The hostess and narrator of the story, Beppa, sadly thinks of the many "sisters" she has lost, and of one in particular, the mysterious heroine who perishes at the arrival of the supernatural Bucentaur. When Beppa finishes her story, she has tears in her eyes, and so does her audience. Suddenly Beppa says, vivaciously,

> Well! What do you have to be so sad about? Is this the effect that fairy tales produce? Haven't you ever heard tell of the *orco,* the Venetian *Trilby*? Haven't you seen it in the evening, in churches or on the canals? It is a good spirit that only does harm to traitors or oppressors. One could say that it is the guardian demon of Venice. But the Viceroy, having heard indirectly of the perilous adventure of Count Lichtenstein, had the patriarch make a great exorcism of the canals, and since that time the *orco* has never reappeared. (599).

Beppa's story, which began realistically, turns supernatural at the end; with the magical appearance of the mythical Bucentaur, it reveals itself to be a fairy tale. "Orco" means "ogre" in Italian, which would not have been any more immediately apparent to Sand's French audience than to a Russian one, so that they could ignore the fairy-tale implications of the title on a first reading. "Trilby" refers to Charles Nodier's fantastic tale "Trilby, or the Imp of Argyle" (1822), in which a Scottish fisherman's wife falls in love with her household spirit; an ancient monk exorcises Trilby from the household, but the wife goes to her death to be united with him.[61] In "L'Orco," the frame tale provokes a rereading that reveals the reader's mistaken involvement with what had appeared to be real life events. This structural device of requiring a rereading for the full import of the tale is even more central to Lermontov's writing of "Taman" than are the plot parallels. Pechorin is a writer, who by writing "Taman" demonstrates his self-awareness as well as his literary sophistication.[62] He writes the story to explore how he allowed his literary frame of reference to obscure reality, endangering his own life. For Lermontov, who presumably experienced some element of this, it represents a real-life instance of the dangers of projective reading that Pushkin had warned against in *Eugene Onegin.*

The narrator's name, Beppa, suggests that Sand's narrator is a female version of Byron's *Beppo* (1818). Also subtitled "A Venetian Story," Byron's poem uses mock-heroic style to reverse a cliché: the husband, disguised as a Turk, returns after many years and confronts his wife and her lover, only to be reconciled over a cup of coffee: where you expect daggers and death you get mundane reasonableness. Sand reinforces her Byronic allusion with the Bucentaur, to which Byron refers in *Childe Harold* (canto 4, verse xi). Here, Byron abandons his fictional hero and speaks of the history of Venice in his own persona. He wonders what his future fame will be, accepting the possibility that his name will disappear by comparing it to the faded glory of Venice:

> The spouseless Adriatic mourns her lord;
> And annual marriage now no more renew'd,
> The Bucentaur lies rotting unrestor'd,
> Neglected garment of her widowhood!
> St. Mark yet sees his lion where he stood
> Stand, but in mockery of his wither'd power,
> Over the proud Place where an Emperor sued,
> And monarchs gaz'd and envied in the hour
> When Venice was a queen with an unequall'd dower.

Lermontov had passed through an apprenticeship to Byron and continued to identify with Byron's vision of himself as poet in exile. Pechorin wrestles with the role of the Byronic hero throughout *Hero,* at once trying to play it and to wrench free of it. In "Taman" Pechorin's persona comes as close to Lermontov's as anywhere in the novel. A fellow author, Pechorin sees himself as a jaded Childe Harold on his travels, but is nonetheless duped by some "honest smugglers." The narrative recreates Pechorin's (and possibly Lermontov's) experience: it draws the reader into his initial Romantic interpretation of events to provide the same shock Pechorin himself received; this shock provokes a rereading that reveals an alternative, realist, interpretation of the same events. Where Sand's tale goes from a tale of "real life" to a fairy tale, Lermontov's undergoes a metamorphosis from a Romantic supernatural tale of unclean spirits and erotic mermaids to a description of an ignominious encounter with some nasty thieves. In both cases it is the authors and their narrators who are the smugglers, of one genre onto the page in the guise of another. Lermontov sophisticates Sand's surprise-ending frame tale by removing the frame and subtly incorporating the dual-genred nature of the story into the stylistic fabric of the narrative. He then includes the tale in a cycle that makes this device a meaningful contribution to his portrait of Pechorin as a man struggling with literary stereotypes.

The fairy-tale element is essential to "Taman" and is conveyed by Pechorin's calling the smuggler girl "my undine," or water spirit (from Latin, *unda,* "wave"). Contemporaries would readily recognize his allusion to La Motte-Fouqué's fairy tale, "Undine," named for its heroine who *is* a water spirit. The tale contains dark seascapes, storms, a dangerous forest teeming with goblins, the constant threatening presence of Undine's family of water spirits and death from supernatural causes. The knight Huldbrand arrives at night at a poor fisherman's hut by the sea, where the fisherman's ward, the beautiful Undine, lures him out onto a sea-lashed islet in the midst of a wild storm. She "throws her arms around his neck," and he "kisses her passionately."[63] They soon marry. She confesses her supernatural identity to her husband and gains a soul through human love but is eventually supplanted in his affections by her human counterpart, Bertalda. Undine reverts to her water sprite condition and is considered dead. When Huldbrand then marries Bertalda, Undine is required by sprite-law to come out of the deep and kill him.

Pechorin's language makes it clear that he is referring to the German tale in Russian translation. He has been told that the house he lodges in is "*nechisto,*" unclean, though he doesn't understand the exact meaning of the word at the time. But in Pechorin's later account of his adventure, he has just mimicked the journey of Zhukovsky's knight, who comes upon the fisherman's house by the sea after passing through an impenetrable forest, "and there were / Terrible rumors about it among the people; it was *unclean* there [*tam bylo nechisto*]: / Evil spirits lived in it and scared passersby so that they didn't dare even go near it."[64] Pechorin has gone around the whole town to find lodging: "After wandering for a long time along dirty alleys where, on both sides, I could see nothing but decrepit fences, we drove up to a shanty on the very edge of the sea" (65–66). He is caught between the ambiguity of material uncleanliness, which doesn't quite make sense, since the whole town is dirty, and the folk meaning, inhabited by "unclean" spirits, as in "Undine." The true (realist) meaning of the word in "Taman" turns out to be dirty (illegal) business, but since the first meaning doesn't seem to explain anything, Pechorin picks the second one, for which he has a model.

Pechorin's undine has a "supple figure" (*gibkii stan*) and reddish hair and runs around "skipping and singing" the first day. When he speaks to her, "She suddenly leaped up, began to sing, and disappeared like a little bird" (*Ona vdrug prygnula, zapela i skrylas', kak ptichka* [75]). This is close to Zhukovsky's description:

> The door suddenly opened wide
> And in burst Undina, blond-haired, with a *light figure,*
> With gay laughter, like something made of air . . .
> Suddenly, *shaking herself like a lively little bird, she ran up*
> To the knight.
>
> [Vdrug rastovorilasia nastezh'
> Dver'; i v nem belokuraia, *legkaia stanom,* s veselym
> Smekhom vporkhnula Undina, kak chto-to vozdushnoe . . .
> Vdrug, *vstrepenuvshis' rezvoio ptichkoi, ona podbezhala*
> K rytsariu.]
>
> (335)

Pechorin uses Zhukovsky's vocabulary to describe his undine's wild playfulness, but while Zhukovksy's Undine runs out of the fisherman's house to the sea because it is her native element, the smuggler girl does so to get rid of an informer. The contrast between the Romantic fairy tale and the reality of Pechorin's experience has the same lowering effect as that between "L'Orco" and "Taman."

The undine is an ambiguous figure in folklore; like mermaids (*rusalki*) and sirens, she can lure men to their deaths in the deeps, or, as in the tales of La Motte-Fouqué and therefore Zhukovsky, she can be seeking an immortal soul through love of a mortal. By using Zhukovsky's poem together with Sand's story, Lermontov creates this ambiguity for Pechorin's "undine." Pechorin calls her "my undine" three times and "the rusalka" twice in the space of five pages, maintaining the mythological ambiguity of the girl's motives. By the end of the story, Lermontov replaces Zhukovsky's innocent Romantic undine with the realist version of a siren, luring her enchanted victim to his doom.

Life as he experiences it is Pechorin's first reading of the events in Taman. In his second reading, Pechorin realizes the third interpretation of uncleanliness. The naive Romantic becomes the rueful realist. This is a reversal of the direction of Sand's device: whereas her narrator initially portrays her heroine as a realistic, politically motivated assassin, on a second reading she takes on the dimension of a mythological siren, and the significance of the story's title is revealed. Sand suggests that we are naive to read literature as if it were life; to write a story is to tell a fairy tale. Lermontov addresses this idea in his foreword to the second edition of *Hero*: "With us the most fantastical of all fairy tales would hardly escape the reproach of being meant as some personal insult" (2). The reading public is like Sand's fictional audience, so naive that it interprets fiction literally. Pechorin's naiveté is the obverse kind; like Pushkin's Tatyana, he initially interpreted reality as if it were literature. And like Tatyana, he realizes his mistake. Unlike Tatyana (but like Pushkin), he is able to write about it, blending his sources into a sophisticated narrative.

Pechorin reveals his sources in his narrative. He points to La Motte-Fouqué with "Undine" and uses Goethe, Pushkin, and Balzac to evaluate the pedigree of his Caucasian "rusalka"/"undine" when admiring her hands and feet and straight nose. His words, "In Russia a straight nose is even rarer than a little foot," clearly refer to *Eugene Onegin*. Goethe's Mignon has an "exceptionally beautiful" nose, and the hands and feet may refer to Balzac's description in *A Woman of Thirty*: "She revealed the indelible weaknesses of woman by the meticulous care she took of her hands and of her feet" (108).[65] Lermontov's naive narrator earlier compared Pechorin to a Balzacian woman in "Maksim Maksimych"; here Pechorin shows that, although at a more sophisticated level, he was just as vulnerable to the habit of superimposing literary types on "real" people. He writes his story to show how he learns that lesson during his stay in "Taman," a lesson he passes on by having us experience it.

The moral of Lermontov's tale is contained in its synthesis of European and Russian literary models and of literature with experience. Like a painting of a reflection in which the surface of the water is conveyed by lateral lines and the reflections by vertical ones, *Hero*'s (vertical) subtexts reflect both the characters' and the author's purposes beneath the (lateral) plotline. In "Taman," it is Pechorin, not Lermontov, who refers to German texts to evoke a supernatural frame of reference, using an example that had already been assimilated into the Russian tradition by translation. Pechorin's recontextualization of La Motte-Fouqué's tale into a low Russian scene makes fun of the Romantic clichés of the supernatural tradition while performing a comic translation of the fairy tale into the Russian everyday world.

Lermontov takes Pechorin's work further, incorporating "Undine" into a network of subtexts and redeploying its devices to build a realist novel out of narrative verse that both includes and supersedes Romantic genres. Pechorin refers to "Undine," a simple fairy tale that is a more accessible representative of the supernatural tradition, but it is Lermontov who refers to "L'Orco," of which Pechorin is unaware. "L'Orco" has more global relevance to the construction of a realist novel because, as a modern fairy tale, it underlines the distinctions between fiction and reality and shows how they interpenetrate one another. Pechorin writes the tale of his own naive errors by pointing to his readings; Lermontov, in turn, points his readers to George Sand's story to reveal his own method of composition. In "Taman," as in *Hero,* the same breaking of generic conventions that Pechorin achieves with "Undine" and Lermontov plays with in "L'Orco" highlights the problems of interpretation in literature and life that Pushkin had treated in *Onegin* and *Tales of Belkin.*

"PRINCESS MARY"

Pechorin's diary constructs a society tale in which he consciously acts out the Byronic role learned from Chateaubriand, Constant, Musset, and others. The game he plays with Mary borrows some plot elements from a story that appeared in the *Revue étrangère* in 1833: "Eglantine," by Philarète Chasles.[66] Chasles's hero courts a woman with the intention of leaving her once he has won her, as Pechorin does with Mary. Frederic Bell is a rich sea captain, who, despite his great talents, has retired early. "He was a sailor of thirty-five to thirty-six years of age, pale, with a worried forehead, struck with a kind of premature age from the habit of dangers, and ennui of society. . . . He had something of the man of the world about him, of the misanthrope, of cynicism and of an amiable man; he scorned men and little esteemed women" (365).

Frederic's friend Albert, a naive young artist who lives with him, is "credulous and trusting, naive and passionate, according all the virtues to a pretty face, always associating in his artist's thoughts physical beauty with moral beauty" (369). He is in love with Eglantine Wilsen [*sic*]; she dominates him, treating him cruelly. Frederic asks to be presented to her. Albert replies, "Willingly. I have already spoken of you to her. . . . This proud character that distinguishes you shocked her considerably" (372). When the "glacial" Frederic meets her, he "contradicted all [her] ideas, and left out nothing to seem in her eyes the most displeasing of mortals" (273). Madame de Wilsen discusses him with her friend who asks:

> "Who is this captain with the Byronic air and morose brow?"
>
> "He's Albert's intimate friend, a man who views society misanthropically."
>
> "This man almost scares me. . . . From his severe and sad glances, one would think that he's doing us the honor of hating us all without exception."

> " . . . In the crowd of our young gallants, whose epigrams are as cold as their compliments and their gallantries as innocent as their malice, one could enjoy meeting someone like that." (373–74)

Frederic pays visits to her over a period of two months, always taking a severe tone; she becomes nicer to Albert in order to see his friend Frederic. Albert realizes she is in love, but doesn't know with whom. For her, Frederic is a model hero and ideal type, great and impenetrable. "Two months of silence and anguish weighed on her heart. Her pride was wounded" (379). She falls passionately in love and agrees to sacrifice all for Frederic; heavily veiled, she comes to his house, prepared to leave with him. There he has her write a letter to Albert, and just as she thinks Frederic is about to leave with her, he announces that he has only been practicing on her the cruelty she practiced on Albert. "You are a terrible man," she says, and leaves.

Chasles's version of the *homme fatale* who deliberately courts an aristocratic woman only to turn her down is closer in plotline than the Romantic versions commonly considered Pechorin's ancestors. The friendship between the naive younger Albert and the Byronic, cold, all-knowing Frederic resembles the Grushnitsky-Pechorin relationship. Frederic's methods of causing the woman he pursues to fall in love with him are similar to Pechorin's, although Frederic alienates Albert's beloved from him to free Albert from his despair rather than to cause it.

"Eglantine" provides the core of "Princess Mary," Pechorin's maltreatment of the heroine, which is the more reprehensible in Pechorin's case because Mary has done nothing to deserve it except read Byron in the original. Seduction by the bored *homme fatale* is also the subject of Charles de Bernard's *Gerfaut.* While Bernard self-consciously derives the hero's type from *René* and *Obermann,* Lermontov takes not plot but phrases from Bernard's novel. Octave de Gerfaut (the name, gerfalcon, suggests a predator) pursues a married woman, Clemence, by pretending friendship with her husband, who challenges him to a duel when he discovers Gerfaut's designs.[67] When Gerfaut kills her husband, Clemence throws herself off her balcony into the river, while Gerfaut, a playwright, goes on to new success.

Tomashevsky notes three moments in *Hero* that he calls "indisputable reminiscences" of *Gerfaut.* First, he cites Pechorin's discussion of women's reasoning: "The woman's way: I should not love him because I am married; but he loves me, consequently. . . . Here there are several dots, because reason has nothing further to say."[68] Bernard's narrator says of Clemence's rationalizations: "By one of those agreements with conscience, the secret of which belongs only to women, she finally began to think: 'Since I am sure that I shall belong only to [my husband], Octave can perfectly well belong to me,' a syllogism that is, perhaps, unorthodox, both premises of which she reconciled with unimaginable art."[69]

Second, Tomashevsky finds correspondences to "Princess Mary" in the duel between Gerfaut and Clemence's husband: when they flip a coin to see who shoots first, Grushnitsky and Gerfaut both choose the eagle and win. Pechorin says: "You're lucky . . . you get the first shot. But remember that if you don't kill me, I won't miss, I give you my word." Gerfaut's opponent says, "Fate is on your side . . . but remember that if after my signal you don't shoot or shoot in the air, I'll exercise my right. You know I rarely miss."[70] (Here Gerfaut corresponds to Grushnitsky.) Furthermore, both duels are arranged at the edge of a cliff so that whoever is shot will be killed. Third, Tomashevsky notes that Gerfaut puts his arm around Clemence's waist when she becomes dizzy on an iceberg, just as Pechorin takes advantage of Mary's dizziness to put his arm around her waist crossing a mountain stream.[71]

In "Taman" Pechorin realized that he had unwittingly acted on the basis of a script written by others. In "Princess Mary" he picks his script in advance, taking the role of *l'homme fatale.* The points of similarity are close enough to suggest that Pechorin uses Bernard's novel to map out the details of his courtship of Mary as well as his duel with Grushnitsky. Gerfaut resolves, "My future conduct shall be so odious that I will force the capricious woman to adore me."[72] As Pechorin does to Mary, he gives a confession full of pathos that causes Clemence to blush:

> My last illusion has vanished. . . . I imagined a universe of which I was to be the sovereign lord. Intent upon the conquest of the world, I embarked on the consecrated barque of love. But my expedition was ineffectual. Less fortunate than Columbus, I was wrecked long ere I attained the promised strand!
>
> I admit that I have faith only in material objects . . . the mind is said to possess a creative power. On the contrary, love is fated to perish of its own exaggerations . . . at length, disappointed and disgusted, we wander through life, desiring but despairing of our conversion. (1:257–60)

As playwright, Gerfaut enjoys his ability to manipulate the emotions of his theater audience in the way Pechorin manipulates the people in his life:

> "How often, concealed in my box, have I participated in the emotions of which I was the origin! The fire of *my* imagination is the cause of those heaving bosoms, those blushing cheeks." But his own was cold and passionless.
>
> . . . involuntarily he retained the dire faculty of analyzing his impressions. In a mirror of scorn, he seemed to behold the reflection of every scene, in which he was both actor and spectator, agitated and calm, enthusiastic and skeptical, impassioned and satiated . . . (1:106)

Like Pechorin, Gerfaut has a friend who is an inferior version of himself. Marillac, a lesser writer, has "pretensions to the classical costume of the middle ages. Costume constituted his highest notions of art. As to intellectual qualities, his mustachios were the most renowned in the lists of literature. . . . To pronounce the word 'art,' he screwed up his lips like M. Jourdain in ejaculating O" (1:98).

Marillac visits Clemence's estate: "Having arranged his curls to his satisfaction, the artist raised his shoulders and drew in his waist. . . . Half stifled by the tightness of his short greatcoat, and swinging in his hand a small grey hat, he stood before them, affecting the distinguished attitude of one of Van Dyck's warriors" (1:44). As a fellow writer, Marillac contributes to the theme of the analogy between theater and real life. When Gerfaut is about to duel with the Baron, Marillac says, "You talk like the fifth act of a melodrama" (2:182).

Other elements are part of the genre of the *roman d'analyse* that conditions Lermontov's choice of detail. To have Princess Mary read Byron in the original is already parodic; in *Gerfaut* a fat coquette at the Baron's dinner party is "a passionate admirer of Byron, a pretension not infrequent among ladies whose beauty and dimensions are considerable" (1:230). Right after discovering Gerfaut's love letters to his wife, the Baron himself is found holding a volume of Byron in English (2:111), unclear whether in quest of explanation or consolation. Like Lermontov's Doctor Werner, Gerfaut's ironical doctor is also associated with Byron; he asks Gerfault, "Are you preparing Calderon, Montesquieu or some Lord Byron for the ladies?" (1:103).

Pechorin acts out the role of the fatal hero in the genre of the *roman d'analyse,* which includes the theme of outmoded Byronism, the innocent victimized heroine, the buffoon of a friend who presents a comic version of the hero's faults, and the ironic doctor, all of whom conveniently lend themselves to his plot, in life and on the page. He records the results of the parody he enacts in his diary, even as he chooses to take the role of one of the stock characters he writes about. To create a portrait of spa society that parodies that of Petersburg, he cobbles together scenes from literature known to all the actors on his stage. Golstein considers that Pechorin's motivation is to shatter harmful illusions; at the very least Pechorin exposes the literary clichés accepted by his entire cast, with the possible exception of Werner, by writing a self-conscious parody of them in his diary.[73]

For Lermontov's purposes too, *Gerfaut* is relevant because its hero and his friend are writers, heightening the close relationship between literature and life central to the characterization of Pechorin. The thin melodrama of *Gerfaut* is easily reducible to its formula; using one of the minor representatives of the genre, Lermontov parodies the type of hero who combines and acts out literary and social clichés. He adds another layer to Pechorin's diary by having it show the impossibility of escaping that formula, because it is the only script all the participants can share.

"THE FATALIST"

Lermontov's title suggests he has written "The Fatalist" with Diderot's *Jacques the Fatalist* in mind.[74] His narrator's plaintive paragraph about man's loss of faith echoes in condensed form a whole epoch of post-Voltairean French literature that laments the death of religious faith in France. Pechorin, gazing at the stars, exclaims,

> What strength of will they derived from the certitude that the entire sky with its countless inhabitants was looking on them with mute but permanent sympathy! . . . But we, their pitiful descendants who roam the earth without convictions or pride, without rapture or fear (except for that instinctive dread that compresses our hearts at the thought of the inevitable end), we are no longer capable of great sacrifice, neither for the good of mankind, nor even for our own happiness, because we know its impossibility, and pass with indifference from doubt to doubt. (188)

Jacques is considered an anti-novel, having no plot, no purpose to the journey of its Don Quixote–like master and his servant Jacques, no narrative coherence, interrupted as it is by the sub-narratives of various characters, no verisimilitude, no moral to the tale. It is a novel of ambiguity, suitable to a world in which nothing is clear or under control, where it cannot be determined whether there is a God or only the material universe.

"Jacques said that his captain used to say that everything that happens to us both good and bad down below was written above."[75] This is the conclusion of the opening paragraph; it becomes a refrain throughout, and testing it is as much of a premise as Diderot's book can be said to have. It is Jacques's verdict on each successive picaresque incident.

The first night Jacques and his master stop at the most miserable inn in a part of the country full of bandits. They are brought a poor supper of turned wine and black bread, because a dozen bandits in the next room have commandeered all the provisions.

> They heard a knock at the door; it was the servant that these insolent and dangerous neighbors had constrained to bring our two voyagers, on one of their plates, all the bones of a fowl they had just eaten. Jacques, indignant, took his master's pistols.
>
> "Where are you going?"
>
> "Leave it to me."
>
> "'Where are you going?' I asked you."
>
> "To put reason into that riff raff."
>
> "Do you know there are a dozen of them?"
>
> "If there were a hundred, the number makes no difference if it is written above that there aren't enough of them."
>
> "May the devil take you with your impertinent old saw! . . ."
>
> Jacques escapes the hands of his master, enters the room of these cut-throats, a loaded pistol in each hand. "Quick, go to bed," he tells them, "the first one who moves gets his head burned. . . ." Jacques had such a convincing manner and tone that these scoundrels, who valued life as much as honest folk, got up from the table without breathing a word, undressed and went to bed. (31–32)

Similarly, Pechorin dives into the hut to seize the Cossack by the arms. For Pechorin, this is a test of Vulich's faith in what is written above.

> It occurred to me to test my fate as Vulich had.
>
> "Wait," I said to the Major, "I shall take him alive." . . .
>
> Suddenly I wrenched off the shutter and flung myself through the window headfirst. A shot sounded above my very ear, a bullet tore off one of my epaulettes; but the smoke that filled the room prevented my adversary from finding his sword. . . . I seized him by the arms . . . and three minutes had not passed before the criminal was bound and removed under guard. . . .
>
> How could one not become a fatalist after all this? I prefer to doubt everything; this inclination of the mind does not impinge upon resoluteness of character. On the contrary, as far as I am concerned, I always advance with greater courage when I do not know what awaits me. For nothing worse than death can ever occur; and from death there is no escape!" (194–95)

Jacques describes his captain's similar attitude:

> Do we lead destiny or does destiny lead us? How many sagely planned projects have failed, and will fail! How many mad projects have succeeded, and will succeed? That's what my captain repeated to me after the capture of Berg-op-Zoom and Port-Mahon; and he added that prudence didn't assure success, but would console us and excuse us from failure: thus he would sleep on the eve of an attack in his tent as if he were in his garrison and would go into combat as if going to a ball. (36)

Both adventures and the captain's words demonstrate the value of decisive action. Golstein interprets Pechorin's response to fatalism as a rejection of the passivity characteristic of Russians in favor of the uncertainty that makes free will, and therefore action, possible; Lermontov attempts to cure readers of "blind reliance on metaphysical certainties," elaborating "a new ethics of behavior based on indeterminacy."[76] *Jacques the Fatalist,* like *Hero,* never resolves the question of the existence of predestination. Vulich, as a Serb, takes an Eastern fatalistic view, like Jacques, who accepts his captain's words.[77]

But Jacques's actions resemble Golstein's interpretation of Pechorin's: "He keeps his eyes open, takes precautions, while remaining ready for any turn of events."[78] Pechorin can articulate his own skeptical metaphysical argument, as the simple Jacques cannot, and take bold, but well-considered, action, as Jacques's master cannot. Lermontov isolates Jacques's fatalist position in Vulich and presents an alternative philosophy on which to base an active position, in the absence of metaphysical certainty.

Like Pushkin's *Tales of Belkin,* where the narratives are presented as separate stories, Diderot's playful account contains long, embedded tales told by narrators appropriate to their subject matter: the hostess of the inn tells the tale of Madame de la Pommeraye, who tricks her faithless lover into marrying a former prostitute. The master tells a story about his friend, the chevalier de Saint-Ouen, involving love, debt, and treachery. Jacques recounts the story of how the mercenary village doctor takes advantage of his injured knee, as well as a tale involving corrupt monks.

The thread uniting three hundred pages of narrative is the master's desire to hear the story of Jacques's loves. Jacques's narratives are embedded in the story of their journey: how he lost his virginity, how he seduced two women at a wedding, and so on. These anecdotes resemble tales of the Chaucer or Boccaccio type, as Diderot signals by mentioning the medieval French story *Lawyer Patelin* (236). Pushkin uses this device of allotting particular genres to appropriate narrators in order to play with their clichés in *The Tales of Belkin;* in modeling his novel on Pushkin's five tales, Lermontov too highlights the relationship among narrator, genre, and the clichés of that genre.

The narrator of *Jacques,* who purveys these varied stories, apostrophizes the reader, justifying himself against their imagined charges of obscenity and bad language.

> If what I've told you doesn't satisfy you, open the preface of Jean-Baptiste Rousseau and you will find my apology. Who among you would dare to blame Voltaire for having written *The Virgin*? . . ."But," you will say, "your *Jacques* is nothing but an insipid rhapsody of some real and some imagined events written without grace and distributed without order." . . . I amuse myself by describing your follies under borrowed names; your follies make me laugh; my story makes you angry. Reader, to speak to you frankly, I find the more wicked of the two of us is not me. . . . Vile hypocrites, leave me alone. (248–49)

Lermontov's preface to the second edition addresses a similar tirade to his readers:

> Some [readers] were dreadfully offended, quite in earnest, that such an immoral person as the Hero of our Time should be set as a model to them. . . . *A Hero of Our Time,* gentlemen, is indeed a portrait, but not of a single individual: it is a portrait composed of all the vices of our generation in the fullness of their development. You will tell me again that a man cannot be as bad as all that, and I shall tell you that since you have believed in the possibility of so many tragic and romantic villains having existed, why can you not believe in the reality of Pechorin?" (1–2)

The traveling narrator's preface to Pechorin's notes mentions Jean-Jacques Rousseau; the reference evokes Diderot's reference to Jean-Baptiste Rousseau, an important eighteenth-century poet who was banished for some defamatory verses in 1707 and spent thirty years in miserable exile. The similar themes, devices, and, especially, philosophic concerns suggest that Lermontov has transposed yet another well-known French text to a Black Sea setting. As David Powelstock says, the books "share the theme of ethical paradox of the roles of freedom and determination in human action."[79] Lotman identifies the oppositions between East and West, Muslim and Christian, tradition and freedom, critical analysis and acceptance of an unknowable fate, volition and passivity as central to Lermontov's consideration of Russian national character.[80] Pechorin, as a Europeanized Russian, is at the boundary between the two worldviews. "The Fatalist" shows the difficulty of reconciling the opposition. By using the French Jacques as a source for the argument presented by the Serb Vulich, and Diderot's book as an argument for accepting uncertainty over absolute faith in anything, Lermontov represents his own duality as a Europeanized Russian in the Eastern, fatalistic milieu of the Caucasus, emphasizing the irreconcilability of the two worldviews.

Lermontov considers the array of French literature outlined above from the point of view of an outsider in space and time. As a Russian, and a post-Romantic, he looks at the body of Romantic prose we have just surveyed with a writer's critical eye, deciding what to make use of and what to reject. Clearly he finds the type of the Romantic hero both misguided and outmoded. Pechorin is the illustration of the impasse of hypertrophied self-consciousness that the Romantic vision of the poet leads to. The literary genres he explores he finds either artificially high-flown (Chateaubriand's eloquent Indians, Sand's Venetian patriot) or trivial (Janin, Chasles, and Bernard's society tales) or outmoded (Diderot's picaresque). He finds useful material in de Vigny's structure, Diderot's discussion of fatalism, and the plots of "Laurette" and "L'Orco" and recasts it to make it part of the Russian experience as well as to create a stylistics appropriate to the new realism he wants to establish. Rejecting the outmoded genres and Romanticism of the French literature he reviews, he proposes Pushkin's prose as a model for the future of the Russian novel. *The Tales of Belkin* provides him with an ideally versatile structure.

Pushkin

In 1830 Lermontov wrote in his notebook: "Our literature is so poor that I can't borrow anything from it." The following year, Pushkin "descended to humble prose," and published *The Tales of Belkin* (*Povesti Belkina*). Lermontov was as attentive a reader of current Russian literature as he was of French. Unlike others among Pushkin's contemporaries, who regarded the tales as frivolous, Lermontov studied them carefully, and, understanding them as a review of the materials available to Russian prose writers in 1831, structured *A Hero of Our Time* on the *Belkin* cycle.[81]

Lermontov's first effort at a novel, *Princess Ligovskaya* (*Kniaginia Ligovskaia,* 1836), may be understood as an attempt to translate *Eugene Onegin* into prose. The hero's name, also Pechorin, is a deliberately transparent analogy to Onegin, the first name derived from a northern river, the second from a northern lake. Lermontov takes his epigraph from chapter 1 of *Onegin.* Pechorin flirts with Varvara as Onegin flirts with Olga; Pechorin and Varvara had been in love, but he leaves her for no clear reason. When they later meet in Petersburg, Varvara is married to an older man and transformed into Princess Ligovskaya, just as Tatyana becomes a "goddess" after marrying her general.[82] Lermontov's novel breaks off after Pechorin and Varvara have had several painful encounters in Petersburg high society, at the corresponding point where the love plot of *Onegin* is (unhappily) resolved through Onegin's letter to Tatyana.

As mentioned, in *Princess Ligovskaya,* Lermontov failed in his attempt to mix Pechorin's romantic life with the naturalist tale of the poor clerk.[83] In *Hero,* however, instead of using Pushkin's novel in verse as a model, Lermontov looked to Pushkin's prose, which provided a way to integrate the naturalist sketch into the society tale.[84] Critics thought Onegin the only one of Pushkin's heroes sufficiently complex to serve as a model for Pechorin, considering *The Tales of Belkin* too laconic a basis for complex psychological portraits. As Tolstoy put it, "Pushkin's tales are rather bare."[85] But Lermontov combined Onegin's character with *Belkin*'s structure to resolve the problem of conflicting genres.

The Tales of Belkin and *A Hero of Our Time* are both made up of an introduction and five stories. The intimate relationship between these two formative prose works has gone unnoticed, but analysis of the correspondence between each part reveals Lermontov's implicit dialogue with Pushkin that shows him to be equally concerned to bring Russian prose to the level of the Western European novel.[86]

Familiar as Lermontov was with European Romantic texts, he would readily have recognized Pushkin's integration of European models in *Belkin* as a step toward constructing a national Russian literature. The *Belkin* tales manage, astonishingly, to be at once a primer for beginning readers and an encyclopedia for writers and critics; Pushkin's five entertaining stories review some of the stock plots, typical heroes, and genres of the time while providing a critical commentary on the nature of literary artifice.[87] Lermontov incorporates these features into a novel, uniting the five stories and narrator's preface around the figure of Pechorin.[88]

Pushkin's story cycle is united by themes, motifs, and method. In *Belkin* the philosophical discussion of fate versus chance is related to the underlying question of fictional artifice by the theme of how to read, a lesson only one of Pushkin's characters learns. This theme is carried in part by the motif of blindness throughout the stories; almost all the characters in the *Tales of Belkin* fail to recognize the stereotypes, and their sources, that determine their fates.[89] The narrator of "The Shot" accepts Silvio as the hero of an adventure tale, even after hearing the Count's side of it; the young lovers of "The Blizzard" act out the elopement plot of French epistolary novels with (mock) tragic results; the "Undertaker" Adrian Prokhorov misses (and therefore will never act upon) the implications of his dream: in the German supernatural genre, it points to his guilt and the possibility of retribution for it; and the poor "Stationmaster" Samson Vyrin never realizes that his expectations of Dunya's ruin are governed by the parable of the Prodigal Son. Only Liza of "The Lady-Peasant" identifies her masks and manipulates them successfully: recognizing Alexey's pretensions to Byronism, she assumes the role of the "exotic" woman, redistributing the national elements: as the peasant Akulina, Liza parodies the French *bergère* masquerade of the court of Louis XIV; as the young lady in her Louis XIV wig, she mocks Russian affectation in mimicking French aristocracy. The plot of "The Lady-Peasant" is a comic version in miniature of the Tatyana-Onegin romance; Tatyana's mature role is made possible by her perusal of Onegin's library, which allows her to realize the discrepancy between her Richardsonian models and his Byronic ones. Tatyana's education comes too late to prevent her unhappiness, while Liza has luckily done her homework on time, allowing her to be the heroine of a comic tale instead of a tragic one.

Lermontov had been dealing with literary stereotypes in *Princess Ligovskaya*; the correspondence between the plot of *Eugene Onegin* and Lermontov's own unresolved love affairs with Sushkova and Lopukhina suggests that Lermontov had been pondering the relationship of literary stereotypes to his own life. But more important than their personal appeal to Lermontov as a man, the *Tales of Belkin* helped him as a poet trying to write prose that could educate a naive reading public. *Belkin* provided a solution to the problem Lermontov never solved in *Princess Ligovskaya*: Pushkin's story cycle, which might seem more problematic material for a novel than Pushkin's "novel in verse," had a built-in means of separating the different genres, and the multiple naive readers in *Belkin* provided motivation for the inclusion of a variety of literary styles, plots, and types. The layered narrative structure of *Belkin* made possible several variations on the problem of the relationship of actual author to authorial persona and of both to the hero, relationships that needed renovation as the Romantic hero, so close to his author, was being replaced by a realist one.

The two sets of five tales are paired by plot and by genre.[90] Lermontov sets up a mirror symmetry, inverting the order of Pushkin's five tales. He matches his last with Pushkin's first, his first with Pushkin's last, the second with the fourth, the fourth with the second, and pairs the two middle stories. Here are the five sets, following Pushkin's order:

1. "The Shot" (*Vystrel*) and "The Fatalist" (*Fatalist*) are adventure tales with mysterious heroes of the type found in Ann Radcliffe's *The Italian.*
2. "The Blizzard" (*Metel'*) and "Princess Mary" (*Kniazhna Meri*) are society tales about the tragic consequences of accepting an unsuitable match.
3. "The Undertaker" (*Grobovshchik*) and "Taman" are parodies of supernatural tales in the German tradition of Hoffmann, Tieck, and La Motte-Fouqué.
4. "The Stationmaster" (*Stantsionnyi smotritel'*) and "Maksim Maksimych" are sympathetic physiological sketches of the low government official.
5. "The Lady-Peasant" (*Baryshnia-krest'ianka*) and "Bela" are variations on the Byronic hero's quest for the exotic.

The analysis of these pairings shows how Lermontov, who began writing *A Hero of Our Time* soon after Pushkin's death, at once acknowledges Pushkin's achievement and uses the *Belkin* story cycle to develop the novel form.

There are clear parallels between both the plots and genres of each pair of tales, but Lermontov departs from Pushkin in structuring the relationship between narrator and narratee. Both authors treat this subject in the introductions that frame their tales (Lermontov's was, however, written only for the second edition of 1841). Pushkin's authorial persona, the editor A.P., and Lermontov as author, address the public, justifying the ensuing material. Both introductions raise the question of authorial impersonation: Pushkin's by signing his own initials but using the voice of a parodied editor; Lermontov's by mocking the accusation that Pechorin is a self-portrait. In A.P.'s introduction, Pushkin spoofs the naive, self-important editor and presents two extremes of naive reader: the housekeeper who uses Belkin's manuscripts for household purposes, and the landowner who regards writing as an indecent activity. Lermontov's foreword also represents the naive reading public, personified as a "provincial" who cannot see beneath the surface forms of discourse and demands morality and realism in artistic prose.

A.P.'s ostensible purpose is to introduce Belkin, the problematic author of the tales (how faithfully is Belkin reproducing what was told to him by his four sources?); Lermontov presents Pechorin who authors three of the five tales, also problematically (is he keeping a diary or writing/acting a drama in "Princess Mary," reminiscing or authoring a tale in "Taman"?). And the first two tales of *A Hero of Our Time* are told by an unnamed narrator who fancies himself the writer of travel notes. The clichés of that genre determine his narrative: the ecstatic stock descriptions of mountains (the Caucasus replacing the Alps of the Romantics) and the condescending drawing-out of Maksim Maksimych ("I know, these old Caucasus veterans love to talk and tell stories, they so rarely have the chance" [9]).[91] His eagerness to publish a good story overrides human compassion, as emphasized in his introduction to Pechorin's journal ("I learned not long ago that Pechorin had died on his way back from Persia. This news gladdened me very much, it gave me the right to publish these notes" [63]). This narrator is a close relation of the narrator of Pushkin's stationmaster, who "hope[s] to publish a curious collection of observations picked up during [his] travels," and so plies Vyrin with five glasses of rum to obtain Dunya's story.[92] Pushkin's narrator too condescends to his subject; Vyrin and his tragic tale move him less than their literary associations: "Such was the story of my friend, the old stationmaster, a story that was more than once interrupted by tears, which, like the jealous Terentich in that beautiful ballad of Dmitriev's, he wiped away picturesquely with the sleeve of his coat. These tears were caused partly by the punch" (116).

The first two tales of *A Hero of Our Time* are twice filtered, once through "Lermontov" as author of the introduction, and then through the unnamed narrator.[93] "Bela" in turn contains narrations within Maksim Maksimych's narration. The narrator tells Maksim's tale of Bela's abduction, quoting extensively from disparate speakers. The traveling narrator is presumably responsible for these generic raisins in the plum pudding of his travel notes.[94]

In this way, Lermontov duplicates the narrative structure of the *Belkin* tales: A.P. (i.e., "Pushkin"), Belkin, and the four people who have told Belkin the stories he records, identified only by their initials in A.P.'s footnote, are matched by "Lermontov," the narrator, and Maksim Maksimych in "Bela." In the second story, "Maksim Maksimych," Maksim is removed as narrator. As Nabokov says, Pechorin is brought gradually nearer (vii). The motivation (which Nabokov does not discuss) is to identify several possible (mis)understandings of Pechorin. In "Maksim

Maksimych" we come to doubt the appropriateness of Maksim's emotions in the scene of reunion. His exaggerated version of his friendship with Pechorin, his tactless reminding Pechorin of Bela's death, his overreaction to Pechorin's polite distance when they meet make us reinterpret everything we have just read in "Bela."

Part 2 of *A Hero of Our Time* does, of course, bring us as close as possible to Pechorin through his journal, but the introduction to part 2 by the narrator of part 1 again establishes a third layer, as in *Belkin.* It is not a narrative layer but an interpretative filter that functions the same way, alerting the reader to the role of interpretation, with an admonitory Lermontov at one extreme, a discredited Romantic narrator at the other, and in the middle a suspect Pechorin calling into question his own perceptions.[95]

These vantage points develop Pushkin's indirectly implied theme of self-awareness. Lermontov suggests that the good reader is potentially the good writer; the analogue in life is that the greater one's awareness, the greater one's self-determination. Pechorin is the only character in *A Hero of Our Time* to demonstrate awareness of his own misapplied stereotypes. "Taman," as we saw, is about the effects of reading too much spooky German literature. The narrative simultaneously conveys the narrator's point of view during the events described, and his later reinterpretation of them that includes an analysis of why he misperceived the situation in the first place. The story Pechorin writes and the sophistication of its author is contrasted to the travel notes of the bumbling narrator of the first two chapters, whose desperate desire to publish something prevents him from evaluating Maksim Maksimych's narrative and undermines his own with its obtrusive, self-centered self-consciousness. While that narrator learns nothing from his travels, Pechorin has learned something from all his reading; like Lermontov himself, Pechorin has read both the Western European Romantics and Pushkin's parodic transpositions of their work to Russian soil and (for better and worse) incorporates that knowledge into his actions. This essentially optimistic adjustment of the themes carried out by the *Belkin Tales'* narrative devices is balanced by the tragic outcomes of the plotlines in *A Hero of Our Time;* the opposition reflects on the one hand the opening out of Russian prose, and on the other the closing down of post-Decembrist Russian politics, a topic beyond the scope of this discussion.

Let us examine the plot parallels between the stories.

"THE SHOT" AND "THE FATALIST"

Lermontov pairs Pushkin's opening tale, "The Shot," with the last tale of *A Hero of Our Time,* "The Fatalist." The heroes of the tales, Silvio and Vulich, have foreign names, unknown pasts, and keep aloof from their fellows. At the end of their tales they are dead, but not through dueling. Silvio is shot at twice by the count, who misses both times: the first shot goes through Silvio's cap, the second through the count's painting. Vulich also shoots twice: his first shot, at himself, misfires; his second hits a cap hanging on the wall. The Count twice draws the first shot in the duel, for which Silvio calls him "fortune's favourite" (*liubimets schastiia*); Pechorin tells Vulich that he's "fortunate in gambling" (*schastlivyi v igre*).

The similarities between the tales are established in order to point to the differences. Silvio plays the role of adventure hero, lending his young officer friends the means to identify him as such: "He had a good collection of books, mostly military histories and novels. He was always willing to lend these, and he never asked for them back" (69). The narrator of "The Shot" is naturally Silvio's best audience, as he himself says: "By nature a romantic, I had been more attached than the others to the man whose life was such a mystery and whom I regarded as the hero of some strange tale" (71). By his own account Silvio provoked a duel with the innocent count out of sheer jealousy and then devoted six years of his life to what he calls "revenge." Yet years later the narrator has never questioned Silvio's tale, as is clear when he asks the count about the "slap in the face by some rake" (79). Even after hearing the conclusion of the duel from the count, the narrator persists in calling Silvio a hero.

Pushkin's tale makes an implicit parallel between literature and life, with its attendant theme of interpretation. Not merely a blasé aristocrat, only the count escapes the restrictions of literary stereotype, but he is nonetheless subject to the dangers of the misinterpretations of others: Silvio takes it upon himself to become, as it were, the count's fate.

Fate is a unifying theme in the *Belkin* tales; as Vyrin says "There's no escaping misfortune; fate is master unto itself" (*ot bedy ne otbozhish'sia; chto suzhdeno, tomu ne minovat* [110]). Lermontov too uses it as the keystone to his construction, considering it explicitly in what is in *Hero* the closing story of the novel, where Vulich is more philosophical than Silvio: he gambles with fate, staking his own life, purely out of interest in the question of predestination. Like Silvio's narrator, Pechorin is both the narrator of Vulich's tale and his fellow officer; as a skeptic, he is inclined to accept the idea of free will over predestination. Vulich and Pechorin reach a new and opposite understanding of the question of predestination within the tale: Vulich's dying words are "he was right," referring to Pechorin's prediction that he would die that night and thus reaffirming predestination, while Pechorin comes to understand that the conflict between free will and predetermination is irresolvable. Pechorin records the experiences leading him to his insight, including Maksim Maksimovich's contradictory judgments; the reader is given material to consider the problem. This presents precisely the challenge that Lermontov's foreword proposes to the "young and naive" reading public, to reconcile the multiple points of view presented in the text. In "The Shot," the reader has to reassess the narrator's idolization of Silvio after reading part 2 of the story; in "The Fatalist" we have to reconcile the conflicting viewpoints of Vulich, Pechorin, and Maksim. Lermontov takes up Pushkin's theme of interpretation as essential to the growth of Russian realist prose and its readership.

"THE BLIZZARD" AND "PRINCESS MARY"

In "The Blizzard" first Vladimir and then Burmin woo Maria; in "Princess Mary" first Grushnitsky and then Pechorin woo Mary (who, as a Russian, is actually also Maria). Maria reads French novels "and consequently is in love"; Mary reads Byron, which affects her choice of beaux. The young and naive Vladimir and Grushnitsky are poor army corporals; neither gets his girl and both die, Vladimir at the impersonal hands of fate, and Grushnitsky at the hands of Pechorin. Burmin and Pechorin are older than their predecessors, the first "around twenty-six," Pechorin twenty-five. Vladimir is not considered suitable by Maria's parents, but they give their blessing when Maria falls sick; Pechorin is also not considered a suitable match for Mary, but her mother accepts him after Mary's illness. In Pushkin's tale the young lovers count on "throwing themselves at her parents' feet"; Pechorin, refusing the weeping Mary, says, "another minute and I would have fallen at her feet" (179).

But while Burmin follows fate's mysterious workings and marries Maria, Pechorin rejects Mary. Pechorin is dead when we begin the novel, independently of any of his actions in the novel. Within it he is the agent of his own, as well as Grushnitsky's and Mary's, fate. Because he knows what literature they base their lives on, he scripts their actions in life and records them in his diary. As narrator of their tale, he has the last word; while all four of these romances are based on literary clichés, only Pechorin is aware of them. Lermontov rescripts Pushkin's use of blind fate, allowing his hero enough awareness to be an author rather than only a character. Vladimir took decisive action but was thwarted by fate; Burmin followed impulse but was rewarded by fate. Pechorin refuses to be fate's pawn and takes action, having analyzed the scripts at play, just as Lermontov decisively chooses his subtexts, having analyzed the traditions, genres, and worldviews at play in Russia in the 1830s.

"THE UNDERTAKER" AND "TAMAN"

Both tales make comic use of the German supernatural tradition to discuss the effects of literary stereotypes on life. Characterizing his gloomy hero, Pushkin's narrator points out that his undertaker departs from the literary model: "The enlightened reader knows that Shakespeare and Walter Scott portrayed their gravediggers as jolly, fascetious people" (97). As a lowly artisan, Pushkin's undertaker Adrian Prokhorov is, not surprisingly, a bad reader who even reads nothing at all. When he dreams that his clients have returned from the grave to accept his Don Giovanni-style invitation, he has no means of recognizing or interpreting his nightmare. Neither life nor art has suggested the possibilities his dream presents, and he quickly dismisses the insight into his own responsibility that it should have provided. Prokhorov knows the German artisans he got drunk with, but not the German tales in which wine and dreams can explain supernatural appearances and their moral implications.

Pechorin, on the other hand, is *too* familiar with German Romantic stereotypes and nearly gets himself drowned by projecting the image of Goethe's Mignon and the Undine onto the smuggler girl. He writes the story of his adventure, laughing at the inappropriateness of the literary images that determined his perceptions. "Taman" is an inversion of "The Undertaker": Prokhorov reads, thinks, and acts too little, Pechorin—too much. Pechorin, refusing to be a passive victim or unaware of stereotype, writes a story to ironize about having become both in Taman. Although Adrian Prokhorov shares Pushkin's initials, he is the victim of Pushkin's narrative: surly and immoral, Prokhorov is doomed to a lowly existence by his lack of conscience. Lermontov allows Pechorin the intellectual and moral means to reverse Prokhorov's fate. The juxtaposition of "Taman" to "The Undertaker" underscores the theme of awareness, showing interpretation to be the crucial theme of both *Belkin* and *Hero.* The placement of "Taman" and "The Undertaker" in the middle of the five tales suggests their thematic centrality.

"THE STATIONMASTER" AND "MAKSIM MAKSIMYCH"

Samson Vyrin and Maksim Maksimych are "simple" men in government service, aged "about fifty" (Pushkin, 108; Lermontov, 4). Both tragically lose their beloved "daughters." Vyrin's Dunya is abducted by a dashing hussar in a Circassian hat; Maksim Maksimych's Bela (whom he loves "like a father" [47]) is abducted by a Circassian on horseback. Vyrin drinks the rum offered by the narrator and eventually drinks himself to death; Maksim refuses the white rum from Tiflis that his narrator offers him—to be drunk in the Caucasus is to risk your life.

Their stories are told to us by travelers who quote their simple speech sympathetically. Vyrin's narrator plays the role of the humane author of physiological sketches, refuting the public's generally unsympathetic view of stationmasters.[96] But he sees neither his own condescension nor the connection between Vyrin's misfortune and the German engravings on the wall that tell the tale of the prodigal son. Similarly, the narrator of "Bela" uses the clichés of the travel-note genre and is condescending to Maksim Maksimych. But while Lermontov's narrator resembles Pushkin's, Lermontov distinguishes Maksim Maksimych from Vyrin. Vyrin does not realize that the hussar is making a deal with the doctor in German or that he himself has projected the story of the prodigal son with its German subtitles onto Dunya. Maksim Maksimych is allowed to be part of the theme of the interplay of literary sources and life; he knows that there is a foreign influence at work, that Pechorin is following some fashion, and he even suspects it comes from "the French." With the narrator's correction—"No, it was the English"—Lermontov has the characters themselves discuss the question of literary influence (41).

Thus Lermontov integrates his dialogue with French literature into his updating of Pushkin's. His French/English joke undercuts the reading and writing narrator—who is as naive in his educated way as the "simple" man the narrator tries to fashion into clichés—since the stereotype was both French and English.[97] The integration of French sources also plays a role in Lermontov's pairing of the two tales. Pushkin's narrator describes Dunya at home in Petersburg using an image from Balzac's *Physiology of Marriage*: "Dunya . . . was sitting sidesaddle on the arm of [the Hussar's] chair like an English equestrienne."[98] Pushkin's hidden quotation emphasizes the social and emotional distance between the narrator and the poor stationmaster. In "Maksim Maksimych" Lermontov, as we saw above, also characterizes his narrator with a description from Balzac that casts Pechorin as a "woman of thirty." Lermontov uses Balzac to undercut the narrator and show how foreign borrowings can mock their user. By pointing to this issue, much discussed by Russian writers and critics since the argument about Zhukovsky's translations of "Lenore" (see chapter 1 of the current book), Lermontov carefully highlights his own implicit discussion of Russian adaptation of foreign sources.

Lermontov treats the narrative of "Bela" and "Maksim Maksimych" as continuous, while pairing each tale with the two *Belkin* plots by matching the genres from which the characters are drawn. Thus the physiological sketch of Maksim Maksimych spans both "Bela" and "Maksim Maksimych" and is paralleled to Samson Vyrin's tale. Bela is therefore made to play a double role: she is Maksim's abducted daughter (parallel to Vyrin's Dunya), while she is Pechorin's exotic woman (parallel to Aleksey's peasant love). The novelist skillfully condenses the redundant heroines of the story cycle.

"THE LADY-PEASANT" AND "BELA"

The last *Belkin* tale, "The Lady-Peasant," corresponds to *A Hero of Our Time*'s first: Aleksey and Pechorin, both recently from Petersburg, court exotic women who come from enemy camps. Aleksey's father, the Russophile Berestov, is at odds with Liza's father, the Anglophile Muromsky; Aleksey falls in love with the "peasant" "Akulina" who turns out to be the young lady (*baryshnia*) Liza. Pushkin's tale is a comedy, in which Aleksey is a would-be Byronic hero who drops his mask easily under Akulina's influence, allowing youth, nature, and tradition to bring about a happy ending, with which the story cycle closes. It is the second happy ending in the *Belkin* tales.

Pechorin fights in the Russian army against the Caucasian tribes, including the Circassians. Pechorin courts the Circassian Bela but finds that "the love of a wild woman [*dikarki*] is not much better than the love of a noble lady" (40). Grushnitsky, the would-be Byronic hero analogous to Aleksey, has already been killed by Pechorin in "The Princess Mary," so that the Bela episode is Pechorin's second love story in the novel and his last; unlike Burmin's and Aleksey's, both his affairs end in tragedy.

Pushkin's *Belkin* tales are fairy tales in which high literature masquerades as part of the oral tradition.[99] Belkin *hears* his tales from their narrators just as he listens to his housekeeper's stories. She is presumably illiterate, as she uses his manuscript to seal up her windows. Lermontov's narrator addresses this distinction between oral and written tales and their tellers in "Bela" when speaking about Maksim Maksimych: "In simple hearts, the sense of the beauty and grandeur of nature is a hundred times stronger and more vivid than it is in us, enthusiastic tellers of tales, oral or written" (30). Lermontov demonstrates the distinctions among life experience, oral tales, and written tales from multiple points of view, each time at the expense of the more literate. The traveling narrator interprets the weather incorrectly in "Bela," retells Kazbich's oral tale in inappropriate, borrowed literary language, and gets character as well as literary image wrong in "Maksim Maksimych"; Pechorin misreads circumstances in "Taman" and smugly acts out a script based on literary cliché in "Princess Mary." Lermontov turns Pushkin's implications about the transition from oral to literary fiction into part of the characterization, plot, and theme of his novel.

Fairy tales have happy endings, and so do all the *Belkin* tales. Of the three deaths, two of them are off-stage: it is said that Silvio was killed in battle, while in "The Blizzard" Vladimir's demise in Moscow on the eve of the entry of the French is mentioned in an aside and is a means to Maria's marriage to Burmin (82, 91). The only tragic figure of the collection is Samson Vyrin; yet despite his death, "The Stationmaster" ends happily with the news of Dunya's remarkable good fortune (three sons, nurse, pug dog).

Lermontov, on the other hand, says in his foreword that the public does not understand fables (*basni*) and jokes—we remember both the poor reception of *Belkin* and his statement that "the most fantastic of all fairy tales with us would hardly escape the reproach of being meant as some personal insult" (2). He rewrites Pushkin's fairy tales as tragedy. By the end of the novel Bela, Grushnitsky, Vulich, and Pechorin are dead; Vera, Princess Mary, and Maksim Maksimych are betrayed in their affections. There are no happy endings. Lermontov even rewrites the zero-ending of Pushkin's "The Undertaker" in a dismal vein—instead of Adrian Prokhorov's dreary, venal life merely going on unchanged, Pechorin is robbed, the smuggling band of "Taman" broken up, and the blind boy abandoned. Lermontov wrote *Hero* after Pushkin's death and his own exile to the Caucasus for his poem, blaming the court of Nicholas I for the tragedy of Pushkin's death. Following in his poet-hero's footsteps, with no change in regime or imperial policy in sight, Lermontov could expect a similar fate. His fiction reflects the dead end of imperial policy in personal and political life, as well as the dead end of late Romanticism that had already run its course in Europe and needed to be replaced by a realism that could somehow assist change in all three realms. The environment made such change unlikely; only Pushkin had risen to that challenge and he had been destroyed.

Synthesis: Foreign and Native

Lermontov provides the mirror of tragedy to Pushkin's comic work in the resolution of his plots and the interpretation of each genre, as would be expected in the period of late Romanticism. The advantage of that later perspective is, of course, the greater awareness afforded by the accumulated models, Western European and Russian. Among the many narrators, editors, and letter writers of the *Belkin* tales and *A Hero of Our Time,* only Pechorin is aware of all the genres, styles, and stereotypes parodied in the story cycles. His review of two generations of Romanticism allows him to interpret, reinterpret, and therefore craft his reality, as well as to write his own tales about his life. In the process, he identifies a central dilemma of the Romantic vision—the division between head and heart that results from self-awareness.[100] Lermontov examines this opposition and shows the futility of the dichotomy through the tragedies Pechorin brings about. Lermontov uses the deliberately ambiguous word "hero" to refer both to life and to art, pointing out that generations of readers had been bred on restrictive Romantic categories. The variations on the theme of the interplay between life and art in the novel suggest that the acceptance of Romantic literary categories has blighted the development of potential real-life heroes.[101] The idea is signaled by Pechorin's statement that Grushnitsky's ambition is "to become the hero of a novel" (85), while the hero of Lermontov's novel himself acts out the role of the hero of his own novel in the amphitheatre of Pyatigorsk, saving Mary from "certain death" by social humiliation at the ball (85, 126). From the life-into-literature direction, the traveling narrator reduces reality to pseudo art, viewing the mountains through the genre of travelogue and Maksim Maksimych as material for a physiological sketch. Pechorin does better than the narrator in his three tales, but for all his self-awareness, he misuses his French models as well as his German ones: the authors truly responsible for Bela's tragedy are Rousseau and Chateaubriand, who provide Pechorin with scenarios of the noble savage, which he tries to enact and finds false. He should have been able to avoid this, given that he had already realized in "Taman" the interplay between Romantic stereotypes and life: he recognizes his own German-colored filter and the effect art can have on random, innocent reality. Perhaps he missed it because the German supernatural material is more clearly marked as literary for Russian readers, while French literature is part of their education and daily life, so that its effects are harder to notice. Only Lermontov is in fine control of the large variety of literary models he uses to differentiate each chapter and character, as well as to create a complex discourse on the nature of literary creation and interpretation.

A Hero of Our Time demonstrates the need for the resolution of oppositions—of head and heart, of art and life, of foreign and native—and at the same time makes clear that such resolution is impossible within the Romantic ethos fostered by the literary models that are parodied in the *Tales of Belkin* and in *A Hero of Our Time.*[102] *The Tales of Belkin* is the most central work Lermontov incorporates into his novel, providing not only its structure but also a reading of Western European Romanticism in the Russian context of the 1830s. Highlighting the effect of literary stereotypes on life, Pushkin's work establishes a new direction for Russian prose; in *A Hero of Our Time,* that cycle determines the movement away from stereotypes and narrowly understood nationalism to achieve a synthesis of the Western European novel with the prose techniques of the best Russian interpreter of that tradition, Pushkin.

In *A Hero of Our Time,* Lermontov finds a solution to the problem raised in the debates over Bürger's "Lenore": he fully integrates the French models of his age into both Russian life and art. He applies his reading of recent French prose from the autobiographical memoir (de Vigny's *Servitude*), the stylized fairy tale (Sand's "L'Orco") and the physiological sketch (Balzac's *A Woman of Thirty*) to his own experience of the Caucasus, and combines it with a fine understanding of Pushkin's language, methods, and purposes. Lermontov completes an apprenticeship to French genres, as well as to Pushkin, who makes him into a critic of Romantic thematics and stylistics. The French works Lermontov deploys in *A Hero of Our Time* enable, by negative as well as positive example, the creation of the first thoroughly Russian novel—a novel that deeply assimilates both its Russian and its French materials.

3

Dostoevsky, *Crime and Punishment*

The French are disgusting.
Fyodor Dostoevsky, 1862

In *Crime and Punishment,* French novels about prostitutes and young men who abandon virtue for vice are set into opposition to the Russian cultural universe in order to be assimilated into it through biblical truth. We will explore four tales of prostitution that contribute to the characterization of Sonya and four tales of sinner-criminals that structure the hero's quest for redemption. In the first group, Balzac's is the most substantive subtext; in the second, Dostoevsky draws on three of Balzac's novels that he arranges in relationship to an important, hitherto undiscovered, governing subtext: Jules Janin's *La Confession.*

Dostoevsky was ambivalent toward things French. He deplored French decadence yet revered French fiction, to which he referred directly in his work far more often than any other national literature.[1] In *Crime and Punishment,* he sets French subtexts into dialogue with the force that was to overcome the moral failure he feels they represent, the New Word of Jesus Christ. Leonid Grossman considers that it was their combination of Catholicism with atheism that caused Dostoevsky's particular antipathy to the French; incorporating a quantity of French novels about prostitution and murder into the tale of the struggle for his hero's soul, Dostoevsky answers French apostasy.[2] We may read *Crime and Punishment* as Dostoevsky's argument with the French literary tradition from Rousseau to Balzac, as well as with French culture as a whole. Dostoevsky pits the numerous works of Russian literature that represent the Saint Petersburg text in *Crime and Punishment* against the French tradition as a subtextual thesis and antithesis, a struggle resolved in *Crime and Punishment* through the biblical subtext of the Gospel of John.[3]

France

"To amass a fortune and possess as many things as possible has become the Parisian's main moral code, his catechism," writes Dostoevsky in *Winter Notes on Summer Impressions* (1862), underscoring the contradiction between materialism and the ideal it negates.[4] In parts six, seven, and eight of his impressions based on the three weeks he spent in Paris in the summer of 1862, Dostoevsky mocks the "simpering, affected, unnatural" Parisienne with a "bird's brain and heart" who has perfected the art of counterfeit. He mocks her husband, who accepts his wife's lovers and has no other desires than to see the sea and roll on the grass. He mocks the public at large, which "cannot live without melodrama," valuing "eloquence" above meaning,[5] and calls Paris "a most boring city."[6]

And yet Dostoevsky had devoured the best French novels as a youth. He spent the summer of 1838 reading everything Balzac had published, and wrote to his brother Mikhail: "Balzac is great! His characters are products of a universal mind. Not the spirit of the times, but the struggles of whole millennia prepared this development in the human soul."[7] Dostoevsky owned two sets of Balzac's complete works, in twenty volumes (1857), as well as a later edition in twenty-four (1869–76).[8] His enthusiasm for Balzac appears in his work throughout his life, from his first publication, a translation of *Eugénie Grandet,* to shortly before his death, when he quoted Balzac in his Pushkin speech. Dostoevsky works out his profound involvement with French literature in the dense layering and interplay of French subtexts embedded in his most perfectly constructed novel.

Crime and Punishment shocks the reader by the intensity of its brutal detail—the beating to death of the mare, the degradation of the prostitute, the bloody ax murder of two women by a crazed former law student. Even against the background of the Russian physiological sketches, the poor clerk tales of the naturalist school of the 1830s and 1840s, and the Russian imitations of the French feuilletons, *Crime and*

Punishment stands out within the Russian tradition for its vivid evocation of the violent lives of the city poor.

To the reader of French literature of the 1820s and 1830s, however, Dostoevsky's novel of the 1860s looks entirely familiar; it is in fact the culmination of the evolution of the French prose tradition that prevailed in the late 1820s. *Crime and Punishment* recombines the themes of prostitution, murder, and redemption typical of the *école frénétique* (or, as Balzac called it, the *école du désenchantement*).[9] *La littérature frénétique* had existed since the seventeenth century in various forms; it explores the irrational forces of human personality beyond the control of social or moral laws, intensifying sensuality and sensibility as it dwells on the passions and the imagination. In the nineteenth century, Romanticism added the fantastic, violence, and melodrama of the German and English *roman noir* to the French tradition, whose proponents, les Jeunes France (Young France—Hugo, Balzac, Chasles), represented the "frenetic" or "furious" school that created the *roman furieux.*[10]

The French intertextual material serves several important purposes in *Crime and Punishment.* While the censorship in Russia had been liberalized after the reforms of the 1860s, it still would not have permitted the publication of explicitly sexual material, or the graphic descriptions of death and dismemberment characteristic of the *école frénétique.*[11] The criminal themes of murder, prostitution, and sexual deviance were at the boundaries of the permissible in fiction.[12] But Dostoevsky could count on his readers to be familiar with these worlds through their reading of French journals and novels.[13] He refers to both the best French authors such as Honoré de Balzac and the now almost forgotten, but then equally well-known Eugène Sue and Jules Janin, whose novels and *romans-feuilletons,* serial novels, were hugely popular in both France and Russia starting in the 1830s.

Janin, Sue, and Balzac show French life at a transitional historical moment from the late 1820s to the mid-1840s, a period of moral uncertainty and spiritual quest. Their work reflects the turbulence surrounding the July revolution of 1830, the triumph of bourgeois culture, and the concomitant loss of religious faith under the reign of the "citizen king" Louis-Philippe that followed it. From his vantage point in the late 1850s when he began thinking about *Crime and Punishment,* Dostoevsky saw France's experience as a warning to Russia, which had been going through an analogous transition from the 1840s to the 1860s.

Some of the greatest Russian scholars have studied the effect of French literature on Russian prose in this period. Viktor Vinogradov,

Grigory Gukovsky, Alfred Bem, and Boris Tomashevsky have established the importance of the French feuilleton and the *roman furieux* for Dostoevsky, focusing predominantly on the history of genre rather than on thematics and the interpretation of particular literary texts.[14] The exceptions are Leonid Grossman and his successors, who examine Dostoevsky's use of Balzac's *Père Goriot.* Reading Janin, Sue, and Balzac through the lens of *Crime and Punishment,* we can fill in the literary genealogy more completely; Dostoevsky understood how much Balzac in his turn responded to the work of his predecessors and enters into dialogue with all three. Balzac draws from his friend and, later, rival, Janin, in writing *Père Goriot, The Wild Ass's Skin,* and *Splendors and Miseries of Courtesans,* as well as from Sue's feuilletons, where the borrowings were reciprocal.[15] Balzac addresses these works individually and recasts them. Dostoevsky in turn interprets Balzac's reaction to Janin's and Sue's *romans-feuilletons.* A close reading of the several texts reveals a discussion among the three most important French writers of the period and Dostoevsky's close tracking of it.

The transition in the arts from Romanticism to realism was related to the growth of cities and of a poor urban class in the beginning of the nineteenth century. In France in the 1820s, literary prose shifted focus to the lives of the city poor and the peculiar role of Paris in relation to the provinces, so that the themes of criminality and the provincial in the city became important. Two principal themes predominate: prostitution, the female crime; and murder (or demonic ambition), the male crime, with the resurrection of the sinner-criminal as goal in both cases.[16] We will first look at French treatments of the prostitute, as material for Dostoevsky's characterization of Sonya, and then at treatments of the sinner-criminal, as contributing to his portrait of Raskolnikov.

Janin takes up prostitution in *The Dead Donkey,* as do Sue in *The Mysteries of Paris,* Regnier-Destourbet in *Louisa, or the Griefs of a Prostitute,* and Balzac in *Splendors and Miseries of Courtesans.* Dostoevsky uses all these to create Sonya's world in *Crime and Punishment.*

THE FEUILLETONS

Dostoevsky wrote in his own feuilleton, "If I were not a casual feuilletonist but a regular, daily one, it seems to me that I should wish to turn to Eugène Sue in order to describe the mysteries of Petersburg."[17] He was an enthusiastic reader of the French potboiler fiction of the frenetic school of the 1830s, published by the feuilletonists who wrote daily inserts for the newspapers.[18] Cheaper than books and journals, the newspapers in which they appeared made fiction accessible to larger circles of readership than ever before and had a democratizing effect on literary production. The feuilleton tradition flourished between 1836, when, for example, *Le Constitutionnel* had a circulation of seventy thousand in all of France, and 1846, when its Paris readership alone was two hundred thousand thanks to Eugène Sue's contributions.[19] By the 1840s, almost all writers appeared in the feuilletons, since it was the best way to reach an audience—between 1837 and 1847 Balzac published about a novel a year in *La Presse.*[20]

The feuilleton form begot the popular feuilletonist, who would write daily four-page installments of novels that might appear over several years. The *romans-feuilletons* relied on stock devices such as the unknown origins of the characters, disguises, terrifying episodes that break off at the peak of suspense, and simplified character types. The tales are action-based, and the characters have little psychological depth. This form of popular literature is full of digressions that fill in earlier events for those who tune in late, opinions on current questions such as prison regime or peasant life, and chapters in which nothing actually happens. The style depends on declamation, frequent tirades, and the indiscriminate use of intensifying adjectives; things keep happening "suddenly," night keeps falling, the dialogue is feeble.[21] As René Bazin describes them, "Almost all the feuilletonists have an exact sense of dramatic movement; a science of the horrible and terrifying; an ability to raise the hair; an aptitude for leaving for dead on the battlefield of action heroes who revive to live a long life; a deftness in the use of suspense; a fidelity to the honorable type of the good mother and the industrious little working girl whose eternal love is not as reprehensible as one thinks."[22]

Grossman discusses Dostoevsky's fascination with popular genres in his essay "Dostoevsky and Europe." He asks, "What did Dostoevsky seek in these so dissimilar aspects of the boulevard and the psychological novel, the picaresque and the sentimental, the adventure and the philosophical, the epistolary and the naturalist confessional novel and the *roman-feuilleton*?" and answers that Dostoevsky was interested in the narrative tone, not the ideas, themes, or structure: "He sets himself the problem of gathering in one work the most varied elements in order to throw them into the whirlwind motion of the catastrophic concept that gives them the unity of a headlong surge" [*sploshnoe ustremlenie'*] . . . subordinating extremely incompatible elements to the unity of philosophical concept" (321, 322–23).

Grossman names many examples of this literature, some of which seem irrelevant, but he does not discuss Dostoevsky's use of it. Close reading shows that he was wrong—Dostoevsky *was* interested in the themes and structure, and even the details, of the *roman-feuilleton.* These details struck Dostoevsky so forcibly that he retained them from his early reading and, even after the bitter experience of prison and exile, found meaning in them that he was driven to incorporate into his work decades later, using both the best and the worst of this material for atmospheric background and subtext for the philosophy central to his novel.

SONYA AND THE NOBLE PROSTITUTE

Jules Janin (1804–1874)

Jules Janin's first book, *The Dead Donkey or the Guilllotined Woman* (1829), is an important (and entirely unexamined) subtext for *Crime and Punishment.* It caused a furor when it appeared in France and then in Russia (in Russian) that same year. Aware that its gruesome descriptions of a Paris abattoir, a hospital for venereal diseases, a prison, and an execution would be controversial, Janin published the book anonymously.

In April 1830 Pushkin wrote to Vyazemsky, "You're right to find the *Dead Donkey* delicious. It's one of the most characteristic works of the moment. It is being attributed to V. Hugo—I see more talent in it than in *The Last Day of a Condemned Man,* where there is a lot."[23]

Janin—who wrote a weekly feuilleton for the *Journal des débats* every Monday for forty years (1829–69) and produced novels, stories, literary portraits, and translations—was an important presence in the French press. His contemporaries had extreme reactions to him: while Mirecourt accuses him of misusing his journalistic influence and calls him a "jealous pygmy" for his treatment of Balzac (who called him "that fat little man who bites"), Piedagnel praises his loyalty to his editor, his generosity as a professional always ready to help young writers, and recalls Twist, a Dutch horticulturalist who named a tulip for him.[24] The Comte de Gobineau, writing in the 1840s, defends Janin's reviews against his detractors, claiming that Janin invented the new genre of the comic literary review; Marc de Montifaud and the poet Théodore de Banville praise Janin's lightness of style.[25] While his reviews may have consisted more of his own flights of fancy than analysis, his influence was broad: Regnier-Destourbet dedicated his tale *Louisa* to Janin, and Alphonse Karr was influenced by his Sternian mix of genres.[26]

Jules Janin (*Revue étrangère* 8 [1833])

Janin was such a well-known figure in Russia in the 1830s that Gogol nicknamed his friend Annenkov "Jules." Vinogradov, Tomashevsky, and Makashin consider the *Dead Donkey* the foundation of the Russian horror novel, just as French critics consider Janin the founder of the frenetic school.[27] Belinsky wrote in the *Telescope* in 1836 that Janin was "a true Frenchman, a good fellow without pretensions, simple, naive, amusing, often witty, often touching," and Pushkin found Janin's novels the most interesting of the French literature of the early 1830s.[28]

Victor Hugo (*Revue étrangère* 5 [1833])

***The Dead Donkey* (1829)** *The Dead Donkey*'s horrifying and sordid details outdid those in Victor Hugo's *The Last Days of a Condemned Man,* which had appeared two months before Janin's book. Janin, however, had begun the book intending merely to parody Hugo's gruesome literary tendency, which had so stunned readers; he even uses Hugo's title for his own chapter 25.[29] His narrator says, "I tried to denature everything without pity or mercy, to make the beautiful ugly, turn virtue into vice, day into night."[30]

Janin's premise is the corrupting effect of Paris on a country girl and her donkey. At the opening of the tale, the unnamed narrator sees Henriette, young and fresh, riding her donkey, Charlot. He is charmed by the way she kisses Charlot's face and by the purity and innocence of the scene. By the end of the tale, Charlot has been dismembered in a charnel house after being torn apart by dogs; Henriette has been guillotined and her dismembered body dug up from its grave to be sold to medical students for dissection. Janin traces Henriette's descent from innocence via debauchery to the hospital, prison, and execution and blames Paris for her corruption: "I have a theory: if everyone could live in vast apartments they would be much less susceptible to crime, much more subject to remorse . . . A man is buried in a space six feet long by six feet wide" (58–59). Dostoevsky both illustrates and refutes this theory: he describes Raskolnikov's room as a "coffin" and discusses man's need for "air" but analyzes this

Henriette and Charlot (Jules Janin, *L'Ane mort* [1842])

motive for murder in spiritual terms—wounded pride in the amoral philosophical atmosphere of St. Petersburg university discourse in the 1860s (discussed below). Dostoevsky presents as counterargument to the materialist determinism of Janin's statement the example of Razumikhin, who, despite the same coffin and air, sees through the German texts he translates and maintains his honesty and humanity.

Henriette's horrifying demise results from her initial seduction, which leads to a life of prostitution. After she emerges from the hospital, she encounters the man who debauched her and kills him in a rage. Janin's narrator explains the cause of Henriette's crime: "It's Paris that leads to this, corrupting the village with its vices" (213). While the idea of the city as corrupting force is an ancient topos widespread in the nineteenth-century realist novel (e.g., *David Copperfield*), here the cluster of images is more specific. Like Henriette, Raskolnikov had led a pure life as a child in the village where, in his dream, he kisses the bloody muzzle of the mare beaten by the peasant. The narrator later sees Henriette's donkey, Charlot, being beaten by a peasant: "I was passing by a heavy-looking peasant—a boor, in the full force of the word—when he cried out to a wretched ass, laden with dung, and which he was beating unmercifully" (23–24). Horse beating too was a routine event and appeared often in literary texts, several of which have been suggested as a source for Raskolnikov's horrifying dream of the peasant beating his mare to death: Balzac's *Un début dans la vie,* Nekrasov's poem "About the Weather" (1859) and its probable sources, Victor Hugo's poem "Melancholia" (1856) and his *Les Misérables* (1862).[31] Dostoevsky has combined elements from all these descriptions, and we can include an earlier one that may have contributed to Hugo's—Janin's shocking description of Charlot's death, staged in an arena at the *barrière du combat*:

The peasant and Charlot (Jules Janin, *L'Ane mort* [1842])

> The first thing the poor ass did was try to maintain his equilibrium: he made one step forward, and then another, . . . let fall his head, and waited . . . four frightfully savage dogs rushed into the arena; they . . . threw themselves on the poor animal. . . . The dogs lacerated his body, and pierced it with their pointed teeth. The champion remained calm and motionless; he gave not one single kick, for if he had done so, he would have fallen; but . . . resolved to die standing. Blood soon flowed; tears ran down the poor thing's face, and a dull hollow sound escaped from its breast. . . . At length the ass fell. . . .
>
> . . . There he lay, gasping on the blood-stained ground . . . He was struggling with the throes of death. (8–10)

Compare the mare's death in Raskolnikov's dream:

> The poor old mare was already in a very bad state. She was gasping for breath, standing still, pulling the cart again, and almost collapsing in the road. . . .
>
> And Mikolka swings again, and another blow comes down hard on the back of the unfortunate mare. She sinks back on her haunches, only to leap up again . . . They were belaboring her from every side with six whips. . . .
>
> "Alive and kicking!" they shouted on all sides.
>
> "Bet she'll fall down any minute now. . . ."
>
> . . . The mare stretches out her muzzle, draws a heavy breath, and dies.[32]

Janin shows the woman's fate comparable to the donkey's, indicting an unfeeling and hypocritical society for its violent desires. One of Hugo's chapters in *Les Misérables,* "The Death of a Horse," creates a similar parallel between the fate of a mare and Fantine; in that scene as in the others there are observers, but only in Janin's are there several active participants in the beating as there are in *Crime and Punishment.*

Dostoevsky intensifies Janin's images. The four dogs become six men who delight in the shared act of beating a creature to death. Like the donkey and Henriette, or the mare and Fantine in *Les Misérables,* the mare and the pawnbroker establish a system of parallels among female victims. In *Crime and Punishment,* this parallel defines Raskolnikov's psyche and the book's religious philosophy. Even though he awakens from his dream asking, "Will I really do *that*?" implicitly aligning himself with the beater and the mare with the pawnbroker, in his dream Raskolnikov identifies with the mare. He remembers himself as a child, running alongside the mare as she is being beaten: "One of the whippers grazed his face with his whip." The dream identifies Raskolnikov with the mare from the outset, and the childhood moment is repeated in the present of his Petersburg experience when the coach driver whips him in the street. The prolonged wrenching violence we experience during Raskolnikov's dream prepares us to react with even greater revulsion to his murder of the two women whom Dostoevsky aligns with Sonya and the mare as his victims. Although after he wakes up Raskolnikov is as revolted by his dream and its implications as we are, he reverts to casting the pawnbroker as victimizer (rather than as his future victim) to justify himself in acting out Mikolka's role, despite his dream. The mare and Sonya are the only two suffering victims for whom Raskolnikov is able to sustain his feelings of compassion.

Dostoevsky presents Sonya as a counterargument to Janin's Henriette, through whom he could elaborate the prostitution theme. Dunya too is a counter to Henriette. A female variant of her brother, her pride and independence distinguish her from the meek Sonya. She represents an alternative to Raskolnikov's, Sonya's, and Henriette's fates: the combination of her village purity and her fierce pride protects her; despite her vulnerability (as woman, as poverty-stricken), she finds the strength to reject marriage to Luzhin and firmly resists seduction by Svidrigailov—although, importantly, not at the price of murder, even in self-defense. Materially, she can earn her living as a governess; morally, she avoids corruption by the material, intellectual, and spiritual effects of the city.

Janin's narrator protests the way Paris crushes purity and then lacks all compassion for its victims. His book ends in despair. Raskolnikov preaches the same despair to Sonya when he tells her she will either commit suicide or go mad from the conflict between her life of prostitution and her purity of spirit. But Dostoevsky endows Sonya with faith in Christ, which provides her with unshakable strength. She is the opposite of Henriette, of whom the narrator exclaims: "Everything was dead in her, heart, soul, spirit, virtue, passion"; "Woe to this divine, mortal envelope that does not contain a soul—and a heart!" (76, 71). In Sonya, Dostoevsky contrasts the material envelope with spirit; Henriette perishes, but Sonya provides Raskolnikov with the means to eternal life. The mare, like Janin's donkey, dies a horrible death, but Raskolnikov's dream of his boyhood compassion for the mare almost prevents him from committing murder and finally provides the potential for his redemption.[33] From Janin's grotesque, debased figures Dostoevsky creates agents of resurrection.

Eugène Sue (1804–1875)

Along with Janin, Sue was one the most prolific authors of the *roman-feuilleton*; Vinogradov calls them the ringleaders of the furious school.[34]

Sue began as a rather cynical producer of popular literature, exploiting the unfortunate as subjects for his feuilletons, but, as Peter Brooks writes, in the process of research he became a dedicated activist who worked to improve their lot. Brooks calls *The Mysteries of Paris,* which appeared in 147 installments over a five-month period in 1843, "perhaps the most widely read novel of the nineteenth century."[35]

Critics briefly allude to Dostoevsky's relationship to Sue's work: he considered translating Sue's *Mathilde* (1841) and read his *Wandering Jew* when it came out in 1845, commenting that it "isn't bad [*neduren*]" but that "Sue is pretty dim [*ves'ma nedalek*]."[36] Dolinin observes that Dostoevsky's *Netochka Nezvanova* is indebted to *Mathilde* for the correspondence between the two girls, which he terms "direct influence, bordering on plagiarism," and Fridlender, without going into detail, considers that *The Mysteries of Paris* contributed to the realist ballast of *Crime and Punishment.*[37] Dostoevsky selected that ballast carefully.

***The Mysteries of Paris* (1843)** Sue's novel was published in Russian and begot many imitations in the 1840s, commissioned by Russian editors.[38] None of these imitators, however, takes up the theme of prostitution, central to both Sue's and Dostoevsky's novels, perhaps because of the censorship. *The Mysteries of Paris* begins in the underworld of Paris, where a mysterious hero, Rodolphe, rescues a young woman, Fleur de Marie, from being beaten up.[39] She tells her history in a tavern: she never knew her parents and can only remember from the age of seven or so being kept by an old woman who beat her, made her go begging, and pulled out a tooth to punish her, "yet she never expressed any feeling of hatred against the atrocious woman who had treated her so cruelly."[40] By the age of sixteen Fleur is forced to become a prostitute, but maintains her innate virtue; telling her tale, she says, "It must be pleasant to be good" (31). The narrator comments, "Misery and poverty, but not crime, had been the ruin of this poor girl" (32). Yet an "innocent, joyous expression . . . shone on this lovely face," and she exclaims, "How good is the Almighty for having given us such a fine day!" (59). Rodolphe, a disguised nobleman, ransoms her from prostitution; she is embarrassed to take his arm "out of delicacy" (54–55). After a series of perilous adventures from which Rodolphe keeps rescuing her, he reveals that he is her father and that she is the Princess Amelia. With her "exquisite sensibility," she cannot accept the love and respect of all around her and takes the veil, but dies in the nunnery, tormented by the contrast between the respect of the nuns and her past shame (410).[41]

Dostoevsky again takes up this discrepancy between bodily degradation and spiritual purity. Fleur de Marie has grown up under inhuman conditions yet maintains her noble spirit: she cherishes nature, is meek, compassionate to others, and, despite her trials, maintains a love of God, apparently because she is, after all, of noble birth. Her princely father who protects the oppressed has almost god-like qualities, and she worships him accordingly: "I bless you and I respect you as I do my God . . . in prison . . . I said . . . 'Mr. Rodolphe succours the unfortunate.' To those who hesitated between good and evil I said ' . . . Be virtuous; Mr. Rodolphe rewards those who are virtuous'" (330).[42] Dostoevsky replaces Sue's deification of French nobility with Christ himself; Sonya's strength of spirit comes from faith; her purity is contrasted to her cheap prostitute's clothing that emblematizes her physical defilement. She is "unconscious of her fourth-hand gaudy silk dress with its long absurd train and the immense crinoline that filled the entire doorway . . . her bright-colored shoes . . . and her foolish round straw hat with the bright red feather on top" (187). But no earthly figure rescues Sonya from her degradation; rather she herself embodies Christ's teachings and can therefore rescue Raskolnikov. Svidrigailov is the *diabolus ex machina* who provides the material part of the solution to Sonya's physical debasement by giving her Marfa Petrovna's money to take care of her half-siblings; Sonya's moral deliverance is provided by Christ's New Word.

Regnier-Destourbet (1804–1832)

A third tale of a prostitute, *Louisa, or the Griefs of a Prostitute* (*Louisa, ou les douleurs d'une fille de joie,* 1830), supplies an element missing from the two just discussed: the sinner's compassion. Regnier-Destourbet, writing under the pseudonym "Abbé Tiberge" (taken from a character in *Manon Lescaut*), dedicated his tale of a corrupted country girl to Jules Janin. In *Louisa* a young woman travels to Paris from the country, but this one has already adopted a life of vice, as is apparent to all in the omnibus she enters. Like Fleur de Marie and other virtuous prostitutes, she is acutely aware of her unworthiness: "Perceiving the effect that her arrival had on the company, she felt quite some embarrassment"; Sonya too is distressed when she is seated in Raskolnikov's room with his friends and family (43). En route to Paris, the omnibus is stopped by an accident: a tilbury knocks down an old woman, breaking her arm. The woman wails, "How am I going to earn my living!" and Louisa gives her a gold louis (twenty francs), her only money. The poor woman exclaims, "May the supreme being recompense your humanity and give you holy benediction! . . . Let me go on my knees to you!" Louisa replies, "Pray God for me, my dear, that's all I ask of you" (51). In the poor woman crushed by a carriage, Louisa-the-sinner's act of spontaneous charity and its potential for redemption, Dostoevsky could find Raskolnikov's charity for Marmeladov; Raskolnikov takes Marmeladov home after he has been run over on the street and gives twenty rubles to the family, asking ten-year-old Polya to pray for him—"I'll pray for you the whole rest of my life," she promises (191). Louisa the prostitute has presumably earned her money through vice. But Raskolnikov's money, as he later reassures Sonya, comes from his mother, not from the pawnbroker. Sinner though Raskolnikov be, the charity he gives is clearly separated from the murder he commits. His compassion is shown to come from a different, contrasting part of his personality. Sonya goes beyond Louisa's charity in her compassion for Raskolnikov, himself nearly run over by a carriage.

Honoré de Balzac (1799–1850)

> The Frenchman is quiet, honest, polite, but false and money is everything for him. He has no ideal.
>
> Fyodor Dostoevsky, 1862

Balzac's novels had even more importance for Russian writers than Janin's *Dead Donkey* and Sue's *Mysteries.* Extremely popular in Russia in the 1830s, Balzac was read in French as well as in translation in a wide variety of Russian journals, from the conservative *Readers' Library* (*Biblioteka dlia chteniia*) to the more progressive *Telescope.* Pushkin borrows details from Balzac in "The Stationmaster" and "The Queen of Spades"; and, as we saw, Gogol's poor clerks owe much to Balzac's descriptions of their French colleagues.[43]

The close relationship between *Le Père Goriot* and *Crime and Punishment* has received much critical attention and takes on further resonance when seen as part of a continuing discussion among Janin, Balzac, and Dostoevsky.[44] By 1830 the theme of the prostitute noble of spirit had been thoroughly exploited in French literature.[45] Balzac takes it up again in 1839 in *The Splendors and Miseries of Courtesans. Splendors* (which has been translated as *A Harlot High and Low*) is far superior to Janin's and Sue's works and, probably because of this, more closely related to Dostoevsky's.[46]

***The Splendors and Miseries of Courtesans* (1843, 1847)** The first two parts of Balzac's novel (1843) treat the tale of a prostitute. The third and fourth parts (1847) relate to Raskolnikov and will be discussed later in this chapter. In parts 1 and 2 of *Splendors,* Balzac returns to the theme of prostitution after it would appear to have been exhausted, perhaps out of rivalry with Sue, whose *Mysteries of Paris* was appearing in the *Journal des débats* at the same time (from June 1842 to October 1843) as the first two parts of *Splendors* were appearing in *Le Parisien* (May and July 1843).[47]

Early in the novel, we find Esther Gobseck, a poor Jewish prostitute nicknamed "the Torpedo," lying on the floor of her poor room, having just attempted suicide. The details of her surroundings convey the grotesque contrasts between the two social levels of Esther's life. Her room has yellow-brown calico bed curtains with a dull-red rose pattern and grey wallpaper speckled with flowers. The simple poverty of the room contrasts with her "delicious hat" and "elegant dress" and "laced half-boots fit for a queen." Balzac describes "these luxuries among the broken fragments, this household so appropriate to the Bohemian life of this limp, half-dressed wench sunk down like a horse dead in its harness, pinned by a broken shaft, caught in the reins" (38). The description contains three features of Dostoevsky's construction of Sonya: the stark room with the "yellowish, stained, shabby wallpaper" and no curtains around the bed; the contrast of the room's austerity to her absurd hat with the red feather; and her identification with the beaten mare of Raskolnikov's dream (309).

Esther is rescued by the criminal Jacques Collin. He has earlier appeared in *Père Goriot* disguised as Vautrin; here he is disguised as the priest Carlos Herrera. For his sinister purposes, he installs Esther in a convent. She agrees to go because she is in love with Lucien de Rubempré, and Herrera promises her, "The day after that on which you are washed in the waters of baptism, you will see Lucien again" (59). Esther is rendered newly virginal by repenting the sins of her life as a prostitute, and she is converted from Judaism to Catholicism. The baptism of the Jewess in the convent is a mock sanctification arranged by Collin as part of his plot to gain power in Parisian society. The criminal intends to translate the prostitute's sensual power into social-political power and gives the whole maneuver a religious disguise.

The young poet Lucien, however, operates within a literary-romantic conception of both the prostitute and the divine: even before Esther's religious conversion, Lucien "had divined the angel in the prostitute, rather brushed by corruption than corrupt" (63–64). Collin is aware of and able to manipulate the categories; speaking to Lucien, he employs the poet's literary rather than religious usage of the word "angel" when he reunites the lovers after Esther leaves the convent, telling Lucien that "that angel who wished to rise up to heaven has come down . . . and awaits you" (68). Esther has achieved the conversion that Sue's Fleur de Marie could not.

Dostoevsky reorders Balzac's system. Dostoevsky had begun writing *Crime and Punishment* using the same model of earthly love between the prostitute and the sinner as Balzac. In the notebooks, Dostoevsky has Sonya write to Raskolnikov: "She wrote him, finally, a letter: I love you, I'll be your slave, she was captivated by his pride and independence and preaching that she is not humiliated (her letter is artistic). He goes to her after that letter."[48] But in the final version, Dostoevsky removes all sexuality from Raskolnikov's relationship to Sonya. Raskolnikov calls her not an "angel" but a "holy fool" (317). Even Sonya's role as prostitute is desexualized; she remains untainted by and apparently unsusceptible to sensuality. Balzac's narrator exclaims that Esther "personifies the myth . . . where a sublime being lies hidden beneath a degraded exterior, typified also . . . in the book of books, the Bible!" (239). But in addition to her selfless loyalty, Esther is voluptuous and manipulative, while Sonya is childlike and guileless.

Dostoevsky separates the sensual aspect of Balzac's couple from its spiritual component. He strips all irony, masquerade, and Romanticism from the religious theme and transforms this sexual, romantic (in both senses) love between Lucien and the converted Esther into Sonya's divine love that enables Raskolnikov's future spiritual resurrection, rather than Lucien's social one. Dostoevsky removes the irony from Balzac's "sublime being" to make it refer to the divine aspect of all human beings and resacralizes the relevance of the Bible, from which Sonya herself reads the Raising of Lazarus to Raskolnikov, modeling for him his future rebirth. Esther's name carries her connection to the Old Testament; Dostoevsky names Sonya for her identity with the New Testament and with the "divine wisdom" of Russian Orthodoxy.

Balzac and Dostoevsky take up Napoleonism in this context, likening the treatment of prostitutes to Napoleon's disregard for human life. Herrera proposes to sell Esther to the Baron de Nucingen. When Lucien expresses horror at this, Herrera preaches the expendability of human life: "How many generals died in the prime of life for the Emperor Napoleon? . . . There is no shortage of women!" (89). Esther too invokes

Napoleon as she prepares to kill herself when Herrera tries to force her again to play the role of prostitute. She tells Lucien, "Men aren't worth the trouble of loving. Napoleon killed them like flies" (284).

Raskolnikov echoes both victimizer Herrera and victim Esther: "People are used up by the millions, and it's considered a virtue" (408). He tries to act with the same indifference to human life as Herrera does, murdering two expendable women in his experiment to see if he is a Napoleon. But Dostoevsky rejects Balzac's scenario: not only does Sonya not commit suicide, as Esther does and Raskolnikov says Sonya will, but she refutes Raskolnikov's Napoleonism with Christ and follows him to Siberia to begin a new life.

Dostoevsky refutes Balzac's analysis of the struggle between men and women—rich and poor—and of the individual, for influence in society; for him this is only part of the trivial material aspect of human existence. Although he keenly felt the humiliations that poverty brings and had shown this in *Poor Folk,* it is much more important for him to reduce the material argument to its essence, in the figure of Sonya, whose poverty and powerlessness should drive her to suicide but whose faith makes her the strongest figure in *Crime and Punishment.*

RASKOLNIKOV: CRIME AND RESURRECTION

The French tales of the prostitute parody the biblical topos of the Magdalene, by contrast mocking both the possibility of the resurrection of the prostitute and the society that has lost the faith in Christ that would have enabled it. Janin and Balzac use biblical references to mock their male sinners as well; their protagonists murder, cause the murder of others indirectly, or choose luxury and debauchery over honesty and the implied values of the novels they inhabit. The French writers never reverse their heroes' path to destruction; the characters can never regain faith in something higher than the world they live in. The authors' role as social satirist demands that they emphasize the dire consequences of a godless society. Balzac reinforces the bitter irony in Janin's mockery of biblical imagery; Dostoevsky counters both of them by reinstating the power of the biblical Word. Europe is a "graveyard" (as Ivan puts it in *The Brothers Karamazov*), but Russia has the spiritual potential of its intuitive Orthodox faith.[49]

Honoré de Balzac

Balzac's *Dead Donkey,* Chapter 30 (1830) While Pushkin could be enthusiastic about Janin's literary talent in 1830, in the 1850s

Dostoevsky was more attuned to Janin's thematics and how they developed out of the ferment of the 1820s–1830s. Janin's *Dead Donkey* is mercilessly materialist, emphasizing physical degradation and decay. The pessimism of Janin's tale reaches its climax when the narrator, wanting to give Henriette a decent burial, goes to her grave:

> The next day I returned alone, my thoughts filled with prayers, my heart filled with pity, my eyes filled with tears, and my hands filled with flowers; but on reaching the spot where a few drops of blood were still visible, there was no longer a tomb. The grave, which had been ransacked and half filled up again, had already delivered up its prey; the School of Medicine had stolen the body. . . . The women of the neighborhood had battled with each other for the shroud. . . . Nothing was left." (141)

Roger J. B. Clark calls this a sacrilegious parody of Jesus's resurrection.[50] That the narrator meets Henriette when she is riding on a donkey also suggests a parodic version of Jesus's entry into Jerusalem. The narrator's lament—"I had followed her to the end of her sad path of candor and vice, of roses and of thorns"—supports the idea. Janin makes a mockery of the mystery of Jesus's absence from the tomb by having Henriette's body taken for the most material purpose of medical research (it was a common practice to use prostitutes' bodies): "How could I hope to snatch her from the surgeon's knife?" wails the narrator. He concludes, "no hope in thy soul, no tears in thy eyes, no flowers in thy hands; not even in this tomb."[51]

Balzac reviewed *The Dead Donkey* for *Le Voleur* in February 1830 and added his own parodic chapter 30 to the *Donkey*'s twenty-nine. In it, he has Janin's narrator receive Henriette's tibia from the medical students. He makes it into a letter knife, on which he has a famous artist engrave "a dead donkey on one side of the handle and a young girl on the other" (147). He takes up Janin's parody, completing the sacrilege with a relic of the sainted martyrs designed for practical everyday use, setting the polarities into extreme opposition, in a grotesque contrast between utilitarian letter-opener and the remains of a human being destroyed by an uncaring society.

Balzac writes his own version of a tragic death scene in *Père Goriot.* Dostoevsky answers and reverses all three—Janin's ending of *The Dead Donkey,* Balzac's parody of *The Dead Donkey,* and Balzac's ending of *Père Goriot*—in the epilogue of *Crime and Punishment,* where he unites the theme of prostitution with the biblical subtext of the Gospel of John to achieve Raskolnikov's future resurrection.

Dostoevsky treats the theme of the ambitious young man more fully than that of the prostitute, responding in detail to two of Balzac's novels, *The Wild Ass's Skin* (*La Peau de chagrin*) and *Père Goriot.* Balzac's novels present a critique of the godless materialism and egotistical individualism characteristic of Paris in 1830 under the reign of Louis Philippe. *Crime and Punishment* contains an analogous critique of the atheistic rationalism of the radicals in St. Petersburg of the 1850s and 1860s.

***The Wild Ass's Skin* (1830)** Much has been written about the effect of Balzac's work on Dostoevsky's, but the relationship between *The Wild Ass's Skin* and *Crime and Punishment* has so far gone unexamined. Nils Åke Nilsson credits Balzac's work with introducing the fantastic of E. T. A. Hoffmann into Russia, citing in particular *The Wild Ass's Skin.* Translated into Russian in 1832, it contributed to the eerie blend of the realistic with the fantastic in Pushkin's "Queen of Spades," whose hero is a literary relation of Raskolnikov's.[52] Balzac's description of his desperate hero Raphael de Valentin is still more important for Dostoevsky's of Raskolnikov; both heroes conclude a Faustian bargain, Raphael literally and Raskolnikov figuratively. Although Dostoevsky has no interest in the supernatural aspect of the magical ass's skin or the love story in part 2 of the novel, "The Woman without a Heart," he draws significant material—thematics, scenes, details of appearance, actions, setting, and motivations—from Balzac's depiction of Raphael in part 1, "The Talisman."

Raphael and Raskolnikov, true to the type of the young man from the provinces, are talented, ambitious, and proud but have fallen on hard times. In their wretched poverty, they are contemptuous of and isolated from everyone around them. The novels' opening sentences provide the city settings that define their desperation. *The Wild Ass's Skin* begins:

> Towards the end of the month of October 1829 a young man entered the Palais-Royale just as the gaming houses were opening.[53]

Crime and Punishment begins:

> In the beginning of July, at an exceptionally hot time, toward evening, a young man left his lair which he rented from tenants on Stolyarny street and slowly, as if indecisively, set off for the Kokushin bridge. (13)

The opening sentences are conventional, but the similarities between them go much farther. Raphael is on his way to a gambling house to fling down his last piece of gold, almost wanting to lose it before he goes to commit suicide; Raskolnikov is going to the pawnbroker's to prepare a slightly different gamble that he almost wants to lose and that will lead him too to consider suicide. Dostoevsky's opening crams more into his introductory sentence: the oppression of the heat and of Raskolnikov's confining "lair," his indecision, and the bridge that becomes a tempting jumping off place for a suicide set up the dynamic of part 1 and will become important motifs in his struggle throughout the novel.

Raphael loses his "last napoleon" (Raskolnikov's murder is his final attempt to become a Napoleon) and goes to the Pont Royal:

> Having reached the middle of the bridge, he gave a black look at the water.
>
> "Bad weather to drown yourself!" a ragged old woman said to him with a laugh, "it's filthy and it's cold, the Seine is!"
>
> . . . But death in full daylight seemed sordid to him, and so he decided to die by night. (30–31)

Prior to this, the narrator had set the scene:

> Every suicide is a poem sublime in its melancholy. Where will you find, emerging from the ocean of literature, a book that can vie in genius with a news-item such as: *Yesterday at four o'clock, a woman threw herself into the Seine from the Pont des Arts.* (29)

Raskolnikov, realizing that he has failed to make himself into a Napoleon after murdering Alyona and Lizaveta, also considers and rejects drowning himself. Standing on the bridge, he actually witnesses a poor woman's attempt to drown herself, which leads him to decide, "No, it's foul . . . the water . . . it's not worth it" (174). The reality of drowning postpones both poor but ambitious heroes' actions.

Raphael's reason for postponing his death is comically trivial (too sordid during the day), while Dostoevsky conveys the pathos of the desperation of poverty by having it acted out for Raskolnikov and the reader. Balzac gives two variants of suicide: Raphael's comically trivial one and the newspaper item, tragic in principle, but not elaborated, and so not experienced by the hero or the reader. Dostoevsky, who drew so much from the newspapers, takes up the challenge: to write a book that can vie with the suicide notice by dramatizing it. Raskolnikov witnesses firsthand a woman's suicide such as is described in Balzac's news item—Dostoevsky combines Raphael's meeting the woman by the Seine with the hypothetical news item. Where the French-educated Balzac is rhetorical, Dostoevsky is dramatic; the scene of the woman's actual and Raskolnikov's contemplated suicides carries the ideological significance of Raskolnikov's connection to the city poor, the "ant hill" he despises but learns to accept his identification with.

At the novel's opening, Balzac describes Raphael as he is seen by the gamblers at the Palais-Royale:

> His youthful features were stamped with a clouded grace and the look of his eyes bore witness to efforts betrayed and to a thousand hopes deceived. The gloomy passivity of intended suicide imparted to his brow a dull, unhealthy pallor, a bitter smile drew creases round the corners of his mouth. . . . The young man had a stylish evening coat, but the junction of waistcoat and cravat was too carefully preserved for one to suppose that he was wearing linen underneath. His hands, dainty as a woman's, were none too clean . . . some of the . . . charm of innocence still bloomed in his slender, delicate proportions, his sparse, fair and naturally curly hair. (25–26)

Raskolnikov is also poor but attractive, without the feminine dainty hands; he is "remarkably handsome, with handsome dark eyes, dark brown hair, above average in height, slim and well-built [*tonok i stroen*]. . . . He had eaten nothing at all for two days. He was so badly dressed that another . . . would have been ashamed to go out in such rags in the daytime" (14).

These externals convey the contradictions of their personalities. Raphael's elegant clothing conceals his hidden poverty. This is reversed in Raskolnikov—his rags make the intelligent, well-educated young man look like a beggar. Raphael is an "angel without his halo" torn between two extremes: "Shadows and light, nothingness and existence battled in producing an impression at the same time of both grace and horror. The young man resembled *an angel without his halo,* who had strayed from his path. Thus all the professors emeritus of vice [in the gambling hall] resembling a toothless old woman full of pity at the sight of a pretty girl who offers herself for corruption were ready to cry to the novice: 'Leave this place!'" (26–27, emphasis mine). The oppositions grace/horror, angel/fallen angel are applicable to Raskolnikov too. He is a "novice" capable of compassion for the suffering poor who also "strays from his path." As Porfiry describes him, "he committed murder, yet continues to consider himself an honest man; he looks down on people and walks around *like a pallid angel*" (440, emphasis mine).

Both heroes' moods shift quickly from joy to contempt for those around them: Walking away from the bridge, Raphael "broke into a smile, philosophically thrust his hands into his waistcoat pockets, and was about to walk on again with an air of proud disdain, when he was surprised to hear some coins jingling . . . in his pocket. A smile of hope stole from his lips to every feature, lit up his brow, and brought a gleam of joy to his eyes and haggard cheeks . . . But his face darkened" at seeing he has only three copper coins, which he throws to two beggars (31). These rapid alternations are the center of part 1 of *Crime and Punishment,* which traces the system of Raskolnikov's oscillations between the pride that moves him toward his crime and the compassion that redeems him from it. In his concern for the seduced girl on the street and for the Marmeladovs, he quickly gives away the few coins he has in his pocket, only to regret the gestures later. Where Raphael gives his remaining money to two random beggars, Dostoevsky once again dramatizes the action; he provides scenes that convey the girl's situation, Marmeladov's personality, and Raskolnikov's dual reactions to both, scenes that begin to establish a complex set of parallels among the cast of characters.

Raphael and Raskolnikov wander the streets in a state of delirium, obsessed with the contrast between their impotent poverty and the absolute power of the great men in history. Raphael goes from the bridge to an antique shop, where he reviews human history through the objects collected there—"A Sèvres vase on which Madame Jacquetot had painted Napoleon was standing next to a sphinx painted by Sesostris"—and meets a "wizened little old man," the proprietor of the shop, whose "pale, hollow cheeks, the implacable severity of his small green eyes . . . might well have made [Raphael] believe that Gerard Dow's *Money-Changer* had stepped down from his frame" (34, 44). The antique dealer thinks Raphael intends to kill him for his gold, but Raphael admits the "innocent piece of deceit" that he had no intention of buying anything but was only waiting for nightfall to drown himself without fuss (47). It is then that the dealer offers him the magical ass's skin.

In this eerie scene the elements of Raskolnikov's crime are assembled: the pawnbroker, a "tiny, dry little old lady with sharp and mean little eyes" (*kroshechnaia, sukhaia starushon'ka, s vostrymi i zlymi glazkami*); Raskolnikov's not-innocent piece of deceit; and his murder of her, apparently for her gold (8). Balzac's reference to Gerard Dow is foreign to the characters' frame of reference; Dostoevsky's narrator sticks to the characters' immediate physical world.

The scene of Raphael's receiving the fateful skin from the Mephistophelean antique dealer sets in motion the action of the novel, Raphael's struggle with his contradictory desires that culminates in his death; Raskolnikov's murder of the pawnbroker sets in motion his journey toward rebirth; as Dostoevsky put it in his notebook, "His moral development begins from the crime itself."[54]

Dostoevsky transforms the scene from supernatural to naturalist without losing a sense of eeriness and shifts its significance from the social and philosophical to the psychological and spiritual planes. The ass's skin that grants Raphael's wishes at the price of shortening his life is replaced with the murder of the pawnbroker, the plot variant that Balzac's antique dealer had feared. Raskolnikov's motives for the crime evolve until they are distilled into the desire for power in human society, as emblematized by Napoleon, but are transformed through his suffering, beyond the boundaries of the novel, into a spiritual transcendence.[55]

Raphael is almost granted transcendence of his worldly passions (for the cold Foedora [*sic*] and for the money, elegance, and status needed to win her) when he moves to the attic of a poor lodging: "Nothing could be more sordid than this attic with its dirty yellow [wallpapered, 110] walls, which smelt of poverty and seemed to await a needy scholar. The roof followed a downward slope and the badly fitting tiles gave glimpses of the sky" (109).

Raphael calls the room "worthy of the *Leads* [prisons] of Venice" and an "aerial sepulchre" (109), the same terms of "prison" and "coffin" that Dostoevsky uses to describe the "needy scholar" Raskolnikov's attic room with its yellow wallpaper.[56] There Raphael meets the landlady's daughter, Pauline, "a little girl of about fourteen, playing at battledore and shuttlecock with one of her companions," whom he continues to refer to as "child" years later (108). When he overhears her praising him to her mother, he says, "The poor child had applied a soothing balm to my wounds" (137). Pauline generously takes care of him, pitying him in his misfortune despite her own poverty. He gives her piano lessons and "see[s] only a sister" in her despite her "maidenly charms." With her mother, she reads the Gospel of John to determine Raphael's fate, using it in a divining ritual. Pauline prophesizes that they will all become rich, which Raphael dismisses as "empty but affectionate words, similar to the meaningless songs with which a mother lulls her invalid child to sleep," but, he says, they "restored me to something like calm" (140). When they meet again after a long absence in the final section, "The Death-Agony," Raphael believes Pauline has delivered him from the pact of the ass's skin: "Your presence has always dispelled my sorrows and brought solace to my soul. At this moment I feel as it were purified by your angelic smile, ready to begin a new life" (217). Compare this to Raskolnikov's reaction to Sonya's ten-year-old half-sister, Polya (the diminutive form of Polina, Pauline), when she runs after him to ask his name:

> He put both hands on her shoulders, and with a kind of joy he looked at her. He felt so good, looking at her.
>
> "Will you love me?"
>
> Instead of answering, the girl . . . reached up to kiss him. Suddenly her arms, as thin as matchsticks, embraced him powerfully.
>
> Five minutes later he was standing at the bridge at exactly the same place where the woman had jumped not long before. (190–91)

And he resolves, "No more phantoms! Life is!"

Dostoevsky considerably abbreviates the sentimentality of Pauline's naive, selfless love, embodying her childlike innocence in the figure of Polya. Pauline's prophecy of riches comes to pass but is useless to Raphael, whose life grows shorter as his wishes are granted. For Pauline's material riches, Dostoevsky substitutes Polya's prayer, which is an adjunct to her sister's religious power, itself more fantastical than the fiction of the ass's skin in its true power to change the world. Raskolnikov will achieve the richness of spirit that Raphael tragically foregoes. Dostoevsky realizes the spiritual potential of Balzac's Pauline in having Sonya too read the Gospel of John, but not for divination: her reading the Raising of Lazarus aloud to Raskolnikov also foretells his fate, his return to a new life, but on a spiritual plane, as Pauline's more primitive use of the Gospel had for Raphael in the material realm.

Both young men write essays on the subject of their obsessions as part of their thirst for greatness. Raphael had renounced law and struggled in abject poverty to write his "Treatise on Will" (*Un Traité sur la volonté*), which was to gain him the reputation of a man of genius. Instead he accepts the antique dealer's magic gift, which yields him earthly wealth at the cost of his life—he is unable to profit from Pauline's selfless (if earthly) love. Raskolnikov also abandons his law studies and writes his article "On Crime" in a similar attic with the aim of becoming a superman; with Sonya's help, his murder of the pawnbroker ultimately leads him to something more powerful than the magic skin and, most importantly, universally available—human community and faith in Christ.

Dostoevsky's changes of Balzac's details are all in this material-to-spiritual direction. Raphael, starving, regrets the condition of his top hat:

> Worst of all, the rain was ruining my hat. How after this could I present myself at [an elegant woman's] salon without a decent top hat? So far, by taking extreme care of it, whilst cursing the absurd and stupid fashion which

> condemns us to hold our hats constantly in our hands and exhibit the lining, I had kept mine in passable condition. . . . But its artificially prolonged life was reaching its end, it was bruised, crippled, done for—a mere tatter, a worthy representative of its owner. (135–36)

The starving Raskolnikov wears an old top hat, referred to by the name of its German maker, Zimmerman, to which Dostoevsky devotes two paragraphs:

> A drunk who was riding down the street in a huge wagon . . . suddenly yelled at him as he passed, "Hey you, German hat!" and roared at the top of his lungs—the young man suddenly stopped and with a shudder grabbed his hat. This hat was tall, round, a Zimmerman top hat, but all worn out already, completely rust-colored, full of holes and spots, without a brim and tilting to one side at a most outrageous angle. But not shame, rather a completely different feeling even resembling fear seized him.
>
> "I knew it!" He muttered in distress, "just as I thought! The last straw! It's just this kind of stupidity, some tawdry detail that can ruin the whole concept! Yes, the hat is too noticeable . . . It's ludicrous, that's why it's noticeable . . . I need a cap to go with my rags, some old pancake or other, and not this freak. No one wears this kind, they'll notice it on meeting me, remember it . . . the main thing is they'll remember it later, and distinguish it. You need to be as unnoticeable as possible in this . . . trivial details are the main thing! It's these details that always ruin everything. . . ." (14–15)

Raphael fears that his hat will betray his poverty to high society; Raskolnikov fears his hat will reveal him as a murderer. The Zimmerman is in fact "a mere tatter, a worthy representative of its owner" in that it reveals Raskolnikov's poverty of spirit, because the German name carries a complex set of meanings in the Russian context.

Razumikhin "for some unknown reason" refers to Raskolnikov's hat as a "Palmerston"; the description of his purchases emphasizes their foreign origins—the United States of America (the trousers—a pun on *shtany/Shtaty*), the boots of foreign workmanship taken to the bazaar by the secretary at the English embassy—and in the notebooks is added: "In autumn, to be sure, all this will fall apart, like the Babylonian monarchy, though not from luxury, but from inner disharmony."[57] Lord Henry John Palmerston, the British prime minister from 1855 to his death in 1865, was both an elegant aristocrat (for whom a top hat would be appropriate) and known for an imperious temper and "extreme acerbity of language."[58] The mention of Babylon suggests the venality of the city; Dostoevsky may have eliminated it as overemphasizing the foreign origins of Raskolnikov's crime, inappropriately mixing the secular and the religious argument, which belongs properly to the novel but not to Razumikhin's frame of reference.

As for the Zimmerman's connotations, throughout the novel, Dostoevsky alludes to several German popularizers of materialist social scientific thought who were being read by the progressive youth of the 1850s and 1860s, among them Adolph Wagner, Ludwig Büchner, and Karl Vogt.[59] Raskolnikov's exposure to their views in Petersburg university circles contributes to his theory that leads him to murder. Heavily censored in Russia during the 1840s–1860s, some of them for their "scientific," materialist approach to religion, the German texts are also part of the basis for the "new ideas" Lebezyatnikov discusses with Luzhin, which parody Raskolnikov's Napoleonism.[60] Thus the German hat on Raskolnikov's Russian head suggests why his friend Razumikhin calls him "a translation," that is, a Russian imitation of the kind of book (parodied by the title *Is Woman Human?*) that Razumikhin generously offers to let him translate in order to earn enough to eat. That scene between the two students also shows the effects of *The Wild Ass's Skin.*

Raphael goes to his friend Rastignac (seen here at a later time in his career than in *Père Goriot*) for financial help when he is at his lowest, and Rastignac takes him to a tavern for breakfast, where he introduces him to a "literary speculator," telling Raphael: "This fellow . . . has received the Legion of Honor for publishing works that he doesn't understand. He's a chemist, a historian, a novelist and publicist. He owns a quarter, third, half shares in quite a number of plays, and he's as ignorant as Don Miguel's mule . . . he's a half-breed in the moral sense—neither wholly honest nor a complete knave" (141–42). For writing for "this fellow," Rastignac will get a commission (which he intends to give Raphael) and Raphael will get an advance. Rastignac arranges for him to write up some historical memoirs for the speculator and pass them off as belonging to his aunt, a marquise once prominent at court. (Raphael is later appalled at selling his aunt's name but manages to get out of that part of the bargain.)

Raskolnikov goes to Razumikhin for some kind of help after committing the murder, and Razumikhin sacrifices some much-needed income for his friend. Recognizing Raskolnikov's poverty, he suggests the translation deal for the bookseller Kheruvimov. The name incorporates the idealist/materialist duality that structures the entire novel: it suggests that Kheruvimov ("of the cherubim") has studied at a seminary, as this is the type of name given to seminarians, yet he is the purveyor of materialist literature.[61] Unlike Raskolnikov, Razumikhin is untouched by the materialist argument of the German works he translates, mocking them and the book dealer who publishes them:

> He does a little publishing—natural science and stuff like that. And does his stuff sell! All you really need is the title! Remember, you always used to say I was dumb? Well, my God, you'd be surprised how many people there are in the world dumber than I am! Now he's taken up the progressive movement too. He doesn't know beans about it himself, but I egg him on, of course. Here you have a little over thirty-two pages of German text. In my opinion it's the most blatant fake. Is woman a human being or not? That sort of thing. Well, naturally, you prove triumphantly that she is a human being. Kheruvimov's getting it ready for his feminist section. I'm translating. He'll expand those thirty-two pages to a hundred. We'll compose the most passionate title, half a page long, and we'll put the thing out for half a ruble. Will it sell! I get about fifteen rubles for the job. I took six in advance . . . take three rubles. Because I received an advance for the whole translation. . . . So three rubles goes straight to you—your share. When you're done you'll get another three. (117)

Rastignac is prepared to have Raphael betray his aunt, but Razumikhin, characterized as impulsively pure and anti-Socialist, only offers the translations, which he views as harmless. Both publicists are purveying the very materialism that Balzac satirizes and Dostoevsky refutes; Raphael takes the bait, while Raskolnikov initially takes the money and leaves with the translation, but immediately comes back and silently returns both.

Razumikhin is "gay and communicative"; "No failure daunts him, and unfavorable circumstances seemed unable to keep him down . . . Though he was very poor, he made his own way entirely, earning money at various odd jobs. He knew a fantastic number of ways of making money" (59). Rastignac is "the diabolical Gascon" whose "ease of manner and imperturbable self-assurance" (141) help him to take advantage of Parisian luxury on credit while being as poor as Raphael. For Dostoevsky, Razumikhin is the counterexample to Raskolnikov, transcending environment, an implicit rebuttal of Balzac's scenario in which Rastignac leads Raphael into the thick of Parisian social emptiness, introducing him to Foedora, whose rejection sends Raphael to the brink of suicide and causes him to accept the ass's skin. Here Dostoevsky reverses the usual material-into-spiritual direction of his transformation of Balzac's material: Raphael's "diabolical" friend who leads the hero astray is replaced by the down-to-earth, rather uncouth Razumikhin who saves Raskolnikov and his whole family in the practical realm by his capacity for an everyday kind of selfless love, the Christian principle applied to daily life.

Balzac too parodies the materialist argument. He pits mathematics against the metaphysical: at Taillefer's party Raphael's friend Emile says, "I'd cheerfully pay a hundred francs to any mathematician who could prove to me the existence of hell by means of an algebraic equation" (77). At a gathering at Porfiry Petrovich's, Razumikhin says, "I'll prove to you . . . that the only reason you have white eyelashes is because the bell tower of Ivan the Great is a hundred yards high" (255). The two scenes appear to be very different. The first is a lavish feast where the journalists, bankers, and wits of Paris are bantering about the total lack of values in the age of Louis-Philippe; the second takes place in a modest apartment in Petersburg. But the discussion in both capitals is about the loss of religion and the new amoral attitude toward crime. Raphael's friends jest about "A Method of Killing an Uncle": "'First, take an uncle, stout and fat, at least seventy years old. . . . ' 'What a hope! My uncle is tall and thin, a miser'" (70). They address the value of a human life:

> "Men and events are nothing. . . . In politics and philosophy only principles and ideas count."
>
> "How horrible! You would execute your friends without compunction for the sake of an *if*?"
>
> "But . . . the man who feels remorse is the real villain, for he has some idea of virtue; whereas Peter the Great and the Duke of Alba embodied systems." (68)

At the gathering at Porfiry's, Raskolnikov first expounds the theory he has published in a journal in a similar dialogue:

> Porfiry: "Can you imagine what we got onto last night, Rodia: is there such a thing as crime or isn't there?"
>
> Razumikhin: "It began with the socialist point of view. . . . Crime is a protest against the abnormality of the social order."
>
> Raskolnikov: "The 'extraordinary' man has the inner right to permit his conscience to transgress . . . certain obstacles."
>
> Porfiry: "What's really original here . . . is that you permit bloodshed *according to conscience.*" (253, 257, 260)

Thus Raskolnikov's theory leads him to commit murder precisely "for the sake of an *if*," that is, to see *if* he is an extraordinary man or not.

In the scene at Taillefer's banquet in *The Wild Ass's Skin,* Balzac presents a more diffuse, more comic, version of the Mandarin argument that appeared in *Père Goriot* four years later. Grossman long ago discussed Dostoevsky's use of the Mandarin in *Crime and Punishment.* The parallel of Raskolnikov's first discussion with Porfiry to the discussion at Taillefer's banquet shows the latter to be another source for the Mandarin idea. This parallel implicitly extends the object of Dostoevsky's critique from socialist ideas to the entire country's loss of faith. Raphael attends the banker Taillefer's banquet because he is being recruited to be an unprincipled journalist, one prepared to take any position to represent an opposition party, "since we don't give a damn whether [the Citizen-King's national government] is freedom or tyranny, religion or irreligion" (58). Raphael struggles against this: "Even if we no longer believe in the devil, we may still regret the Eden of our youth, that period of innocence when we used to extend our tongues devoutly to a good priest to receive the precious body of Our Lord Jesus Christ. . . . Ah! My good friends, if we drew so much pleasure from committing our first sins, it was because they had remorse to embellish them, to give them spice and savor; whereas now . . ." (59–60).

Dostoevsky sets up Raskolnikov's struggle between these polarities, his childhood trips to the village church at one extreme (the "Eden of his youth") and his first sin, the killing of his Mandarin in Petersburg's materialist atmosphere at the other. The whole novel is concerned with Raskolnikov's (saving) inability to shed remorse, a contradiction of Raphael's plaint, in which he regrets the loss of "spice and savor" remorse causes, not the loss of innocence.

Balzac would seem to set materialism in opposition to the mysticism of the magic ass's skin. But Raphael uses supernatural power for material purposes and prays to God only to keep him from dying. "Recoiling in dread from the prospect of meeting the fate of Faust, he impulsively invoked Heaven, for like all dying men he believed fervently in God and the Blessed Virgin" (207). As in *Père Goriot,* God and the devil can only be parodies of metaphysical forces in the Paris of the 1830s. Balzac packs the novel with evidence of the triumph of the material world—the realist detail of the gambling house, the horribly opulent banquet, Raphael's poor garret and Foedora's elegant house—to show a society that has lost its principles and source of meaning. Raphael's pure strivings are thwarted by material need: "I had decided to give my life to study and thought, but they have not even provided me with food"; he trades his pure life of scholarship for power and will, and his first wish upon obtaining the skin is for a Bacchanalian feast (54).

Balzac paints the lush canvas of Nebuchanezzar's feast, emphasizing his hero's initiation into the sensual venality of Parisian society. Dostoevsky replaces Balzac's social critique with, on the material side, a psychological analysis of the effects of poverty on a young man of talent, and, on the spiritual, the substitution of a moral-religious redemption for Balzac's earthly love. He rejects Balzac's implied salvation from within society for the promise of a future salvation to be found in the very process of seeking it. Raskolnikov's motive for murder is gradually revealed to be the thirst for power, not money, with selfless Christian love as the antidote to his disease. Dostoevsky replaces Balzac's love story and death by magic skin with Christian love and miraculous resurrection, and for the satire of Parisian materialism substitutes a critique of the (British) Crystal Palace and all it stands for—rationalism, scientific positivism, and utilitarianism—in the context of Russian Radical thought of the 1850s and 1860s.[62] He takes Balzac's sinner's words about the remorse that comes from youthful faith and leads Raskolnikov to a higher, eternal truth. Dostoevsky extends this aspect of his dialogue with Balzac by incorporating *Père Goriot* even more fully than *The Wild Ass's Skin* into *Crime and Punishment.*

***Père Goriot* (1834–35)** Immediately after *Père Goriot* appeared in French, first in the *Revue de Paris* from December 1834 to February 1835 and then as a separate work in two volumes in March 1835, it was published in Russian, both by the *Readers' Library* (February 1835) and the *Telescope* (1836). The translator for the former altered it significantly to conform to the journal's anti-French politics and changed the ending to have the hero set out for Victorine's house instead of Delphine's.[63] *Père Goriot* was the first book Dostoevsky recommended to his new bride, Anna Grigorievna, four months after he completed *Crime and Punishment.*

Grossman was the first to outline the relationship between the two novels. He notes the parallels between the French and Russian casts of characters: both young law students from the provinces leave beloved mothers and sisters at home; in the capital they are torn between compassion, whose objects are Goriot and Marmeladov, on the one hand, and immorality, represented by Vautrin and Svidrigailov, on the other. Grossman's discussion focuses, however, not on textual detail but on the moral question of the superman.[64]

Balzac's hero Rastignac asks his friend Bianchon: "Have you read Rousseau? . . . Do you remember the passage where he asks the reader what he would do if he could make his fortune by killing a mandarin living in China without stirring from Paris?" (Balzac is under the impression that Rousseau was the one who formulated this question. As has been shown, the idea comes from Chateaubriand, but Dostoevsky is happy to highlight the immorality of Rousseau's *Confessions* by contrast with Raskolnikov's.[65])

Dostoevsky has Raskolnikov overhear a student ask an officer if he would kill the old pawnbroker to use her wealth to aid thousands of struggling young people. Typically, Dostoevsky lowers the scene: Balzac's version of the hypothetical mandarin becomes a greasy-haired Petersburg pawnbroker with yellow varnished furniture.[66]

Grossman does not pursue the parallels and says he is "far from having exhausted all the questions" raised by the comparison.[67] Further details show how specifically Dostoevsky responds to Balzac's novel, suggesting the angle of his interpretation. Throughout, Dostoevsky again renders what is literal in Balzac metaphorical, metaphysical: Vautrin plans to go to America to become a slave owner and start a tobacco plantation, while Svidrigailov, speaking of "going to America," is contemplating suicide; Dostoevsky thus represents "two variants of false salvation," as Toporov puts it, the literal journey and the figurative one to the other world (160).[68]

This pattern governs the many correspondences between the two novels. Grossman discusses the "sister motif" as part of the heroes' motivation for their respective crimes. Both heroes in the capitals receive letters from home in the village; he points out that Rastignac calls his sisters "angels" as Raskolnikov's mother calls Dunya an angel.[69] Pursuing Grossman's parallel reveals a detailed system of correspondences: Rastignac's mother tells him, "Love your aunt; I won't tell you all she's done for you" (96). Raskolnikov's mother writes, "Love your sister Dunya, Rodya. Love her as she loves you, and know that she loves you infinitely more than she loves herself" (47). Rastignac's sisters are happy to sacrifice their savings out of their ecstatic love of their brother. Raskolnikov's mother writes that Dunya is prepared to sacrifice her entire life for Raskolnikov by marrying Luzhin, a man she cannot love. Rastignac happily takes his sisters' money to buy clothes so that he can enter high society; Raskolnikov, in despair over his mother's letter, refuses Dunya's sacrifice, one she hoped would help her brother to a career in law.[70] Rastignac eagerly turns his sisters' and mother's gifts to use in visiting Madame de Beauséant; Raskolnikov, in an act of spontaneous compassion, gives his family's money to the Marmeladov family. What is material and morally faulty in Balzac becomes redemptive in Dostoevsky.

Dostoevsky's recasting of the material aspect of human motives is particularly striking in his description of Marmeladov's death; rewriting Père Goriot's deathbed scene, he links the scenes by several details. Rastignac and Raskolnikov send for the doctors and provide for the funerals of the fathers. Both deathbed scenes are illuminated by "a single candle" (*Père Goriot,* 269; *Crime and Punishment,* 187). Rastignac supports Goriot while Bianchon changes his shirt; Raskolnikov "carefully supported Marmeladov's head" as he is carried from the street and "wipes Marmeladov's face with a moistened towel" (*Père Goriot,* 268, *Crime and Punishment,* 187). After Goriot's death, dinner at the maison Vauquer proceeds as usual: "Fifteen diners were soon chattering in their usual way. . . . But the sounds of forks and spoons, the laughter and the talk, the varied expressions on the gluttonous impassive faces of the boarders, their lack of concern, froze the young men with horror" (271). Raskolnikov is similarly appalled by the uncaring rowdy guests at Marmeladov's wake: "Amalia Ivanovna stormed around the room, shrieking, wailing, and throwing everything she could get hold of on the floor in a fuming rage. The lodgers shouted in an incoherent medley of voices—some commenting each in his own way on the events that had just taken place; others arguing and swearing; others struck up songs" (394). Madame Vauquer demands that Rastignac pay Goriot's 144-franc debt for his bed sheets; Dostoevsky's Amalia Ivanovna repeatedly threatens to throw the family out of their lodgings, so that Katerina Ivanovna runs off to her death on the street.

Most important is the inverse relationship between the fathers and the daughters. Joel Hunt has shown Goriot and Marmeladov to be similarly obsessed outcasts who are responsible for their own misery, guilt-ridden and driven to confession and self-punishment.[71] To this may be added some dramatic parallels: Goriot, dying, calls out for his daughters—"Nasie! Fifine!" (268)—but they don't come; in contrast, Marmeladov's daughter immediately runs to his bedside, where he cries out: "Sonya! My daughter! Forgive me!" (189). Goriot's daughters don't want to compromise their social positions by associating with their father. Marmeladov's daughter, who has already compromised her own position to maintain him and his second family, comes despite her shame at appearing at Amalia Fyodorovna's apartment: "Sonya . . . looked like a lost soul, not understanding, apparently, anything, forgetting her fourth-hand silk indecent bright dress with the long and absurd train and huge crinoline that filled the entire doorway, and the bright-colored shoes, and the parasol unnecessary at night . . . and the silly little round straw hat with the bright flame-colored feather" (187).

Dostoevsky's detailed description of Sonya's prostitute's finery implicitly parodies Balzac's elaborate depictions of Goriot's daughters' clothing, the expense of which contributes to their father's ruin.[72] The implication that Goriot's daughters are simply expensively kept prostitutes, conveyed by the boarders' gossip about their backstairs visits to Goriot, is inverted by Dostoevsky's rendition of Sonya. She is an honest prostitute, sacrificing herself out of love for her family, strengthened by her religious faith; her finery is so external to her spiritual nature and love for her family that she is able to forget about it entirely when she runs to her father's deathbed.

The systematic similarity between the two novels highlights the conspicuous point of departure from Dostoevsky's elaborate parallel: Sonya, the most important character for Dostoevsky's philosophy in *Crime and Punishment.* In *Père Goriot* she has her counterpart in Victorine, a devout, pale, "excessively slim" young woman who resembles a medieval statuette and whose eyes "express Christian gentleness and resignation" (17). But Dostoevsky uses the favorite device of the *école frénétique,* combining opposites: Sonya is "a very small, thin girl of about eighteen . . . blonde," "still very young, almost like a child, with a meek and modest manner," imbued with Christian faith—and is a prostitute (187, 234). Dostoevsky's contrast goes beyond the startling effect to argue with all the prostitute tales: unlike Esther Gobseck, who has faith imposed on her by the false priest Herrera, or Fleur de Marie, who learns a faith from the beneficent priest and her father that leads her to suicide, Sonya has found faith, strength, and love through suffering, loving others as herself, and reading the Bible.[73] Dostoevsky gives us two examples of vulnerable females who are not ruined by prostitution: Dunya and Sonya. Faith is Sonya's equivalent of Dunya's pride; she answers Raskolnikov's reasonable prediction: Polya will not go that way too! And her faith is rewarded through the most improbable means—Svidrigailov, the embodiment of faithlessness, cynicism, and amorality, whose view of hell is a bathhouse with spiders, provides the means for the orphaned Polya's maintenance.

The diabolic Vautrin proposes that Rastignac marry Victorine to make his fortune: Vautrin will have Victorine's brother killed so that she will inherit millions, the equivalent of killing the mandarin. In *Crime and Punishment,* Dostoevsky recasts this social and monetary "salvation" that is to be attained through murder: Raskolnikov's moral and spiritual salvation is brought about not by killing his mandarin, the pawnbroker, but through his compassion and eventual acceptance of suffering. The character of Sonya is the point at which the French genre of the prostitute with a heart of gold intersects with the detective thriller; through her Dostoevsky rewrites both genres to reject their insistently materialist interpretation. He finds more material of the detective thriller kind, "the awful drama of a criminal inquiry," in the second half of *The Splendors and Miseries of Courtesans.*

***The Splendors and Miseries of Courtesans* (1847)** The third and fourth parts of Balzac's later novel contain a prolonged cat-and-mouse game played between the Napoleonic criminal Jacques Collin and the chief prosecutor. They also describe the examining magistrate's interrogation of Lucien de Rubempré, material that contributes to the scenes of Raskolnikov's interrogation by Porfiry Petrovich.

Collin, who had been disguised as Vautrin in *Père Goriot,* reappears in *Splendors* disguised, as we have seen, as the Spanish priest, Carlos Herrera. He schemes to acquire wealth and power in Paris society using the handsome Lucien to court influential women, but by the end of part 2 both men have been arrested. Parts 3 and 4, which take place mostly in the Concièrgerie in Paris, are based in part on the life story of the astonishing criminal François-Eugène Vidocq, who was a friend of Balzac's. Vidocq repeatedly escaped from prison and became a notorious criminal but finally, tired of the criminal life while confined in the Concièrgerie, confessed his identity to the chief of police, asking to become a police spy.[74] Collin does the same. He says to the chief of police: "You see me with three ways before me: suicide, America and the rue de Jerusalem" (543). The rue de Jerusalem was the actual location of the office of the Special Investigative Division of the Paris Prefecture, for which Collin proposes to work. The street name contains the ambiguity between the practical resurrection from prosecuted criminal to police investigator and spiritual renewal by pilgrimage to the holy city. When he had become an investigator, Vidocq, after winning a case trumped up against him by jealous enemies in the Prefecture, hung a sign outside the office of his investigating agency that read "Resurrection!" Like Vidocq, by the end of *Splendors* Collin is resurrected as an honest member of society.

Collin's three choices are similar to Svidrigailov's. Incapable of choosing the spiritual pilgrimage implied by the rue de Jerusalem, Svidrigailov combines Collin's first two alternatives. Collin had earlier proposed to the chief of police: "I could, with a passport, go to America and live in solitude" (542). When Dunya definitively refuses him,

Svidrigailov redefines his journey from Collin's literal America to a figurative one and commits suicide.

The young Lucien's interrogation by Camusot, the investigator in charge of their case, is the opposite of Collin's. Collin is aware of every detail of Camusot's words and looks, while Lucien is gullible and vulnerable. Introducing the two scenes, the narrator explains,

> A small detail . . . may indicate to those who have given the matter thought how vital, interesting, curious, dramatic and terrifying a battle judicial inquiry may be, a battle waged without witnesses but recorded as it takes place. God knows what remains on paper of these scenes so glacially ardent, where the eyes, the tone of voice, a quiver of the facial muscles, the slightest change of color caused by a new feeling, are signs of no less danger than those noted by savages mutually seeking out to kill each other. . . .
>
> The reader must have already noticed how excessively out of proportion are the armaments deployed in these battles between prisoner and examining magistrate. . . . The moment denial fails to account for certain evident facts, the prisoner is entirely at the judge's mercy. Take the case of a half-criminal, like Lucien, who, preserved from the initial shipwreck of his virtue, might amend and become useful to his country; he may yet perish in the pitfalls of judicial inquiry. The magistrate draws up a bare report, a faithful verbal analysis of the questions and answers, but of his insidiously paternal speeches, of misleading admonitions . . . nothing remains. (352, 378)

Balzac gives us Camusot's clever interrogation of Lucien in uninterrupted dialogue in which the examiner's respectful politeness easily lulls Lucien into betraying Collin's identity. The narrator reports: "Lucien remained gloomy, pale, he saw himself at the bottom of the precipice, pitched there by the examining magistrate, whose friendly manner had beguiled him" (381). Realizing his error, he says to Camusot, "Between the physical torture of olden days and the present day's moral torture, . . . I'd prefer the sufferings formerly inflicted by the headsman. What do you still want of me?" (381). The latter is uttered "proudly," for in defeat the poet suddenly becomes arrogant.

Similarly, Raskolnikov undergoes the agonies of a peculiar kind of interrogation by Porfiry. On his first visit to the police station to give Porfiry his statement about the pawned objects, he is so rattled by Porfiry's erratic behavior that he tells him, "I believe there's a kind of juridical rule of thumb . . . sort of a tradition that the investigating attorneys follow—you start off obliquely, trifles, or serious matters . . . so long as they're absolutely irrelevant, just to encourage or, you might say, divert, the man you're interrogating, put him off guard—then all of a sudden you take him completely by surprise, the most crucial, dangerous question, bang on the head—isn't that right?" (327). Porfiry uses precisely the devices Balzac describes in interrogation "where the eyes, the tone of voice, a quiver of the facial muscles" carry so much weight: "'There's no hurry, no hurry at all,' muttered Porfiry Petrovich as he paced up and down beside the desk, aimlessly it would seem, darting now to the window, now to his bureau, now back to the desk, sometimes evading Raskolnikov's suspicious gaze, sometimes suddenly stopping dead still and looking at Raskolnikov point blank" (326).

The description of Porfiry's odd laughter and mannerisms pervades the scene (in contrast, all of this is absent in their final talk in Raskolnikov's room when there is no longer any question in Porfiry's mind that Raskolnikov committed the murders). During his interview with Porfiry, Raskolnikov alternates between nervous self-consciousness and rage. He tries to leave, but Porfiry lures him into staying: "Raskolnikov put down his cap and went on listening, silent, serious, and sullen, to Porfiry's vacuous, confused babble" (329).

Balzac's and Dostoevsky's ambitious young men turned criminals feel similar fear, humiliation, and proud rage at their prosecutors. Lucien, realizing he has betrayed Collin, hangs himself in his cell immediately after his interrogation. But Dostoevsky takes what Balzac calls the interrogator's "insidiously paternal speeches, [and] misleading admonitions" and makes them genuine in Porfiry's treatment of Raskolnikov. At their first meeting at Porfiry's apartment, Porfiry asks Raskolnikov, "So you still believe in the New Jerusalem?" (258). At their final meeting at Raskolnikov's, he urges him to find faith in God as he offers Raskolnikov a reduced sentence if he gives himself up, asking for a "brief but circumstantial note" in case he decides to commit suicide (443, 445). Lucien's crimes have been passive, inadvertent—two prostitutes die for him—while Raskolnikov kills two women in cold blood, yet Lucien commits suicide, while Raskolnikov takes up the cross of suffering for his crimes and may yet see the New Jerusalem he has faith in, a spiritual redemption that replaces Collin's worldly one on the rue de Jerusalem.[75] Dostoevsky aligns Svidrigailov with Lucien as a character whose lack of a moral position leads to suicide, while the criminals Raskolnikov and Collin will change, redeeming their actions, Collin within the legal system and Raskolnikov on the spiritual plane.

The analysis of Dostoevsky's dialogue with Balzac's three novels shows that he recasts the French versions in every tiny detail to reject the material focus of the novels' characters as well as the author's focus and approach: Balzac is no less disgusted with Parisian decadence than Dostoevsky is, but he can only satirize it: he considers that God and the devil can no longer be potent enough forces in the Paris he depicts to provide an alternative moral universe. Dostoevsky writes *Crime and Punishment* precisely to reveal that alternative. He makes this central motive clear by his use of a little-known novella by Jules Janin, who addresses the heart of the matter in *The Confession,* a book analyzed here for the first time in Dostoevsky scholarship.

Jules Janin

***La Confession* (1830)** Jules Janin's second book, *The Confession,* appeared a year after *The Dead Donkey. The Confession* is as important to *Crime and Punishment*'s moral and psychological universe as *Père Goriot* was to Dostoevsky's structuring of the cast of characters. *Crime and Punishment* is the story of the realization and acknowledgment of guilt; from the moment he commits murder, Raskolnikov struggles between proud isolation and a desire to confess his crime.[76] Confession is his first step toward salvation, and *The Confession* addresses that moral psychology.

In a letter to his brother written in 1859, Dostoevsky excitedly reported his intention to write a confessional novel, "*ispoved'-roman,*" which he had thought up in prison, "lying on his bunk [*lezha na narakh*]," to be called *The Confession* (*Ispoved'*).[77] The commentators to the *Collected Works* consider that the title refers to what became *Notes from Underground,* an opinion shared by Joseph Frank. But their argument is inconsistent: the editors say that the image of Raskolnikov arose only in 1865, yet they cite as evidence for their position Dostoevsky's 1859 statement that he is abandoning the novel about "a young man . . . who goes to Siberia." They point out that *Notes from Underground* is a first-person narrative in two parts (though Dostoevsky had spoken of three for his *Confession*) but don't mention in this context that *Crime and Punishment* began as a first-person narrative. The editors further assume that the "sensual [*strastnyi*] element" in the projected *Confession* must confirm that the title refers to *Notes from Underground,* but it has other interpretations, as we will see. There is insufficient evidence to controvert Grossman's earlier conclusion: "Hints sprinkled throughout Dostoevsky's letters and notebooks show that by 'Confession' he meant the story of Raskolnikov."[78] An examination of Janin's *Confession* provides support for Grossman's claim.

Grossman suggests four other confessions as well, but their content bears only generic, not thematic, relationship to *Crime and Punishment.*[79] The editors of the *Complete Collected Works* consider that Dostoevsky's projected title for *Crime and Punishment* alludes to Jean-Jacques Rousseau's *Confessions.*[80] Here we will see that it refers at least equally to Jules Janin's *Confession.*

As we saw, Pushkin too had been impressed by Janin's *Confession,* which was published in Russian the year after its publication in France. He even translated chapter 4 of it into verse in a variant of "*Tebia poiu na tomnoi lire*" (1830).[81] Despite Janin's importance to Russian writers, this remarkable work has received little attention, but then even the French had paid it little attention until Janin's centenary in 1974.[82]

Early in *The Confession* Janin throws out a challenge to writers of his generation, who find themselves caught between past faith and present spiritual vacuum: "The history of this painful hesitation is a lacuna in the psychological novel; others than I, philosophers much better at expressing themselves, will doubtless try to render intelligible . . . this deplorable position between being and non-being, incredulity and doubt, in which we find ourselves."[83] Dostoevsky took up that challenge.

The hero of *The Confession* is an educated young murderer, Anatole, who is torn between remorse and the desire to conceal his crime as he searches for a way to appease his conscience, a theme shared with *Crime and Punishment.* The plot is simple: Anatole comes from a rich family that counts on him to reestablish its prerevolutionary station. He is "simple and good, thoughtful and ambitious when there was nothing better to do," and has a "superior intelligence" (*une intelligence avancée* [28]). He marries at the wish of his parents, but on his wedding night in a moment of (ambiguous) passion strangles the wife his mother had chosen for him. The motive for the crime is unclear and never examined. The murder is merely the pretext for the rest of the book, which chronicles the excruciating remorse Anatole experiences and his attempts to find a priest whom he considers sufficiently spiritual to confess to.[84] Faulting the priest is Anatole's way of disguising his own ambivalence about confessing guilt and accepting punishment for his act. Each time Anatole seems about to achieve relief from his agony, he finds the priest deficient and at the last minute decides not to confess to him. In the short final chapter, his parents put him in a madhouse. He eventually recovers and himself becomes a priest: "He prays, he sings, he sleeps; he gives himself over to a well-being that is not of this earth, and when he gets out of his carriage he abandons himself to his lackeys with the soft languor of a woman who has just gotten up from childbed" (260–61). He has become as self-indulgent and dead to the world of the spirit as the priests he had spurned.

The points of contact with *Crime and Punishment* are clear: a heretofore decent young man, intelligent and proud, commits a murder, goes unsuspected, and is plunged into despair by pangs of conscience; he oscillates between his pride and his desire to free himself from guilt, ultimately to pass from painful incarceration to an ambiguous spiritual peace. Janin and Dostoevsky are concerned with the spiritual condition of their generations in a society that has abandoned its former religious and moral ideals in favor of "calculation" and intellectualization.

The one critic to pay attention to *The Confession* is V. V. Vinogradov, who discusses a passage in it that describes a five-story house whose tenants' social class corresponds to the floors they inhabit. He probably selected that description for analysis because Janin himself excerpted it in the *Revue de Paris* in 1830 to illustrate the new naturalist poetics. Vinogradov accordingly cites it as evidence of the influence of the French school on Russian physiological descriptions, an observation Donald Fanger repeats without elaboration in *Dostoevsky and Romantic Realism* some forty years later.[85]

The house description was indeed used by various Russian writers, and here again Janin's ideas pass through Balzac to Dostoevsky.[86] V. G. Reizov considers that while Janin's house plays no active role in *The Confession,* Balzac is inspired by it to make the Maison Vauquer an active "hero" of *Père Goriot,* a terrifying symbol of the hypocrisy and mercantilism of daily Parisian life.[87] Dostoevsky takes up both Janin's critique of the godlessness of French society and Balzac's social critique in designing his stage set for an analysis of the pressures on the hero's psyche.

In *The Confession,* Janin's hero goes into the five-story house seeking spiritual solace. Dostoevsky is indeed interested in the scene that takes place on the fourth-floor landing of that house at the end of the book. Janin's description of the mocking tenants in the midst of squalor provides Dostoevsky inspiration for the scandal scenes at the Marmeladovs'. Anatole has gone in quest of a Spanish priest who lives in the building.

> Anatole arrived at the fourth floor out of breath; he found himself facing a labyrinth of doors, large and small; some noise, some silence: which to knock on?

He knocked on a door that seemed more decent than the others; it had been varnished not long ago, a faded colored ribbon was attached to the bell; there was a rug at the door, which was a bit of elegance for that place.

He knocked, the door didn't open; and by I don't know what echo effect the neighboring door suddenly opened. . . . Anatole was almost afraid.

The woman who stood at that open door was apparently a fat and jovial busybody, a kind of improvised police headquarters in this little world, which had its flatterers, administrators, opposition, friends, council, its parties and balls . . . she was the one who had the surveillance in this department, the care of directing the great and small highroads. . . .

The old woman let out a great cry, a cry of distress; all the neighboring doors opened at this cry. . . .

It was a spectacle to behold: these men and women on the thresholds of their doors; these interiors which offered up at first glance all the carelessness of the morning state; these half-naked women, dirty and wrapped in old shawls, these children interrupted at their breakfast, all these curious looks, all these stupefied faces. "Who of you knows a Spanish abbé here?" the old woman asked.

The whole assembly answered with a burst of laughter.

The assembly didn't understand what use one could have for an abbé.

The men frowned, the children took bites of their bread, the girls shrugged their shoulders.

There was a joker among them: . . ."Monsieur," he said gravely to Anatole, "your Spanish abbé lives here." And he pointed with his finger at the door that had remained closed.

"Here!" said the whole crowd, extending their hands in a solemn manner.

The joker started knocking on the door:

"Hey! Monsieur priest, open up; there's a young man here who . . . has come to confess a great sin you'll be glad to hear; open up!" . . .

And the crowd kept bursting with laughter, and would have stood there all day, if they hadn't heard someone coming up the stairs. (292–93)

The decorated door presumably belongs to the apartment of a prostitute, and the crowd's laughter comes from the joker's juxtaposition of the harlot to the priest. Dostoevsky writes a Russian version of this scene when describing how Raskolnikov first brings Marmeladov home:

They came in through the courtyard and went up to the fourth floor. The higher up the stairs they went the darker it got. . . .

A little sooty door was open at the end of the stairway at the very end. A candle end illuminated the poorest room about ten paces long; all of it was visible from the entryway. Everything was thrown around in disorder, especially various children's clothes. A sheet with holes in it was strung across the rear corner. The bed was probably behind it. . . . It turned out that

> Marmeladov lived in his own room, not in the corner, but the room was a passageway. The door to further rooms or cages, into which Amalia Lippewechsel's apartment was broken up, was open. It was noisy there and full of shrieking. They were laughing. They were playing cards and drinking tea. The most unceremonious words would sometimes fly out of there. (34)

After a description of the Marmeladov family and of Katerina Ivanovna's anger, the lodgers appear:

> The young man hurried to leave, not saying a word. Besides, the inner door opened wide and out of it glanced several curious neighbors. Brazen laughing heads, with pipes and cigarettes, in skullcaps peered out. You could see figures in bathrobes completely open, in summer costume to the point of indecency, some with cards in their hands. They laughed especially loudly when Marmeladov, pulled by the hair, yelled that he enjoyed it. They even began to come into the room; finally there was heard an ominous scream: it was Amalia Lippewechsel herself pushing forward in order to bring order in her own way and for the hundredth time to frighten the poor woman with the order to leave the apartment tomorrow. (36)

The landlady who runs the fourth-floor establishment, the scene of indecent poverty in which skimpily clad, raucously mocking adults mix with children, and Raskolnikov's thoughts about prostitution as he leaves ("They have their Sonya") echo Janin's description written thirty years earlier.

But the realistic sociological description is neither typical of Janin's narrative nor essential to it. *The Confession* is not a naturalistic physiological work but a despairing deliberation on the loss of religion in post-revolutionary France. There are many deeper correspondences between the two works in which an idea of Janin's can be seen to give rise to Dostoevsky's fuller exploration of it. First let us look at the points of similarity.

By chapter 15, Anatole is considering having himself executed on the scaffold. "This was at first a vague and confused religious idea, a vain caprice; then it soon became a need" (87). He recalls his childhood faith: "First he remembered the beliefs of his early years, his lively, pure faith, and his childlike joy when at the first silvery sounds of the bell he would set out on Sunday towards the church of his village, all proud of giving his arm to his grandmother" (88). There follows a happy description of praying, singing with the women, leaving the church through the crowd, village dances in the evening; he remembers being his sister's godfather at age eight, when the priest asks him to renounce the Devil and his works (90). This closely resembles the scene of Raskolnikov at age seven in his village that provides the setting for the mare-beating in his dream; Raskolnikov recalls his childhood pleasure at the family's twice-yearly visits to attend mass for his grandmother and his love of the village church, whose bells become part of an important motif in the novel, and its icons.

Robert Belknap writes of the role of memory in *The Brothers Karamazov* as "an actual moral force, latent for years . . . but offering the immortality on earth" and "a rationally acceptable repository for the good whose preservation was indispensable to his theodicy."[88] He shows the theme of childhood memory in that novel to be accompanied by motifs of family and blessings (a mother and child, sacred stories, icons, slanting rays of sunlight, holy scriptures), connecting memory to "immortality on earth." Similarly, in the earlier *Crime and Punishment,* the material of Raskolnkov's dream, like that of Anatole's, has the capacity to redeem him through memory of compassion, associated with the church and its bell ringing.

The seeds of faith present in both heroes from childhood allow them to turn to faith as a remedy for their agonies; Janin embodies the idea in a realistic village scene as an idyll of purity and community, but after Anatole commits the murder, these are "bitter memories" (90). Dostoevsky makes that bitterness part of the village scene in Raskolnikov's dream of the mare beating. He shows Raskolnikov's village childhood to be the source of his religious faith and love of family but equally the source of murderous violence.

Anatole is conscious that his crime has isolated him totally: "The criminal has friends no more; the presence of a man is killing to me" (108). But his desire to confess is countered by his former pride: "Yes, it's me . . . this pale, thin face, it's me; this lost reason, it's me, this boundless despair, it's me. . . . This man who wants to confess to you . . . is me, the same Anatole that you have seen so proud of his knowledge [*sa science*], so proud of his wit [*ésprit*]. This man who made a religion of his own all alone, here he shares the religion of the lowest beggar [*dernier lazzarone*] who repents having missed mass" (103).

Anatole encounters an array of characters on his quest. One of them, characterized only as a "young skeptic," addresses the idea of the man-God explicitly: "It was perhaps not too much for the ambitious of our times to want to make themselves gods when there was no one who hadn't been king once in his life; hence the sects, heresies, new theogonies, a bourgeois Olympus. . . . Who of us has not been Mahomet? . . . One is a prophet even in his own country now" (176–77).

One of the possible new religions is socialism. The "young skeptic" continues: "You want to believe? Do you want a brand new religion, my son? Saint-Simon extends the hand to you, Saint-Simon whose ardent disciples began with industrialism and ended up with mysticism" (178). Another continues, "everything is connected: Mahomet and Bonaparte, St. Augustine and J.-J. Rousseau, Aristophanes and Judas, Anitus and Luther" (179). The world will end "when all intelligences will be equal in the moral world"—the idea of Dostoevsky's ant heap, also identified with Mahomet, Napoleon, and, less directly, Rousseau (180).

Not only the social analysis but also the psychological portrait of the hero can be seen to be a progenitor of Raskolnikov. Anatole, finding himself isolated, despairing, "thinks first of turning himself over to human justice to satisfy the law he has violated, to have his fellow man [*semblables*] say 'You are a murderer'" (85); Dostoevsky incorporates the idea and has an actual fellow man, the artisan, call Raskolnikov "murderer" on the street. The thought of the shame he would cause his family, especially his sister, prevents Anatole from confessing. He discovers when he sees a chained group of prisoners pass by that he regards them as more honest than he (86); Dostoevsky enlarges upon the theme of Raskolnikov's isolation from the human community through both the artisan's accusation and Raskolnikov's rejection by his fellow prisoners in Siberia.

Janin reports Anatole's dreams:

> Whoever could describe Antole's sleep and give a history of his dreams would arrive at a horrible story: a hidden nervous pain, a pain without tears, and worst of all, an inexorable obstinacy at remembering that wedding night, so vivid that he felt again between his two hands the warm young imprint of a woman's neck; he would hear the death rattle; he would see again the funeral cortège followed by so many tears.
>
> It was always the same scene, always the same horror, always, always the same ghost in the same dim, sad light, a light that is not from heaven, that comes from the earth, that has neither movement, nor life, nor heat. . . .
>
> Always before his eyes, immobile and pale. Poor child whom he had seen so joyous and alive, and who reached out her hand to him with the affection of a sister! (91–92)

Dostoevsky deploys this material in two separate dreams: The horror of repeating the crime endlessly is taken up in Raskolnikov's dream of smashing Alyona with the ax over and over again "while the old hag laughed, spluttering like a blown flame"; Dostoevsky distills Anatole's recurrent dream into one dream and has his hero relive his crime with intensified violence (274). The "sensual element" implied by the murder of a wife in bed on the wedding night is addressed in a separate dream. In Svidrigailov's dream Anatole's "poor child" of a wife, "immobile and pale," becomes the five-year-old whose pallor becomes a flush as she turns into a "venal French whore" (490).

As one of Raskolnikov's amoral doubles, Svidrigailov represents the venal aspect of the "sensual element" Dostoevsky mentions in his letter to Mikhail. In Janin's work, the murder clearly relates sexuality to violence. Anatole's horror at murdering his wife is intensified by the victim's innocence, childlikeness, and purity. In Svidrigailov's dream Dostoevsky combines the innocence with the sensuality—the five-year-old child turns into a mocking prostitute. Raskolnikov's dream of smashing the laughing hag with the ax is doubled by Svidrigailov's dream of the girl, suggesting the psychological link among innocence, sensuality, and violence in Raskolnikov's emotions. His murder victims reveal this same ambivalence: Alyona is an old crone, but Lizaveta is always pregnant. She is a holy fool (pure, innocent), but she is also a sensual being; as with Sonya, the characterization emphasizes the disparity between body and spirit. But Dostoevsky suggests a psychological relationship between childlike helplessness and murderous impulses: Sonya's naive faith infuriates Raskolnikov, leading him to reduce her to tears with his verbal brutality. Sonya is Lizaveta's closest friend, doubled with her by the contradiction of their faith and innocence on the one hand, and their sensual aspect (Sonya's prostitution, Lizaveta's pregnancies) on the other.

Like Anatole, who suddenly finds himself murdering his blameless wife on their wedding night, Raskolnikov is unexpectedly precipitated into murdering the pawnbroker's sister. He murders Lizaveta, but Sonya gives him a second life. In Dostoevsky's geometric logic, the aspect of Anatole's wife that "reached out her hand to him with the affection of a sister" is given to Sonya, while the imponderable impulse that drove him to violence is allotted to Lizaveta. Dostoevsky suggests this complex of emotions through the exchange of crosses. Sonya gives Raskolnikov her cross and keeps Lizaveta's.

Anatole is comforted by his mother's crucifix: "He could get comfort only by gazing at an ivory Christ that his mother had given him. It was a rather large image of the Passion from the chisel of an Italian artist; the face of Christ was beautiful, crowned with thorns and bent like the head of a God, but of a God who is about to die" (95). The crucifix represents a mortal Christ, and the description emphasizes its aesthetic aspect. It is a comfort, but not a means of salvation, because Anatole has yet to confess his sin. Raskolnikov receives Sonya's cross only when he decides to go to the police. Unlike Janin, Dostoevsky shows that the sinner can find no comfort unless he takes up the cross. Furthermore, Sonya's exchange of crosses with Lizaveta permanently associates the cross Raskolnikov receives with his crime.

Like Raskolnikov, Anatole considers suicide, but decides it would be too much of a cliché at a time when it was "everyone's monomania," an excuse similar to the one Balzac gives Raphael in its comic triviality (210). Raskolnikov's rejection of suicide because he is repelled by the foul water of the Neva is also trivial, but of course there is a deeper dimension of Raskolnikov's character. Unlike Anatole (or Raphael), Raskolnikov is worthy of Sonya's sisterhood and capable of regeneration because of his innate capacity for compassion and the seeds of faith planted in his childhood. The counterexample is his double Svidrigailov, who lacks a moral basis, making him unworthy of Dunya. Dostoevsky thus differentiates Raskolnikov from Svidrigailov, the meaninglessness of whose existence drives him to suicide despite his wealth and freedom. This is where Dostoevsky rejects Janin's sardonic resolution of his hero's dilemma and takes up its implications.

Just as Raskolnikov has not repented when he goes to the police, Anatole "felt rather unhappy that he wasn't more ashamed. For a long time he had wanted to finish with doubts . . . to repent the way a Christian repents" (96). He thinks that "formerly one would go to the Holy Land, build a monastery, and peace would return on the banks of the Jordan or on the last steps of a chapel" (212). Dostoevsky realizes this thought at the climax of the novel when Raskolnikov begins to accept Sonya's faith and achieves peace on the bank of the biblically peaceful Irtysh, where "time seemed to have stood still, as though the age of Abraham and his flocks had not yet passed" (526). The steps of the chapel are echoed by the stairs Raskolnikov mounts to the police station—only a way station to repentance.

Anatole's scene of confession is the climax of his tale. Its method resembles Dostoevsky's psychological realism: it is initially unclear that the dialogue with his confessor is a dream, that the severe Spanish priest who appears to Anatole in his bedroom is the product of Anatole's inflamed imagination and agonized conscience. Anatole is slowly awakening from his first peaceful sleep since the crime, when suddenly someone pulls open his bed curtains:

> When he could distinguish objects, he perceived two paces from his bed a pale and austere face, a lively firm gaze. The man was tall, dry, dressed in black and patient enough to discourage a corpse.
>
> He had closed the door to the room, and he stood immobile near the trembling young man.
>
> . . . [Anatole] felt dominated by this iron gaze that didn't leave him for an instant. (251, 252)

Instead of rejoicing at the arrival of this priest whom he had failed to find in the five-story house described above, Anatole suggests they talk so he can judge if the priest is worthy. But the priest is stern: "Confess yourself, sinner!" he insists. "As certain as that there is a God, before I leave here you will confess!" (254). Anatole resists: "Impossible today, father! Today I feel too happy." This is his final oscillation between avoiding confession and confessing. But the priest says he reads "ineffable traces" on Anatole's forehead.[89]

> "What do you read on my forehead, Monsieur?"
>
> " . . . I read on your forehead very little, almost nothing: a moment of error, an innocent sally, a casual epigram, a murder; what could be more innocent?"
>
> Anatole trembled. A secret that had been his alone—discovered!
>
> "What is that to you, young man? One woman less. . . . After all, why do you need to confess? You need joy, lively pleasures, girls to seduce, the transports of ambition. . . . Come, free man, what's become of your will? Order your servants to throw me out. I am an impostor." (255–56)

The scene resembles the end of part 3 and beginning of part 4 of *Crime and Punishment* when Raskolnikov first encounters Svidrigailov. He awakens terrified from the dream of killing the pawnbroker:

> He was breathing heavily. Strange though. The dream seemed still to be going on. His door was wide open, and a man he didn't know at all stood on the threshold and was examining him intensely.
>
> . . . The stranger stood in the same place and continued to gaze at him. All of a sudden he stepped cautiously over the threshold, closed the door carefully behind him, went up to the table, and waited a moment. All this time he did not take his eyes off Raskolnikov. . . . [I]t was apparent that he was prepared to wait a long time. (275)

In the conversation that follows, Svidrigailov justifies his crimes in the same ironic tone that the priest uses to mock Anatole for his. Dostoevsky embodies Raskolnikov's bad conscience in Svidrigailov, who is introduced as his dream-hallucination ("'Is the dream still going on or isn't it?' he thought"), just as Anatole dreams his confessor, and for the same motive of their internal struggle with excruciating feelings of guilt (275). Anatole at first resists admitting his guilt; Raskolnikov can see Svidrigailov's guilt clearly despite the latter's sophistry but cannot see through his own rationalization or recognize his murder as a sin.

But Anatole ends by confessing to the unrelenting priest, who asks: "When you refuse God as judge, when you deny that supreme justice which comes to you, do you think that human justice is satisfied? . . . Divine law or human law claim you; one or the other must be satisfied" (257–58). The priest's knowledge of Anatole's crime and his contrasting two kinds of law is allotted to Porfiry, during their final interview in Raskolnikov's room, as eerie a scene in its way as the one with Svidrigailov, which it echoes. "You committed the murders, yes," Porfiry tells Raskolnikov (440). Raskolnikov keeps running his fingers through his hair as he sits silently resisting Porfiry's request that he confess.

Anatole makes the same gesture while he continues to resist the priest's demand that he confess: "He kept passing his hand through his hair which was still beautiful and which he found obedient as before" (254). The priest takes up the gesture in mocking his unwillingness to confess: "You kill, and when a priest comes to you, you run your hand through your hair, you uncover your murderer's forehead, and you say to him insolently: What do you read on my forehead?" (257). In Janin's context, the gesture more clearly refers to the mark of Cain, which is at once the token of his sin and the sign of divine mercy accorded the murderer; in Dostoevsky's version, the gesture could seem to be merely a realistic sign of Raskolnikov's tension under a detective's gaze.[90] But with the insight afforded by Janin's tale, the gesture can be taken to refer not only to the mark of Cain but equally to the mark of the Beast from the Book of Revelation 13:17–18, which signifies acceptance of the false prophet.

When Porfiry says, "Give yourself up and confess" (441), he is advising Raskolnikov both to give himself up to human law and to find faith in God (443). Dostoevsky examines the hero's movement toward confession by embodying his motives in distinct characters: the despised aspect of self, which Janin merely summarizes in a final paragraph (259–60), becomes Svidrigailov, who confesses readily to his heinous acts but can neither see his guilt nor repent.[91] Dostoevsky renders the stern Spanish confessor, a man who has left human society and acts only as God's intermediary, as the "used up" Porfiry, the bachelor intermediary of human justice. Like Dostoevsky's peasant Marey, Porfiry has an "almost maternal" (248) compassion for Raskolnikov; a New Testament mercy replaces the severity of Janin's Spanish priest.

For Janin, the only place left to look for genuine Catholic faith was Spain. Spanish faith had not been shaken as the French had been by the Enlightenment, so Janin could view it as a source of religious purity, the highest possible spiritual authority remaining for a Frenchman by 1830. The Spanish priest represents an unrealized ideal in the book—Anatole never actually meets him; he can only imagine him, and he conceives him as the strictest judge, an absolute representation of conscience. In *Notes from the House of the Dead,* written three decades after *The Confession,* combining his reading with his own experience in prison camp, Dostoevsky wrote about "an educated young man with a sensitive conscience, with awareness, heart. The pain in his heart will be enough to do away with him, long before any punishment is inflicted upon him. Far more mercilessly than the sternest law, he condemns himself for his crime."[92] Dostoevsky presumably valued *The Confession* for Janin's view of human conscience as an inner force that these words describe. But he had no sympathy with Roman Catholicism. He viewed it as antithetical to the true Christian meaning of the Holy Writ, in part because of the doctrine of papal supremacy. "The papacy much more deeply and fully entered into *the entire West* than is thought . . . Even the earlier reformations are the product of the papacy, and Rousseau, and the French revolution are products of Western Christianity and, finally, socialism with all its formalism . . . is a product of Catholic Christianity."[93] If the spiritual leader is infallible, and the church holds the answers to everything, then it is clear that all are subject to the pope. Dostoevsky parodies these ideas in Ivan's depiction of another Spanish priest in "The Legend of the Grand Inquisitor," as Nina Perlina has shown.[94] So Dostoevsky must replace the absolute pope-based authority of Janin's (and Anatole's) Spanish priest with another form of spiritual authority. He makes Porfiry into an urban variant of the peasant Marey, an embodiment of the essential Russian Orthodox Christian spirit. Porfiry's "almost maternal" compassion carries the selfless, pure love, mercy, and faith in redemption that Dostoevsky (and others) saw as the essence of Orthodoxy. This intuitive understanding of Christ's words is to be found among the Russian peasants, the criminals Dostoevsky met in prison, and even the Petersburg official, the representative of secular authority who uses psychological understanding as a means not only to detection but also to redemption. Janin's Spanish priest is for Dostoevsky a misguided French version of an ideal of conscience because the Roman Catholic figure is authoritarian, an external force commanding confession. In his place he puts Porfiry. The bachelor official, first with his clowning interrogation and later with his simple direct appeal to a fellow human being, is a kind of Russian Holy Fool, who knows the truth intuitively, through "psychology." Redemption must come from the freedom to choose Christ; Porfiry Petrovich allows this as the Spanish priest does not. The royal purple (porphyry) and the Russian tsar Peter implied by his patronymic implies imperial, secular power, which he indeed possesses, but it is the alternate meanings, the rock of the church (porphyry and Peter both mean "rock"), that allow Raskolnikov to render unto Caesar that which is Caesar's (arrest, imprisonment), while rendering unto God that which is God's (repentance).

In *Crime and Punishment* Dostoevsky elaborates Janin's premise: even a misguided young man, if he has a moral basis in religion, will suffer such pangs of conscience for a crime that he will be driven to confess. He answers Janin's challenge to examine the psychology of a man born at the border between a religious generation and a new, faithless one, by showing both sides of that border at once. Dostoevsky makes explicit Anatole's implicit ambivalence by showing clearly both impulses; the will to confess is taken up in Raskolnikov's intense battle with Porfiry as well as in his relationship to Sonya. The resistance to confession, which Anatole rationalizes as the fault of corrupt priests, is represented by Svidrigailov, whose absence of remorse is a result of his lack of belief in any form of meaning. As Dostoevsky says in *A Writer's Diary,* "Without faith in one's soul and its immortality, human existence is unnatural, unthinkable, and unbearable."[95]

Dostoevsky accordingly changes Janin's cynical ending. In *The Confession* Anatole becomes one of the priests whose lack of religiosity had appalled him; rather than be elevated by his ordeal, Anatole capitulates to the spiritual vacuum, becoming a fat, languid priest. The "well-being not of this earth" he achieves is at best ambiguous but more likely a bitter irony. In *Crime and Punishment,* Svidrigailov cannot tolerate meaninglessness and has to make "not of this earth" literal by leaving it; Raskolnikov, however, at the novel's close, is on the brink of "gradual renewal and rebirth, of . . . gradual transition from one world to another, of . . . acquaintance with a new reality of which he had previously been completely ignorant" (528), an "immortality on earth" in Belknap's phrasing. Like *The Brothers Karamazov, Crime and Punishment* ends with faith in the resurrection of the spirit. Thus Dostoevsky turns Janin's flippant picaresque tale (and Balzac's parody of it in *Père Goriot,* whose hero has no pangs of conscience) into both a psychological novel and a kind of modern gospel, genres that before *Crime and Punishment* would have appeared antithetical.[96]

The close relationship between Janin's and Dostoevsky's novels suggests that the strong impression that *The Confession* made on Dostoevsky remained with him in Siberia, where it found confirmation in his own experience. Dostoevsky wrestled with Janin's cynical formulation of the question of the psychology of conscience, repentance and redemption until he distilled it into the projected novel of "a young man who goes to Siberia." *The Confession* became one of the most important of the French realist works whose detail Dostoevsky used to translate the French postrevolutionary spiritual crisis into Russia of the 1860s.

French prose furnished *Crime and Punishment* with a literary rendition of the background of urban social reality, the thematics of prostitution, of the young man from the provinces, and most importantly, in Janin's novel, the narrative of an explicitly spiritual quest in a secular context. Dostoevsky systematically rebuts the French novels by resolving the characters' conflict beyond the social plane of his novel. To convey a positive, not ironic, spiritual universe, Dostoevsky had to turn to an altogether different source, the Gospels.

A Modern Gospel

Those who have renounced Christianity and rebelled against it are of the same image of Christ . . . such they have remained.

Brothers Karamazov

In *A Writer's Diary* of 1876 Dostoevsky made explicit the religious ideas that underlie his polemic with French literature. He writes of "the true exaltation of Christ . . . and the ultimate word of Orthodoxy, at whose head Russia has long been standing. . . . One can seriously believe in human brotherhood, in the universal reconciliation of nations, in a union founded on principles of universal service to humanity and regeneration of people through the true principles of Christ." Dostoevsky calls this the "'new word' that Russia at the head of a united Orthodoxy can utter to the world."[97]

Dostoevsky had already uttered that word in *Crime and Punishment*: the novel may be read as a modern gospel, in particular, the gospel according to John, from which Sonya reads at such surprising length to Raskolnikov.[98] In *Crime and Punishment,* Dostoevsky translates John into modern dress in order to have the Word made, if not flesh, then at least newly vital; by "lowering" the Good News into the world of the Petersburg poor, he shows Raskolnikov's miraculous transformation to be possible for any contemporary reader. Even the sudden change of tone and focus from that teeming world in the much-criticized epilogue has its origin in the conclusion of the Gospel of John.[99]

Christ is the Word made flesh who brings the "new word" of the New Testament, the idea of Christian love and forgiveness. Raskolnikov represents a parody of this ideal: he wants to utter a new word by means of murder, by assuming the power of life and death that properly belongs to God, as Sonya tells him.[100] Dostoevsky leads Raskolnikov through a series of events that parody moments in the life of Jesus as recounted by John in his Gospel. Michael Holquist has argued that Raskolnikov's tale is made up of two distinct kinds of narrative, the detective story in historical time and the "wisdom tale" in eternal time, which must be made to merge in order to complete Raskolnikov's story.[101] These levels may also be seen in terms of Tynyanov's original text and its parody, in which John is the original wisdom tale and Raskolnikov's odyssey a grotesque distortion of the ideal path revealed to us by the "genuine image of Christ."[102] Only when the two tales merge in the epilogue and "the second level becomes visible through the surface of the work" can the reader finally see past the parody to its high purpose.[103]

John had particular significance for Dostoevsky. In mid-January 1850, on his march to Siberia, a wife of one of the Decembrists gave Dostoevsky a copy of the New Testament. He kept it under his pillow during the four years he spent in prison. In it, John has the largest number of marginal markings of any of the gospels, fifty-eight as opposed to Matthew (twelve), Luke (seven), and Mark (two).[104] He takes the epigraph to the *Brothers Karamazov* from John 12:24 and bases *The Idiot* on John. As he wrote in a letter, "In the world there is but one absolutely beautiful individual: Christ, and consequently the very existence of this infinitely good individual is in itself an incomprehensible miracle. The whole of the Gospel according to St. John is in this thought: It finds the whole miracle solely in the incarnation of the good, in its perfect incarnation in blood and flesh."[105]

Analyzing Dostoevsky's markings in his New Testament, Geir Kjetsaa and Irina Kirillova consider that Dostoevsky values John for its "affirmation of Christ's sonship made manifest in the 'theology of love'" central to it, its valuing of compassion.[106] In keeping with Russian

Orthodoxy, Dostoevsky emphasizes John over the first three gospels.[107] His Gospel demonstrates the connection between God and human life and maps the stages of believing into life's stages. God's word works in the inner heart and is then manifested in actions that ultimately lead to community. In the second part of the gospel, despite the treachery and violence surrounding Jesus's passion, love and the power of life gain ascendancy.[108]

It is understandable, then, why Dostoevsky chooses John as text for *Crime and Punishment.* He reveals but conceals its importance in part 4, chapter 4, when he has Raskolnikov ask Sonya, "where's the passage about Lazarus?" and she answers, "It's in the fourth Gospel" (318). The raising of Lazarus is clearly meant to parallel the redemption of Raskolnikov: Jesus raises Lazarus four days after he has been in the tomb; Sonya reads to Raskolnikov four days after he has committed murder (the parallel is clearer when Raskolnikov's later understanding—"I killed myself"—is taken into account).[109] Here Sonya plays the role of Jesus to Raskolnikov's Lazarus; through her Raskolnikov begins his day-to-day journey toward faith and community.

Dostoevsky integrates John's gospel into *Crime and Punishment* by recasting the passion story in novelistic terms of character and plot. Luzhin plays the role of Judas, Porfiry is Pilate, although both are also briefly identified with Peter. Sonya and Raskolnikov play dual parts, one secular and the other sacred. In the first of these, they follow the prototypes of French novels, and in the second, of the Gospels: Sonya is a prostitute and hence associated with Mary Magdalene, while Raskolnikov, as an ambitious young man from the provinces (compare this with Renan's interpretation in *La vie de Jésus*), is a mock Jesus who tries to play the role of God and fails. Balzac portrays diabolic temptation in the character of the criminal who has the trappings of a mock devil out of a melodrama (Jacques Collin's red hair), while Dostoevsky's represents diabolic traits in an utterly mundane character (Svidrigailov's bathhouse with spiders). Dostoevsky's novel adds a genuinely sacred plane to Balzac's, in which Svidrigailov represents the lack of any faith and Sonya the ideal of Christ toward which Raskolnikov moves from the opposite pole of false Christ.

CHARACTERS

Crime and Punishment is designed in the spirit rather than the letter of John. The parallels are fluid, overlapping, and not always clearly marked. John is integrated into the novelistic plane by subliminal evocations, for example by giving the patronymic of John (Ivanovna/ Ivanovich) to six characters apparently indiscriminately: Alyona and Lizaveta; Katerina; Svidrigailov; and the two German ladies, Louisa at the police station and the Marmeladovs' landlady, Amalia. Dostoevsky calls our attention to the patronymic twice at Marmeladov's wake, first when Katerina Ivanovna disputes Amalia's right to call herself "Ivanovna" (possibly because she is a German and would not be Russian Orthodox) and later when Luzhin thinks Sonya's patronymic is Ivanovna instead of Semyonovna. In the same way, attributes of biblical personages and markers of scenes from the life of Jesus are not always intended as precise identifications but as barely perceptible evocations and therefore may be distributed freely.

In John, Judas has a kind of double in Simon-Peter, who denies Jesus three times before the cock crows.[110] The role of Peter as betrayer is played by Peter Petrovich Luzhin when he frames Sonya at her father's wake.[111] His impending betrayal is heralded by one of Katerina Ivanovna's irrelevant guests: when she says that the dying Marmeladov had a cookie in the shape of a rooster in his pocket for the children, the guest screams, "A rooster? You were pleased to say a rooster?" (*Petushka? Vy izvolili skazat' petushka?*).[112] Marmeladov shares aspects of the martyred Jesus, and the drunken guests as well as Pyotr (Peter) and Andrey (Andrew) Semyonovich Lebezyatnikov betray him by their lack of love and indifference to his fate, as "rooster" is shrieked twice. The apparently random details of the scandal scene carry biblical undertones that maintain our subliminal awareness of the ideal of compassion against which they are contrasted. Dostoevsky gives the names of Jesus's first disciples, Peter and Andrew (who lived in Capernaum), to the disciples of the false faith of the "new ideas," that is, socialism, and hence are here revealed equally as betrayers of the ideals of Jesus.[113]

In John, unlike the synoptic Gospels, Peter is redeemed in the final chapter when Jesus asks him three times if he loves him, and Peter affirms it thrice, balancing his earlier denial. In *Crime and Punishment,* Peter's role as loving disciple is played by Porfiry Petrovich. As mentioned above, both "Peter" and porphyry, a kind of purple granite, mean "rock."[114] Both Luzhin and Porfiry have the patronymic "Petrovich." Luzhin's role as Judas, who wants to incriminate Sonya in order to strike at Raskolnikov, is contrasted to Porfiry's as Peter: Porfiry could hand over Raskolnikov to the authorities he represents, as suggested by the "purple" meaning of porphyry, the purple of the robe worn as an emblem of authority from the time of the Roman emperors, but three times chooses not to.

As the highest civil authority in the novel, Porfiry also plays the role of Pilate. Raskolnikov's last encounter before going to give himself up is with Porfiry; it is his third tormenting interview with him. In John, Pilate interrogates Jesus three times and each time finds him innocent.[115] Porfiry has a compassionate view of the law and, although he knows he is guilty and must be condemned for his crime, allows Raskolnikov to go free out of faith in his nature—he knows that Raskolnikov's anguish will eventually lead him to turn himself in. Again, Dostoevsky reverses the cruel aspect of Jesus's story to emphasize hope in the capacity of the human spirit to be regenerated.

John writes his Gospel to testify that Jesus is the Christ whose spiritual power he contrasts to earthly power. In answer to Pilate's interrogation, Jesus repeatedly distinguishes divine law from human law ("My kingship is not of this world" [18:36]). Dostoevsky uses John's Gospel to make the same distinction. He reverses the roles of Pilate and Christ in Porfiry's interrogation of Raskolnikov: as interrogator, Porfiry urges the life of the spirit on his unbelieving prisoner. Raskolnikov asks Porfiry, "What kind of a prophet are you?" Porfiry repeatedly uses the phrase "Don't you believe?"—apparently in its conversational sense of "Don't you think?"—but it becomes clear in the context of the rest of his words that the "belief" also alludes to the problem of faith. Saying that his words sound "as if they were part of a sermon" (442), Porfiry tells Raskolnikov that he needs faith and that "perhaps God is keeping [him] for something," encouraging Raskolnikov to take up his cross in the hope of a future life.[116]

Pilate finds the innocent Jesus guilty, and Porfiry finds the guilty Raskolnikov guilty, but while Pilate nonetheless hands Jesus over to be crucified despite faith in his innocence, in Dostoevsky's version the interrogator has faith in the guilty one's integrity and is merciful to him. Dostoevsky contrasts the legal aspect of Raskolnikov's trial and sentencing to divine judgment and mercy as part of the novel's moral-philosophical argument with the legal reforms of the 1860s and with socialist radicalism.[117] Again Dostoevsky gives his modern gospel a happier outcome: while Jesus is condemned to death, the necessary preliminary to his resurrection, Porfiry is able to persuade Raskolnikov to take steps that will allow him spiritual rebirth within earthly life.

SCENES FROM THE LIFE OF JESUS AND RASKOLNIKOV'S JOURNEY

Crucial moments in Jesus's life as told by John—a composite Passover feast, Jesus's resurrection, Pilate's interrogation of Jesus, and Jesus's third appearance to his disciples—provide the basis for scenes in *Crime and Punishment.* Marmeladov's wake is a travesty of the composite feasts Jesus attends. Unlike the synoptic Gospels, which each encompass one year of ministry, John describes three years of Jesus's ministry, marked by three feasts. In *Crime and Punishment,* Marmeladov's funeral feast takes features from several feasts in John, including a Passover.

At the first Passover, Jesus drives the moneychangers from the temple and says he can rebuild the temple in three days. He is speaking of the temple of his body, which will be resurrected in three days. Dostoevsky gives the metaphor flesh in Sonya, whose earthly body is defiled but whose spirit remains untouched by her sin. While this idea is reinforced by her implicit resemblance to Mary Magdalene, it is also realized by a parallel to Jesus, whose body is crucified but whose spirit is eternal. Her father refers to her as his only daughter, using an adjective usually applied to Jesus's relationship to God: "*edinorodnaia.*"[118] At her father's wake, Sonya's position as a prostitute (Dostoevsky uses the biblical word, *bludnitsa,* harlot) makes her vulnerable to Luzhin's slander in the eyes of the assembled mob; Luzhin plays the role of Judas, planting one hundred rubles in Sonya's pocket instead of accepting thirty silver pieces from Caiaphas, so that Sonya is put on trial.[119] The feast is Sonya's "last supper," at which she is to be handed over to the authorities. As Sonya fulfills the role of Jesus, Raskolnikov simultaneously plays a mock Jesus: while Sonya undergoes her ordeal; he stands "with his arms *crossed,* looking at her with a fiery gaze. 'Oh Lord!' burst from Sonya" (*slozhiv* nakrest *ruki, i ognennym vzglyadom smotrel na nee. 'O Gospodi!' vyrvalos' u Soni* [6:303; 383, emphasis mine]).

Raskolnikov is further likened to Jesus at Marmeladov's wake by the role Jesus plays at two other feasts. The first is the wedding at Cana, where he turns the water into wine. Dostoevsky's description of the funeral feast begins: "There was not a multitude of wines, nor madeira, but there was wine" (*Vin vo mnozhestvennom chisle ne bylo, madery tozhe, no bylo vino* [6:291; 386]). The description of the food is introduced by the Old Church Slavonic word for edibles, *iastvo*: "Of edibles there were two or three dishes" (*Iz iastv . . . bylo tri-chetyre bliuda* [6:291; 368]), echoing Jesus's words in John: "He who eats my flesh and drinks my blood has eternal life" (*iadushchii Moiu Plot' i piiushchii Moiu Krov' prebyvaet vo mne* [John 6:56]), a passage Dostoevsky marked in his bible.[120] In John, the word *iadushchii* is repeated three more times (6:50, 51, 54). Its association with the crucial rite of communion and transubstantiation signals Raskolnikov's potential for resurrection through the Christian compassion he has shown in providing the money for the funeral feast.

Raskolnikov's impulsive gift offered at Marmeladov's last rites evokes both the miracle of turning the water into wine and the miracle of the loaves and fishes that takes place at the second feast in John. Five thousand followers gather around Jesus. His disciple Andrew tells him, "there is a small boy here who has five barley loaves and two fishes" (6:10). From these, Jesus miraculously provides food for the multitude. It is the small-boy aspect of Raskolnikov, identified in the mare-beating dream, that has the faith and compassion that lead him to provide the wherewithal for Marmeladov's feast and ultimately make possible his own transformation.

The wake scene is built around the contrast between bodily and spiritual food, the metaphor of the sacrament of the bread and the wine; its grotesqueness comes from the exaggeratedly petty and venal level of the earthly sphere in the context of the subtle presence of the biblical text. Sonya's mock trial prefigures Raskolnikov's actual one and is a source of hope: its climax is the exoneration of Sonya and the indictment of Luzhin before the fickle crowd. The outcome reverses the climax of the third feast in John, when Judas hands Jesus over to the authorities and the crowd chooses to condemn Jesus to death rather than Barrabas.

RASKOLNIKOV'S PATH TO FAITH

The details along Raskolnikov's path that hint at the parallel to the life of Jesus as told by John are often found in inverted form. Raskolnikov commits the sin of which the Jews accuse Jesus when they say, "You, being a man, make yourself God" (10:33). Raskolnikov does this by passing judgment on Alyona Ivanovna, claiming that he benefits mankind by ridding it of the moneylender. Jesus, by contrast, says, "I come not to judge the world, but to save the world" (12:47). Jesus prepares a whip from cords in order to chase the moneychangers from the temple; Raskolnikov sews his ax-loop and binds his fake pledge in twine, preparing to murder the moneylender (2:15–16). Raskolnikov's "victory over the whole ant heap" is an arrogant parody of Jesus's "I have overcome the world" (16:33). Dostoevsky has Raskolnikov confuse earthly power (physical force, economic power, the intellect) with moral and spiritual power, a force that engenders the convicts' humble respect for the frail Sonya.

Capernaum is the administrative center of Galilee. Svidrigailov calls Petersburg "the administrative center." In Petersburg, Svidrigailov lives next door to Sonya, who rents from the Kapernaumovs, themselves reminiscent of the mute and the lame who come to Jesus to be healed, as M. O. Altman points out.[121] Capernaum is mentioned five times in John (as compared to seven times total in the three synoptic Gospels); the name means "village of consolation" and is the site of two of Jesus's miracles: he cures an official's son without even seeing him, and he walks on water to Capernaum on the Sea of Galilee (4:46, 6:17). Capernaum, then, is an appropriate association for Sonya. She offers consolation and miracle by reading to Raskolnikov from John at the Kapernaumovs'. This is the beginning of Raskolnikov's movement toward relinquishing his pride in favor of Sonya's faith. When Jesus meets Lazarus's sister Martha, she says, "Had you been here, my brother had not died" (11:21). In *Crime and Punishment,* Marfa Petrovna could say this of her husband Svidrigailov: had he had faith in Jesus, he would not have committed suicide. He failed to find a redeemer in Dunya; Raskolnikov finds his in Sonya.[122] The parallel correlates physical with spiritual death: as Jesus says to Nicodemus, "He who believes is not condemned, he who does not believe is condemned already" (3:18).

Jesus says, "Unless one is born of water and the spirit, he cannot enter the kingdom of God" (3:5). This text supplies the positive dimension of the water motif in *Crime and Punishment;* its complement is the dirty water of the Neva, in which Svidrigailov and Raskolnikov contemplate drowning themselves. Of all the books in the Bible, water is mentioned most frequently in John, where it is used eleven times, two more times than in Genesis. In *Crime and Punishment,* Svidrigailov chooses death and shoots himself during a downpour, while Raskolnikov chooses life on the bank of the Irtysh River.

From the moment Raskolnikov kills Alyona Ivanovna, the tension builds until he confesses. Will he confess? Will he be arrested? A similar tension grows throughout the Gospel of John, generated by the expectation of Jesus's arrest: "But no one arrested him, because his hour had not yet come" (8:20). This is repeated four more times until Jesus says, "Father, the hour has come" (17:1). When Raskolnikov visits his mother for the last time, already preparing to give himself up, she says, "as soon as I saw you, I thought, well, apparently the fateful hour has come" (497). Raskolnikov's giving himself up to the police is equated to Jesus's crucifixion; Raskolnikov relinquishes the materialist basis of his "new word" in favor of a path to spiritual truth as Jesus relinquishes his earthly form in order to attain eternal life of the spirit.

From the beginning of the gospel, Jesus knows that he must "drink the cup which the Father has given me" (18:11). Raskolnikov is first offered the "yellow glass with the yellow water" by Nikodim

(Nicodemus) Fomich at the police station when he faints and also by Porfiry, who twice tries to get him to drink some water, using the biblical form of the verb *ispit',* and then twice using the more normal form, *vypit'* (6:264; 110). On both occasions Raskolnikov refuses to drink. Even after he finally takes up Sonya's proffered cross and mounts the stairs to the police station for the final time, he again pushes away the glass of water he is offered (511). This suggests that his confession does not complete his passion; he has yet to "drink this cup," as he says himself, words taken up by the narrator: "if he had to drink, then he might as well drink the whole thing at once" (501).

Raskolnikov's evidence at his trial contains further parodic inversion of Jesus's life. When on the third day the stone is removed from Jesus's tomb, all that remains of Jesus's earthly self are the linen cloths and the cloth that had been on his head, indications of the resurrection of his body (20:6). When Raskolnikov's evidence is investigated, they turn back the stone in the yard on Voznesensky (Ascension) Prospect to find Raskolnikov's hidden booty and "several extremely damaged banknotes" (*bumazhki chrezvychaino poportilis'* [6:410, 510]). In *Crime and Punishment,* money is the emblem of earthly power as well as of compassion; here the booty from the murder rots as the unresurrected body rots. As Tatiana Kasatkina writes, "The whole novel is dedicated to the mystery that takes place in the cave with Lazarus, still not having heard Jesus's call, and then what happens to him when he has just heard it. *Crime and Punishment* ends at the moment when 'the dead man came out and Jesus said: unbind him.'"[123] The decaying banknotes are a metaphor for the rotting flesh; they presage the potential, through confession, for resurrection of the spirit. The essence of the Lazarus tale is that even his rotting flesh is capable of resurrection through his spiritual aspect. Raskolnikov's "Golgotha," as Dostoevsky noted in his notebook for the novel, or his physical "death," comes when he confesses to Nikodim Fomich, but Raskolnikov has yet to achieve resurrection.[124] Similarly, in John, it is not the climax of Jesus's tale when Nicodemus gives Jesus the traditional Jewish burial at the end of chapter 19. Completion of the miracle of Jesus's resurrection takes place only in chapter 21.

THE EPILOGUES OF JOHN AND *CRIME AND PUNISHMENT*

As Joseph Frank notes, most commentators "vigorously condemn" the epilogue to *Crime and Punishment.*[125] Some find it an artificial appendage unmotivated by the rest of the novel.[126] Frank himself feels that

Raskolnikov's "conversion" is "brushed in too rapidly and perfunctorily to be really persuasive" and therefore "invariably leaves readers with a quite justified sense of dissatisfaction."[127] More recently others have identified continuities between the epilogue and the body of the novel; Robert Belknap, for example, finds what Mochulsky called a "pious lie" to make "good religious sense."[128] In his analysis of the novel's narrative structure, Gary Rosenshield points out that an account of a "miraculous conversion" can hardly be presented with the same verisimilitude as Raskolnikov's preparations for the murder.[129] He convincingly reads the final two pages of the epilogue (the offendingly nondialogic climax) as a completion of the scene in which Sonya reads the story of the raising of Lazarus to Raskolnikov, as a "fulfilled prophecy." By the end of the novel, "the raising of Lazarus has become a vital reality for nineteenth-century Russia and thus for all time."[130]

Chapter 21 of John is conventionally called the epilogue by biblical scholars. It is devoted to Jesus's actions after his resurrection and unique to John's gospel. The disciples Simon Peter, Thomas, Nathanael, and two others are fishing by the Sea of Tiberias:

> Just as day was breaking, Jesus stood on the beach; yet the disciples did not know that it was Jesus. Jesus said to them, "Children, have you any fish?" They answered him, "No." He said to them, "Cast the net on the right side of the boat, and you will find some." So they cast it, and now they were not able to haul it in, for the quantity of fish. That disciple whom Jesus loved said to Peter, "It is the Lord!" When Simon Peter heard that it was the Lord, he put on his clothes, for he was stripped for work, and sprang into the sea. (21:4–8)

Jesus cooks the disciples a breakfast of fish on a charcoal fire: "Jesus said to them, 'Come and have breakfast.' Now none of the disciples dared ask him, 'Who are you?' They knew it was the Lord" (21:12–13).

Dostoevsky catches the everyday simplicity of this miracle in the climactic scene of Raskolnikov's epiphany:

> Early in the morning, about six o'clock, he went off to work on the bank of the river in a shed where there was a kiln for baking alabaster and where they used to crush it. Only three prisoners went there. One of the prisoners, accompanied by a guard, went back to the fortress for some tools; the other one was chopping wood and putting it into the furnace. Raskolnikov came out of the shed to the bank of the river. He sat down on a pile of timber by the shed and began looking at the wide, deserted expanse of the river. . . .
>
> Suddenly Sonya was beside him. She had come up noiselessly and sat down close to him. It was still very early. . . . Her face still showed traces of illness. She smiled at him joyfully and tenderly. . . .

> How it happened he did not know, but suddenly something seemed to seize him and throw him to her feet. He embraced her knees and wept . . . she understood, and she had no doubts at all about it, that he loved her, loved her infinitely. (526–27)

Dostoevsky's scene of silent recognition at dawn by the shore is modeled on chapter 21 of John.[131] Raskolnikov has accepted the truth of Jesus's message as represented by Sonya, the "divine wisdom," just as the disciples recognize the truth of the miraculous appearance, in the midst of their everyday labor, of their teacher after his crucifixion. Dostoevsky's scene, like John's chapter 21, bodes the "dawn of a renewed future, of a full resurrection to a new life" (527). Both epilogues are the necessary completion of their heroes' sufferings.[132] While they open out into an unknown future, the outcome is clear.

John's purpose is to witness the truth of Jesus's teaching and identity. He insists on the truth of the events of Jesus's life: "We know that his testimony is true," he writes. "These are written so that you may believe that Jesus is the Christ" (21:24, 20:30).

Sonya takes on John's role of recorder when she writes letters describing Raskolnikov's actions in the epilogue. Her letters are "based in solid fact" as she dispassionately describes the gradual miracle of Raskolnikov's rebirth in Siberia (in a town that, like Capernaum and Petersburg, is "one of Russia's administrative centers" [513]).

John emphasizes the incompleteness of his account of Jesus's life in the final verse of his Gospel: "But there are also many other things which Jesus did; were every one to be written, I suppose the world itself could not contain the books that could be written" (21:25). The final sentence of *Crime and Punishment* echoes this idea and intonation: "But that is the beginning of a new story, the story of the gradual rebirth of a man, the story of his gradual regeneration, of his gradual passing from one world to another, of his acquaintance with a new and hitherto unknown reality. That might be the subject of a new story—our present story is ended" (528).

The opening out of the time scale of this conclusion has its precedent in the "reminiscence passages," as Gary Rosenshield calls them, that appear throughout the first six parts of the novel.[133] The narrator tells us what Raskolnikov recalled "afterwards," "later," on twenty different occasions.[134] This echoes the repeated "afterward" of Jesus in John: "What I am doing you do not know now, but afterward you will understand" (13:7). After Raskolnikov has gained faith, he will recall events with a new understanding.

As the most mystical gospel, which nonetheless shows Jesus as human and part of day-to-day human life, John gives Dostoevsky's "detective thriller" deep power, an eternal dimension that the richness of the many literary, philosophical and publicistic materials cannot convey. The omnipresent intonations of John's gospel maintain the atmosphere of divine potential throughout the intense French-inspired naturalism of the novel; once the reader is sensitized to the presence of John in the first six books, the epilogue becomes the inevitable and essential completion of the work.[135]

Synthesis: Novel and Gospel

Those who have written about the quandary of post-Enlightenment literary prose generally conclude that the word had lost its sacred dimension after the close of the medieval period. Peter Brooks, writing principally about Western European literature, describes Balzac, Dickens, Dostoevsky, and others as "social melodramatists" who give a "dual representation of man's social existence, the way he lives in the ordinary, and the moral drama implicated by and in his existence. [They] refuse to allow that the world has been completely drained of transcendence; and they locate that transcendence in the struggle of the children of light with the children of darkness, in the play of ethical mind."[136]

Brooks writes of the post-Enlightenment thirst for resacralization but says that for these social melodramatists, "mythmaking could now only be individual, personal; and the promulgation of ethical imperatives had to depend on an individual act of self-understanding that would then—by an imaginative or even terroristic leap—be offered as the foundation of a general ethics . . . the individual ego declares its central and overriding value, its demand to be the measure of all things."[137] Russian critics agree that this desacralization of the word occurred in Western Europe but that it collided with Russian literature at the beginning of the eighteenth century. The conflict of world views led Russians to develop "defense mechanisms" in the instinct of self-preservation, which helped them to maintain a sacral relationship to the word that they found lacking in Western European literature.[138]

Dostoevsky's dialogue with his subtexts shows that his motive in embedding so much of French literature of his epoch in *Crime and Punishment* was indeed to resacralize it, to refute the Western form of ego that Balzac describes and Raskolnikov embodies. Dostoevsky shared the Slavophile view that Russia's great superiority over the decadent West resided in her innate faith in the Russian Orthodox Church, and seeks to "reanimate the authoritative word of conventional Christianity" in his fiction.[139]

Dostoevsky embeds the rich network of French allusions in his novel in order to refute their material vision of human existence with the eternal truth of the Gospel of John. He rewrites the French theme of prostitution by combining Henriette's victimization, Fleur de Marie's aristocratic nobility, Louisa's compassion for the wounded beggar, and the converted Esther's sacrifice of her life for Lucien in Sonya Marmeladova. The wretched details of Sonya's apartment, dress, shame, and desperation echo the French prostitutes', while her form of nobility, compassion, and self-sacrifice is modeled on Jesus Christ. Dostoevsky combines the French theme of the young man from the provinces with Janin's portrait of the ambivalence of conscience in a world of waning faith in order to render Raskolnikov's oscillations between Napoleonic ambition and selfless compassion. The French detective genre casts Raskolnikov's spiritual guide as a police investigator, and the feuilleton-inspired suspense tale disguises a religious allegory. Neither dimension of the novel can exist in the absence of the other. Dostoevsky wants the reader to identify with the characters' psychological drama, enacted against the backdrop of the French subtexts' physical universe. But the identification is only a means to the end of bringing the divine into the everyday.

Dostoevsky's tale of murder is a parable for his time designed to turn his contemporaries away from a false view of the nature of man already dominant in the West, one he feared would become predominant in Russia at a point in history when he saw the intellect being enshrined at the expense of the human spirit.[140] By bringing readers along Raskolnikov's tortured path, Dostoevsky prepares us to accept John's message and to view the world of St. Petersburg that we have experienced intensely at close range from a new, and higher, perspective.

4

Tolstoy, *Anna Karenina*

What is a Frenchwoman going to talk to the children about? Nasty, stupid things; in her affected way she'll infect them with her vulgar, corrupt, ridiculous and imbecile code of manners, and her distorted notions about society, about religion. . . . The Frenchwoman will introduce a new and vile French element.

Fyodor Dostoevsky, letter to Varvara Mikhailovna Dostoevskaya-Ivanova, 1868

Rousseau and the Gospels have been the two great and beneficent influences of my life.

Lev Tolstoy, letter to Bernard Bouvier, 1905

The richness and ambiguity of *Anna Karenina* arises from the conflict between its sympathy with both the adulteress and the family. In his novel, Tolstoy at once empathizes with Anna and reaffirms the biblical understanding of adultery as sinful, while including a vision of family that could prevent it. Tolstoy's antidote to the decadence he found in the French novel of adultery is made up of the ideals of Rousseau and the eternal authority of the Gospels; he needed them to answer the question that increasingly tormented him as he was writing *Anna Karenina*—the meaning of life and how to live. Tolstoy sets this conflict into dialogue against the background of a variety of literary, philosophical, and sacred texts; he builds his response by recasting the most minute details of each work in such a way that the novel both forgives Anna and enshrines the holy ideal of the family.

Since *Les Liaisons Dangeureuses* first appeared, adultery has been a particularly French theme. To portray an adulteress, Tolstoy, who followed French prose closely throughout his life, drew from Rousseau as well as from French works published during the twenty years preceding his writing *Anna Karenina.* Tolstoy's novel of adultery in the European style became a "philosophico-moral" one as he set the relationship among Karenin, Anna, and Vronsky into dialogue with the ideas of a range of French novels.[1] Tolstoy's counterexample to the adulterous triangle, the story of the successful marriage of Kitty and Levin, explicitly contradicts these French models and uses the Gospels to suggest the mysteries of the sacrament of marriage.

The novel of adultery was a widespread genre in European literature of the nineteenth century, sharing many features: adulteresses go mad or, more often, die—by disease, in childbirth, or by murder—while adulterous men perish on the battlefield, in a train crash, in exile, and a child often serves as a source of grace.[2] The problem of a woman's role in marriage becomes a paradigm for the problems created by interrelating patterns, with marriage as mediator attempting to harmonize the natural, the familial, the social, the religious, and the transcendental realms.[3] As Tony Tanner puts it in *Adultery and the Novel,* "The tension between [Old Testament] law and [New Testament] sympathy . . . holds the great bourgeois novel together."[4] While marriage brings harmony in a mythologized society such as those depicted by Shakespeare, in nineteenth-century Western European society marriage *is* the mythology that the novel of adultery demythologizes. The generic commonalities, however, are insufficient to explain Tolstoy's highly specific response to particular representatives of the genre. Of the many literary sources for *Anna Karenina,* Tolstoy used French material as a baseline against which to consider adultery; he builds the relationship among Karenin, Anna, and Vronsky in dialogue with Rousseau, Dumas, Zola, and Flaubert.

Most of the French subtexts for *Anna Karenina* address the problem of the adulteress from the point of view of the betrayed husband. Only Flaubert's *Madame Bovary* conveys the adulteress's experience predominantly from her point of view, which contributes to making it the most important of the novel's subtexts. Each work relates to particular aspects of adultery in *Anna Karenina*: Rousseau's *Emile and Sophie, or Les Solitaires* considers the moral questions faced by the husband when the wife is in all other respects an honorable woman. Dumas' two works on adultery presuppose a dishonorable wife: his essay *Man-Woman* (*L'Homme-femme*) stimulated Tolstoy's thinking about the "woman question"; his polemical play *Claude's Wife* (*La Femme de Claude*) provides scenes of unhappy married life. Zola's *Thérèse Raquin* and *Madeleine Férat* contribute a few structural and stylistic elements. Flaubert's *Madame Bovary,* a deeper, more artistic work than these five, considers causes of adultery and ultimately the meaning of life from the woman's point of view. In all but Rousseau's *Emile and Sophie,* the women are unredeemable, egotistical adulteresses and the men their victims. Although Tolstoy's firm views on woman's role as wife and mother should have made (and in early drafts did in fact make) him unsympathetic to Anna, Tolstoy set out to write of an adulteress who was "only pitiable and not guilty"; he responds to the French works, and restores Rousseau's ideals, by creating in Anna a complex, sympathetic adulteress with a moral sense, whose values are made explicit through the parallel story of Levin.[5] But Levin's quest for how to live is not set into dialogue with the French novel of adultery; to describe Levin's struggle toward new insight, Tolstoy draws from Rousseauian ideals and from the Gospels.

Anna Karenina was seen by French contemporaries as part of their own tradition. Although, as Boris Eikhenbaum says, Tolstoy overcomes the French "love" novel rather than imitating it (i.e., treats it as background, not an influence), the French texts he was overcoming contribute so much to his Russian novel that his contemporaries' confusion is understandable.[6] Tolstoy does not adapt the French novels; rather he responds to them and orders them in a hierarchy: at the bottom are Zola's novels, which are part of the context of the adultery novel but function only as sources for some dramatic moments. Tolstoy rejects Dumas' view of the battle of the sexes, which functions as a subtext for Kitty and Levin's relationship, as well as some scenes surrounding Anna's betrayal of Karenin. The fullest subtextual relationship is reserved for *Madame Bovary.*[7] Tolstoy's eldest son, Sergey, explains in his memoirs of his father, "My father was a very selective reader, which is not very usual. He remembered everything that he had read, and knew how to get the essence out of a book and what to discard."[8] In *Anna Karenina,* Tolstoy recalls these books on adultery in fine detail and recasts what for him was their social and moral essence, taking up not only their arguments but their imagery and motif systems.

The French and Adultery

JEAN-JACQUES ROUSSEAU (1712–1778)

While Dostoevsky loathed Rousseau and frequently parodied his *Confessions,* Tolstoy was devoted to him from his early youth.[9] "I have read all of Rousseau, all twenty volumes, including the *Dictionary of Music,*"

Tolstoy said in an interview in 1901. "I did better than adore him, I made a veritable cult of him: at fifteen, I wore his portrait around my neck like a holy image. I knew pages of his writing by heart. I think that I could have written them myself."[10]

Tolstoy listed the *Confessions, Emile,* and *Julie, or the New Heloise* as the top three on a list of about fifteen books that made a big impression on him between the ages of fourteen to twenty.[11] After his stay in Paris in 1857, Tolstoy even made a pilgrimage to Clarens, "the same village where Rousseau's Julie lived."[12] And in 1905, near the end of his life, Tolstoy wrote, "Rousseau has been my master since I was fifteen. Rousseau and the Gospels have been the two great and beneficent influences of my life. Quite recently I had occasion to reread some of his works and I felt the same elevation of the spirit and admiration as when I read him in my first youth."[13] The ideals of Rousseau and the Gospels enable Levin to overcome the impulse to suicide; their absence from Anna's life make hers inevitable. Tolstoy adds the religious dimension missing from Rousseau's consideration of adultery.

Emile and Sophie (1762–1765)

Tolstoy never experienced a betrayal by his wife, but he manages to convey Karenin's pain and contradictory feelings toward Anna's adultery in compelling detail. Catherine II had banned the sale of the French edition of *Emile* when it first appeared in 1762, so that *Emile and Sofia, or the Well Brought-up Lovers from the Works of Rousseau* was published in Russian only in 1779.[14] Tolstoy's "twenty volumes" would have included the little-known sequel to *Emile, Emile and Sophie: Les Solitaires,* which appears to have contributed substantially to Tolstoy's depiction of Karenin's struggle with the problems faced by a betrayed husband.[15]

Emile was finished in 1760; Rousseau wanted to complete the sequel in 1768 but never did.[16] *Emile and Sophie* comprises two letters written by Emile to his tutor after he has been married to Sophie and has had two children by her, of whom a son survives. They have moved to Paris from the country to distract Sophie from her grief at the deaths of her parents and daughter: "Approaching the capital, I was struck by a dire impression that I had never yet experienced. . . . I was afraid to expose such a pure union to so many dangers. . . . I trembled, looking at my sad Sophie, to think that I myself was dragging so many virtues and charms into this gulf of prejudice and vice where innocence and happiness would be lost" (294). He is of course right. In Paris Sophie, led astray by the capital's permissive attitude toward infidelity, confesses to Emile that she has "sullied his bed" and is pregnant (302). The remaining three quarters of Rousseau's fragment is devoted to an analysis of the feelings of the wronged husband, one who, like Karenin, has up to this point loved his virtuous wife. What will society think? How should he behave toward his wife? His son? What feeling can he have for the child of his wife's lover? These are the same questions Karenin is forced to face once Anna confesses her infidelity during their carriage ride home after the steeplechase. Rousseau examines the moral basis for answering them; Tolstoy addresses Rousseau's judgments by adding a Christian dimension.

Rousseau takes Emile through a series of responses. Emile's first reaction is that as a virtuous woman who has fallen, Sophie is more to be censured than a frivolous adulteress. But then he wonders, "By what right have I dared to judge her so severely before having been judged myself, before knowing what I should reproach myself for in her wrongs? . . . Her inconstancy is the result of my own. . . . You abandon her and you want her to remain for you! You scorn her, and you want to be honored still! It is your cooling, your neglect, your indifference, which have plucked you from her heart" (311). In this admission of his own shortcomings, he differs from Karenin, who never considers Anna's point of view. Indeed, it is Karenin's "neglect," however unwitting, that makes her need Vronsky's love. Emile, however, blames himself for having dragged Sophie against her will to Paris, "where all that is honest is derided" (312). He realizes that her honesty forces her to her courageous confession and decides that "she is guilty without being vile" (compare Tolstoy's "only pitiable and not guilty"). Emile becomes sympathetic to Sophie: "Despite the horror of my fate, I felt a kind of joy in imagining Sophie worthy of esteem and unhappy" (314). Karenin briefly experiences this joy when he is able to forgive Anna's adultery at what appears to be her deathbed.

Putting aside the intensity of his first emotions, Emile decides to think through his situation "with as much sangfroid as if it were another's" (316). "Everywhere morals are valued, women's infidelities dishonor their husbands. . . . But does the honor of a man . . . depend on his wife? . . . Can he be dishonored by the vices of another? Was I not by my principles above public opinion?" (317). Karenin makes it clear to Anna that public opinion of their situation is important to him, and Tolstoy affirms, differently, that it is an inevitable factor in Anna's fate. But Emile decides this is cowardly reasoning designed to allow him to return to a faithless Sophie. Society is right to impute a wife's bad conduct to the husband; to leave her unpunished shows indifference to honest morals. His "sangfroid" has led him astray, as Karenin's has been the origin of his woes in his relations with Anna. Emile struggles with the desire for revenge. He realizes that their son forms an indissoluble knot between them, a natural argument against divorce, but, as with Karenin, the thought that his wife will share her love for their son with the child of her lover provokes new rage in him, and he resolves to leave her. From this resolution follows the next, also like Karenin's, to take their son from her, but Emile comes to understand that this is worse for his son. He flees France to avoid seeing his family and to forget his shame.

Emile records his deliberations in his first letter to his master, which contain his thinking in isolation from interaction with Sophie and society; Tolstoy presents Karenin's thoughts, often in the third person, though directly from Karenin's mind, in nine chapters throughout the book, in which he interacts with Anna, Vronsky, Oblonsky, and others as the consequences of her adultery develop.[17] *Emile and Sophie* is a philosophical monologue in epistolary form, whereas *Anna Karenina* is a philosophical novel built on dramatic scenes. Yet Karenin's thoughts excerpted from their dramatic context read very much like Emile's attempts to reason with his own painful emotional response to the same events. Both husbands confront the situation of a wife with a lover, a legitimate son, and an illegitimate infant; honorable men, they try to apply reason to their emotional reactions in order to behave justly, struggling with their humiliation and jealousy that turn to anger and the desire for revenge. The principal philosophical difference in Tolstoy's treatment is the inclusion of the religious aspect of the question, the sacrament of marriage that binds the couple in the sight of God.

Tolstoy responds to Emile's questions. The premise of *Anna Karenina* is suggested by Emile's idea that "the adulteries of the *femmes du monde* are nothing more than intrigues; but an adulterous Sophie is the most odious of all monsters" (311). Anna is contrasted precisely to the adulteresses of Petersburg's Liza Merkalova–Betsy Tverskaya variety; what causes her tragedy is that, like Rousseau's Sophie, she takes marriage seriously and is an honest woman. Tolstoy examines Anna's motivation for adultery; Rousseau is not interested in it beyond Emile's insight into Sophie's behavior that "her inconstancy is the result of my own . . . neglect" (311). Anna, through no fault of her own, has married a man who inspires no passion, for which he cannot be faulted, any more than he can be said to "neglect" her. This addresses Emile's question, "Does a cruel husband merit a faithful wife?" recasting it in terms of mutual satisfaction and suggesting that even the wife of a technically faultless husband may have understandable motives to be unfaithful (323). In both cases, the atmosphere of the capital affects women whose incomplete marriage makes them vulnerable, Petersburg society ladies having acquired from Paris looser attitudes toward adultery.

Karenin sees his duty to his wife in different terms from Emile: "As head of the family I am the person whose duty it is to guide her, and who is therefore partly responsible" for her morals.[18] He formulates the speech he will make to her upon her return from Betsy's, where she and Vronsky have scandalized the company by their behavior even before they become lovers. Like Emile, Karenin tries to use reason to cope with the emotionally charged situation: "I must make the following clear. First, the importance of public opinion and propriety; secondly, the religious meaning of marriage; thirdly . . . I must refer to the harm that may result to our son; fourthly, allude to her own unhappiness" (131). Although Tolstoy makes fun of the formality of Karenin's logical treatment ("the form and sequence of the speech he had to make shaped itself in his mind . . . as though it were an official report") and has him crack his knuckles twice, by the end of the novel he shows him to be right in each point. In particular, Tolstoy endorses Karenin's most powerful statement to Anna in their subsequent interview: "Our lives are bound together not by men but by God. This bond can only be broken by a crime, and that crime brings its punishment" (133).

Emile tries to ignore public opinion: "What did it matter what others think of me, provided that in my own heart I did not cease to be good, just, honest? Is it a crime to be merciful? Is it cowardly to pardon an offense? Have I disdained the prejudices of man for so long to sacrifice my happiness to them? . . . She who expiates her error by her regret is more worthy of pity than of hate; one can . . . pardon her without shame" (317–18). Later he considers this to be sophistry. Emile does not test the above proposition, since he neither talks to Sophie again after her confession nor reenters society. Karenin, though having cited public opinion first in his list of concerns, does indeed go against it when he pardons Anna at what all think is her deathbed. For that moment, Vronsky sees the deceived husband, instead of being ridiculous, as worthy of veneration: "That husband in his lofty elevation turned out to be, not only not cruel, false, or absurd, but kind, simple and dignified" (378). But Karenin knows that a potent "coarse power" will take his humble peace from him, that this "coarse power [of which Betsy Tverskaya is the personification] would rule his life in the eye of the world . . . he felt powerless; he was aware in advance that everybody would be against him and that he would not be allowed to do what seemed so natural and good" (385, 387). He is eventually reduced to helpless misery by the contempt he perceives all around him, "left alone, disgraced, ridiculed, not wanted by anyone and despised by all" (459). "He felt he could not divert from himself people's hatred, because that hatred was caused not by his badness . . . but by his disgraceful and repulsive misery" (460). Tolstoy answers Emile's question, "What did it matter what others think of me, provided that in my own heart I did not cease to be good, just, honest?" by showing that while Rousseau and Karenin are right that public opinion is unjust and responds to the wrong thing, the victim of adultery is unavoidably affected by it.

Emile considers that the son forms an indissoluble knot between the parents and is a natural argument against divorce. Certainly Tolstoy agrees. He shows this to be true from the father's, the mother's, the son's, and the lover's points of view: Karenin cannot relate naturally to his son after Anna's betrayal; Seryozha pines for his mother, falls sick after she pays her birthday visit to him, and finally struggles to forget her: "He took pains to drive [his dreams and memories of his mother] away" and responds angrily to Oblonsky's fatuous question, "Do you remember your mother?" (657, 658). Anna's loss of Seryozha is the most painful and insuperable aspect of her attempt to start a new life with Vronsky—the two loves are distinct and equally essential to her happiness but cannot be allowed to coexist for long (indicated by Anna's use of Vronsky's photograph to push out Seryozha's from her album); Vronsky is unable to marry Anna and so has no legal relationship to his own daughter (490, 58).

Emile initially wants to take his son from his wife but realizes that "to take his mother from his son is . . . to sacrifice the child to revenge himself on the mother; it is an act of passion, never of reason. . . . It is certain that the resolution to take my son from his mother had been the effect of my anger" (332–33). But Emile is also tormented at the thought of his son as part of a new family with his wife's lover: "I would have preferred to see my son dead than to see Sophie with one from another father. This idea made me more bitter, more alienated from her than everything else that had tormented me thus far" (324). The son is inevitably a reminder of both parents, so letting Sophie keep hers can also serve Emile's desire for revenge: "May he remind the faithless one every day of her life of the happiness of which he was the pledge, and of the spouse she has left" (333).

Karenin's feelings about his son are made of a similar mix: "The feeling of anger with his wife [after Vronsky comes to the house] . . . gave him no rest. She had not fulfilled his condition and he was obliged to punish her and carry out his threat: to divorce her and take away his son" (330). Karenin admits to Anna, who says he only wants to hurt her by taking Seryozha, "Yes, I have even lost my affection for my son, because he is connected with my repulsion for you. But all the same I shall take him away" (332). Tolstoy accepts Rousseau's understanding of the injured husband's natural psychological reactions.

Emile finally rejects the idea of taking his son from Sophie because he understands it would harm his son to take him from his mother. Karenin too tries to separate his feelings from consideration of his son's well-being: "In case of a divorce, what would become of his son? To leave him with his mother was not possible; the divorced mother would have another, illegitimate family, in which the position and education of a stepson would in all probability be a bad one. Should he keep him himself? He knew that would be revengeful and he did not wish for revenge" (392). At Anna's bedside Karenin tells Vronsky, "I confess I was haunted by a desire for vengeance," but now he is granted the joy of forgiving (377). In that state Karenin tells Oblonsky that he will grant a divorce and even give up his son, and only later under the influence of Lydia Ivanovna and her charlatan psychic does Karenin change his mind and refuse both (393). Tolstoy as novelist introduces another character into the drama that Rousseau outlines only in a philosophical way. Through Lydia Ivanovna, Tolstoy creates a necessary conjunction between man's law and God's. She personifies the pressure of society and also appears to represent the spiritual side of the argument, but her particular sentimental, mystical brand of Christianity cannot override her self-interest. Her faith is not tempered by the reason that Tolstoy so valued, so that her attachment to Karenin distorts her judgment, and his emotional dependency on her prevents him from seeing that.[19]

When Anna writes to ask to see Seryozha, Lydia Ivanovna exclaims to Karenin, "I am learning to understand your loftiness and her baseness." Karenin asks, "But who will throw the stone?" (471). By referring to the Gospel of John, Karenin suggests that he does not have the right to judge Anna, to cast a stone at the woman taken in adultery. In this he concurs with Emile's self-questioning: "By what right do you punish her, by what authority? Are you her judge?" (323). Tolstoy's epigraph suggests that only God may judge the consequences of breaking the vows made to Him. As Karenin says to Anna, these vows are an even more important bond between husband and wife than their children are.

Tolstoy's morality was formed under the "beneficent" influence of Rousseau, so that we expect his reading of *Emile and Sophie* to follow his master's precepts. Tolstoy allows Rousseau to frame the dilemma of how to regard the virtuous adulteress who is "worthy of esteem and unhappy." Rousseau does this in a philosophical deliberation by his reasonable hero; Tolstoy is writing a novel and creates a more fallible cuckold in Karenin. Karenin's indifference to Seryozha's pain becomes part of his portrait as hypocritical Christian, a characterization that increases our sympathy for Anna as we understand Karenin's inadequacy as a husband. Tolstoy dramatizes the schematic questions Rousseau raises in Emile's monologue and engages our emotions, often agreeing with Rousseau's analysis, but introduces the idea of the sacrament: a marriage is sanctified by God, and it is not for the wife or the husband to dissolve it. While this appears to be Tolstoy's response to Rousseau's framing of the question of the adulteress in *Emile and Sophie,* his novel is far richer in ambiguity than the comparison of the two texts suggests. Additional subtexts add other considerations to the framing of our judgment of Anna.

ALEXANDRE DUMAS FILS (1824–1895)

Eternal God who joinest them that were separate . . . hast ordained for them an indissoluble union in love.

Anna Karenina

Tolstoy began *Anna Karenina* in part from a desire to respond to the intense debates of the 1860s and 1870s about the "woman question," the nature of marriage, and the proper treatment of the adulteress. Eikhenbaum considers Alexandre Dumas fils's essay *Man-Woman, Response to Monsieur Henri d'Ideville* (1872) one of the stimuli that led Tolstoy to begin writing a novel about these problems that had bothered him since he had finished writing *War and Peace.*[20] Eikhenbaum cites Tolstoy's letter of March 1, 1873 to his wife's sister Tatyana Kuzminskaya: "Have you read *Man-Woman*? This book startled me. One couldn't expect from a Frenchman such loftiness of understanding of marriage and in general of the relation of man to woman."[21]

Eikhenbaum points out that Tolstoy mentions Dumas directly in drafts of *Anna Karenina* and says that his treatise was useful specifically in relation to the problem of women's rights, in which "the story of Anna and Kitty looks like a polemical answer to all arguments" on the

Alexandre Dumas fils (*Revue étrangère* 6 [1833])

subject.[22] But he considers that after the novel had evolved through its many drafts, the plot and the images were "freed of ties with Dumas' treatise."[23] A close reading of Tolstoy's response to Dumas' essay, as well as his play, suggests, on the contrary, that both the treatise and the play became more deeply embedded in the novel, governing Tolstoy's choice and interpretation of scenes of married life.

Dumas' verdict on what to do with the adulteress is "[k]ill her!" Eikhenbaum interprets the biblical epigraph to *Anna Karenina* as an answer to Dumas' idea: God, not man, must be the judge. But Tolstoy responds not only in the epigraph. Reading *Anna Karenina* alongside *Man-Woman* shows that Tolstoy not only rejects a husband's right to avenge himself by murder, but also contradicts the premise of Dumas' essay, that woman wins the grand struggle between the sexes that is marriage. Tolstoy refutes this in the story of Levin's marriage to Kitty.

Man-Woman

Alexandre Dumas and Tolstoy went through a similar evolution in their moral relationship to their art. In his youth, Dumas lived a dissipated life, which is recorded in his novel *The Lady of the Camellias* (1848). At twenty, Dumas fell in love with the courtesan Marie Duplessis, the model for Marguerite, the Lady of the Camellias. Unlike the novel, in which Marguerite nobly renounces the poor Armand Duval at the request of his father, in life it was the poor Alexandre Dumas who broke off the relationship. When Marie died of tuberculosis six months later at the age of twenty-three, he wrote the *Lady of the Camellias* in three weeks. It is understandable then, why the novel is so sympathetic to the courtesan, in contrast to Dumas' later work. The dramatization of the novel in 1852 was a huge success and made him famous. It was the beginning of a prolific and successful career of writing about women of easy virtue: Dumas produced sixteen plays and seven novels.

Dumas was the illegitimate son of a seamstress, abandoned by his father. While his mother, as he said, "comforted me and healed my soul," his father led a wild life.[24] But when Dumas père at last became successful, he took his seven year-old son from his mother and sent him to school. There Dumas suffered six years of such persecution for his illegitimacy that he became ill and his father withdrew him, an experience that may have contributed, along with the conflict between his prodigal father and reliable mother, to his later bouts of depression. In the 1860s Dumas had a prolonged emotional crisis and contemplated suicide; George Sand's physician, Dr. Henri Favre, helped him recover, in the process encouraging Dumas' dogmatic, mystical, prophetic tendencies. As Dumas said to Leconte de Lisle, "I have always been a sermonizer."[25] In 1867, with his moral mission clear, Dumas proposed to found *le théâtre utile,* a kind of theater that rejected "art for art's sake." He had come to believe that "all literature that does not have as its goal perfectibility, morality, the ideal, in a word, the useful, is stunted and unhealthy, born dead."[26] As Tolstoy was to do, he rejected his former art in favor of moral teaching, taking the Gospels as the basis of his social thought.

Dostoevsky followed French opinion when he wrote in 1862 that Dumas' novels contain "an extraordinary amount of smutty, cynically blatant and crudely perverted matter."[27] Certainly Dumas treated a subject not discussed in print in Russia; he coined a term for the world of kept women, *"le demi-monde,"* which he used as the title of a play produced in 1855 about the effects of prostitution on marriage. From 1867 onward, his prefaces and pamphlets contained indictments of the declining morals of the Second Empire; he maintained that prostitution and adultery were undermining faith in the sanctity of the marriage bond that is unbreakable by the law of the church and state, a view of adultery close to Tolstoy's.

Man-Woman is Dumas' response to a newspaper article in *Le Soir* by Henri d'Ideville on Leroy Dubourg's murder of his adulterous young wife, Denise MacLeod, for which Dubourg was sentenced to five years in prison.[28] Calling it barbarous, d'Ideville protests the French law that finds "excusable" a husband's murder of a wife caught in flagrante delicto. He describes Denise's sad case: When she was nineteen, her parents dead and her sisters married, she married a man whom she soon came to find repellent. D'Ideville reproduces her letter to her husband in which she politely asks him to let her live separately. He also prints her touching letter to a friend, in which she resigns herself to a solitary existence. But when she was twenty-two her husband found her in a student's attic and killed her. D'Ideville says divorce is the remedy. But divorce was impossible in France from 1816 to 1884.[29]

Dumas argues with d'Ideville; he sees the relationship between the sexes as a battle in which the woman dominates: "the struggle of the masculine and the feminine, formidable, eternal, daily, incessant, a struggle all the more terrible in that the combatants begin by adoring each other" (17). He demonstrates this in a play-by-play description of each step of marriage, starting with the wedding ceremony:

> Look at the man, peasant, worker, merchant, duke and peer, this is certainly the day of his life where he looks the most foolish [*où il a l'air le plus bête*] in his black suit, white tie and the atmosphere of the wig-maker that always surrounds him. Does he understand the grandeur, the eternity of the step he is taking? . . . He has just declared himself sacrilegious and a perjurer, since to contract this definitive engagement he has had to immolate in his thoughts and certainly in reality his former amours that he had also promised eternity! Ah! Poor man, foolish and coarse, this is what you bring to this virgin in body and spirit![30]

Tolstoy's description of Levin's feelings about this problem on the eve of his marriage to Kitty responds to these ideas point by point. The "foolishness" of the clothing is divided into two types; Levin is in a "fearfully foolish" (*uzhasnom duratskom*) position missing a clean shirt, pacing around "like a caged beast" (the Russian "beast," "*zver',*" corresponds to the French "beast" in "*l'air bête*"), while the frivolous society men in the church wear the white ties and frock coats (408, 413). Oblonsky presents Dumas' view when he says, "How foolish people become in these circumstances!" (409). But Levin, unlike Dumas' stupid bridegroom, is "foolish" throughout the ceremony due to his obliviousness to the externals of the ritual; his "foolishness"—his inability to understand which hand to take, or how to exchange rings—comes from an almost trancelike, holy, foolishness: he is shown understanding precisely the "grandeur, the eternity" of the step he is taking and rejoicing in it.

Tolstoy takes up Dumas' "sacrilege" and "perjury" but applies it to the sacrament of marriage. The novel's biblical epigraph can only have meaning if marriage is understood as a sacrament, blessed by God, and not merely as a civil legality. Levin's doubts about going to confession underscore the importance of the religious dimension of the marriage vows and hence their irrevocability. His eventual conscious acceptance of God is presaged by his intuitive divine rapture on the morning before he makes his formal proposal to Kitty: "And what he saw that morning he never saw again. He was moved in particular by the children going to school, the silvery-grey pigeons that flew down from the roof to the pavement, and the little loaves of bread, powdered with flour, that some invisible hand had put outside a baker's shop. Those loaves, the pigeons, and the two little boys seemed not of this earth" (367). The doves are icons of the Holy Spirit; an invisible hand puts out bread, and Levin communes with that which is not of this earth. Levin's vows, then, taken in a transcendent state in church after his meaningful confession to the sweetly reasonable priest (and Tolstoy wrote in a letter that he was "of course, on the priest's side"), are neither sacrilege nor perjury.[31] Levin neither shows lack of faith in the sacrament, nor does he deceive Kitty, whose simple faith in Levin's goodness, however unconventional he may be in church observance, is shown to be justified.

Dumas' horror at the sacrifice of the virgin to the sexually experienced man is acted out in Kitty's sorrow upon reading Levin's diaries before they are married. The "former amours" of Dumas' discussion of the groom on the wedding day are addressed from Levin's point of view: "He felt the abyss that separated his tainted past from her dove-like purity, and was appalled by what he had done" (371–72). But Tolstoy's groom confesses his impurity to his bride to be, eliminating the dishonesty and thereby removing the hypocrisy that Dumas deplores. Dumas' idea is given voice by one of the women onlookers at the wedding: "What a darling the bride is, like a lamb decked for the slaughter" (415). But Levin's moral honesty and Kitty's forgiveness before the wedding remove any sacrificial aspect from their wedding night.

Dumas' analysis of the wedding night depicts the man as murderer of the woman: "She does not share what she gives. She is twice duped; such is the first impression that follows your violation [*attentat*] and her metamorphosis" (41). But the woman quickly realizes that this is a false victory of the man, her conqueror. "Happy victim! Poor executioner!" exclaims Dumas. Tolstoy employs this image not for the married couple but for Anna's adulterous union with Vronsky, who feels "what a murderer must feel when he looks at the body he has robbed of life" (135). Tolstoy negates the idea of the slaughter of the sacrificial lamb in marriage by treating it comically through the naive language of the peasants about Kitty, while Anna is the unhappy victim not of marriage but of her adultery, which leads to her literal death.

Tolstoy addresses Dumas' idea of the "incessant, daily struggle": "As a bachelor [Levin] had watched the conjugal life of others, the petty cares, the squabbles, the jealousy, with an inward smile of contempt. In his own future married life, he was convinced, there could be nothing of that sort. . . . But now, lo and behold, instead of life with his wife having an individual pattern, it was, on the contrary, made up of all those petty trifles" (436). Kitty's zeal for trifles is opposed to Levin's "early ideal of lofty happiness." Their first two months of married life are remembered as "the bitterest and most humiliating period of their lives," but their quarrels "afford both disenchantment and new enchantment," as Levin realizes that his wife is part of himself (439, 437). The struggle is not for dominance, but comes from the difficulty of merging two lives.

Tolstoy has Levin note his own initial irritation at Kitty's inactivity: "She does nothing and is quite content" (442). But the narrator knows she is "building her nest for the future" (442). Levin loses an early struggle, when Kitty insists on going with him to help Nikolay, but Tolstoy shows that his resistance was based on false scruples, and the happy outcome is his recognition of Kitty's deeper, specifically feminine wisdom in helping the dying: "He could not help knowing that he had more intellect than his wife and Agatha Mikhailovna. . . . He knew too that many great and virile minds, whose thoughts on death he had read, had brooded over it and yet did not know one hundredth part of what his wife and Agatha Mikhailovna knew. Different as those two women were . . . in this respect they were absolutely alike. Both knew, without a shadow of a doubt, what sort of a thing death was . . . they were never under an instant's uncertainty as to how to deal with the dying, and felt no fear" (451). Thus Tolstoy agrees with Dumas about the painful conflict between the masculine and feminine in marriage but disagrees that the two are irreconcilable. The intellect and instinct are complementary, not hostile forces.

Dumas' description of married life moves on directly to pregnancy. "All the feminine of the two families . . . gathers around her to isolate her from you. She is so inexperienced! So delicate!" (40). There is no equality with woman in childbirth. "Is it you who will be torn up right to your entrails? Is it you who will lose the grace of your contours and the purity of your shape? Is it you who could die of it?" (46). These ideas are allotted to Anna's attitude to childbearing in her adulterous relationship, not to Kitty's in her marriage to Levin. Furthermore, Dumas continues, during childbirth, "the doctor says the husband is more of a nuisance than a help. Men aren't strong enough to bear this spectacle" (48). When you finally see her, she wants to be spoiled, "'because, you know, I'm going to be nursing.' . . . And that's it for a year" (49–51).

The story of Levin's marriage to Kitty naturally follows the same sequence of wedding–married life–childbirth and acknowledges some of the truth of Dumas' words about "the feminine of the two families" in his account. Book 6 begins with Kitty pregnant at Pokrovskoe, where Dolly and her children, their mother the princess, as well as Kitty's friend Varenka have come for the summer: "All these people were friends or relations of Levin's wife, and though he liked them all he regretted a little his own Levin world and order of things, which was being smothered by this influx of the 'Shcherbatsky element,' as he called it to himself . . . the Levin spirit was completely suppressed" (500). As in Dumas' version, the feminine element does prevail over Levin in moving Kitty to Moscow to give birth and does gather, excluding Levin at one point when he comes onto the veranda as they are discussing Vronsky. "'I'm sorry to have broken in on your feminine parliament,' he said, glancing around at them all with vexation, perceiving that they had been discussing something which they would not talk about before him. For a second he found himself sharing Agatha Mikhailovna's discontent at having to boil the jam without water, and with the alien Shcherbatsky element in general" (505). But Levin and Kitty immediately set off to join the children picking mushrooms and have a tender talk full of mutual understanding: "He had quite forgotten the momentary unpleasant impression, and alone with her experienced, now that the thought of her approaching motherhood was never for a moment absent from his mind, a new and delicious bliss, quite pure from all alloy of the senses, in being near the woman he loved" (506).

Tolstoy refutes each of Dumas' points about woman's winning a battle over man in marriage and childbirth. Levin shares as much as possible the agony of Kitty's labor. The doctor, rather than excluding Levin, sympathizes with him: "We husbands cut a sorry figure at such times," and Kitty, rather than wanting to be spoiled, is concerned about Levin's condition after she gives birth: "She took his hand and asked him if he had slept" (643, 649). Rather than separating husband from wife, Kitty's first nursing of their son moves Levin to tears and in a later scene is the occasion for Levin's new recognition of his love for his son after his fright during a thunderstorm. All of these moments are associated with a religious sense of the great mystery of birth, paralleled with the mystery of death:

> He only knew and felt that what was happening was similar to what had happened a year ago at the deathbed in a provincial hotel of his brother Nikolay. . . . But that sorrow and this joy were equally beyond the usual plane of existence: they were like openings through which something sublime became visible . . . the soul soared to heights it had never attained before, while reason lagged behind, unable to keep up.
>
> "Lord have mercy on us and succour us," he repeated incessantly, appealing to God, in spite of his long and, as it seemed, complete alienation from religion. (646)

Like marriage and death, childbirth is associated with a sacrament, baptism, and Levin is closest to accepting God at those mysterious transitions in his life. Thus Tolstoy rephrases Dumas' terms. Dumas, more trivially, views religious forces as allied with woman against the man: "Woman begins to escape man through the priest . . . he does not leave her solely under the jurisdiction of her husband. The man, *occupied with serious things,* always entrusts the children's souls to the woman. . . . The priest has but one adversary, the lover" (20).

Tolstoy shows not a struggle between man and woman, or man and priest (and in any case, the Orthodox priest's relationship to his parishioners is different from the Catholic priest's), but the struggle of man to give up his intellect to attain the wisdom that woman, unburdened by intellect-inspired doubts, attains intuitively—in the same way Kitty knows how to help the dying Nikolay, in labor she is confident and joyful despite her pain. Furthermore, Tolstoy shows the care of the children's souls to be of crucial importance, contrasting Dolly's attention to her children's moral and spiritual qualities with Anna's inattention to Annie and making Levin's son the focus of his spiritual epiphany.

In the story of Kitty and Levin, Tolstoy rejects Dumas' overall formulation about the embattled relationship between the sexes. The novel, however, accepts Dumas' sociological formulation dividing woman into three types, women of the temple (virgins); women of the household (wives); and women of the street (courtesans) (8). Sergey Tolstoy reports his father telling him the same thing, without attribution to Dumas: "About women he said that there are three categories," enumerating the same three.[32] In the course of *Anna Karenina,* Varenka remains in the first category; Kitty moves from the first to the second, in keeping with the church sacraments; and Anna moves from the second to the third, breaking the sacrament of marriage and going against that of christening, implicit in motherhood. Both Dumas and Tolstoy condemn their adulteresses to death. But Dumas is happy to have the husband take it upon himself to kill his adulterous wife, while since for Tolstoy it is precisely the sacrament that is broken, it is for God to judge, and certainly not for man to execute. Hence the epigraph points, as Eikhenbaum says, to the divine pronoun: "Vengeance is *mine.*"[33]

D'Ideville wrote a letter to Dumas that prefaced his first letter to *Le Soir,* adding an epigraph from the Gospel of John: "Let him who is without sin cast the first stone" (8:7). He concludes with a response to Dumas' long deliberation on Adam and Eve in *Man-Woman*: "You are a man of the Bible, monsieur, the man of Jehovah and Moses. . . . We are the disciples of Christ the merciful [*Christ-doux*], the servants of him who pardoned the adulterous woman." As we saw, Karenin uses John 8:7, d'Ideville's epigraph, in claiming (possibly hypocritically) that he refuses to judge Anna. But Levin does judge fallen women: "Christ would never have spoken those words if he had known how they would be misused!" (38). Whatever sympathy Tolstoy had with Dumas, his epigraph, drawn from both the Old Testament, where it is spoken wrathfully by Jehovah (Deuteronomy 32:35), and the New, where it is interpreted mercifully by Paul (Romans 12:18–19), is closer in intent to d'Ideville's New Testament one and to the many who opposed Dumas.[34]

Dumas' extreme position led his critics to propose a solution, and an argument arose over the issue of divorce. D'Ideville believed that divorce was the remedy for situations that led to adultery, but Emile de Girardin in *his* letter to Dumas saw problems with it: "Divorce, without regard to modesty, invites [the judges] and the public into the mysteries of the conjugal alcove and the most intimate secrets of the life of families whose walls it demolishes. Divorce makes marriage into a school for scandal."[35] Tolstoy addresses the subject in Karenin's investigation of divorce; Karenin's objection to granting Anna's request makes the same argument as Girardin. When he goes to Moscow armed with Vronsky's letters to Anna in order to consult a lawyer, he pales when he learns that "letters may certainly serve as partial confirmation, but direct evidence is required—that is, of eye-witnesses" (336). Karenin's shame is shown to be focused on what others think of him rather than on his feeling for Anna—he is excessively concerned with his public position. Tolstoy's unsympathetic portrait of the smug divorce lawyer catching moths and resolving to reupholster his furniture in velvet conveys Tolstoy's view of divorce as a legalistic tinkering by man with a pledge made before God, which cannot obviate the sin of adultery. But at the same time, he engages with Girardin's part of the debate in his sympathy for the anguish of women trapped in unsuitable marriages, which is at the heart of *Anna Karenina.*

Dumas' play *Claude's Wife,* like his essay *Man-Woman,* analyzes the problem of adultery from the husband's point of view. Tolstoy addresses the relationship between Dumas' adulteress Césarine and her husband Claude in his treatment of Karenin and Anna.

Claude's Wife

The Dubourg murder case inspired Dumas to write *Man-Woman* because, as he explains to d'Ideville at the beginning of the essay, he had been planning to write a play about an adulteress for four or five years, and thus "your article is a pretext to write, and my letter is like an advertisement for my play" (2).

Claude's Wife appeared the year after *Man-Woman,* with a preface this time addressed to Monsieur Cuvillier Fleury, who had attacked Dumas' "Kill her!" in the *Journal des débats,* of which he was the editor. In his preface, Dumas explains *his* interpretation of John 8:7: "All my life I have tried to reconcile in my life and in my soul the [Civil] Code and this Gospel." Jesus did not pardon the adulteress, he argues, He just said: "Let him who is without sin cast the first stone." If anyone had announced he was sinless, Jesus would have said, "Strike!" ("*Frappe!*") "So my 'Kill her' that so scandalized everyone is only a paraphrase of Christ's word."[36] Dumas says his play is a symbolic work. Its heroine, Césarine, is the Beast—prostitute, infanticide, adulteress. Times are perilous, and his play is needed. "I am convinced that the future has never been more menacing, and that the Beast has never been more insatiable" (80).

In Césarine Dumas constructs the worst possible adulteress. Tolstoy's words about wanting to depict an adulteress who was "only pitiable and not guilty" were addressed to his wife in 1870, but after reading Dumas' essay, in 1873 he began by making Anna not only unredeemably evil but unattractive as well (1873). Like Césarine, Anna has, as the commentator to the variants says, "too strong an egotistical thirst for personal happiness."[37] As Tolstoy worked on the novel, while incorporating his response to Dumas, his initial impulse took precedence and Anna evolved into an attractive woman. In this third stage, Tolstoy appears to be in dialogue with *Claude's Wife* as well, as he examines a woman's *understandable* adultery.

Dumas' play opens with a scene that Tolstoy places later in Anna's drama: the return of the adulteress to her home. After three months away, the wayward Césarine knocks at the French windows of the grand salon of her former house at seven in the morning. She has not let anyone know she is coming; she has left her luggage at the station and come on foot. Admitted by the maid, Césarine tells her, "I have been sick. I almost died . . . so sick that I took confession"; while sick, she says, "I saw nothing but [Claude]."[38] She has read of her husband's important invention in the newspapers. The maid, her confidante, tells her that Claude has maintained absolute silence about her since she left, saying that she has gone to her sick grandmother. Césarine asks if Claude has taken up with Rebecca, a young woman living in the house with her father, Daniel. The maid answers, "You forget that your husband is the most honest man on earth" (6).

In Tolstoy's version of this scene Anna is indeed pitiable as well as guilty. When she returns secretly to the house after her trip to Italy, unlike Césarine, she feels the guilt of the adulteress but is drawn irresistibly to see her son on his birthday. Although Seryozha has been told that his mother is dead, for him she is "not dead"—in him lies the potential for her moral resurrection. Césarine hopes to resurrect her husband's love for her, but only in order to steal his patent on a design for a small cannon (a humanitarian invention that will somehow reduce casualties in war). Further, Césarine's having almost died, taking confession, and attempting to reunite with Claude are in Tolstoy's rendition made sincere: Anna, in a feverish state, is reconciled with Karenin, who experiences true Christian forgiveness commensurate with her sincere repentance. Tolstoy rewrites even the maid's role: Césarine tells the maid Edmée, who eavesdrops on all the household conversations, about her plans of amorous conquest. In contrast, after confessing her adultery to Karenin in the carriage, Anna is ashamed before everyone:

"She could not bring herself to ring for her maid, and still less to go downstairs and see her son and his governess. The maid, who had long had an ear at the door, at last came in unsummoned. Anna glanced inquiringly into her face, and blushed with alarm" (262–63). Anna's relation to her maid becomes more like Césarine's to Edmée only after she enters into her life with Vronsky. Her maid is with her at Vronsky's estate at Vozdvizhenskoe, marking Anna's descent into adultery.

Césarine has literally abandoned the child of one of her many adulterous affairs, visiting it twice in three years and leaving it to die at the home of its wet nurse. Of her child's death, her husband says, "When it died, you saw only one thing, that there was no more proof of your guilt, and you rejoiced; I cried!" (64).

Like Claude, Karenin is able to feel compassion for the illegitimate infant, identifying with its abandonment and guiltless in relation to it. Tolstoy isolates the moral and psychological aspects of Anna's feelings, contrasting her intense love for her legitimate son (whom she nonetheless abandons for her lover) with her lack of feeling for her illegitimate daughter. The baby Annie is, in contrast to Césarine's, surrounded by every luxury money can buy, but her nursery at Vronsky's estate is a sterile place that Anna is unfamiliar with. That the maternal instinct can be driven out by sexual passion is the most reprehensible aspect of her conduct and is the proof of the sacrilegious nature of adultery for Tolstoy. Anna herself recognizes this: "If I ran away and abandoned my son, I should be behaving like the most infamous and wickedest of women. He knows that, and knows I could never do it" (267). Yet she does, and the shame of it makes religious solace impossible. "She knew . . . that she could find no help in religion unless she were prepared to renounce that which made up for her the whole meaning of life" (263). The separation from her husband, and hence her son, separates her from God.

Césarine is unmitigatedly perfidious and never gains our sympathy. We see no cause for her behavior, whereas Anna's desire for passionate love that Karenin is incapable of giving her is understandable. Nonetheless we sympathize with Karenin despite his sanctimoniousness, because he has done no wrong, and he suffers.

> His wife's words, confirming his worst suspicions, had sent a cruel pang to his heart. . . . But to his surprise and delight he felt completely freed . . . from the doubts and agonies of jealousy that had been torturing him of late.
>
> He felt like a man who has had a tooth out that has been aching for a long time . . . The agony had been strange and terrible but now it was over; he felt he could live again and think of something other than his wife. (254)

Claude says something similar: "It is this woman . . . who has forever killed the smile on my lips. She would have killed me if I hadn't conquered her and exterminated her in me" (18). Dumas allows this to stand without any irony or ambiguity; Claude is absolutely in the right.

While, like Claude, Karenin is an honorable member of the aristocracy whose work is publicly esteemed, unlike Claude, he is shown to bear some responsibility for his wife's faithlessness. He is perfectly innocent in only the legal sense. Anna's resentment of him is exaggerated, but not without foundation.

Claude is genuinely selfless and able to forgive Césarine her adultery, and she reproaches him for it: "You pardoned me, but from on high, from a distance, in disengaging yourself from me, in withdrawing, in ceasing to be a man. You should have insulted me, thrown me at your feet and pardoned me like a man. . . . I don't understand grand sentiments and half-pardons" (64). When Césarine attempts to get her husband's pardon and he refuses, she rails: "Ah! Implacable Christian in your conscience and righteousness, I'll lead you like myself to blasphemy and curses" (66). Anna is similarly angry with Karenin: "Of course, he's always in the right; he's a Christian, he's magnanimous! Yes, the mean, odious creature!" (266). Dumas' heroine is angry that her plan fails; Anna's anger expresses her guilt that she can no longer see herself as a righteous Christian.

Karenin infuriates Anna with his dry, distant attempt to cope with her faithlessness. "What does he care, if he can talk so calmly? If he were to kill me, if he were to kill Vronsky, I might respect him. But no. All he cares about is pretence and propriety" (189). Unlike Césarine, Anna feels guilt toward her husband, which leads her to exaggerate his alleged faults. Césarine tells Claude she feels "anger, the need to revenge myself on you, to make you suffer" (65). Tolstoy reverses this—Karenin had wanted revenge on Anna and Vronsky (440). Later Anna, in her deranged state, wants revenge against Vronsky, not Karenin, and kills herself in part to punish him.

Asked why he did not divorce Césarine, Claude replies: "Separated from me, she would have taken my name with her. This name which I received in an honorable state and which I wanted to leave as I received it . . . she would have dragged publicly through all sorts of mud, and I would have come upon it every moment in the scandals of society. . . . And then I have long hoped that I would enlighten her and save her!" (19).

Karenin too is concerned about his good name: "I shall ignore [Anna's infidelity] as long as the world knows nothing of it, so long as my name is not disgraced" (291). He too thinks of reforming his faithless wife—"I shall devote part of my energies to her reformation and salvation"—but the narrator tells us that Karenin is "perfectly aware that . . . an attempt at reformation could lead to nothing but lies" (257). Again, where Dumas makes a black-and-white case for the husband's legitimate anger and right to murder his wife, Tolstoy presents ambiguities and conflicts: Karenin does not, at least initially, delude himself, and although the book endorses his Christian impulses, they are irrelevant to Anna's feelings and so ultimately incapable of changing anything.

Both authors treat the question of religious hypocrisy. Dumas' villain Césarine is the hypocritical Christian in Dumas' play: asked whether she plans to seduce Daniel, she replies, "A Jew! Me, who has just taken confession!" (3). Until Tolstoy's first attempt to publish the novel, Anna too was to have been a religious hypocrite, the star of a Petersburg circle of the "Khomyakov-Orthodox-feminine-court-slavophile-virtuous" sort (variant No. 19), such as Lydia Ivanovna later becomes, speaking, like her, in an affected, ecstatic elevated tone.[39] But as Anna became a more attractive and ambiguous character, Karenin correspondingly became less pitiable, making it more possible to sympathize with Anna's adultery. In this process, he took over her attribute of hypocritical Christianity, one that Anna may have initially inherited from Césarine. First Karenin uses religion to justify maintaining the "nominal status quo" with Anna and to satisfy his desire to punish her: "Though in passing through these painful moments he had not once thought of seeking guidance in religion, now that his decision corresponded, as it seemed to him, with the requirements of religion, this religious sanction to his decision afforded him complete satisfaction . . . no one would be able to say that he had not acted in accordance with the principles of that religion that he had always held aloft" (257–58). After Anna has left him, Karenin's pseudo-Christianity becomes even more marked, as in his abandonment he falls into the manipulative hands of Lydia Ivanovna. Through her, Karenin allows himself to be cruel to Anna and Seryozha in the name of a vague faith of the sort popular among the intelligentsia in the 1870s: As Karenin instructs Oblonsky in Petersburg, "We are saved through Christ who suffered for us. We are saved by faith" (666).[40] Karenin decides the question of whether to grant Anna a divorce on the instructions of the charlatan Landau, issued during his "real or pretended trance" (668). Unlike Claude's Christianity, Karenin's is fallible, subject to irrational forces, as any belief must be.

Oblonsky proves correct when he tells Karenin that the divorce is a matter of "life or death" for Anna (655). Karenin indirectly condemns her to death by refusing Oblonsky's request. In an early draft Karenin (then called Stavrovich, and not yet a hypocrite) loads a pistol and goes to see Anna, who lives with her lover. But even as Tolstoy wrote this scene, he rejected the idea of the wronged husband shooting his wife; by the end of the scene Stavrovich is trying to save her through religion, but Anna nonetheless subsequently kills herself as she does in the final version.[41] When Claude finds Césarine seducing his protégé to learn the secret of the cannon, he shoots her, because she has proven herself beyond saving.

In *Man-Woman,* Dumas builds his justification for murdering the adulteress on a lengthy analysis of the female principle in the Bible, in which woman is man's inferior, the temptress who leads Adam astray. In *Anna Karenina,* no women are temptresses or inferior to their mates as Césarine is, and religion itself is shown to be vulnerable to interpretation and misuse, a reflection of the practitioner. Self-interest can generate hypocritical acts allegedly inspired by Christian faith; an avowed agnostic may act in accordance with Christian precepts. Tolstoy puts his belief in the unlikely mouth of Oblonsky, who says blithely, "Faith without works is dead" (665). In *Anna Karenina,* Tolstoy adds complexity to Dumas' too-easy portrait of a virtuous Christian husband faced with an unredeemable wife. In Tolstoy's novel, adultery's relationship to Christianity is based on the sacraments that are the foundation of family life; both men and women err when they break them. And yet the whole problem of the novel is that this truth cannot solve Anna's dilemma, created by the legal system, social custom, circumstance, and human personality. How can Christian truth be reconciled with the natural, human needs, however "disgusting" Tolstoy may find them, described in French novels? The collision of these worlds, emblematized by Kitty's reading of Levin's diaries before their wedding, creates the tension in *Anna Karenina.* Despite the Christian decency of almost all the characters, the sexual dimension of man-woman relationships creates problems in the happy marriage of Kitty and Levin as well as the unhappy one of Dolly and Oblonsky, causes the failure of Varenka and Koznyshev to become engaged, and leads to the tragedy of all involved in Anna's and Vronsky's adultery.

Although Dumas' moral stance on the woman question impressed Tolstoy, he was unwilling to accept his characterization of the battle between the sexes. In his account of Kitty and Levin's courtship and marriage, he presents a touching (and idealized) counterexample of a more Rousseauian kind: a prelapsarian Emile and Sophie, based on the early stages of his own marriage. He answers Dumas' somewhat simplistic polemics in novelistic form that has greater potential for identification and entails more ambiguity; we owe some of the most moving moments in *Anna Karenina* to Dumas' stimulus. In those scenes Tolstoy, with his remarkable capacity to identify with women, rejects Dumas' cynical view of Woman's manipulation of Man. Tolstoy gives a more profound and far-reaching response to Flaubert's novel, *Madame Bovary.*

GUSTAVE FLAUBERT

Madame Bovary

Did Tolstoy intend a dialogue with Flaubert's *Madame Bovary* when he wrote *Anna Karenina*? Eikhenbaum quotes S. de Pirelée's "Leon Tolstoy" as an example of judgments widespread in the French press that *Anna Karenina* "makes one recall" *Madame Bovary.*[42] George Steiner, adducing several important parallels, concluded that "all that can be said is that *Anna Karenina* was written in some awareness of its predecessor."[43] But the evidence of that awareness is so abundant and suggestive that it is worth examining the possibility of a more detailed dialectic than Eikhenbaum and Steiner propose.[44]

Tolstoy arrived in Paris on February 21, 1857. Less than a month earlier, on January 29, Flaubert and the editors of *La Revue de Paris* had been taken to court for "outrage to public and religious morals and to morality."[45] The defendants were acquitted of all charges, which verdict was announced on February 7.[46] Tolstoy alludes to none of this in his diary, noting on the day of his arrival, "spent a lot of money, saw absolutely nothing. Diarrhea."[47] In Paris he spent a lot of time with Turgenev, went frequently to the opera, and admired the many plays of Molière he attended. He also read a lot of Balzac—*Cousine Bette,* as well as the foreword to the *Human Comedy,* which he finds "petty and arrogant" (*melko i samonadeiano* [April 10]), and deplores Balzac's "depravity" (*depravatsiia* [April 20]). While Tolstoy was reviling Balzac, Michel Levy brought out *Madame Bovary* in book form (in mid-April), which was followed by a flurry of reviews, in Sainte-Beuve's regular Monday column for *Le Moniteur Universel,* and in all the major journals; later there were responses by George Sand, Baudelaire, and many others. Fifteen thousand copies of the novel were sold in two months.[48] As Francis Steegmuller put it, "since the death of Balzac, no novel had so impressed the public."[49]

But Tolstoy says nothing about all this in his diaries. In fact, he who says so much about so many things over so many decades says almost nothing about Flaubert's novel.[50] When G. A. Rusanov spent two days talking about literature with him in August of 1883, he mentioned Flaubert: "*Madame Bovary* T. had forgotten, but he remembers that when he read it, he had 'liked it'" ("'*ponravilos' eto*'").[51] Forgotten it!

Tolstoy did, however, express his admiration for Flaubert years later. In an interview with a French journalist in 1904, he said, "One of my most favorite writers is your incomparable Flaubert. There is a truly magnificent artist, strong, exact, harmonious, full-blooded, perfect. His style is filled with the purest beauty. Can one say this of many writers?"[52] Furthermore, Tolstoy's library contained a copy of the Russian translation of *Madame Bovary* published in *Biblioteka dlia chteniia* in 1858.[53] Interestingly, it had been torn out of the journal and bound together with Shakespeare's *Othello,* suggesting that Tolstoy did indeed read Flaubert's novel in the context of the adultery question that so occupied him in the early 1870s.[54]

The fact that both Flaubert's and Tolstoy's novels belong to the genre of the novel of adultery could account for some of the similarities of plotline: a woman in her twenties with a young child is married to a man she finds dull (and who becomes ludicrous and pitiful in her eyes once betrayed); she takes a passionate lover, and the relationship deteriorates into sensuality, in part due to its illicit nature. The women begin to imagine the decline of their lovers' ardor; with Emma Bovary it is her second lover, Leon, who brings out her fears of losing him—like Anna, Emma becomes more and more demanding, increasing her lover's alienation. Both Leon's and Vronsky's mothers oppose their sons' liaisons—the women are jeopardizing their sons' careers. The adulteress tries to be ever more physically alluring but becomes jealous and desperate as she feels she is losing her lover. With nothing meaningful left, she commits suicide in a moment of frenzy. The novel passes judgment on her—she has broken both divine and human law, but she has our sympathy inasmuch as we are made to consider society's complicity in the adulteress's unresolvable dilemma.

No doubt it is this fairly elaborate and precise set of parallels that has led many critics to note, en passant, certain similar features between the two novels—the whole description of the decline in the relationships between Emma and Leon and Anna and Vronsky, for example.[55] But none of them has proposed an overall relationship of *Anna Karenina* to *Madame Bovary.* Steiner, for all his initial disavowal that no more can be said, seems to be nursing a suspicion: he writes that Anna's inability to focus on reading her book on the train ride home to Petersburg "seems to derive directly from Tolstoy's remembrance of *Madame Bovary.*" And when Anna suddenly notices the absurdity of Karenin's ears at the station, Steiner queries: "Is this not Tolstoy's version of Emma Bovary's discovery that Charles makes uncouth noises while eating?"[56]

It is worth pursuing Steiner's speculation that Tolstoy incorporates remembered details of Flaubert's novel into *Anna Karenina.* The two sets Steiner mentions cannot be said to be central in themselves. Given the extensive congruence of the novels' plots, it would be unlikely that these would be the only details to correspond in over eight hundred (English) pages. There are remarkable parallels between the two novels, not only in theme and plotline but in character description, motifs, and central emblems, suggesting a carefully structured polemic.

Heroines There are several similarities in appearance between Emma and Anna, though they may carry different meanings in the text; it will be possible to infer what Tolstoy might be suggesting by these parallels once they are sketched out. Emma surprises Rodolphe by being "turned out like a Parisian!"; her elegance of dress and manner is remarked by all throughout the book. She has a "bird-like tread" and dark hair.[57] At her father's farm, the wind ruffles "stray wisps of hair at the nape of her neck" (30). Her eyes are "made to look black" by her "long curving lashes" (28, 148). During her relationship with Rodolphe, Emma is repeatedly described with narrowed eyelids or half-closed eyes (159, 36, 175, 210). These features will recall Anna's elegance of figure, light tread, black hair with "the willful little curls that always escaped . . . on the nape of her neck" (72), and her habit, which grows after she enters into adultery, of narrowing her eyes, squinting through her "thick lashes" (56).[58]

The break in the heroines' lives is located in a ballroom scene.[59] The viscount's ball at La Vaubyessard gives Emma her fatal taste for luxury, aristocracy, and sensuality, emblematized by the greenness of the silk border on the cigar case Charles finds in the road on the way home to Tostes. This green is related to the color of both of Emma's lovers' coats: Rodolphe is wearing a "green velvet frock coat" when Emma first sees him, and Leon wears a green coat to his tryst with Emma at the Rouen cathedral, which leads to the infamous carriage ride (140, 250). An elegant ball also determines Anna's fate: there Vronsky forsakes Kitty for her. The ball scenes are naturally characterized by luxuriousness, which in both is indicated by hothouse plants: it is winter in Moscow when Kitty wears a rose in her hair and Anna has pansies in hers; the landing with the mirror at which Kitty pauses is lined with "growing plants," and the staircase is "flower-decked" (70, 72). The ladies at La Vaubyessard wear in their hair "forget-me-nots, jasmine, pomegranate blossoms, wheatears or cornflowers," while Emma, like Kitty, wears "a rose" in her chignon; the guests are served pomegranates and pineapple (63, 62). The elegant foreign influences in Moscow are French or English, while Anna wears Venetian lace; in France the old chateau at La Vaubyessard has been torn down and a "modern building in the Italian style" erected in its place (59). Emma's fatal dance is a sensual waltz with the Viscount, which leaves her dizzy and panting; the waltz is the determining dance for both Anna and Kitty, for it is the dance that makes Vronsky's preference for Anna clear to Kitty (66, 73).[60]

Anna shares another determining scene with Emma: the opera. Both Flaubert and Tolstoy maintain an ironic distance from the opera, describing it as the meeting place of the best society. Flaubert stresses the provincialism of the audience and the performance of the celebrated tenor Lagardy, who combines "ingredients of the hairdresser and toreador" (235). Tolstoy focuses on the hypocrisy and affectation of members of high society who condemn Anna for crimes they themselves commit. The performance by Patti is incidental, but the apparently random bit of social chitchat that closes the scene echoes Flaubert's Lagardy: Vronsky's friend Stremov says to Anna, "There are no more tenors. *Le moule en est brisé* [the mould for them has been broken]" (499). The opera scene determines Emma's next adulterous affair: from being in love with the legend of the tenor Lagardy, she begins to imagine herself his mistress; at that point Leon appears in her box and her fantasy devolves to him. The failure of Emma's second attempt to find love leads to her demise. For Anna, her evening at the opera reveals conclusively the impossibility of her position in society, which contributes to her final tragedy.

There are more similarities, for example, the way their husbands summon them to bed. Charles says, "Come on, Emma, it's time" while she is waiting for Rodolphe (181). Karenin comes in to Anna's room at midnight in his bedroom slippers and says, "Time for bed now" with a "special smile," and Anna, thinking of how Vronsky looked at Karenin at the station, goes into the bedroom with her usual fire "quenched or hidden far away" (103). We can add to Steiner's soup-slurping / ears protruding parallel Charles's "stubby" fingers and Karenin's habit of cracking his knuckles, Charles's "common" manner and Karenin's pedantic one (199).

Tolstoy uses several motifs to characterize Anna that Flaubert had used for Emma. Vronsky's relations with his racehorse Frou Frou are clearly meant to relate to his affair with Anna; Emma's affair with Rodolphe begins when they go riding together on his horses. The horses and heroines are linked by a bird motif: In Tolstoy's novel, after Frou Frou falls, she begins "fluttering on the ground . . . like a wounded bird," while Anna in the stands is described a few pages later as "fluttering like a caged bird" (182, 192). Emma has a "bird-like step," swallows dart by when Emma comes to Abbé Bournisien for spiritual guidance; Rodolphe's house has two "swallow-tailed weathervanes"; and Emma's dreams are said to "[drop] in the mud like wounded swallows" (120, 124, 176, 197). Flaubert names the coach that takes Emma to Rouen for her trysts with Leon the Hirondelle, which means "swallow" in French. Thus the bird motif connects the heroines to their adulterous affairs.

Anna and Emma share another motif—fog, haze, mist. When Emma takes Rodolphe as her first lover, she is ecstatic: "A misty blue immensity lay about her" (175). The scene of her first tryst with Rodolphe is surrounded by mist, from the "haze in the poplars" to Emma's features, which are discernible "in a haze of blue" through her blue veil; her vision of eloping with Rodolphe "hovered on the horizon . . . in a haze of blue" (171, 172, 208).[61] Flaubert's narrator is the creator of the motif, while in Tolstoy's novel Anna herself speaks of the blue haze, associating it with the innocence of first love: "'I remember that blue haze, like the haze on the mountains in Switzerland. That haze which envelops everything at that blissful time when childhood is just coming to an end and its huge merry circle narrows to a path which one treads gaily yet with dread into life's corridor.' . . . Kitty smiled. . . . 'How did she go through it? How I should like to know the whole romance of her life!' she thought, recalling the unromantic exterior of Anna's husband" (67). Tolstoy uses the Russian word "*tuman*" in all instances of the motif, sometimes assigning a color. We can use "haze" throughout except for Levin's fields ("*tuman*" is sometimes rendered both as "haze" and "mist" within a single translation), giving its color when it is specified. The motif appears again when Kitty realizes the growing attraction between Anna and Vronsky at the ball and "a haze spread[s] over the ball and the whole world in Kitty's soul" (74). Tolstoy uses the blue haze for what he deems a genuine form of ecstatic love; by contrast, the violent break of the natural order through adultery he associates with the shrieking, whirling snowstorm surrounding the future lovers' meeting on the platform, though Vronsky's pursuit produces "joyful, glowing and exhilarating" visions in Anna, similar to Emma's delight at her new role of adulteress (95). Tolstoy's recasting of the haze motif is hinted at just before Kitty refuses Levin: for her "a future with Levin appeared wrapped in haze," which appears at this point in the novel to be a neutral image (43). Tolstoy reserves grey mist for another kind of bliss on Levin's estate, of which more in a moment (138).

These similarities between Anna and Emma not only make us aware of their resemblance but underscore how very dissimilar they are. Emma is hopelessly shallow and selfish, as is shown by her relationship to her daughter, Berthe. Before her affair with Vronsky, Anna is intelligent, direct, unpretentious, and a devoted mother. Emma's downfall, like Tatyana's in *Eugene Onegin,* is caused not by reading romantic novels, as her mother-in-law suggests, but rather by misreading them, identifying with their heroines in a particularly sensual and indiscriminate way. Anna, by contrast (here is Steiner's parallel again), is unable to read her English novel on her train ride home after dancing with Vronsky. "She was too eager to live herself. If she read how the heroine of the novel nursed a sick man, she wanted to be moving about a sickroom with noiseless tread herself" (115). When she does identify, it is to make an unconscious moral judgment: "The hero of the novel had nearly attained to his English happiness of a baronetcy, . . . and Anna wanted to go to the estate with him, when she suddenly felt that he must have been ashamed, and that she was ashamed for the same reason" (92). It is only the trivial Betsy Tverskaya and her circle who read like Emma and project role-playing onto Anna. Betsy reports that Liza Merkalov "raves" about Anna, who is "like a real heroine out of a novel" (271).

And this suggests Tolstoy's idea: Emma is conceived by Flaubert as an imitation, the product of *idées reçues,* of undigested clichés drawn from a hodgepodge of literature (much as Razumikhin accuses Raskolnikov of being a "translation"). After Emma first enters into adultery, "she remember[s] the heroines of books she had read, and that lyrical legion of adulteresses began to sing in her memory with sisterly voices that enchanted her" (175).

But Tolstoy wants to consider the dilemmas faced by the adulteress at the deepest level possible, and to do that he has his appealing heroine reject the accepted practice of deceiving her husband. The change from the early drafts of *Anna Karenina,* where Tolstoy described his adulteress as unattractive both physically and morally, suggests that as the novel evolved, he came to identify with her need for passionate love (to which his story "The Devil" testifies so vividly that it was only published after his death, in 1911). Her stature grew as his sympathy (and desire for complexity) increased.[62]

It is possible to understand Anna as an ideal version of Emma. Emma admires and imitates luxury; Anna already has it. Emma wants a passionate aristocratic dashing lover but finds only imitations of one; Anna gets Emma's wish in Vronsky.[63] Emma wants to be the heroine of a novel; Anna is seen as one by her peers. Emma fantasizes eloping to Italy with the pseudo-aristocrat Rodolphe (who clenches his teeth in predatory passion); Anna and the truly aristocratic Vronsky (of the "regular," "compact" teeth) actually do elope to Italy (173, 160, 164). In this way, Tolstoy isolates and distills the moral and psychological aspects of adultery for a young married woman, purifying it of the concern with social status and material luxury that obsess Emma and positing an intelligent, self-aware heroine.

The unfulfilled young woman with small child and uninspiring husband who takes a passionate lover and commits suicide is the obvious point of contact between the two novels. But Tolstoy incorporates a large array of more complex details and structures that show he had *Madame Bovary* in mind while writing *Anna Karenina.* An analysis of them will reveal Tolstoy's subtle reading and reinterpretation of Flaubert's novel.

Emblems Much has been written about the centrality of the railroad to Tolstoy's novel.[64] Anna and Vronsky meet at the Moscow station, where a peasant is killed by a train; their understanding is sealed during the snowstorm on the platform on the return trip; Anna throws herself under a train; and we see Vronsky for the last time on his way to war back again at the Moscow station. The train from the outset is associated with metallic clanking, with incipient romantic passion, and with the peasant's death, in which Anna sees an omen. Anna and Vronsky both dream of a dirty peasant with a matted beard, and, oddly, in both their dreams, he is speaking French. Vronsky "vividly recalled the peasant again and the incomprehensible French words the man had muttered, and a chill of horror ran down his spine" (324). In her dream Anna can make out the words *"il faut le battre, le fer; le broyer, le pétrir* [it must be beaten, the iron: pound it, knead it]" (329). And as Anna falls to the rails, "A little peasant muttering something was working at the rails" (695). The grotesqueness of the dream has to do in part with the incongruity of the muzhik, that essence of Russianness, speaking French. Throughout the novel the corrupt characters speak or read French, while the innocent ones are distorted by having to use French in elegant society, starting with the Tatar waiter who translates Levin's soup and kasha into "*kasha à la Russe*" (47). Like the French language, the railroad is an artificial foreign graft onto Russia causing, among other things, exaggerated centralization in the cities, as Levin says (510). The city in *Anna Karenina* is associated with luxury and debauchery; Levin has called Moscow a Babylon, as Countess Nordston tauntingly reminds him at Kitty's (45). And Flaubert does the same with Rouen: "that ancient Norman city lay outspread beneath [Emma's] eyes like an enormous metropolis, a Babylon awaiting her" (274).

The Yonville priest Bournisien warns against Emma's proposed trip to the opera in Rouen in language close to Tolstoy's in "What Is Art?": "'Where you have these couples brought together in luxurious surroundings, with all the adornment of worldly display, the barbarous dressing-up, . . . all that must breed a certain laxity, and give rise to unclean thoughts, impure temptations!'" (229).

The Hirondelle is the conveyance that makes impure temptations available to Emma Bovary. From the outset, the carriage has ominous dimensions, marking key moments in Emma's decline toward suicide. Charles and Emma arrive in Yonville on the Hirondelle to meet the members of the cast assembled at the Golden Lion (91). The Hirondelle passes as Leon brings Emma a cactus and while Rodolphe begins his verbal seduction of Emma at the fair (112, 159). Like the railroad, the Hirondelle is accompanied by the "rattle of old iron" (340). Tanner makes this connection too, noting that iron is "an inexplicably ominous part of [Emma's] surroundings."[65]

The railroad for Anna is associated with the French-speaking peasant; an analogous figure follows Emma alongside the Hirondelle:

> Up the hill, in the midst of the carriages, trudged an old tramp with his stick. A mass of rags covered his shoulders, his face was hidden by a battered beaver hat stuck on like an inverted bowl. When he removed this, he revealed where his eyelids should have been a pair of gaping holes all stained with blood. The flesh was shredded into red ribbons, discharging matter which had congealed in green scabs down to his nose. His black nostrils

> twitched convulsively. To address you, he threw back his head with an idiot laugh; and then his glaucous eyeballs, rolling in perpetual motion, shot up towards his temples and knocked against the open sore.
>
> As he followed the carriages he sang a little song:
>
> "When the sun shines warm above
> It turns a maiden's thoughts to love"
>
> And the rest of it was all birds and summertime and green leaves. (278)

The love song is in grotesque contrast to the revolting beggar, like the muzhik and the French-speaking world. The heroines' quests for romantic love are far removed from the reality of the world around them. The heart of both novels is contained in this emblem of adulteress, conveyance, and grotesque peasant; components of the image map the novels' denouements.

When Anna first meets Vronsky, she immediately thinks that the death of the peasant under the train is an omen. Emma too begins to sense something uncanny when the hideous beggar appears:

> Sometimes he would appear suddenly behind Emma, with his head uncovered. She would spring back with a cry . . .
>
> Often he would thrust his hat in at the window as the coach was moving off, clinging to the footboard with his other arm and getting splashed by the wheels. His voice, at first a feeble whine, rose shrilly, rending the darkness like a plaintive utterance of some obscure distress. Heard through the jingle of horse bells, the murmur of the trees and the rumbling of the empty carriage, it had a suggestion of remoteness that upset Emma. It penetrated the very depths of her being like a whirlwind in an abyss. It swept her away into the vast spaces of a limitless melancholy. However, Hivert . . . lashed out at the blind man with his whip. It cut across his sores, and he dropped in the mud with a howl of pain. (278)[66]

The jingling horse bells are part of a motif that culminates in the tolling of the church bells at Emma's death, just as the motifs of clanking metal accompany Anna's trajectory toward death. The muzhik reappears at Anna's death, and it is ambiguous whether she sees him in reality, or in her imagination:

> She tried to get up, to throw herself back; but something huge and relentless struck her on the head and dragged her back. "God forgive me everything!" she murmured, feeling the impossibility of struggling. A little peasant muttering something was working at the rails. And the candle by which she had been reading the book filled with trouble and deceit, sorrow and evil, flared

> up with a brighter light, illuminating for her everything that before had been enshrouded in darkness, flickered, grew dim, and went out forever. (695)

Emma's peasant also reappears at her deathbed scene just before the darkness:

> Suddenly there was a clumping of sabots on the pavement outside, the scraping of a stick, and a voice came up, a hoarse voice singing:
>
> "When the sun shines warm above,
> It turns a maiden's thoughts to love."
>
> Emma sat up like a corpse galvanized, her hair disheveled, her eyes fixed, gaping.
>
> "All across the furrows brown
> See Nanette go bending down,
> Gathering up with careful hand
> The golden harvest from the land."
>
> "The blind man!" she cried.
>
> And Emma started laughing, a ghastly frantic desperate laugh, fancying she could see the hideous face of the beggar rising up like a nightmare amid the eternal darkness.
>
> "The wind it blew so hard one day,
> Her little petticoat flew away!"
>
> A convulsion flung her down on the mattress. . . . She was no more. (337)

The song traces Emma's descent into gross carnality. By the end of the novel, the final realist image of Nanette bending over with no petticoat has replaced the earlier Romantic "thoughts of love" and "all the rest . . . about birds, sun and leafiness."[67] Tolstoy emphasizes the difference between Anna and Emma in his choice of the recurring image associated with Anna's death. Anna reacts with compassion and dread when the peasant is killed by the train. Her dream is associated with the guilt she feels from the beginning of her relationship with Vronsky, despite the real possibility of marriage to him, and the presence of the peasant at her death is emblematic of "the book filled with trouble and deceit, sorrow and evil" that her life has become. Unlike Emma, Anna has never deluded herself. Emma has no desire to marry either of her lovers and feels no sense of sin or remorse; Anna's honesty and conscience keep her from accepting the breach of the sacrament of marriage and doom her from the start.

Flaubert and Rousseau

> We only know life in this world and this is because if there is meaning in our life, then it is here in this world.
>
> Leo Tolstoy, 1880s

Tolstoy began his novel with the adultery story but was discontented with it and set it aside, even after having sent it off to the printer. Gradually he built what he called the novel's "scaffolding," the story of Levin.[68] What scaffolding does his story provide, and can a relationship be found here too to Flaubert's novel?

When the poet Fet read the first installment of *Anna Karenina,* he wrote Tolstoy, "Fools will carry on about Flaubert's realism, but here everything is ideal."[69] Indeed, this is why the novel resists any dramatic rendition that perforce focuses on the plotline; Anna's story seems merely to echo Emma's, but throughout *Anna Karenina,* Tolstoy infuses his ideals into every aspect of the life he depicts. His impulse is not to show the low aspect of the everyday, the evidence of a falling away from an ideal world, but a Matisse-like distillation of what its beauty consists in—Dolly's love and care of her children, Levin's cherishing of family tradition and farming his land, Karenin's dutiful government service and well-ordered life; the beautiful, loving embodiment of the life force in Anna and even in its undercut form in the jovial, kindly Oblonsky. *Anna Karenina* moves us particularly because it presents an *almost* ideal world of decent members of the Russian aristocracy, a portrait that is the opposite of Flaubert's ironic rejection of the restrictive pettiness of provincial France.

From the catalogue of similarities that point to differences between Flaubert's novel and Tolstoy's, it appears that Tolstoy restores the ideals that Flaubert shows are being lost. Both authors seem to locate the formulation of these ideals in Rousseau's work. As Milan Markovitch has noted, several of the incidents in *Anna Karenina* may have their source in *Julie*: like Levin, Wolmar works with his peasants, struggles with the question of faith, and begins to lose some of his skepticism when faced with the possibility of his wife's death.[70] With Rousseau's ideals so much in mind, how might Tolstoy have read *Madame Bovary?*

Flaubert lampoons Rousseau, displaying the degradation of Rousseau's ideals. Charles's first wife, the scrawny widow Dubuc, is named Héloise but is the antithesis of either a romantic lover or a wifely ideal, neither *une ancienne* or *nouvelle* Héloise. Homais invokes a confused version of Rousseau's ideas about education from *Emile* when he encourages Charles to agree to Emma's piano lessons so that she can teach her daughter: "It's my opinion that children ought to be taught by their mothers. It's an idea of Rousseau's, still a bit new, perhaps, but one that's bound to prevail in the end, like mother's milk and vaccination" (272). The lessons, of course, are a cover for Emma's adulterous trysts; and the novel shows Romantic literature to be the source of her malaise.[71] Another of Rousseau's views travestied is his argument against the theater made in his *Lettre à d'Alembert*: Flaubert puts it in the mouth of the inadequate priest Bournisien, where it is trivialized but proven in some sense to be valid—Emma *is* corrupted by going to the theater.

Flaubert shows the absence of Rousseau's ideas in contemporary French life. In *Madame Bovary* the reader can infer the possibility of Rousseauian ideals, in religion, in art, in true science, and in nature, through their travesty by the shallow characters' actions. Leon's seduction of Emma begins in the glorious Rouen cathedral, travestying religious ideals. The only place these ideals are present in positive form in the novel is in the perfection of Flaubert's verbal medium, which he famously agonized over. Not the characters but the author finds meaning in *Madame Bovary,* as in this impersonal evocation of natural beauty seen from the hill over Yonville: "The water flowing along beside the grass makes a streak of white between the meadow and the plowland, and the whole effect is that of a large mantle spread out before you, its green velvet collar trimmed with a silver braid" (82). The green and the velvet that had betokened luxury and romance for Emma and that Charles therefore uses for Emma's shroud occurs in its only pure role in Flaubert's narration; here the green velvet carries no pretensions, but rather functions as a metaphor that creates a synthesis between man and nature in artistic prose. Man plants the meadow but God makes it grow; the novelist, "like God in the universe," makes the metaphor and divine inspiration assists it to unify the novel's levels of meaning.[72]

While Flaubert leaves the glories of nature and his own description of them beyond the ken of his characters, Tolstoy uses Levin's world as scaffolding to integrate the ideals contained in *Julie* and *Emile* into the life of the Russian landowner. Flaubert's location of meaning in his own artistic synthesis is antithetical to Tolstoy's views, but Flaubert's green velvet fields are the point of origin of Levin's quest for meaning:

> On the Thursday the wind fell and a thick grey mist [*tuman*] rose as if to hide the secret of the changes nature was carrying on. Beneath the mist the snow-waters rushed down, the ice on the river cracked and moved, and the turbid, foaming torrents flowed quicker, until on the first Sunday after Easter toward evening the mists dissolved, the clouds broke into fleecy cloudlets and

> dispersed, the sky cleared, and real spring was there. . . . Last year's grass grew green again and the young grass thrust up its tiny blades. . . . Invisible larks broke into song above the velvety green fields [*nad barkhatom zelenei*] and the ice-covered stubble-land. . . . Spring had really come. (138–39)

This is the description of spring on Levin's estate, where, after Kitty has refused his offer of marriage, Levin locates his hopes for the future, first without Kitty, but by the end of the novel, together with her. Like Levin's economic analysis, in which agriculture is the basis of the wealth of a nation, his spiritual analysis bases moral existence in working his land.

The scene of Levin's joy on that spring morning brings together several motifs that are crucial to both novels: green, velvet, haze/mist, and cigars. All four motifs depict Emma's moral decline throughout *Madame Bovary*; Tolstoy redeploys them. In this scene, the first three motifs convey the joy of man's cooperation with nature while the fourth is made to travesty the first three as well as the morals that Tolstoy associates with Levin's farming.

Tolstoy continues the long description of Levin's spring with another "vast expanse of smooth, velvety green carpet" (*barkhatnym kovrom zelenia*) spreading before Levin as he goes about his estate planning to get the manuring done before the first planting (142). And then Oblonsky arrives: "[Levin] showed his guest into the spare bedroom, where Oblonsky's things—his bag, a gun in a case, and a satchel for cigars—were also brought" (145).

In *Madame Bovary,* cigars connote worldliness, luxury, and sensuality, originating in the aforementioned viscount's cigar case found on the road after the ball.[73] The priest has tobacco stains on his chest; Rodolphe smokes a cigar after he first seduces Emma in the woods; Emma gives Rodolphe a cigar case "just like the viscount's"; Leon lights a cigar waiting for Emma at the cathedral before their carriage ride (125, 174, 202, 250). And Emma goes out on the street in Rouen with a cigarette in her mouth, which marks her moral decline (204).

In *Anna Karenina,* cigars play a similar role, and Oblonsky is most frequently found smoking them. He calls them "the crown and hallmark of pleasure" (147). He lights one after dinner at Levin's, when he opines that "a pretty maid is better than an old nurse" (145). It is part of his moral blindness: Oblonsky "enjoyed his newspaper, as he did his after-dinner cigar, for the slight haze it produced in his brain" (6). This reminds us of his sister, who, as we have seen, associates blue haze with young love. So it is emblematic that Oblonsky should arrive at Levin's with an entire separate satchel for cigars, which, against the background of the twice-mentioned green velvet fields, is perceived by the reader as their antithesis. In this way, the luxury that Flaubert associates with the viscount's green-trimmed cigar case is transferred in *Anna Karenina* to the true source of well-being, the well-tended fruit of Levin's honest toil. Anna acquires a tortoise-shell cigar case by the time she meets Levin; it contains the cigarettes she now smokes, associating her with Oblonsky's sensuality and thereby tracing her decline as cigarettes do Emma's (631).

In *Madame Bovary,* the motifs shared by the two novels—haze, green, velvet, and cigars—are associated with Emma's descent into debauchery, but Tolstoy redistributes them: The first three are transferred to Levin's estate, while Oblonsky obtrudes upon them with his own tobacco haze.[74] Interestingly, the drafts for this scene do not combine the "green" with the "velvet," nor do they contain Oblonsky's satchel for cigars.[75] Instead of the latter, Tolstoy had only "[Oblonsky's] elegant things—straps, suitcase, bag, gun—. . . were carried in."[76] Later Tolstoy gave Oblonsky a cigar case (*sigarochnitsa*), which became a satchel (*sumka dlia sigar*) only when he prepared the first edition of the novel for publication as a separate book.[77] Anna's tortoise-shell cigar case is also absent from the published drafts of the scene.[78] The late addition of this system of details, which links the shared sensual aspect of the brother's and sister's personalities, suggests the importance of the motif for Tolstoy and his awareness of Flaubert's famous cigar case.

Another motif focuses the essential difference between Flaubert's and Tolstoy's novels: manure. Dmitri Merezhkovsky connects Tolstoy's love of manure to Rousseau in *Tolstoy as Man and Artist*: "The idyllic perfume of manure moved . . . Jean-Jacques Rousseau almost to tears. Leo, too, loves its savour."[79] Levin's joy in the mystery of spring in the scene is coupled with his concern that the manuring be done properly, and the word *manure* is repeated three times in two pages, in perfect keeping with the elevation of Levin's soul and our fresh amazement at nature's miraculous self-renewal. It is the same juxtaposition that had gotten Wordsworth and then Pushkin, into such trouble years earlier, that of the lofty with the lowly.[80]

Flaubert plays with this juxtaposition, also using manure, but to comic effect. Rodolphe begins his seduction of Emma at the Agricultural Fair in Yonville. He entrances her with talk of souls ordained to meet by fate against the counterpoint of the speeches from the Fair's tribunal. Both lines in the counterpoint are made up of horrendous clichés, each set designed to manipulate their audience. Romantic love and political idealism are equally travestied:

> "We, now, why did we meet? What turn of fate decreed it?
> "General Prize!" cried the Chairman.
> "Just now, for instance, when I came to call on you . . ."
> "Monsieur Bizet of Quincampoix."
> " . . . how could I know that I should escort you here?"
> "Manure!" (161)

Manure and fertilizers are mentioned three times in as many pages from the Yonville tribunal: "Work above all at the improvement of the soil, at producing rich fertilizers, at breeding horses, cows, sheep, pigs! [*les races chevalines, bovines, ovines et porcines!*]" (160).

What Flaubert uses to mock cynical political exploitation of a bovine peasantry Tolstoy makes the basis of Levin's faith, Levin who thinks joyfully of his future herd of cows bred from Pava even during his despair over Kitty's refusal. In Tolstoy's drafts for *Anna Karenina,* Levin was to have come to Moscow not to propose to Kitty but to show Pava at an agricultural fair. Oblonsky was to have met him there by chance, in the company of one of his mistresses.[81] In the draft we have the same intersplicing of the adulterous couple with the agricultural concerns as in *Madame Bovary,* with the same redistribution of censure: while Flaubert mocks both, Tolstoy shows the agricultural, marked by the manure motif, to embody an elevated moral ideal, while adulterous love is a travesty of the ideal of married love that is based in nature and ordained by God.

Thus in *Anna Karenina* Tolstoy examines the question of what men live by in order to consider the problem of adultery, returning to Rousseau for a basis. Anna's great tragedy is that she is condemned by the very honesty that constitutes Levin's virtue: both characters adhere to Tolstoy's Rousseauian ideals by refusing to abide by public opinion and meaningless social convention. But while Levin flouts the frivolous conventions of society, he comes to accept the wisdom of those related to God; Anna flouts both and is repaid accordingly.

Flaubert does not make this distinction; the villain of his novel is his bête noir, the *idée reçue,* the cliché, the unexamined view, and all the damage it can do. *Madame Bovary* ends not when Emma dies but after the chemist of Yonville, Monsieur Homais, has received the Legion d'Honneur.

Homais is the chief agent of events in the novel. He talks Charles into performing the operation on the clubfoot Hippolyte because he has read about a new method in the newspapers. Homais talks Charles into taking Emma to the theater in Rouen. It is among Homais's chemist supplies that Emma finds the arsenic to kill herself. Finally, it is Homais who tells the blind beggar to come to Yonville so that Homais can apply ointment to his eyes, which culminates in Homais having him imprisoned. Homais and the pseudoscience he preaches are a parody of Him who would make the lame walk and the blind see.

In *Anna Karenina,* Oblonsky acts as go-between, the agent of all the important interactions of the novel: he summons Anna to Moscow; brings Kitty and Levin together; obtains Karenin's consent for a divorce; and introduces Levin to Anna, to mention the most important. He corresponds in many ways to Homais, and even has the same number of children (six). Tolstoy endows Oblonsky with many loveable characteristics so that the reader tends to accept him as uncritically as Oblonsky's friends do but nonetheless shows that he lives without any moral basis for his actions and lacks the capacity for independent thought.[82]

Oblonsky is also a purveyor of the accepted view. A materialist like Homais, he gets all his opinions from the newspapers: "And although he was not particularly interested in science, art or politics, on all such subjects he adhered firmly to the views of the majority, as expressed by his paper. . . . The Liberal Party said, or rather assumed, that religion was only good as a curb on the barbarous part of the population; and indeed Oblonsky could not stand through even a short church service without aching feet, or understand the point of all that dreadful, high-flown talk about the other world, while one can live in this one so merrily" (6).

As a man of science, Homais has no use for religion and constantly baits Bournisien. Homais is a chemist, while Oblonsky is head of a government board, but the language describing him smacks of the pseudo-medical: Oblonsky, "who had a leaning towards physiology," is said to act "by a reflex action of the brain" and to "have a physical effect" on the people he meets (2, 13).[83]

Homais and Oblonsky are linked by a shellfish motif. In Moscow Oblonsky takes Levin to dinner against his will at a restaurant whose elegance seems to defile Levin's feelings for Kitty. They have three dozen oysters, described so as to emphasize Oblonsky's sensuality: "'Not bad,' he said, tearing the quivering oysters from their pearly shells with a silver fork and swallowing them one after another. 'Not bad,' he repeated, turning his moist and glittering eyes now to Levin, now to the Tatar" (32).

Homais arrives in Rouen and drags Leon off to a long lunch at a pretentious restaurant. Leon is in despair because he knows Emma is waiting for him but is forced to listen to Homais "expound immoral theories on women" (62). Red lobster claws had lain over the edge of the platter at La Vaubyessard as part of the abundant luxury; by the end of the book, via a series of permutations, the crustacean motif, like other motifs in the book connoting luxury, has descended along with Emma to become a ludicrously defiled token of elegance and romance: Homais and Leon "could see in the broad sunlight a little fountain gurgling into a marble basin, where among watercress and asparagus three torpid lobsters were stretched out with some quails lying on their side all in a heap" (290).

Madame Bovary closes with Homais's reward for his destructive meddling. In the final part of *Anna Karenina,* we learn that Oblonsky has won the post at eight thousand rubles a year he has been discreetly lobbying for.[84] He is to be secretary of the committee of the consolidated agency of credit balance of the southern railways, which he describes to Karenin in Homais-like journalese as "a new institution of undoubted utility" (653). Given the role of railways in the novel and Levin's view that their premature proliferation is detrimental to agriculture, Oblonsky's post and the entire agency suggests that its utility is precisely dubious, and that Oblonsky's phrase is a piece of high-flown obfuscation. He is rewarded with the post for his readiness to employ the readymade phrase, idea, way of life unquestioningly, while the railroads that will supply him extra income have also been the means of his sister's destruction.

Homais is master of the cliché, which he assembles with demonic rapidity for the articles he writes for the local newspaper, the *Rouen Beacon.* "'C'est là la question,' as the paper was saying the other day," he prattles, immune to the irrelevant (to him) source of his tagline (221). In *Anna Karenina,* Vronsky's friend Petritsky uses "That is the question!" fatuously, but Oblonsky also employs readymade tags, quoting Levin the same verses about a young man in love that he later repeats to Vronsky (163, 33–34, 53).[85] In both books, there is ironic meaning for the reader. But while Homais cannot know that Hamlet's suicide soliloquy pertains to Emma, Oblonsky does know that Levin and Vronsky are apparently both in love with the same woman and therefore bears moral responsibility for his utterance, though it has no consequence. Flaubert's characters are his victims; Tolstoy's are autonomous moral beings.

If Emma's story illustrates the tragic results of acting out her projective reading of romances, Homais displays the destruction caused by misapplied materialism, embodied in his apothecary's faith in science.

Emma is a degraded version of Chateaubriand's René; she devalues his romantic quest for an ideal by embodying it in tawdry reality; Homais, on the other hand, presents the degradation of Rousseau's progressive views and of Enlightenment ideas.[86] Emma is guided by sensuality, Homais unrestrained by any moral principle. Oblonsky combines these features. As Anna is the best possible adulteress, he is the best possible sensualist, enjoying oysters; women; hunting; and his friends with appealing good health, energy, and bonhomie. But he is nonetheless the Enemy; he represents the destructive force in Tolstoy's novel, for it is this life force and sensual appetite, unrestrained by any moral principles, that precipitates Anna's ruin.

Tolstoy's polemic with European literature, focused on the "woman question" and the novel of adultery, is, as Eikhenbaum wrote, "a dialectic unity, the result of a complex mental process."[87] That complexity includes applying values absorbed from Rousseau to the problem of adultery, values elaborated specifically in dialogue with Flaubert.

The parallels between *Madame Bovary* and *Anna Karenina* show both authors to be concerned with the decline of cherished ideals; emblematized by the adulteress in the conveyance accompanied by the grotesque peasant with his inappropriate language, a people is shown to betray its own best nature and traditions through shallow understanding of them. Instead of Flaubert's trivial heroine, Tolstoy posits the best possible case, but Anna is no less doomed than Emma by the inherent contradictions both of her society and, especially, of adultery itself.[88]

Tolstoy, then, may be said to be restoring Rousseau's views by giving them a dignity, freeing them from the parody with which Flaubert degrades them. Levin is a true Emile, learning from his own experience the cost of luxury, the superiority of things made by oneself, the freedom to enjoy black bread and not to be a slave to public opinion.[89]

EMILE ZOLA (1840–1902)

> Une tempête sous un crâne est un spectacle sublime; une tempête dans les reins est un spectacle ignoble.
>
> "Ferragus"[90]

Zola made his name as the theorist and leader of a naturalism so lurid that "Ferragus" (the pseudonym of Louis Ulbach, a contemporary critic) called his novels "putrid literature," accusing them of appealing to the basest human instincts.[91] But as Flaubert said of Zola, "He is a colossus with dirty feet, but a colossus nonetheless," and Tolstoy accordingly read and responded to him, even as he deplored his work.[92] As with his silence about *Madame Bovary,* and despite incorporating early Zola into *Anna Karenina,* Tolstoy only begins to mention Zola in print in the 1890s. In 1893, in a letter to his friend, the writer N. S. Leskov, he wrote, "I have long thought that all that literature including, especially, all those Zolas, Bourgets and so on, is useless nastiness, and now that has become an absolute certainty for me."[93] Four years later in "What Is Art?" (1897–98), he recounts that, preparing to write that essay, he read works praised all over Europe, by "Zola, Bourget, Huysmans, Kipling . . . novels with the most wrenching plots, [which] didn't touch me for a moment, rather I was constantly irritated at the authors. . . . From the first pages you see the intention and all the details become unnecessary, boring. . . . You know that the author had no other feeling than the desire to write a story or a novel, so you get no artistic impression."[94] In a variant to "What Is Art?" he calls these works (and Monet's paintings, Verlaine's and Mallarmé's poetry, Wagner's music, Ibsen's plays) a "perversion of art," saying of Zola's work that "everything in it is cold, artificial and there isn't a spark of infectious feeling."[95]

At the meeting point of the Anna-Levin plotlines in book 7, chapter 6, Anna and Levin have a similar response to Zola and the French naturalists:

> Levin said that the French had carried conventionality in art further than anyone else and therefore attributed special merit to a return to realism. In the fact that they had left off lying they perceived poetry. . . .
>
> "What you have said quite characterizes present-day French art, painting and even literature: Zola, Daudet. But perhaps it is always like that—they form their conceptions from imaginary conventional figures, and when they have made every possible combination of these, they tire of the conventional figures and begin to devise more natural, correct ones." (632)

Tolstoy's allusions to moments in two of Zola's early novels show how he consciously reverses this characterization in writing *Anna Karenina.* In part because he bases his characters on his own family and acquaintances and not on "imaginary conventional figures," it is natural—not a mere literary manipulation—for him to infuse emotional power and richly ambiguous meaning into the devices he takes from Zola.

Zola published *Thérèse Raquin* and *Madeleine Férat* in rapid succession in 1867 and 1868, and the two novels are structurally similar: the powerful woman caught between a delicate husband and a sexually potent lover is driven to suicide, urged on implacably by a vengeful older woman. Both tales are related to the theme of adultery and provide material for *Anna Karenina.* Because, like Tolstoy, Zola too uses Flaubert's singing beggar in *Madeleine Férat,* we will begin with the second of his two adulteresses.

Madeleine Férat

Madeline Férat is located temporally and artistically between Flaubert's *Madame Bovary* and Tolstoy's *Anna Karenina.* Zola's novel is based on the premise that he says he took from Michelet's *Woman*: "A woman, once impregnated, will carry her husband with her everywhere," and "The first union is never over."[96] Zola's heroine considers that her first lover, Jacques, is her true husband and that she betrays him by her subsequent marriage to Guillaume. Zola's novel posits a physiological form of adultery, which leads to the same consequences as the conventional one. The ending of the novel, in which Madeleine, overcome with guilt and grief, commits suicide, has features taken from Flaubert that Tolstoy uses in *Anna Karenina.*

Two female figures represent Madeleine's conscience: Geneviève, an old Protestant fanatic who lives in Guillaume's house, and her former comrade Louise, a loose woman who has become a hideous beggar. The former torments Madeleine's domestic life with nightly readings from the Old Testament; her refrain, "God the Father does not forgive!" is the final line of the novel. The beggar woman, now known as Vert-de-Gris, appears for the first time clinging to the lantern of the couple's carriage when they are fleeing their home for an inn to avoid Jacques. Vert-de-Gris enters the inn and talks to Madeleine in her room, reminding her of old times. She next appears at their house, her hideous face glued to the railings of their park:

> A smile revealed her yellowed teeth, and she began to sing a song that the two young women had once together pitched to the echoes of the Verrières woods . . . returning from their pleasure parties. Her hoarse voice shrilled:
>
> There was a rich pasha
> Called Mustapha.
> For his seraglio he bought
> Mademoiselle Catinka.
> And tra la la, tra la la
> Tra la la la, la la la la. (250)

Vert-de-Gris makes her third and final appearance when Madeleine is returning home from a visit to Jacques and contemplating suicide. She again sings her verse. "The 'tra la las' . . . took on a tone of sad irony. One would have said it was the laughter of a madwoman who was touched and drowning in tears. Madeleine stopped, as if nailed to the spot," recalling how she and Vert-de-Gris used to sing the song (281).

> She heard Vert-de-Gris' steps approaching; she began to retreat in order not to find herself face to face with this woman whose pitiful silhouette she could already distinguish. After a silence, the madwoman again raised her voice:
>
> For his seraglio he bought
> Mademoiselle Catinka.
> He paid thirty sous:
> She was worth less than that. . . .
>
> Madeleine, horrified by the mad laughter of the singer, shaken to tears by this hoarse, sad voice that sang her youth in the freshness of the evening . . . ran off across the fields. (281–82)

Zola has appropriated the blind beggar from *Madame Bovary*; in his version the beggar provides direct psychological motivation for the heroine's suicide by representing the past that Madeleine shared with her but has tried to escape. Zola also uses Emma Bovary's method of suicide: driven to despair, Madeleine poisons herself in front of her husband, who instantly goes mad. As we have seen, Tolstoy makes far greater changes to Flaubert's heroine's final journey, but *Madeleine Férat* contains one scene that was useful to him.

After Madeleine has betrayed Guillaume with Jacques in Paris, she walks along the street blindly, talking to herself like a madwoman: "She began to walk feverishly, with bowed head, not knowing where she was going. . . . The noise of the carriages, the elbowings of the passersby, all the jostling and movement which surrounded her was lost in the whirlwind of sensations and thoughts that transported her" (279).

She is revolted at having just given herself to her former lover: "'What kind of a woman am I? . . . I am cursed. . . . My flesh is base. Ah what filth!' And she made gestures of disgust, walking along the houses like a madwoman" (279). She decides to go home to explain to her husband why she is going to commit suicide.

> She took a train that was just leaving for Mantes. During the two hours of the trip, a sole thought pulsed in her brain: "I'll kill myself at Noiraude [home], she told herself, when I have proven to Guillaume the necessity of my death." The regular and monotonous joltings of the carriage, the deafening noises of the train's motion, in a strange fashion lulled her idea of suicide; she thought she heard the grinding of the wheels repeat echoingly: "I'll

> kill myself, I'll kill myself." At Mantes, she got into a coach. Leaning her elbow on the door, she looked at the countryside, recognized along the road certain houses she had seen at night several months earlier when she had passed in the cabriolet with Guillaume. And the countryside, the houses, everything seemed to her to repeat the sole thought that throbbed at the base of her being: "I'll kill myself, I'll kill myself." (280)

This is the point at which the beggar woman reappears for the third time, as the beggar does at Emma Bovary's carriage during her final return home from Rouen to Yonville, where she poisons herself.

On Anna's final journey toward suicide, she observes the shops and the passersby in semi-delirium. Like Madeleine, she recalls her betrayal and is revolted by the thought of love in its several forms, her husband's, her son's and her lover's: "Remembering Karenin . . . and the feeling that had once existed between them and which had also been called love, she shuddered with revulsion." She remembers her love for Seryozha: "'[I] exchanged his love for another's, and did not complain of the change as long as the other's love satisfied me.' And she thought with disgust of what she called 'the other love'" (691).

Metallic sounds and the rhythm accompany Anna's delirious train ride to Vronsky's mother's estate at Obiralovka: "At last the third bell rang, the engine whistled and creaked, the coupling chains gave a jerk. . . . She looked out the window. . . . With rhythmic jerks over the joints of the rails, the carriage in which Anna sat rattled past the platform and a brick wall, past the signals and some other carriages; the sound of the wheels slightly ringing against the rails became more rhythmical and smooth" (693). Anna, in part motivated by the desire to punish Vronsky, kills herself on arriving at the station, unlike Madeleine, who is punishing herself; both heroines' journeys convey the incoherent misery that adultery has brought them, which can only be resolved by death.

Tolstoy and Zola take the same scene from *Madame Bovary* and transpose it to the railway, but Zola does little more than update his material, while Tolstoy builds an important motif out of the railroad, connecting the adultery theme to Russian economic and social development in *Anna Karenina.* But Zola is the first to answer Flaubert's Hirondelle with a railroad carriage; his scene sets the delirious thoughts of his tormented heroine among the clanking railway sounds, the rhythm of the wheels of the journey toward suicide. Tolstoy condenses Madeleine's drawn-out suicide and delays Vronsky's reaction until part 8. He uses the device of the interior monologue to show Anna's distorted view of

Vronsky and the world around her to be rooted in her guilt just as Madeleine's is and that indeed, "God the Father does not forgive!"

Thérèse Raquin

Thérèse Raquin, first published as a separate volume in 1867, relates the passionate affair between Thérèse, married to her sickly cousin Camille, and Laurent. They tacitly agree to kill Camille, and Laurent throws him off a boat into the Seine, where he drowns. To avoid suspicion, the lovers wait a year to be married, but are unable to enjoy their long-awaited union because they suffer the torments of guilt and terror, so agonizing that they finally commit suicide, taking poison together.

Balzac's work had been called "the sublime manure on which all those mushrooms grew."[97] If Tolstoy found Balzac's work disgusting, he must certainly have been even more repelled by the "puddle of mud and blood called *Thérèse Raquin.*"[98] Thérèse and Laurent, brutish members of the urban poor, commit a murder in order to indulge in gross sensual passion. However little his lovers resemble them, Tolstoy nonetheless found something in Zola's novel that he could use in *Anna Karenina.*

A year after Camille's murder, Laurent begins to be terrified at night by the drowned man's ghost. He has a recurring nightmare in which, as he tries to embrace her, Thérèse is replaced by the drowned man, who opens his arms to Laurent. "The same sinister denouement which awoke him each time, gasping and distraught, didn't diminish his desire; several minutes later after he had gone back to sleep, his desire forgot the cadaver who awaited him, and he again ran to find the warm, supple body of a woman." Each time the shock awakens him. "The final [shock] was so violent, so painful, that he decided to get up, not to struggle any longer. Day was dawning; a dreary grey light came in the window. . . . Laurent dressed slowly with dull irritation. He was exasperated at not having slept, exasperated at having allowed himself to be seized by a fear that he now called infantile" (108–9). When he goes to see Thérèse that evening, he learns that she too "has seen the drowned man rise up before her" (111). In *Anna Karenina,* Vronsky, tired from hosting the foreign prince, lies down for a nap in the afternoon:

> The memory of the disreputable scenes at which he had been present during the last few days became jumbled and connected with pictures of Anna and a peasant who had played an important part as a beater in the bear-hunting; and Vronsky fell asleep. He woke up in the dark trembling with fear, and hurriedly lit a candle. "What has happened? What horrors I

> dreamt! Yes, yes, the peasant, the beater—I think he was small and dirty with a tangled beard—was stooping down and doing something or other, and suddenly began to say strange words in French. . . . But why did it seem so terrible? He vividly recalled the peasant and the incomprehensible words that the man had uttered, and a shudder of terror ran down his back. "What nonsense!" he thought, glancing at his watch. It was already half past eight.
>
> He rang for his valet, dressed hurriedly, and went out into the porch, having quite forgotten his dream. (324)

He drives straight to Anna's, where (in a conversation in which Anna is jealous of his former amour Thérèse, whose name is mentioned twice) he learns that Anna has had a similar dream.

Tolstoy complicates Laurent's dream, in which his sexual passion is thwarted by the vision of his murder victim. Vronsky's memory of the debaucheries he has attended with the prince merges with his passion for Anna before he falls asleep and confronts the terrifying image of the peasant, which reminds us (and presumably him, although he fails to figure out the cause of his terror) of the peasant killed at the railway station when he first meets Anna. In the course of the novel, the peasant becomes an emblematic murder victim associated in turn with Anna, Karenin, and finally Vronsky, so that on the symbolic level Vronsky and Anna can be said to have committed murder.[99] On waking, Laurent and Vronsky try to dismiss their terrifying dreams, dress, and go to their mistresses only to find that their mistresses have had the same dream. Even after Laurent and Thérèse are married, they are unable to indulge their passions: "The specter of Camille would come to sit between the newlyweds. . . . Thérèse and Laurent would again sense the cold, damp smell of the drowned man in the hot air they were breathing; they told each other that the corpse was there, nearby. . . . They didn't open their lips, they looked at each other, and the two of them had the same nightmare at the same time. . . . Their taut nerves threatened a crisis; they could shout, perhaps fight" (136).

After Vronsky has his dream of the French-speaking peasant beater at the bear hunt, Anna tells him hers:

> Her face was full of horror. And Vronsky, remembering his dream, felt the same horror filling his soul.
>
> "He fumbles about and mutters French words, rapidly, you know, lisping: *"Il faut le battre le fer, le broyer, le pétrir . . ."* . . .
>
> "What nonsense, what nonsense!" said Vronsky, but he himself felt there was no conviction in his voice. (329)

Vronsky and Anna still hope for happiness and, like Madeleine Férat and her husband, have a respite of domestic tranquility. But like Zola's characters, they have committed a crime that can only continue to haunt them. Zola imitates Flaubert in having both Thérèse and Madeleine take poison; for Tolstoy it is important to the structure and worldview of the novel that Anna uses a train to destroy herself.

In the 1890s Tolstoy objected to the French naturalist school for showing all "working people" as animals.[100] Even though they are beset by anguish for their deeds, the characters in Zola's two novels, and indeed throughout his monumental twenty-volume Rougon-Macquart (as well as in *La Bête humaine* [1890], which is in Tolstoy's library at Yasnaya Polyana in Russian translation), are shown to be driven by their passions.[101] As late as 1906 Tolstoy was still inveighing against what he considered Zola's "indifferent, even contemptuous relationship to the basic questions of life."[102] In *Anna Karenina,* he incorporates Zola's devices—the shared dream, the presuicide delirious interior monologue—into his own treatment of adultery to present the deep humanity of his heroine. The passion that binds her to Vronsky is legitimated (unlike Madeleine's conflict between Jacques and Guillaume) as a natural aspect of a woman's nature (like Thérèse) and connected to murder only figuratively (unlike the case of Thérèse and Laurent). In contrast to Zola's simple heroines, Anna has many of the noble qualities of an ideal Russian aristocrat—generosity of spirit, maternal love for her son, a capable intellect, a Christian conscience—and Tolstoy's desire to tell her tale is motivated not by Zola's idea that human beings are inevitably governed by their animal nature but by a profound search for the meaning of human existence in their higher nature.

The Gospels

The world began and so it will end, with farming.
Bamana proverb, Mali

Tolstoy's antidote to adultery and indeed to all the decadence that these French novels represent required not only the ideals of Rousseau but also the eternal authority of the Gospels.[103] After finishing *Anna Karenina* in 1877, Tolstoy went through a religious crisis that generated four related works, starting with his *Confession* (begun in 1879) and *Criticism of Dogmatic Theology* (1880), in which he sets out his understanding of the meaning of the Gospel teachings. This led him to embark on a retranslation of the Gospels, for which he studied Greek and Hebrew, working intensely from January 1880 to July 1881.[104] Like many post-Enlightenment thinkers, he wanted to isolate the truth in the Gospels for himself by purging them of miracles and mystery, to formulate what he considered Jesus's authentic teachings.[105] This is what is meant by speaking of Tolstoy's Gospel as "materialist," a use of the word distinct from the "materialism" of the Radical Russian writers of the 1860s. This quest produced his monumental *Unification and Translation of the Four Gospels*. At the time, the work could not be published in Russia, where religion was one of the most sensitive categories for the censorship, which had rejected Gogol's title *Dead Souls* as blasphemous in 1842. Tolstoy considered the *Unification* unfinished and probably unfinishable when he finally stopped correcting it, and it appeared in a mistake-riddled two-volume edition printed in Switzerland only in 1892–94. It was finally published in Russia in 1906.[106]

It is agreed that Tolstoy exaggerated the degree of his religious conversion in his *Confession*.[107] Father Florovsky points out that as early as 1852 Tolstoy was already writing, "I believe in one, incomprehensible and good God, in the immortality of the soul and in the eternal reward for our deeds," and on March 4, 1855, Tolstoy wrote in his diary about establishing a new religion that "a conversation about divinity and faith led me to a great, gigantic thought, to the realization of which I feel capable of dedicating my life. This thought is the creation of a new religion, in accordance with the development of mankind, a religion of Christ, but cleansed of faith and mystery, a practical religion which does not promise future bliss, but which provides bliss on earth."[108]

In 1859 Tolstoy wrote Countess A. A. Tolstaya his "*profession de foi*," reporting the results of an initial religious quest: "I found that there is immortality, that there is love and that one has to live for another in order to be happy eternally. These discoveries surprised me by their similarity to the Christian religion, and instead of discovering them for myself, I began to look in the Gospels for them, but found little. I found neither God, nor the Redeemer, nor *mysteries*; nothing."[109]

In 1860 in a continuation of this line of thought, Tolstoy, in his project to "renovate Christianity," considered writing a "materialist Gospel," a "life of Christ the materialist."[110] Andrew Wachtel points out that Kitty sees in Levin "precisely the presence of church ethics without church dogma," and this could be taken further: Tolstoy's account of Levin's quest for faith is itself a kind of "materialist Gospel."[111]

Dragan Kujundzic writes that *Anna Karenina* "thematizes, represents and performs its own relationship to the Biblical texts."[112] Several critics have identified themes, moments, and phrases in *Anna Karenina* that evoke the Gospels; together the Gospel references describe Levin's movement toward faith.[113] Referring to the Gospels, we can see that the peaks of Levin's journey are established in parallel with three pivotal moments in Jesus's life: his crucifixion, his birth, and the second coming—paralleled by Nikolay's death, Mitya's birth, and Levin's epiphany at Kolok. Tolstoy's diary entry of January 24, 1894, suggests why this should be so:

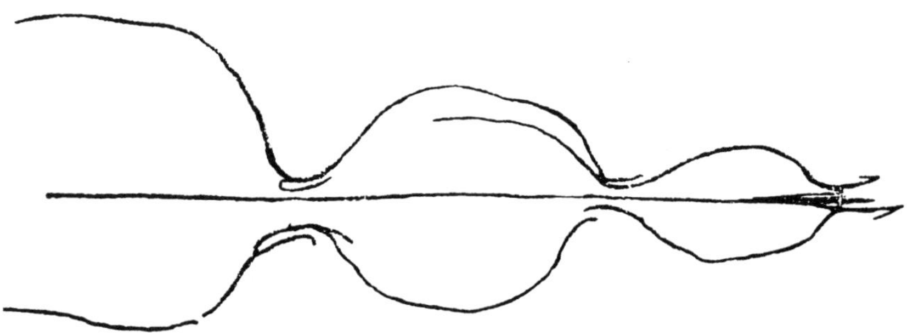

> The straight line is God. The narrow places are the approach to death and birth. In those places God is closer. He is not hidden by anything. But in the middle of life He is obscured by the complexity of life.[114]

Kitty and Levin's story "takes place in a context of Christianity."[115] Tolstoy depicts Kitty through Levin's eyes as a Virgin Mary:

> He could imagine her vividly . . . the splendor of that blond little head, with its expression of childlike goodness and clarity, so freely placed on her stately maidenly shoulders. The childlike expression of her face . . . created her special splendor. . . . But what always amazed him unexpectedly about her was the expression in her eyes, meek, peaceful and just, and in particular, her smile, which always carried Levin into a magical world where he felt himself moved and softened the way he could remember himself on rare days of his early childhood.[116]

The distinctly non-sexual depiction of Levin's love for Kitty, consistent with Levin's falling in love with Kitty when she is still a child, his faithfulness to her even when he has lost all hope that they will marry, and their wedding, which leads him to take confession, suggest that for Levin Kitty is invested with the Virgin Mary's saving grace. The idea is also consistent with Tolstoy's later demystification of the miracle of

Jesus's birth in the *Unification.* Tolstoy rewrites the Gospel so that "of the virgin birth there is left only the germ of what might have become an adultery novel":[117] "There was a girl named Mary. This girl became pregnant by someone unknown. Her affianced husband took pity on her and, hiding her shame, accepted her. From her and the unknown father a boy was born. They called the boy Jesus" (*Pss,* 24:48).

Kitty is present in Mary's role at the series of death-birth-resurrection scenes crucial to Levin's growing faith. Jessica Frank's fine analysis, which I will summarize here, shows the textual parallels between the Gospels and three crucial scenes in *Anna Karenina.*[118]

Nikolay is depicted as a fallen Christ figure when on his deathbed. Levin remembers how, "despite the ridicule of his fellow students his brother had lived like a monk while at the University and for a year after, strictly observing all the religious rites, attending service, fasting, avoiding all pleasures and especially women: and then how he suddenly broke loose, became intimate with the vilest people and gave himself to unbridled debauchery" (77–78).

Jesus is accused of similar sins and responds, "The Son of man has come eating and drinking; and you say, 'Behold, a glutton and a drunkard, a friend of tax collectors and sinners!'" (Luke 7:34). Mary Magdalene is, according to tradition although she is not explicitly identified in the gospels, one of these sinners; she first appears when Jesus is dining at the home of one of the Pharisees. Seeing her supplicating Jesus, Simon says, "If this man were a prophet, he would have known who and what sort of woman this is that is touching him, for she is a sinner" (Luke 7:39). Similarly, when Levin enters Nikolay's home, where he is dining and drinking wine, he sees "a young pock-marked woman in a woolen dress without collars or cuffs . . . his heart sank painfully at the thought that Nikolay lived among such strange people" (78). Jesus and Nikolay read their companions' thoughts and defend the prostitutes who show them such devotion. Jesus says: "'Do you see this woman? . . . I entered your house, you gave me no water for my feet, but she has wet my feet with her tears, and wiped them with her hair. . . . You did not anoint my head with oil, but she has anointed my feet with ointment. Therefore I tell you, her sins, which are many, are forgiven, for she loved much.' . . . And he said to her, 'Your sins are forgiven . . . Your faith has saved you: go in peace'" (Luke 7:44–48, 50).

Nikolay defends Maria similarly: "And this woman . . . is my life's companion, Maria Nikolaevna; I took her out of a bad house . . . But I love and respect her and beg all those who wish to know me . . . to love and respect her. She is just the same to me as a wife . . . So now you know whom you have to deal with, and if you feel you will be degraded—there is the door." And he dismisses Maria to fetch the supper wine as Jesus dismisses Mary Magdalene: "You may go" (80).

Jesus accuses Simon of neglecting him as well as of disapproving of Mary; Levin feels he has neglected Nikolay, leaving Maria to take care of him: "instead of looking him up, I dined out and came here" (77). Jesus, actively, and Nikolay, inadvertently, teach those around them forgiveness: "For if you forgive men their trespasses, your heavenly Father also will forgive you" (Matthew 6:14); "Levin felt that his brother Nikolay in his soul, despite the depravity of his life, was no worse than those who despised him. . . . 'I will show him that I love and therefore understand him'" (78).

As E. B. Greenwood says, "this scene dramatizes a crucial formative experience in Levin's religious quest."[119] Tolstoy surrounds Nikolay's deathbed scenes with motifs from Christ's Crucifixion. Maria and Kitty attend Nikolay's last days as Mary Magdalene and the Virgin Mary do Jesus's. The doctor tells Kitty "he can't live more than three days" and "another three days of torture" pass (451, 457). Jesus is crucified "in the third hour" and predicts, "After three days, I will rise again" (Mark 15:25, Matthew 27:63). Kitty's nursing of Nikolay evokes imagery surrounding Jesus on the cross: "Instead of the foul smell there was the odor of vinegar and of scent, which Kitty—pouting her lips and puffing out her rosy cheeks—was blowing through a little glass tube . . . on the table medicine bottles and a bottle of water were neatly placed, also a pile of folded linen which would be required later. . . . On another table there was a glass of some refreshing drink and some powders" (448). Jesus is given vinegar to drink while on the cross and Joseph of Arimathea wraps Jesus's body "in a clean linen shroud" when he is taken from the cross (Matthew 27:48, Matthew 27:59). The powder echoes the spices the women bring to the tomb to anoint Jesus (Mark 16:1, Luke 24:1).[120]

Levin's brother is a fallen Christ, a warning to Levin of what he might become by choosing reason over faith ("step by step modern scientific explanations of the phenomena of the universe had driven out [Nikolay's] faith" [454]). Kitty's compassionate alleviation of Nikolay's suffering echoes that of the bystander at the crucifixion who succors Jesus when he cries out, "My God, my God, why hast thou forsaken me?" (Matthew 27:47). His motives in giving Jesus the poor man's wine (vinegar) are ambiguous—either he takes pity on Jesus's suffering or he wants to revive him in order to have him suffer a little longer.[121] Kitty succors Nikolay spiritually by having him receive Communion and Extreme Unction; her care for his body that alleviates his ordeal is also ambiguous: it allows him to cling to life a little longer despite the hopelessness of his condition. The saving grace of her maternal role as Mary is underscored by the connection between Nikolay's death and the news of the advent of Levin's son. Tolstoy reverses the sequence of birth and death in a direction that relieves Levin's despair in the face of death with the hope and joy of a literal new birth that later takes on the significance of a spiritual one. When the child is born after Kitty's long labor, "on [Kitty's] face was the same change from the earthly to that which was beyond earth, as is seen on the faces of the dead; but in their case it is a farewell, in hers it was a welcome" (649). Levin feels he would not have been surprised if he had been told that "they had angel children, and that God was present with them. . . . Whence and why had he come? Who was he?" this "human being who had so incomprehensibly appeared from some unknown realm" (648). Tolstoy replaces the unbelievable (to him) miracles and mystery of the Gospels with a natural mystery, the birth of a child. This is the direction Tolstoy takes in his later Gospel; in *Anna Karenina* the natural miracle of Mitya's birth eventually brings both mother and father closer to a spiritual awareness.

The birth is not an end in itself, it is a means. Mitya's birth initially inspires no real change in Levin, who, "gazing at this tiny piteous being, vainly searched his soul for some indications of paternal feeling. He felt nothing for it but repulsion" (650). After the birth, Levin still "suffered so much [from not knowing what he was or why he lived in the world] that he was afraid he might commit suicide" (717). Levin "reviewed the whole course of his thoughts during the last two years, beginning with the clear and obvious thought of death at the sight of his beloved brother hopelessly ill" (721). His suffering is finally turned to joy by the peasant Fyodor's words about Platon who "lives for his soul and remembers God" (719). He realizes that truth, which is goodness, is revealed to him by Christianity and is outside reason, and that the law of goodness is an "indubitable manifestation of the Deity" (739, 738).

He is briefly distracted from this state of joy by everyday pettinesses, until he realizes that Kitty and Mitya are trapped in Kolok wood in the midst of a thunderstorm. "In that short time the center of the cloud had already so moved over the sun that it was dark as during an eclipse" (734). Jesus, foretelling his Second Coming, says, "The sun will be darkened, and the moon will not give its light, and the stars will fall from heaven, and the powers of the heavens will be shaken" (Matthew 24:29).

As Levin reaches Kolok, "suddenly everything burst into flames, the earth seemed on fire, and just overhead the vault of heaven seemed to crack . . . and there was a flash of lightning" (735). Jesus foretells that "as the lightning comes from the east and shines to the west, so will be the coming of the Son of man" (Matthew 24:27).

Levin sees "two figures in dark dresses . . . bending over something. They were Kitty and the nurse" (735). Barbara Lønnqvist writes that "the scene with the two women bent over the child recalls the well-known religious motif of Anne and Mary with the Christ child, and it works as a revelation for Levin."[122] She also finds the icon motif of the "Milk-Giving Mother of God" in the subsequent scene of Kitty's breast-feeding Mitya, in which Levin says "today, after that fright during the storm, I realized how much I love him" (738). It takes the lightning bolt to fuse Levin's new spiritual understanding with his love for the immediate world around him.[123] In this way Tolstoy unites Levin's love for his own child with love of Christ. Levin realizes that his "new feeling . . . be it faith or not . . . is just like my feeling for my son" (740). This is the essence of Tolstoy's materialist Gospel: the realization of goodness in the everyday, the spirit of Christ in every child.

Tolstoy repeats what can be understood as the import of this vision in *Anna Karenina* in a diary entry written over twenty years later:

> There is only one unique teaching, that of truth—that universal and eternal teaching so perfectly expressed, for myself no less than others, in the Gospels. This teaching calls man to recognize his sonship to God, and to realize . . . both his freedom and his service, since in freeing himself from the influence of the world he enters the service of God and His will. And as soon as a man has understood this teaching, he enters into free communication with God and has nothing more to ask from anyone. (November 1899)[124]

This is what Levin has understood by the end of *Anna Karenina.*

Tolstoy believed that Jesus was the son of God only in the same sense that we are all God's children: "The expression 'Son of God' is accepted by the church as exclusively the name of Jesus Christ. But according to the Gospels it does not have this exclusive sense; it is equally applied to all people as well. This meaning is clearly expressed in many places in the Gospel."[125]

Man's purpose in life is to reach understanding (*razumenie,* which Tolstoy uses to translate "logos" in John 1:1) of the nature of the kingdom of God and how to live in it. Tolstoy interprets Jesus's conversation with Nicodemus in the Gospel of John stressing sonhood: "That spirit in man, originating in the infinite and relating to him as son to father . . . is what replaces an imaginary God with this real and unique God. . . . To glorify the son of God in man, to rely on him, to live in truth means to live in the kingdom of God."[126] Tolstoy allows Levin to reach this truth by placing him in relation to God and to his own son as part of a continuum of divine and earthly fathers and sons. This is the good news that the Gospel (*vozveshchenie blaga liudiam*) contains, and the definition of that goodness (*blago*) is the most essential part of the Gospels for Tolstoy.[127]

Other elements associated with the Gospels contribute to the definition of the good. Galina Galagan identifies the ripening of grain as a motif in Tolstoy's treatment of the stages of spiritual evolution in man in the *Unification,* mentioning as illustration Jesus's parable of the sower.[128]

> Listen! A sower went out to sow. And as he sowed, some seeds fell on the path, and the birds came and ate them up. Other seeds fell on rocky ground, where they did not have much soil, and they sprang up quickly, since they had no depth of soil. But when the sun rose, they were scorched; and since they had no root, they withered away. Other seeds fell among thorns, and the thorns grew up and choked them. Other seeds fell on good soil and brought forth grain, some a hundredfold, some sixty, some thirty. Let anyone with ears listen! (Matthew 13:3–10)

Jesus interprets his parable for the disciples:

> Hear then the parable of the sower. When anyone hears the word of the kingdom and does not understand it, the evil one comes and snatches away what is sown in the heart; this is what was sown on the path. As for what was sown on rocky ground, this is the one who hears the word and immediately receives it with joy; yet such a person has no root, but endures only for a while, and when trouble or persecution arises on account of the word, that person immediately falls away. As for what was sown among thorns, this is the one who hears the word, but the cares of the world and the lure of wealth choke the word, and it yields nothing. But as for what was sown on good soil, this is the one who hears the word and understands it, who indeed bears fruit and yields, in one case a hundred fold, in another sixty, and in another thirty. (Matthew 13:18–23)

Tolstoy's translation of the parable of the sower in the *Unification* speaks to Levin's growth of understanding throughout *Anna Karenina,* which enables his joyful epiphany:

> As the sower knows that there are ruts, stones, burdocks in his field, that much of his grain perishes, he knows nonetheless to sow the whole field, that, notwithstanding the loss, much grain will grow and there will be a harvest—thus the life of understanding is sown in people: there will be loss,

> but there will also be a harvest . . . The same way the life of understanding is sown in all people: some lose this life, others return it a hundredfold.[129]

After Kitty refuses Levin and he returns from Moscow to rejoice in the pure country life, he is so filled with the joy of manuring his fields in spring that

> he was not irritated by the sight of a peasant's horse and colt treading down the young growth . . . nor by the jeering and stupid answer the peasant . . . gave him in reply to his question:
>
> "Well, Ipat, is it time to sow?"
>
> "We must plow first, Konstantine Dmitrich," said Ipat. (142)

Having understood the Gospel parable, we can see the unconscious wisdom of Levin's not minding the loss of the trodden-down shoots—"there will be loss, but there will also be a harvest"—as well as the truth of Ipat's apparently impertinent words. Levin is not ready yet for the revelation of meaning he will receive; first he has to plow his ground so the seeds can take root. For Levin this entails his confession and wedding, Nikolay's death, and Mitya's birth. His revelation finally takes place in the summer following Mitya's birth, at "the most pressingly busy season of the year," when it is time "to mow or reap the rye and oats, and cart them, to finish mowing the meadows, to replough the fallow land, to thresh the seed corn and sow the winter rye" (717). Levin has been spending his day in the harvest of the grain when he talks to Fyodor, who precipitates Levin's epiphany with his words about Platon, who "lives for his soul and remembers God." They are standing "beside the neat yellow freshly-reaped stack of seed-rye on the threshing floor" (719). Despite the seeds that were crushed by the peasant's horse, there is a rich harvest (precisely of *seed*-rye), both material and spiritual. Even the infant Mitya participates in a growth of understanding: that evening after the thunderstorm Mitya shows that he "recognizes his own people," which is a source of joy to all around him, to Kitty, Levin, the nurse, and Agafya Mikhailovna (737).

The Gospels announce the coming of the Son of God. In *Anna Karenina,* the divinity in every man makes each a son of God like Jesus; Levin in his painful search for understanding takes on Jesus's role as Tolstoy's bearer of the Good News.

Answering the French novels of adultery with Rousseau and the Gospels, Tolstoy reinfuses idealism into the realist novel, which he felt had become distressingly naturalistic, as his remarks about Balzac and responses to Zola suggest. While the Romantics insisted on the unattainability of a Platonic Ideal in the real world, and materialists denied the existence of God, Tolstoy shows another possibility: the continuous approach toward the ideal and the divine in the everyday: both the Romantic and the holy ideal of the beloved can be united, painfully and gradually, with the actual wife; the "strange, limp, red creature" (650) that is his son can reveal the divinity in the everyday, and the novel of adultery can be transformed into a *profession de foi.*

Conclusion

The intertextual achievement of the novels we have discussed involves, as Laurent Jenny puts it, "not a confused, mysterious accumulation of influences, but the work of transformation and assimilation of various texts that is accomplished by a focal text which keeps control over the meaning."[1] Russian literary prose, developing only in the second third of the nineteenth century, assimilated French genres that had been absent in the Russian tradition, as were their themes and casts of characters: the Romantic hero, the poor clerk, the prostitute, the young man from the provinces, the adulteress. The Russian writers admired the great French authors whose work they assimilated (Lermontov and Sand, Dostoevsky and Balzac, Tolstoy and Flaubert), even as they purposefully transformed the French material; the very necessity of turning to the French for models in creating a national Russian literature made the desire to highlight their own distinctiveness even more acute than the difference between worldviews alone would have done. The tension between admiration of the French artistic achievement and rejection of the world it depicts contributes to the rich ambiguity of the Russian synthesis of the two cultural universes.

From Romanticism to Realism

In the 1830s, its early phase, Russian prose recast the vocabulary of European Romanticism and assimilated it into a realist discourse, a process that continues from Lermontov's work through Tolstoy's. Romantic writers in quest of the sublime, that which transcends daily life, used elevated language appropriate to the realm of the ideal; physical reality would undercut that vision, with its petty, everyday details. The ideal could be found in nature, not in the city: man makes the city; God, or some transcendent force unknowable by man, creates nature. The realists translate the quest for the sublime into the everyday, recasting the stylistic elevation and natural surroundings so that the ideal dimension becomes almost invisible. Harry Levin said that every realist is a failed idealist; the Russian rewriting of French fiction in the nineteenth century lowers the imagery and diction of the Romantics in the direction of realism while giving a fuller, more clearly implied, formulation of the ideal than either the French Romantics or the French realists.

Taking *René* as the *point d'origine,* Lermontov, Balzac, Dostoevsky, Flaubert, and Tolstoy move the quest for the ideal from the wilds of America into the small town and the city, incorporating the ugly, coarse, vulgar, lowly, and using a much more specific language to designate the material world. But while the French employ the imagery of Romanticism to show the failure to attain the ideal in the everyday, the Russians use it to show its possibility. Emma Bovary is blind to the beauty of nature, but Pechorin experiences ecstasy while alone in the mountains of the Caucasus; Raskolnikov has his mare-beating dream outside the city, under a bush, and Levin achieves bliss mowing with his peasants. As so many Western writers since the Romantics have done, the Russian novelists apply the Romantic questions and images to their own worlds. The entire body of Romantic texts is a subtext for the nineteenth-century realist, but the Russians, more than the Europeans, are uniquely able to infuse this transformation with hope in the transcendent.

SEA, SAILS, SAILORS, BOATS

Single words and images became markers of the Romantic tradition. The sea, sails, and boats of Romanticism depict the solitude of the Romantic hero in the face of the grandeur of nature where he relishes the struggle to achieve the sublime. Lermontov's poem "The Lone White Sail" (1832) encapsulates this Romantic image with characteristic efficiency:

> A lone white sail gleams
> In the haze of the pale blue sea!
> What does he seek in a distant land?
> What has he left in his native land?
>
> The waves play, the wind whistles,
> And the mast bends and creaks . . .

Alas! he does not seek happiness,
And is not running from happiness!

Below him a stream brighter than azure,
Above him a golden ray of sun . . .
But he, rebellious, asks for a storm,
As though there were peace in storms!

The poem underscores the degree to which Lermontov's later creation, Pechorin, is cast as a belated questing hero of the René type. In *A Hero of our Time,* Lermontov exhausts Pechorin's models by taking the contradictions of the type to their logical dead end, stripping them of the elevated stylistics that disguise self-deception.

Writing in the 1850s, Flaubert also lowers the Romantic tradition. Emma Bovary, as a variant of a failed René, reads Romantic literature and wants to be part of it: "She loved the sea only for its storms" (56). When pining for a more exciting life, "Like sailors in distress, she gazed at the solitude of her life with despairing eyes, seeking some white sail in the far-off haze of the horizon" (79). Flaubert makes tragic fun of her blind attempt to bring this imagery into her daily life when she and Leon make love in the carriage, which is "shut up more tightly than a tomb and tossing about like a boat"; in "the bed [that] was a large mahogany one shaped like a boat"; and finally when her coffin "advance[s] in a series of jerks like a boat tossing at every wave" (234, 250, 313). Lowering the elevated Romantic image of the quest for the ideal, Flaubert uses boat imagery in at least ten places in the novel to show how Emma adopts and distorts Romantic topoi: she pines for a lover and luxury, rather than for the immaterial sublime. Only when she is dead does the boat imagery suggest a transcendent world, off-stage, apparently unattainable by any of the novel's characters.

Tolstoy too uses the sea and boats, but while Flaubert travesties the Romantic imagery in everyday provincial life, Tolstoy reverses the relationship of the paired Romantic categories of ideal/real and high/low. Levin is a true René, in quest of the highest, yet everyday, ideal: how to live. It includes the day-to-day struggle (manuring the fields) to run his estate effectively. When Levin despairs at his ability to get the peasants to do what he tells them, the narrator comments, "He had seen that the boat was leaking but had not found or looked for the leak" (293). Tolstoy uses the same metaphor the same way when Levin struggles to make his marriage work: "At every step he took he felt as a man would feel who, after admiring the smooth, happy motion of a little boat upon the water, had himself got into the boat. He found that besides sitting quietly without rocking he had to keep a lookout, not for a moment forget where he was going, or that there was water under his feet, and that he had to row, although it hurt his unaccustomed hands" (436).

Tolstoy purposefully lowers the metaphor from the glorious wind-driven sailboat to the prosaic little rowboat—true ideals require daily, mundane maintenance. The boat image can also indicate the falling away from the ideal. Dolly's day at Anna and Vronsky's estate contrasts Vozdvizhensk to Pokrovskoe in many details, departing from Levin's ideals in every respect. For Levin, the rowboat is a prosaic metaphor for an ideal end; at Vronsky's an actual rowboat excursion after tea is an attempt to entertain an idle company: "When, after a row in the boat at night-time, Dolly entered her bedroom alone, . . . she felt great relief" (575). Dolly is happy to return to Levin's estate, where the work of living is carried on. In contrast, when her husband, Oblonsky, lands at Levin's "peaceful shore" to do some hunting and transact some business, it is clear he is not in quest of an ideal, even as Levin's estate is the locus of it.

The original Romantic form of the sailor image is reserved for the most important dimension of the ideal in the novel: family, motherhood, faithfulness. The presence of Seryozha "evoked both in Vronsky and in Anna a feeling such as a sailor might have who saw by the compass that the direction in which he was swiftly sailing diverged widely from the right course . . . This child with his naïve outlook on life was the compass which showed them the degree of divergence from what they knew, but would not recognize, as the right course" (169–70).

The ideal is not to be found in the solitary Romantic hero's experience of the transcendent in a dramatic natural setting of storm-tossed seas, on crags, on boats, but in a life well-lived within moral dictates, as measured by the unerring instinct of an innocent child.

BELLS

Another Romantic motif connects the books we have discussed: the bell. Chateaubriand's use of it combines with its natural setting to give it specific importance: village churches use bells to summon the faithful and mark the serving of mass, so that the tolling of church bells is inevitably associated with weddings, christenings, ordinations, and funerals, as well as regular worship. René describes the importance of the sound of church bells, recalling his childhood:

> On Sundays and holidays I often stood in the deep woods as the sound of the distant bell drifted through the trees, calling from the temple to the man of the fields. Leaning against the trunk of an elm, I would listen in rapt silence to the devout tolling. Each tremor of the resounding bronze would waft into my guileless soul the innocence of country ways, the calm of solitude, the beauty of religion, and the cherished memories out of my early childhood! Oh! What churlish heart has never started at the sound of the bells in his birthplace, those bells which trembled with joy over his cradle. . . . All is embraced in that magical revery which engulfs us at the sound of our native bell—faith, family, homeland. (87–88)

The state of childhood innocence and family warmth is connected to the magical beauty of religious faith, and church bells evoke all of this together. In *Atala* the sound of the bell again summons up those feelings. The young Indian maiden Atala and the half-Indian Chactas are about to consummate their passion but are stopped by the ringing of the bell in the midst of a storm, just as the convent with its tolling bells separates René, sitting on a rock by the stormy sea, from his sister Amelia. Both of Chateaubriand's tales use bells and the religious ideals they carry to preserve a state of innocence in the midst of the sublime, the storm.

Dostoevsky preserves this imagery in *Crime and Punishment* and adds a secular, earthly dimension to the ideal signification of Chateaubriand's bells. On Raskolnikov's first visit to the pawnbroker's apartment, "he rang the bell to the old woman's apartment. The bell rang feebly, as though it were made of tin and not of brass. In the cramped little apartments of such houses, there are always bells that sound like that. Its tone had slipped his mind. Now this peculiar tone reminded him suddenly of something" (16). After the murder, he returns at night while the workmen are there: "He seized the bell and pulled. It was the same bell. It made the same tinny sound. He pulled again, and again. He listened. It came back to him. That previous horrible, agonizingly hideous sensation came back to him more clearly and vividly. At every ring he shuddered" (176). At the first visit, the tone of the bell may remind him of the tinny sound of village church bells; at the second, Raskolnikov obsessively evokes the memory of his crime by repeatedly ringing the tinny bell. But as with all of Dostoevsky's motifs, the bells have a complement. They also contain their ideal counterpart: lying on his bed, "[Raskolnikov] thought about nothing. Faces seen long ago in childhood; the bell tower of a church; a back staircase drenched with slops; and from somewhere Sunday church bells ringing" (270). Thus Raskolnikov's dichotomy is set out through bells: through them the murder is opposed to the saving faith he learned in childhood in his village.

The belfry unites these two sides of the bell motif. Razumikhin, arguing against a rational, materialist interpretation of how environment determines human nature, parodies socialist logic: "I'll prove to you right now that the only reason we have white eyelids is because the bell tower of Ivan the Great is a hundred yards high, and I'll prove it clearly, precisely and in a progressive manner, and with liberal overtones even!" (255). The logic of socialists and those spreading the "new ideas" is mocked using the belfry, an emblem of irrational faith. Porfiry unites Raskolnikov's association of bells and murder with the church and the belfry when he says, "I understand what makes a man sometimes want to jump out of a window or from a belfry. . . . It's the same with ringing doorbells" (337). Porfiry understands the two sides of Raskolnikov's crime: the potentially redemptive belfry juxtaposed to the murdered women's doorbell.

The Russian word for bell is *kol*okol. The syllable can be found in Ras*kol*nikov's surname, as well as in the names of two opposed characters: (1) Mi*kol*ka is the name of the peasant who beats the mare in Raskolnikov's dream. He is aligned with Raskolnikov's murderous aspect and with his not wearing a cross. (2) Ni*kol*ay is the house painter and schismatic (ras*kol*nik) who, out of an excess of religious fervor, confesses to a crime he didn't commit, seeking redemption, as Raskolnikov himself eventually is on the brink of doing. The syllable, in both related words, contains opposed meanings for Raskolnikov: "*kol*ot'," to chop, to split, is connected to his axe murders, as well as to the idea of the "ras*kol*nik," the schismatic who splits off from the church. "*Kol*okol," bell, relates both to the murders and to the potential redemptive force of the church.[2]

Dostoevsky uses the redemptive church bell as it appears in Chateaubriand's tales (and others, such as Janin's *Confession*) for the ideal dimension of his novel. Transferring the Romantic quest to the poor streets of Petersburg, he places it in opposition to the moneylender's doorbell, designating the two aspects of Raskolnikov that struggle throughout the novel.

In *Madame Bovary*, bells track Emma from cradle to grave, also setting up an opposition between the potential for the true sublime and Emma's misguided attempts to achieve a false sublime through her adulterous affairs. The narrator describes Emma's thoughts after she has become disillusioned with marriage: "How sad she was when they rang Vespers on Sunday. She would listen in an attentive stupor to each cracked chime of the bell. . . . Once in a while a dog would howl in the distance and the bell would continue its monotonous, evenly spaced ringing, which faded off into the countryside" (80). The bell is a potentially positive image, but her response is sadness at her own disillusionment.

Another potentially ideal image of the bell accompanies Emma's visit to the village priest to seek help: "[the children's] voices could be heard across the booming of the bell, which diminished with oscillations of the thick cord as it fell from the heights of the steeple and was dragged on the ground by its tip. Swallows were flying by and chirping" (79). Emma is not susceptible to the loveliness of the moment that Flaubert enjoys describing; neither the bell nor the swallows has any appeal for Emma. Rather, they are linked in the Hirondelle (swallow) that takes Emma to her adulterous trysts in Rouen accompanied by "the jingle of the horse bells."

In the same way that Dostoevsky creates a double bell motif, Flaubert connects bells to Emma's negative aspect as well as to the potential for something transcendent. Emma values everything for its sensual dimension: Paris "resounded in her ears like a cathedral bell"; she fantasizes eloping with Rodolphe to somewhere with "the bells ringing and the mules braying, the murmur of guitars and fountains"; the theater bell calls the actors to rehearsal in Rouen (74, 192, 252). In all three cases, the bell is connected to a false sublime: the glamour of Paris, the exotic background for adultery, the provincial theater where she takes up with Leon. Bells relate to the divine for Emma only in the tolling Yonville church bell that frames her funeral (312).

In *Anna Karenina,* too, bells signal both the everyday and the sublime. Just as the Levin-Kitty tale presents the positive, ideal plotline and the Anna-Vronsky the negative, the bell motif marks peak moments of the love of the first couple and the death of the second. To be sure, bells are an inescapable part of daily life; the Russian writers, however, employ them in dialogue with the Romantic tradition.

Levin awakens on the haycock thinking how to lead a pure life "in the period of gloom just before daybreak and the complete triumph of light over darkness" and suddenly hears the "tinkling of bells" that herald Kitty's carriage as she passes on her way to Dolly's (252). Again early in the morning, Levin in the hotel room waiting to go to Kitty's to propose, gazes at "the beautifully-shaped silent cross, full of meaning for him" and hears "the church bell ringing for service" (366). The holy ideal of faithful marriage signaled by the church bell is framed on either side by the waiter being called away when the bell rings—the everyday, but not negatively weighted, bell.

Bells, and not just church bells, are associated with death: Anna on her way to the station for her fatal ride hears the three bells ring for the train's departure, as they do for Vronsky's train departure to the Serbian war.

The bell motif travels from a Romantic setting to a realist one, where a conflict is shown between the ideal version (church bells) and the mundane, everyday one set out variously by Flaubert, Dostoevsky, and Tolstoy. Flaubert parodies Emma's Romanticism, Dostoevsky disguises the divine element in the lowered setting, and, Tolstoy sets out the distinction between ideal and real without denigrating reality itself at the expense of the ideal to show how, either through the intuition of women, children, and peasants or the seeking of the male intellect, it can be embodied in reality.

The Everyday

The realist lowering of that which the Romantics had elevated progresses from writer to writer. Although Lermontov rejects the Romantic hero of the *Adolphe* type, the young man in search of himself who sacrifices others egotistically, Pechorin is nonetheless stuck with it, lacking a means to create a new one. Lermontov, however, debunks the typologies by transforming all his French models into a realistic rendition of life in the Caucasus, ranging from the pettiness of spa society to the everyday deaths in the army, in duels, in tribal life. The juxtaposition of the French and the Russian variants acts as covert propaganda for a new, active stance enabled by self-awareness, to be applied both in aesthetic practice and in a way of life that refuses false authority.

Dostoevsky rejects Balzac's view of life in *Père Goriot, The Splendors and Miseries of Courtesans,* and *The Wild Ass's Skin,* crafting *Crime and Punishment* in part to refute the lack of spirituality of Balzac's heroes: he insists that it is a travesty of human nature to reduce a society's concerns to money, social standing, and the willingness to use women to gain it. To each character Dostoevsky adds a metaphysical aspect: Vautrin wants to go to a literal America; Svidrigailov's America is the next world. Raskolnikov's mistake is to frame his ambition in terms of earthly power, but Sonya shows him the path to spiritual riches.

Tolstoy refuses to accept Flaubert's views of humanity and the nature and purpose of art. In creating the captivating Anna Karenina he rewrites the trivial, misguided Emma Bovary. To isolate the religious and philosophical questions surrounding adultery, he dismisses Dumas' and Zola's venal characters. We admire Anna as we cannot admire any of the French adulteresses, as she struggles against adultery, feels guilt for it, and is condemned for it by a complex of forces beyond her control. Furthermore, Tolstoy adds the scaffolding of Levin's tale not only to offer a happy counterexample to the adulterous pair but also to consider the central question of how to live justly. The book ends not with Homais's Legion of Honor or even Oblonsky's similar eight thousand rubles a year but with Levin's enlightenment: the ideal can be found in everyday love and work. Not all humankind is as contemptible as the characters in French novels. And literature is made of more than beautiful language: the very writing of it is part of a quest for moral truth.

In part, this progression describes the movement from Romanticism to realism, which took place in both France and Russia. But Russia's distanced evaluation of French Romanticism, which rejected the world and diction of the solitary solipsist and of French realism, with its tendency to sensational sociological exposé, helped Russian writers define both their sense of national identity and their conception of the purpose of literary art.

The Hierarchy of Subtexts

The Russian writers make their evaluation of each of their materials quite clear. Nina Perlina shows that Dostoevsky does something similar in *The Brothers Karamazov,* in which she identifies a hierarchy of subtexts. At the top of the hierarchy stands the Bible: "In the text of the novel, quotations from Holy Scripture appear as words of unshakeable authority, as ideal models of indisputable truth, and as a 'living bond' between the eternal and the temporal."[3] She identifies Pushkin as the highest aesthetic authority; a character's misquotation of Pushkin reveals his alienation from Truth. Dostoevsky said in his Pushkin speech that he is "the ultimate ethical and esthetic manifestation of Russian universality . . . an esthetic revelation of truth."[4] Perlina shows how Dostoevsky's characters are measured by their "quotations" from these (and other) texts. Not surprisingly, these same two authorities govern the three novels we have discussed, with the difference that it is the authors rather than the characters who use the Bible and Pushkin's work to define the truth of their books, setting the French subtexts they select into dialogue with them. In Perlina's analysis, "the narrator and his characters can incorporate authoritative words into their discourse in only one way: by quoting directly from an acknowledged source." Here it is each author's allusions, which are hidden, indirect and more diffuse, that similarly "combine to produce the multivoicedness of his novel."[5]

Lermontov, Dostoevsky, and Tolstoy each root their novels in Pushkin: *A Hero of Our Time* and *Anna Karenina* are inspired by *The Tales of Belkin* (Tolstoy additionally by the fragment "The guests were arriving at the dacha") and *Crime and Punishment* builds crucial scenes on "The Queen of Spades."[6] The Bible becomes more important for the latter two authors, who respond to the events of the intervening decades.

The predominant concern for the earlier writers, Pushkin and Lermontov, was of necessity more technical and aesthetic than for the later writers. Dostoevsky and Tolstoy not only had the benefit of their work but also had seen the values of the 1840s give way to the utilitarian materialism of the 1860s and were more overtly concerned with the moral aspect of their novels. All three selected French works by theme and genre to structure their novels and define their arguments.

Tolstoy noted the generic uncertainty peculiar to the Russian novel: "From Gogol's *Dead Souls* to Dostoevsky's *House of the Dead,* in the recent period of Russian literature there is not a single artistic prose work rising at all above the level of mediocrity, which quite fits into the form of a novel, epic or story."[7] These three Western genres that Tolstoy names had not developed independently in Russia; in assimilating them, the Russians construct variations of these genres appropriate to their own purposes.

In *A Hero of Our Time,* Lermontov models each chapter on distinct Western European genres—travel notes, the conquest of the *sauvageresse,* the travel adventure tale, the society tale (subspecies spa romance), the philosophical tale. His novel's review of Western genres critiques each one individually and constructs yet another Western genre out of them, the novel, but a novel "with ellipses," that forces the reader to order the fragments and construe the interconnections.[8]

In *Crime and Punishment,* Dostoevsky converts the secular tales of prostitutes and ambitious young men into a novel of resurrection, with the help of Janin's philosophical novel, and Balzac's early novels that themselves incorporate the lesser genres. The resolution of Dostoevsky's novel is not effected through plot, that is, the character's death, as in *The Wild Ass's Skin, Père Goriot,* or *The Splendors and Miseries of Courtesans,* but in a non-novelistic epilogue that opens out into an unknowable future.

In *Anna Karenina,* Tolstoy uses French philosophical essays as well as novels to create another alteration of the French novel genre. Donna Orwin analyzes the restaurant scene as a recasting of Plato's *Symposium* and Svetlana Evdokimova has discussed *Anna Karenina* as "a Platonic dialogue on the nature of love."[9] Rousseau's and Dumas' essays contribute to the dimension of philosophical discourse in the novel. Just as Chateaubriand's *Genius of Christianity* contains the tales *René* and *Atala, Anna Karenina*'s plotlines can be seen as illustrative stories embedded in a philosophical essay, stories themselves structured on different French novels of adultery. The greatest of these is *Madame Bovary,* which Flaubert concludes with a brief postscript describing Homais's ironic success and the sad fates of the characters still alive after Emma Bovary's funeral. But *Anna Karenina* requires book 8 to build the climax of Tolstoy's resurrection tale, as *Crime and Punishment* requires an epilogue after Raskolnikov has turned himself in to the police. The Russians use the French to novelize their philosophical and religious deliberations.

THE BIBLE

The French were the first to raise the problem of loss of faith in literary fiction; whether directly, like Janin, or ironically, like Balzac, they point to it as the source of the sexual and criminal deviance that is the stuff of their novels. The culture described in the French prose these novels refer to (as opposed to that of the Catholic revival in France) is conspicuously secular—Anatole cannot find a spiritual priest in all of Paris; the priest Carlos Herrera is a criminal in disguise. Dostoevsky and Tolstoy are repelled by this vision of human nature, the obsession with externals and the absence of an ideal, and reinfuse the Word into daily existence by embedding the absolute authority of the Gospels into their characters' universes, "saturating occurrences of everyday life with the spirit of eternity."[10]

TOLSTOY AND/OR DOSTOEVSKY

"On the highest level of [*The Brothers Karamazov*'s] structure, the final result of polyphony is not the annihilation of an incorrect utterance, but its transformation. This is a process whose final aim is the regeneration of an incorrect word into a true one."[11] Nina Perlina's insight applies to the artistic transformations of the three novels we have discussed. The

French material, admired for its artistry and deplored for its "depravity," dissolves into the Russian authors' moral vision. Dostoevsky's words about *Anna Karenina* apply equally to his own oeuvre: "The book in my opinion directly assumed the proportions of a fact capable of giving Europe an answer on our behalf."[12] That answer is that "evil in mankind is concealed more deeply than the physician-socialists suppose; . . . that the laws of the human spirit are so unknown to science, so obscure, so indeterminate and mysterious . . . that there is only He who saith: 'Vengeance is mine; I will repay'" (792–93).

Dmitri Merezhkovsky, followed by George Steiner and Mikhail Bakhtin, constructed an elegant opposition between the artistic methods of Tolstoy and Dostoevsky, but it is equally possible to see the unity of their vision. Both emphasize the moral authority of the Bible as the source of the Truth that could save Raskolnikov and Anna, were humans either purely rational or purely spiritual beings. Both authors see the representation of this Truth as the deep import of their work, the essence of its "answer to Europe." Yet if this were all, the novels would not continue to involve readers intensely. The characters face unresolvable dilemmas, which both authors allow us to empathize with variously, changing our responses from reading to reading. However authoritative Tolstoy's narrator may be, he cannot tell us what Anna should do, or even allot blame to the characters in a fixed way; the problem is too complex, dependent on a mix of disparate causes in various stages of evolution.[13] The fly-catching lawyer may be simply absurd, but Tolstoy nonetheless shows the law to be out of sync with the changing conditions of life; some members of society are clearly satirized as hypocritical, but others are simply honorable or even compassionate, and Tolstoy does not always judge their decisions or pronouncements. And however Dostoevsky's "voice-ideas" may take on an existence independent of a narrator, the position that the implied author would like to endorse is no less clear than Tolstoy's. As Caryl Emerson writes, "It could be argued that the unrelieved life-confusion of your typical Tolstoyan hero or heroine is more genuinely open, vulnerable, and in process than is the more articulate idea-confusion of any voice-idea in Dostoevsky."[14]

Dostoevsky has his characters read his biblical subtext out loud and act it out conspicuously; Tolstoy hints at *Anna Karenina*'s in his epigraph and embeds it more subtly into his novel. Both clothe the spiritual aspect of their novels in complex blends of the genres, themes, and plots of French (and other) novels and ground their polemic with French culture in the arguments of French philosophers. Dostoevsky loathes and parodies the Rousseau of the *Confessions,* while Tolstoy reveres the Rousseau of *Emile* and the *Social Contract.*[15] Dostoevsky detests Renan for his materialist interpretation of Jesus; Tolstoy criticizes Renan for failing to discuss Jesus's teachings. But far more important, both reject French Enlightenment faith in reason in favor of the intuitive Russian Orthodox vision of the human spirit.

RUSSIAN ORTHODOXY

The Russian nationalist self-definition of Orthodox Christian *narodnost'* and *sobornost'* as distinct from Western Roman Catholic decadence colored the perception of French culture and suffused Russian literature with a peculiar sense of spiritual mission. The realism of Janin, Balzac, Flaubert, and Zola implicitly bemoans the loss of faith in France by 1830 through parody or gruesome depictions of reality, but Balzac can find no devil any more potent than Jacques Collin, a homosexual king of the underworld who lacks any supernatural dimension, or the old antique dealer who acts out a typical Mephistophelean role while his victim gains no moral revelation. Dostoevsky and Tolstoy, despite their own struggles to gain faith in God, arguing with the French writers who meant the most to them for either aesthetic or ideological reasons, insist on faith's possibility. In this respect, adopting French literature as an interlocutor performed the role of Ivan Karamazov's devil in the "Grand Inquisitor"—it was a way of externalizing their own struggle for faith. At the same time, the extraordinary literature produced in France from the 1830s through the 1860s stimulated the best Russian writers of the period to artistic emulation; to take on their opponents on their own terms, they had to create an art that was as powerful and sophisticated as that of the French. Reading French literature with heightened sensitivity, and the ambivalence of the outsider, they wrote some of the greatest novels not just in the Russian, but in the Western tradition.

Appendix

"The Flood at Nantes"

MADAME AIMÉE HARELLE

The added emphases in my translation indicate points of contact with Pushkin's *Bronze Horseman.*

"Inondation à Nantes," 24–25

The wind turns to the west, and presses from the ocean rain clouds that for three weeks have torn the grey veil of a harsh winter. The sky has regained all its brilliance; it is under the influence of a pure sun, of a warm and balmy air that opens the month of March of the year 1789. It is about seven o'clock in the morning; great activity reigns in the port of Nantes: and yet, an extraordinary thing, none of its numerous dockyards contains a song, nor the blows of carpenters' hammers. The caulkers no longer smoke their tar by the quayside filled with ships leaning against the piers. The sailmaker has stopped assembling large bands of canvas along which just yesterday his hand ran so hastily. Construction, repairs, rope-making are all suspended: these are unaccustomed labors that at this moment are occupying a crowd of workers of all classes; and while they are occupied, distress is imprinted on each face. All movements are precipitous. No joyous words are exchanged; voices aren't raised except for mutual advice about what is urgent to do.

Take a look at the Loire, and you will learn the cause of this sad agitation. The river, suddenly enlarged by the melting of the snow and by long rains, *roils its troubled waters impetuously.* It overflows everywhere. Charming islands covered with rich plains and numerous flocks, which, just yesterday, offered gracious scenes on its left bank, are today no more than *a surging sea from which stick out here the tops of trees filled with dabs (flocons) of foam, there a group of houses against which the waves surge and break.* From moment to moment the flood makes frightening progress: it has already *penetrated several low quarters of the city,* and will not hesitate to cover the quays. However much a crowd of arms hastens to remove from riverside houses objects that *the water could take off or destroy,* the river mounts so rapidly that it seems impossible to save everything. *And every owner is distressed thinking about the ruinous damage that he tries in vain to prevent.*

Equally as active as the nervous inhabitants of Nantes, but animated by a different motive, the sailors *of all countries* move along the shore and make preparations for a departure too long delayed by contrary winds. At the command of the captain, the *national flag is deployed on each ship*: the cables are unfurled, the masts are covered with sails; and the anchor is at last weighed.

Notes

Introduction

1. In this sense, Russia is the colony and Europe the imperium of Said's *Orientalism.*

2. Hohendahl, *Building a National Literature,* 198.

3. Or perhaps, as Andrei Zorin suggests, the subject was neglected because few Soviet scholars knew French.

4. B. G. Reizov and Vera Milchina have also contributed a valuable body of work on the interrelationship between Russian and French literature in the eighteenth and early nineteenth centuries.

5. Lotman, "Russkaia literatura na frantsuzskom iazyke," in *Izbrannye stat'i,* 2:368. All references to Lotman's work will give volume and page numbers in Arabic.

6. Lotman, "K postroeniiu teorii vzaimodeistviia kul'tur," *Izbrannye stat'i,* 2:117.

7. Fonvizin, letter to Petr Aleksandrovich Panin, 29 September 1778, in *Polnoe sobranie sochinenii D. I. Fonvizina* (hereafter *Pss*), 904.

8. Seton-Watson, *Nations and States,* 5.

9. Cracraft, "Peter the Great and the Problem of Periodization," 11.

10. Rogger, *National Consciousness,* 5–9. Much of my discussion of the eighteenth century here represents a condensation of the first two chapters of Rogger's book.

11. Shcherbatov, *Neizdannye sochineniia,* 126.

12. Rogger, *National Consciousness,* 45–84.

13. "We are beginning and they are ending." Fonvizin, letter to Ia. P. Bulgakov, 25 January 1778, *Pss,* 914.

14. Shishkov, *Rassuzhdenie,* 8.

15. Karamzin, *Letters of a Russian Traveler,* 3.

16. Anderson, *Imagined Communities,* 19–21.

17. Hastings, *The Construction of Nationhood,* 3–4.

18. For a discussion of mythological orientation, see Lotman, "Tekst v

tekste," *Izbrannye stat'i,* 1:148–60. For a study of the biblical basis of five Russian novels, see Bethea, *The Shape of Apocalypse.*

19. Rachel Polonsky addresses the same issues in the introduction to her *English Literature and the Russian Aesthetic Renaissance,* especially 2, 6.

20. Schelling, *System of Transcendental Idealism,* pt 6, p. 219–36, especially 222–24.

21. Belknap, *The Genesis of* The Brothers Karamazov, 2.

22. Nina Perlina (*Varieties of Poetic Utterance,* 55–58) also applies Taranovsky's method of poetic analysis to prose.

23. Thomas Barran (*Russia Reads Rousseau,* xxiv) uses "intertext" this way, quoting Laurent Jenny ("The Strategy of Form," in *French Literary Theory Today,* ed. Tsvetan Todorov [Cambridge, MA: Cambridge University Press, 1982], 34–63, 37).

24. Eliot, "Tradition and the Individual Talent," 13.

25. Taranovsky, "Concert at the Railroad Station," 18.

26. Ronen, *An Approach to Mandel'shtam,* xvii-xviii.

27. Riffaterre, "Syllepsis," 625–38, Riffaterre, "Flaubert's Suppositions," 2–11; Toporov, "O Strukture romana Dostoevskogo," 225–302.

28. The terms are Riffaterre's. See *Semiotics of Poetry,* 4–6.

29. See Meyer, "Gogol and Hoffman," 62–73.

30. Frow, "Intertextuality and Ontology," 46.

31. Bakhtin, *Problems of Dostoevsky's Poetics,* 69–73.

32. René Wellek long ago reached this conclusion. See "Bakhtin's View of Dostoevsky," 232–35.

33. Tynianov, *Arkhaisty i novatory,* especially 87–227.

34. Rushdy, *Neo-Slave Narratives,* 17.

35. Pushkin, *Eugene Onegin,* 1:xxvi.

Chapter 1. From Poetry to Prose

1. Reizov, *Bal'zac,* 297.

2. Lichtlé, "Balzac et la *Revue étrangère,*" 55.

3. Reizov, *Bal'zac,* 297.

4. Ibid., 294.

5. Ibid., 297.

6. This is according to Evgenii Borisovich Belodubrovskii. See Modzalevskii, "Biblioteka A. S. Pushkina," 369.

7. Kahn, *Pushkin's* "The Bronze Horseman," 3–8.

8. Lednicki, *Pushkin's "Bronze Horseman"*; Jakobson, *Pushkin and His Sculptural Myth,* 26.

9. Eidelman, *Pushkin: Istoriia i sovremennost',* 142–48.

10. Lednicki, *Pushkin's "Bronze Horseman,"* 25–42.

11. Vernadsky, "Pushkin and the Decembrists," 45–76; Blagoi, *Sotsiologiia tvorchestva Pushkina;* Jakobson, *Pushkin and His Sculptural Myth,* 25.

12. Briggs, *A Comparative Study,* 106–7.

13. Akhmatova, "Pushkin i nevskoe vzmore," 119–26.

14. Stroganova, "Otgoloski dekabristskoi temy," 110–18.

15. Mirsky, *Pushkin,* 209–10; Lednicki, *Pushkin's "Bronze Horseman,"* 13–14; Kuleshov, *Zhizn' i tvorchestvo A.S. Pushkina,* 331.

16. Jakobson, *Pushkin and His Sculptural Myth,* 26.

17. Harkins, "The Place of *Domik v Kolomne,*" 201–2.

18. This is in keeping with Lotman's observation that Pushkin's thinking about the historical process in the 1830s took the form of a tripartite paradigm. See Lotman, "Zamysel stikhotvoreniia *'O poslednem dne Pompei,'*" in *Izbrannye stat'i,* 2:445–51.

19. Mirsky, *Pushkin,* 212.

20. Lednicki, *Pushkin's "Bronze Horseman,"* 137.

21. Pushkin, quoted in Lednicki, *Pushkin's "Bronze Horseman,"* 12; Kahn, *Pushkin's* "The Bronze Horseman," 5.

22. Jakobson, *Pushkin and His Sculptural Myth,* 25.

23. Lednicki, *Pushkin's "Bronze Horseman,"* 11–12.

24. Vera Milchina has shown the degree to which Pushkin incorporated French prose works into his poetry and prose in "Frantsuzskaia literatura v proizvedeniiakh Pushkina," 244–54.

25. Pushkin, letter 495, first half of September 1832, *Pss,* 10:416.

26. Madame Aimée Harelle, "Inondation à Nantes," 1:24–41.

27. Pushkin, "Mednyi vsadnik," *Pss,* 4:377–98.

28. Vernadsky, "Pushkin and the Decembrists," 74.

29. Harkins, "The Place of *Domik v Kolomne,*" 205.

30. Harelle, "Inondation à Nantes," 26.

31. Ibid., 37.

32. Ibid., 38.

33. Eidelman, *Pushkin: Istoriia i sovremennost',* 111.

34. Frank, "Pushkin kak politicheskii myslitel'," 396–422.

35. Pushkin, "John Tenner," *Pss,* 7:434–35.

36. Karpovich, "Pushkin as an Historian," 196. I am grateful to Timothy Binyon and Vera Milchina for their remarks on this topic.

37. Kuleshov, *Zhizn' i tvorchestvo A. S. Pushkina*; Meilakh, "Pushkin i dekabristy posle 1825 goda," 2:196–213.

38. Blagoi, *The Sacred Lyre,* 307; Kuleshov, *Zhizn' i tvorchestvo A.S. Pushkina,* 312–14.

39. Pushkin, "André Chénier," *Pss,* 2:259–60.

40. Pushkin, "Ezersky," *Pss,* 4:344.

41. Harelle, "Inondation à Nantes," 28.

42. Jakobson, *Pushkin and His Sculptural Myth,* 10; Belknap, "A Likely Story, Pushkin's *Bronze Horseman,*" 26–33; Nepomnyashchy, "The Poet, History, and the Supernatural," 34–46.

43. Zhekulin, "On Rereading the *Bronze Horseman,*" 230.

44. Harelle, "Inondation à Nantes," 41.

45. Nepomnyashchy, "The Poet, History, and the Supernatural," 37.

46. Arkhangel'skii, *"Mednyi vsadnik,"* 8, notes that prose is the source of the realism of *The Bronze Horseman.*

47. Balzac, "La Transaction," 149–76; 223–41. Page numbers in the text refer to the *Revue étrangère* edition.

48. Honoré de Balzac, *La Comedie Humaine*, 3:1333–35n.
49. Gogol, *Polnoe sobranie sochinenii*, 2:753.
50. Nilsson, *Gogol et Pétersbourg*.
51. Nilsson, "On the Origins of Gogol's 'Overcoat,'" 67.
52. Lotman, "Pushkin i 'Povest' o kapitane Kopeikine," in *Izbrannye stat'i*, 3:45–47.
53. On this topic see Nilsson, "On the Origins of Gogol's 'Overcoat,'" 66. He also identifies Balzac's "Les Employés" as a source for the "Overcoat," 67.
54. Robert, *Le Nouveau petit Robert*.
55. Nabokov, *Nikolai Gogol*, 144.
56. Balzac, "La Transaction," 149.
57. Gogol, *Diary of a Madman*, 10. Hereafter, page numbers in the text for "Diary," "The Nose," and "The Overcoat" refer to this edition.
58. E. T. A. Hoffmann also uses this detail in "The Golden Pot." See Meyer, "Iz 'Zolotogo gorshka' Gofmana," 336–44.
59. Balzac, *La Comedie Humaine*, 1342n, 1346n.
60. Nilsson compares this feature of "The Overcoat" to Odoevsky's tale "The Brigadier" (1833), in which a clerk appears after his death to accuse men of indifference, though the phantom appears only to the narrator. See Nilsson, "On the Origins of Gogol's 'Overcoat,'" 69.
61. Nilsson, "On the Origins of Gogol's 'Overcoat,'" 63.
62. In *Dostoevsky and Romantic Realism*, Donald Fanger divides nineteenth-century Russian literature into these periods.
63. N. K. Gudzii, "Istoriia pisaniia i pechataniia *Anny* Kareninoi," in L. N. Tolstoi, *Pss*, 20:578.
64. Belknap, *The Genesis of* The Brothers Karamazov.

Chapter 2. Lermonotov, *A Hero of Our Time*

1. As many have noted, for example, Eikhenbaum, *O proze*, 231–304; Fiodorov, *Lermontov i literatura ego vremeni*, 198–200.
2. Vinogradov, "Stil' prozy Lermontova," 517–628.
3. Tomashevskii, "Proza Lermontova," suggests that Lermontov left his early prose unfinished because he outgrew his works as he wrote them (495).
4. Lermontov, letter of 8 June 1838, *Pss*, 2:349.
5. Gershtein, *Geroi nashego vremeni*, 25–31; Kiiko, "*Geroi nashego vremeni*," 189.
6. *Biblioteka dlia chteniia*, April 1844. Quoted by Belinsky in his review of the third edition of *A Hero of Our Time* in *Literaturnaia gazeta* in 1844, translated by Neil Cornwell in his edition of *A Hero of Our Time*, 148–49.
7. See Nabokov, "Translator's Foreword," in Lermontov's *A Hero of Our Time*, v–xix.
8. See Eikhenbaum, *O proze*, 231–304; and Vinogradov, "Stil' prozy Lermontova," for a detailed discussion of this transition.
9. See Vladimir Golstein's excellent discussion of "marlinism" in *A Hero of our Time* in *Lermontov's Narratives of Heroism*, 133–53.

10. Haumant, *La culture française en Russie*; Duchesne, *Michel Iourievitch Lermontov.* See especially 301–24 (French edition); Rodzevich, *Lermontov, kak romanist.*

11. Tomashevskii, "Proza Lermontova," 469–516. Tomashevskii traces a variety of Western literary sources in Lermontov's prose: in *Vadim* he finds elements of Sir Walter Scott's historical novels as purveyed by Balzac's *Les Chouans*—English literature is received through the French.

12. Woronzoff, "The Pattern of Discovery," 51–61. See also Haumant, *La culture française en Russie*, 389; Tomashevskii, "Proza Lermontova," 500–501; and Mersereau, *Mikhail Lermontov*, 91.

13. See Schmidt, "Psikhologiia *Geroia nashego vremeni*," 59–74, 64. He considers the French borrowings, of which he names only a few, to be mere appropriations clumsily stitched together by the immature Lermontov.

14. See Rodzevich, *Lermontov, kak romanist*, 70, 73 on *Adolphe*; 91 on *Memoirs d'un enfant du siècle.* Tomashevskii only enumerates the bored Western literary heroes who contribute to Pechorin's character in *A Hero of Our Time*, considering that Lermontov is perfecting, not imitating, French models ("Proza Lermontova," 502).

15. As Tomashevskii says ("Proza Lermontova," 497–48), all references to the French Romantic heroes are mediated by Pushkin's use of them in *Onegin*, as Onegin's melancholy is itself inherited from Western models. He notes that although Lermontov knew *Onegin* before writing *Princess Ligovskaya*, the break in Lermontov's work occurred later (500). Perhaps the *Tales of Belkin*, which carried the parody even further in "The Lady-Peasant," were instrumental.

16. Sainte-Beuve, *Avant-propos.*

17. Chateaubriand, *Les Natchez*, 2:105. In-text citations refer to volume and page number.

18. Musset, *La Confession d'un enfant du siècle*, 299. Further references to this work are cited parenthetically in the text.

19. Todd, *Fiction and Society*, 143.

20. Reid, "The Society Tale," 53.

21. Todd, *Fiction and Society*, 137–63.

22. Rodzevich, *Lermontov, kak romanist*, 74.

23. Haumant, *La culture française en Russie*, 381.

24. Lermontov, *A Hero of Our Time*, trans. Nabokov, 126–27. All quotations cited in text are from this translation with minor alterations.

25. Constant, *Adolphe*, 38, 40, 41. All quotations cited in text are from this translation with minor alterations.

26. Hasty, *Pushkin's Tatiana*, 11.

27. Ibid., 64.

28. Rodzevich, *Lermontov, kak romanist*, 61. Chapters 3 and 4 outline the parallels between *Adolphe* and *Hero*; chapters 6–8 do the same for *The Confession* and *Hero.*

29. Golstein, *Lermontov's Narratives of Heroism*, 88–89.

30. Durylin, *Geroi*, 130–32.

31. Belinsky, *Pss*, 4:265.

32. Eikhenbaum, *M. Iu. Lermontov,* 148.
33. Dubshan, "'Bela,'" 270.
34. Mikhailova, *Proza Lermontova,* 203–381, especially 219–20.
35. For a thorough discussion of Pushkin's treatment of the "Caucasian epidemic" in Russian literature, see Layton, *Russian Literature and Empire,* 36–53.
36. Peter Scotto ("Prisoners of the Caucasus," 246–60) says the tale should be read as "an interrogation of the discourse and practice of imperialism" that transcends the discussion of romantic/realist and Western European models; Pechorin is to Bela as Russia is to the Caucasus (247).
37. The critics who have identified "The Red Seal" as a source for *Hero,* Duchesne (*Michel Iourievitch Lermontov,* 319), Tomashevskii ("Proza Lermontova," 500–501), and John Mersereau (*Mikhail Lermontov,* 91), say only that Lermontov draws three things from it—the image of Maxim Maximych, the narrative strategy and the setting. Only one critic has devoted more than a paragraph to exploring de Vigny's role in *Hero*: Alexander Woronzoff finds similar themes in the two books and establishes the parallels between the old soldier, the traveling officer and the young woman but doesn't analyze the intertextual relationship between the two stories.
38. de Vigny, *Servitude and Grandeur of Arms,* 20. Further references to this work are cited parenthetically in the text.
39. Lermontov, *Sobranie sochinenii v 4-kh tomakh,* 4:475–79, 475.
40. Lermontov, "Bela," 167.
41. Similarly, he smuggles in a reference to the exiled Decembrists in his description of Werner's "philosophical-metaphysical" discussions in a "numerous and noisy circle of youth" that referred to their political discussions in Stavropol (Durylin, *Geroi,* 133).
42. This point is not always understood by early commentators, who sometimes even conflate Lermontov and his narrator-editor. Robin Aizelwood, however, calls the narrator "a hack ruthlessly in search of material to publish" ("*Geroi nashego vremeni,*" 40).
43. Ibid., 39. See also Drozda, "Povestvovatel'naia struktura *Geroia nashego vremeni,*" 5–34.
44. Rodzevich, *Lermontov kak romanist,* 50–58.
45. Bela's and Vera's love for Pechorin and the undine's for Ianko may be selfless but cannot be called ideal in the Romantic sense.
46. See Vinogradov, "Stil' prozy Lermontova," 573–79; and Aizelwood, "*Geroi nashego vremeni,*" 41.
47. Tomashevskii ("Proza Lermontova," 508) and Dominique Millet-Gerard ("Dandys et coquettes," 43) point out that Lermontov could have known any of the five editions of variations of *Scènes de la vie privée* or *Même histoire* that appeared between 1832 and 1838, where the heroine is named Madame de Vieumesnil, before being renamed Madame d'Aiglemont.
48. Balzac, *La Femme de trente ans,* 108–9. Further references to this work are cited parenthetically in the text.
49. Millet-Gerard, "Dandys et coquettes," 44–47.
50. Balzac, avant-propos to the 1834 edition of *Même histoire, Scènes de la vie privée.* Millet-Guerard notes that the function of Balzac's two forewords to the

1832 edition (*Scènes de la vie privée*) and the 1834 edition (*Même histoire*) function the same way Lermontov's foreword of 1841 does ("Dandys et coquettes," 61–62).

51. For the details of this, see Drozda, "Povestvovatel'naia struktura *Geroia nashego vremeni*," 5–9.

52. Lotman, "Problema Vostoka i Zapada," *Izbrannye stat'i*, 3:9–23.

53. Lermontov, "Primechaniia," *Pss*, 4:663.

54. Quoted in Durylin, *Geroi*, 208–9, from Tseidler, Untitled, *Russkii vestnik* 9 (1888): 135–36.

55. Excerpts from chapters one and three were first published in *Biblioteka dlia chteniia* in 1835; *Undina, starinnaia povest', razskazannaia v proze baronom Lamot Fuke, na russkom v stikhakh V. Zhukovskim* appeared as a separate book in 1837.

56. Zurov, "'Taman' Lermontova i 'L'Orco,'" 278–81.

57. Sand, "L'Orco," 584–99. Page numbers refer to the French edition.

58. I am grateful to Robin Aizelwood for this observation, which connects Lermontov's use of "L'Orco" to Peter Scotto's reading of *Hero* as a critique of Russian imperialism.

59. Noted by Zurov, "'Taman' Lermontova i 'L'Orco,'" 279.

60. Quoted in Durylin, *Geroi*, 208.

61. I am grateful to Jenefer Coates and Norman Shapiro for their help with "Trilby."

62. See Arian, "Some Aspect," 28–29.

63. La Motte-Fouqué, "Undine," 66.

64. V. A. Zhukovsky, "Undina," *Sobranie sochinenii v 4-kh tomakh*, 2:331–400, 332. Further references to this work are cited parenthetically in the text.

65. Goethe, *Wilhelm Meister*, 85.

66. Chasles, "Eglantine," 364–83. Further references to this work are cited parenthetically in the text.

67. Tomashevskii, "Proza Lermontova," 506.

68. Ibid., 502–7. He says that *Gerfaut* is only a "literary relative" (507) of *Hero*.

69. Ibid.

70. Ibid., 503.

71. Ibid., 505–6.

72. de Bernard, *The Lover and the Husband*, 1:241. Citations in the text refer to the English translation by Mrs. Gore.

73. Golstein, *Lermontov's Narratives of Heroism*, 148–53.

74. I am grateful to David Powelstock for suggesting the relationship to Diderot and for allowing me to read his manuscript. See Powelstock, *Becoming Mikhail Lermontov*, 329–397.

75. Diderot, *Jacques le fataliste*, 25. Further references to this work are cited parenthetically in the text.

76. Golstein, *Lermontov's Narratives of Heroism*, 131, 124.

77. Lotman, "Problema Vostoka i Zapada," 9–23.

78. Golstein, *Lermontov's Narratives of Heroism*, 129.

79. Powelstock, *Becoming Mikhail Lermontov*, 337.

80. Lotman, "Problema Vostoka i Zapada," 15–17.

81. See Belinsky, *Pss,* 1:139–40; and others discussed in Bocharov, "O smysle *Grobovshchika,*" 199. Lermontov's structuring of *Hero* based on the *Belkin* cycle has gone unnoticed by excellent critics like Viktor Vinogradov ("Stil' prozy Lermontova"), who discusses the interplay of Gogol's and Pushkin's modes through Lermontov's prose. Boris Eikhenbaum places the structure of *A Hero of Our Time* in the context of the development of the Russian story cycle and emphasizes Lermontov's achievement in creating a psychological novel out of that genre (*O proze,* 427–30). V. Turbin investigates the constant use Pushkin and Lermontov made of the work of secondary writers; he pays particular attention to genre in noting the interplay between poetry and prose, but does not examine the story cycle (*Pushkin, Lermontov, Gogol'*).

82. Pushkin, *Eugene Onegin,* 1:xxvii.

83. U. R. Fokht compares Lermontov's treatment of Krasinsky to Pushkin's of Samson Vyrin in "The Stationmaster," as well as to Gogol's of Piskarev and Poprishchin, noting that Lermontov deepens Pushkin's realism (*Lermontov,* 145, 156).

84. Pushkin himself suggests that direction in *Tales of Belkin,* taking his epigraphs from poetry and answering them in prose tales. See Bethea and Davydov, "Pushkin's Saturnine Cupid," 14.

85. Discussed by Fiodorov, *Lermontov,* 209.

86. Tomashevskii mentions Belkin as one of the many "false authors" current in literature of the period but does not discuss the *Tales* ("Proza Lermontova," 509). U. R. Fokht compares the economy of Pushkin's portrait of Belkin in "From the Editor" and of Vyrin in "The Stationmaster" to that of Lermontov's portrait of Maksim Maksimych in order to emphasize the analytic aspects of the portrait of Pechorin in *A Hero of Our Time* (*Lermontov,* 153). S. Durylin says that Lermontov learned his realist narrative devices from the *Tales of Belkin* in writing *Princess Ligovskaya* (Durylin, *Geroi,* 9). Vinogradov ("Stil' prozy Lermontova," 564–65) comes the closest to establishing a relationship, seeing in *A Hero of Our Time* a return to Pushkin's realist manner in the *Tales.* Vinogradov emphasizes the differences: Pushkin uses the three prisms of narrator, Belkin, and editor, while Lermontov uses two (a point disputed in this chapter), and while Pushkin's tales are not about Belkin, Lermontov's are about Pechorin. These, as well as Vinogradov's parallels between *Onegin* and "Princess Mary," are debatable readings.

87. "Beginning readers" is Bethea and Davydov's term ("Pushkin's Saturnine Cupid," 14). The idea of Belkin as an overview of available plots and genres is discussed by Vinogradov, "Stil' prozy Lermontova," 564–65, and taken up by Bethea and Davydov.

88. Although Lermontov published "Bela" (March 1839), "The Fatalist" (November 1839), and "Taman" (February 1840) in *Otechestvennye zapiski* before the novel appeared in April 1840, it is clear from the manuscript of *A Hero of Our Time* that he conceived the five stories as a united whole: the notebook containing the final versions of "Maksim Maksimych," "The Fatalist," and "Princess Mary" bears the title "One of the Heroes of the Beginning of the Century." See Mikhailova, *Proza Lermontova,* 192; and Durylin, *Geroi,* 10.

89. See Turbin, *Pushkin, Lermontov, Gogol'*, 68–76; Bethea and Davydov argue that the count, Burmin, and Dunya outgrow their youthful flightiness and are rewarded, while Silvio, Vladimir, and Vyrin "are punished because they are flat and non-developing, too ready to translate literary novels into life" ("Pushkin's Saturnine Cupid," 13), but the authors do not claim that the rewarded characters gain any awareness of literary stereotypes.

90. Herbert Eagle discusses the genres of the tales comprising *A Hero of Our Time* in his article "Lermontov's 'Play' with Romantic Genre Expectations," 299–313).

91. On the Caucasus replacing the Alps, see Layton, *Russian Literature and Empire*, 36–53.

92. Pushkin, *The Complete Prose Tales*, 106. Further references to this work are cited parenthetically in the text.

93. In the first edition, the actual author beyond the text is only indirectly evoked by the narrator's foreword to Pechorin's journal; Lermontov's foreword to *A Hero of Our Time* first appeared in the second edition of 1841.

94. On Russian versions of the genre of the *récit de voyage* see Layton, *Russian Literature and Empire*, 54–70.

95. Language is called into question in the same way. The repeated phrases and epithets that Nabokov attributes to Lermontov's stylistic immaturity (xiii) are constantly being reset into new contexts from story to story. The device is indicated by Pechorin's repetition of Grushnitsky's courtship of Mary; using the same methods and clichés self-consciously, the more sophisticated imitator of the Byronic hero gets the girl.

96. Turbin (*Pushkin, Lermontov, Gogol'*, 69–73) lists three tales of stationmasters with which Pushkin takes issue: V. Karlgof's "Stantsionnyi smotritel'" (1826); F. Bulgarin's "Ivan Vyzhigin" (1829); and Prince Vyazemsky's "dictator of the posting station" from his poem "The Station" ("Stantsiia," 1829) quoted in Pushkin's epigraph.

97. Vinogradov ("Stil' prozy Lermontova," 564–65) writes that in "Maksim Maksimych" Lermontov makes fun of Pushkin's ignorance about the Caucasus in *Journey to Arzrum*, in which Pushkin has an excessive eighteen oxen harnessed to a cart.

98. Tomashevskii, "Pushkin i frantsuzskaia literatura," 68.

99. But they aren't disguised enough that the peasant children in Tolstoy's school could understand them. See Bocharov, "O smysle *Grobovshchika*," 200.

100. On this question in general see Hartman, "Romanticism and Anti-Self-Consciousness," 46–56.

101. This reading suggests that the term "superfluous man" is itself an inappropriate and restrictively socio-historical category. Vladimir Levin has effectively argued against the term on its own grounds in "Dostoevskii, 'podpolnyi paradoksalist' i Lermontov," 142–56, especially 151–56.

102. Lotman shows that toward the end of his life Lermontov moves toward the resolution of opposition, to synthesis, in his work ("Problema Vostoka i Zapada," 21–23). The conflict between free will and predestination, however, reflects Lermontov's enthusiasm for Schopenhauer, who endorses action as the expression of free will and relates to the social restrictions of the period. This

opposition remains irresolvable; even Pechorin acknowledges that ultimately everyone is controlled to some indeterminable degree by fate.

Chapter 3. Dostoevsky, *Crime and Punishment*

1. Chapple, "Catalogue of Dostoevskii's References to French Literature," 335–53.
2. Grossman, "Dostoevskii i Evropa," in *Sobranie sochinenii,* 2:193–94.
3. Toporov, "O strukture romana Dostoevskogo," 255–302.
4. Dostoevskii, *Polnoe sobranie sochinenii,* 5:76. I have translated in-text citations from the Russian.
5. Dostoevskii, "Zimnye zametki," *Pss,* 5:92.
6. This chapter's epigraph—"Frantsuzy, ei-bogu, takoi narod, ot kotorogo toshnit"—comes from the same letter: F. M. Dostoevsky, letter to N. N. Strakhov, 26 June/8 July 1862, *Pss,* 28.2:27.
7. Dostoevskii, letter of 9 August 1838, *Pss,* 28.1:51.
8. Grossman, *Seminarii po Dostoevskomu,* 32.
9. Balzac, *Oeuvres completes,* 26, 470.
10. "La littérature frénétique," in *Grand Larousse Encyclopédique,* 5:267.
11. Choldin, *A Fence around the Empire,* 196–98, shows that sexual content was by far the most important factor in banning the importation of foreign books during the second half of the nineteenth century. She tells of a mid-century German traveler to St. Petersburg whose copy of Balzac's *Parents pauvres* was confiscated at the border (1).
12. In the freer atmosphere of the 1860s, a number of articles appeared that treated the problem of prostitution; after the censorship was lifted in 1905, there was an even sharper increase of public discussion of the "sexual question." See Stites, "Prostitution and Society," 349, 359.
13. Robert L. Belknap refers to this kind of subtext/intertext as a "literary instrument" (*The Genesis of* The Brothers Karamazov, 65).
14. Vinogradov examined the influence of Janin's *The Dead Donkey and the Guillotined Woman* on Gogol's "Nevskii prospekt" in "Romanticheskii naturalizm Zhiul' Zhanen i Gogol'," in *Evoliutsiia russkogo naturalizma,* 153–204.
15. Honoré de Balzac, *Splendeurs et misères des courtisanes;* text references are to this English translation by Rayner Heppenstall. On Eugène Sue, see Ian Pickup, "Elements of Balzacian Portraiture in the Novels of Eugène Sue," 34–45; Charles Bernheimer, *Figures of Ill Repute,* 46.
16. Peter Brooks (*Reading for the Plot,* 155–162) and Charles Bernheimer (*Figures of Ill Repute,* 34–68) have discussed the French treatment of prostitution in helpful detail.
17. "Petersburg Visions in Poetry and Prose," quoted in Fanger, *Dostoevsky and Romantic Realism,* 149.
18. See Vinogradov, *Evoliutsiia russkogo naturalizma,* especially 291–390; Frank, *Dostoevsky: The Miraculous Years,* 96–97, 101; Fanger, *Dostoevsky and Romantic Realism,* 135–36, 151.
19. Atkinson, *Eugène Sue et le roman-feuilleton,* 11.
20. Ibid., 8.

21. See Eco, "Rhetoric and Ideology," 134.

22. Bazin, *Questions littéraires et sociales*, 18.

23. Tomashevskii, "Pushkin i frantsuzskaia literatura," 65; also in Tomashevskii, "Frantsuzskaia literatura v pis'makh Pushkina," 377.

24. Mirecourt, *Jules Janin*, 31; Balzac, quoted in Bailbé, *Jules Janin*, 13; Piedagnel, *Jules Janin*, 61.

25. Gobineau, "Jules Janin," in *Etudes critiques*, 115–30; Montifaud, *les Romantiques*, 68–73; Banville, *Mes souvenirs*, 53–62.

26. Abbé Tiberge (pseudonym of Regnier-Destourbet), *Louisa*, 3.

27. Tomashevskii, "Frantsuzskaia literatura v pis'makh Pushkina," 377; Makashin, "Literaturnye vzaimootnosheniia Rossii i Frantsii," v–lxxvii, xxxvi.

28. Belinsky quoted by Haumant, *La culture française en Russie*, 361.

29. Banville, a neighbor of Janin's, reports Janin's remark that he could never write the books he meant to: "When I've decided to marry my heroes, it turns out I kill them; and if I've condemned them to death, they suddenly marry" (56).

30. Jules Janin, *L'âne mort et la femme guillotinée*, 44. This passage is absent in the first edition (Paris: Baudouin, 1829), suggesting that Janin wanted to emphasize the parodic aspect of his work after it was attacked in the press for its depiction of gruesome detail. Further in-text citations are from *The Dead Donkey and the Guillotined Woman.*

31. Joel A. Hunt suggests that Balzac's *Un Début dans la vie* is the source for Dostoevsky's scene of the mare beating ("Balzac and Dostoevsky," 440). On Hugo's "Melancholia," see Lapshin, *Estetika Dostoevskogo*. For the relationship between the two poems, see Serman, "Nekrasov i Viktor Giugo," 128–36. Natalie Babel Brown considers the interrelationship among Nekrasov's, Hugo's, and Dostoesvky's horse-beating scenes (*Hugo and Dostoevsky*, 92–105).

32. *Crime and Punishment*, 65–66. English translations (some slightly amended) are cited from Dostoevsky, *Crime and Punishment*, trans. Sidney Monas.

33. See Blackmur, "Murder in Your Own Room," 119–40.

34. Vinogradov, *Evoliutsiia russkogo naturalizma*, 303.

35. Brooks, *Reading for the Plot*, 146.

36. F. M. Dostoevsky, letter to M. M. Dostoevsky, 4 May 1845, *Pss*, 28:110.

37. See Fridlender, *Dostoevskii i mirovaia literatura*, 31. G. Gukovskii discusses Sue's similar effect on Dostoevsky's contemporary, Nekrasov: "From Eugène Sue Nekrasov took a new way of describing the depths, the world of criminals and beggars, the city as a place of vice, dirt, poverty, misfortune" (*Zhizn' i pokhozhdeniia Tikhona Trosnikova*, 360).

38. Donald Fanger lists four published in 1845: Kovalevsky, *Day and Night*; Nekrasov, *Petersburg Corners*; Krestovsky, *Petersburg Slums* (1846); Butkov, *Petersburg Summits*. He includes Dostoevsky's *Poor Folk* (1846) in the list (*Dostoevsky and Romantic Realism*, 135). The last hints at the threat of prostitution.

39. Victor Terras identifies Fleur de Marie as a source for Sonya in *Reading Dostoevsky*, 53.

40. Eugène Sue, *The Mysteries of Paris*, 27. Further references to this work are cited parenthetically in the text.

41. Bernheimer discusses this topos of the prostitute tale as dictated by the male author's desire to contain the female's "unruly energy" (*Figures of Ill Repute*, 52).

42. Jean-Louis Bory notes this (*Eugène Sue*, 281).

43. Gregg, "Balzac and the Women in *The Queen of Spades*," 279–82.

44. On the connection between *Le Père Goriot* and *Crime and Punishment*, see Sicher, "The Boundaries of Space in the Modern Literary Text," 306–9; Walker, "The Cramped Room in the City," 288–93; Blinoff, "Dostoevskii et Balzac," 342–55; Hunt, "Balzac and Dostoevsky," 307–24; and Hunt, "Color and Imagery in Dostoevsky and Balzac," 411–23.

45. Bernheimer (*Figures of Ill Repute*, 42) identifies four works employing this archetype: J.-J. Rousseau, "The Loves of Milord Edouard Bromston" (1780); Madame de la Charrière, *Lettres écrites de Lausanne* (1788); Restif de la Bretonne, *Contemporaines de commun*, "La Courtisane vertueuse, ou la vertu dans la vice"; J. H. Meister, "Betzi, ou l'amour comme il est" (1801).

46. Citations are from Balzac, *A Harlot High and Low*, trans. Rayner Heppenstall.

47. Bernheimer, *Figures of Ill Repute*, 45.

48. Rozenblium, "Tvorcheskaia laboratoriia Dostoevskogo," 46. See also Dostoevsky, *The Notebooks for* Crime and Punishment, 44.

49. F. M. Dostoevskii, "Brat'ia Karamazovy," *Pss*, 14:210.

50. Clark, "Parody and Revolt," 254–55.

51. On using prostitutes in medical research, see Bernheimer, *Figures of Ill Repute*, 47.

52. Nilsson, *Gogol et Pétersbourg*, 33.

53. Balzac, *The Wild Ass's Skin*, trans. Hunt, 21. Further references to this work are cited parenthetically in the text.

54. Dostoevsky, *The Notebooks for* Crime and Punishment, 46.

55. They evolve as they did for Dostoevsky in the course of composing the novel (ibid., 6).

56. *Pss*, 6:25; *Crime and Punishment*, trans. Monas, 37–38. See also Knapp, "The Dynamics of the Idea of Napoleon," 31–40, where the development is charted.

57. Dostoevsky, *The Notebooks for* Crime and Punishment, 161–62.

58. "Palmerston, Henry John Temple," in *Encyclopedia Britannica*, 1911, 20: 645–49.

59. See Ludwig Büchner (1824–1899), *Darwinismus und Socialismus* and *Kraft und Stoff* (*Force and matter; or, Principles of the natural order of the universe. With a system of morality based thereon*). The latter book is the basis of the "nihilist" Bazarov's views in Turgenev's *Father's and Sons*. The geologist Karl Christoph Vogt (1817–1895) was the author of *Lectures on Man: His place in creation and in the history of the earth*. Adolph Wagner (1835–1917) was an economist and popularizer of the concept of "moral statistics"; he wrote *Theoretische Sozialökonomik oder, allgemeine und theoretische Volkswirtschaftslehre. Grundriss tunlichst in prinzipieller Behandlungsweise*. His statistical sociology is the source for Raskolnikov's ironic words about prostitution: "A certain percentage go that way."

60. Choldin, *A Fence around the Empire,* 187–95.

61. The name furthermore suggests that the publisher is part of a circle of seminarists known to be close to democratic circles of *raznochintsy* (F. M. Dostoevskii, "Primechaniia" (Notes), *Pss,* 7:371).

62. See Frank, *Dostoevsky: The Stir of Liberation,* 238–42; "The Genesis of *Crime and Punishment,*" 124–143; and *Dostoevsky: The Miraculous Years,* 120.

63. Reizov, *Bal'zak,* 169–70. Reizov points out that Grossman assumed that Dostoevsky read *Père Goriot* in this translation, and further that this was originally Balzac's own ending, which Reizov shows to be false.

64. Grossman, *Balzac and Dostoevsky,* 32–47.

65. On this question, see Isabelle Naginski, "Intertexts: The Old Mandarin," unpublished manuscript. I am grateful to the author for this information. Robin Feuer Miller finds the dialogue between Rastingnac and Bianchon important to Ivan's "confession," his formulation of the philosophy underlying his "Legend of the Grand Inquisitor" in *The Brothers Karamazov* (*The Brothers Karamazov: Worlds of the Novel,* 62–63).

66. Bem, *O Dostoevskom,* 47.

67. Ibid.

68. Toporov, "O strukture romana Dostoevskogo," 251n52.

69. Grossman, *Balzac and Dostoevsky,* 41.

70. I am grateful to my students Angela Ng, Dan Goldberg, and John Moore for their observations on these parallels.

71. Hunt, "Balzac and Dostoevsky," 312–17.

72. Ibid., 316.

73. Karl Marx and Friedrich Engels, *Die Heilige Familie oder Kritik der kritischen Kritik: gegen Bruno Bauer und Consorten* (1845). Quoted and discussed by Brooks, *Reading for Plot,* 153; and Eco, "Rhetoric and Ideology," 131.

74. See Stead, *Vidocq.* Vidocq went on to a hugely successful career as a detective, working with trusted friends who were former criminals, and founded the French *Sûreté.*

75. Scholars have suggested that here the "New Jerusalem" refers to Saint-Simon's socialist utopia (e.g., Kirpotin, *Razocharovanie i krushenie,* 111), but as Gary Rosenshield points out (*Crime and Punishment,* 112n5, 130), this makes no sense in context. Berdiaev has a religious meaning in view when he says it is the vocation of the Russian people to reach the New Jerusalem. There is, however, an implicit comparison between the old part of Paris on the Isle de la Cité and the Haymarket slum area in Petersburg. For a discussion of Dostoevsky's dialectic between Paris and Petersburg architecture in *Crime and Punishment,* see Lindenmeyr, "Raskolnikov's City and the Napoleonic Plan," 99–110.

76. Hunt, "Balzac and Dostoevsky," 311.

77. F. M. Dostoevskii, "*Selo Stepanchikovo* and *Unizhennye i oskorblennye,* Primechaniia" (Notes) *Pss,* 3:493, 7:308n1; Frank, *Dostoevsky: The Miraculous Years,* 61.

78. Grossman, *Dostoevskii,* 331. Konstantin Mochulsky agrees with Grossman (*Dostoevsky,* 271).

79. They are Alfred de Musset, *La Confession d'un enfant du siècle;* Georges

Sand, *La Confession d'une jeune fille*; Frederic Soulié; *Confession générale*; and de Quincey, *The Confessions of an English Opium Eater*. See Grossman, *Sobranie sochinenii*, 2:143.

80. F. M. Dostoevskii, "*Zapiski iz podpol'ia*, Primechaniia" (Notes), *Pss*, 5:378.

81. Tomashevskii says that Pushkin's variant takes "But Anatole didn't understand" as a refrain ("Pushkin i frantsuzkaia literatura," 66).

82. See Bailbé, *Jules Janin*, 11.

83. Janin, *La Confession*, 25–26. Further references to this work are cited parenthetically in the text.

84. Compare Marmeladov's words to Raskolnikov, whom he selects to tell the tale of his sins to in the tavern: "I am looking for a sensitive and educated man" (25). But inversely to Anatole, Marmeladov confesses to everyone while continuing to commit the same sins, taking up Janin's theme of the psychological need to confess that Dostoevsky elaborates on.

85. Fanger, *Dostoevsky and Romantic Realism*, 23–24. The only other Russian critical notice of *The Confession* I have found is for its brief mention of opium in the context of Gogol's "Nevskii prospekt" and de Quincey's *Confessions of an English Opium Eater* in Vinogradov, *Evoliutsiia*, 89–126, especially 91.

86. Nilsson says that Janin in turn has drawn from the feuilletons of Victor-Joseph Jouy who himself borrowed from L. S. Mercier, *Tableau de Paris* (1781), for this description (*Gogol et Pétersbourg*, 39).

87. Reizov, "K istorii romanticheskogo urbanizma," 139.

88. Belknap, *The Genesis of* The Brothers Karamazov, 87. Robin Feuer Miller also discusses the role of memory and forgetting, in *The Brothers Karamazov*, 19–21.

89. In *Crime and Punishment* the word "traces" is taken up by the narrator in pt. 2, chap. 1 (95–97) and answered by Raskolnikov, just as here Anatole repeats the dream-priest's word. Anatole's internal struggle takes place within a dream dialogue. Raskolnikov's internal dialogue moves from a first person confession in the drafts for *Crime and Punishment* to a dialogic form of third-person narrative. Svidrigailov takes up the motif when claiming that there were "no traces" of his having beaten Marfa Petrovna (278).

90. Cain says to the Lord: "Whoever finds me will slay me." The Lord replies, "'Not so! If anyone slays Cain, then vengeance shall be taken on him sevenfold.' And the Lord put a mark on Cain, lest any who came upon him should kill him" (Genesis 4:14–15). Note George Gibian's comment that "Raskolnikov realizes that his trends of thought have banished him, like Cain, from the brotherhood of men" ("Traditional Symbolism in *Crime and Punishment*," 984).

91. Where in the context of all his other sins, the murder becomes merely "*un peché presque vulgaire*" (an almost vulgar sin), just as Svidrigailov, without faith, can see all his misdeeds (e.g., his various depraved acts of womanizing, wife-beating, swindling, and causing Filip's suicide) as ordinary (259).

92. Translation from Frank, "The Genesis of *Crime and Punishment*," 129–30.

93. F. M. Dostoevskii, "Neizdannyi Dostoevskii," 29 August 1876, 244.

94. Perlina, *Varieties of Poetic Utterance*, 97–115; Dostoevsky, *A Writer's Diary*, 214.

95. Dostoevsky, *A Writer's Diary*, 733.

96. Iurii Lotman describes this pattern of difference between the plotting of Western European novels and the Russian (the "Cinderella" fairy-tale structure with a happy ending versus the cyclical nature of time in mythological plot patterning), in "Siuzhetnoe prostranstvo russkogo romana XIX stoletiia," in his *Izbrannye stat'i,* 3:91–106, especially 97–98. I am grateful to Otto Boele for pointing this out.

97. Dostoevsky, *A Writer's Diary,* 530.

98. That several of the passages Sonya reads were inserted in the final stages of composition to replace censored material substantiates the importance of John for the novel (see Notes to *Crime and Punishment, Pss,* 7:326, 386).

99. Others have noted Dostoevsky's use of particular gospels in his fiction: Robert Louis Jackson points to the origins of Marmeladov's "mighty prose poem" in Luke 7:36–50 (*The Art of Dostoevsky,* 191); Sergei Hackel notes Alyosha's interpolation of Matthew 22:1–10 into chapter 14, "Cana of Galilee" (taken from John 2:1–11), in *The Brothers Karamazov* ("The Religious Dimension," 159); Nadine Natov has traced gospel sources in *The Brothers Karamazov* ("The Ethical and Structural Significance," 3–44). Post-perestroika Russian scholars have written extensively on the religious dimension of Dostoevsky's works since my work on John was first published in *Dostoevsky Studies;* see the series of collected conference papers, *Evangel'skii tekst v russkoi literature XVIII–XX vekov,* and *Russkaia literature XIX veka i khristianstvo,* especially Dudkin, "Dostoevskii i evangeliia ot Ioanna," 337–48; and Kasatkina, "Voskreshenie Lazaria," 176–208. These valuable analyses are based on the same premise and reach similar conclusions but do not suggest a systematic textual parallel between novel and gospel.

100. Harriet Murav has noted the parody of the biblical new word in *Crime and Punishment* in *Holy Foolishness,* 67. Dudkin emphasizes the New Word's basis in love and freedom ("Dostoevskii i evangeliia ot Ioanna," 341).

101. Holquist, *Dostoevsky and the Novel,* 75–103. See also Cassedy, who sees the body of the novel as a Greek tragedy and the epilogue as a Christian resurrection tale ("The Formal Problem," 171–90).

102. Tynyanov, "Dostoevsky and Gogol," 101–17; Dostoevsky, *A Writer's Diary,* 525.

103. Tynyanov, "Dostoevsky and Gogol," 117. Susanne Fusso has called this type of parody "restorative parody" ("Maidens in Childbirth," 261–75).

104. Kjetsaa, *Dostoevsky and His New Testament,* 5–8; Kirillova, "Dostoevsky's Markings," 41–50, 42; Dudkin, "Dostoevskii i evangeliia ot Ioanna"; Kasatkina, "Voskreshenie Lazaria."

105. Quoted by Kjetsaa, *Dostoevsky and His New Testament,* 9. Translation slightly altered (see Dostoevskii, letter to S. A. Ivanova, 1(31) January 1868, *Pss,* 28.2:251).

106. Kirillova, "Dostoevsky's Markings," 50. See also Kjetsaa, *Dostoevsky and His New Testament,* 9–10.

107. See also Dudkin, "Dostoevskii i evangeliia ot Ioanna," 337–38, on Russian Orthodoxy's and Dostoevsky's preference of John over the synoptics.

108. Brodie, *The Gospel According to John,* 32.

109. Dostoevskii, "*Prestuplenie i nakazanie,* Primechaniia" (Notes), *Pss,* 7:386.

David Matual points out the timing of Sonya's reading to Raskolnikov ("In Defense of the Epilogue of *Crime and Punishment,*" 32).

110. See Brodie, *The Gospel According to John,* 445, 453, 527.

111. Antony Johae also attempts to interpret Luzhin's name in relation to the disciple Peter's in "Towards an Iconography," 184–86.

112. In *Père Goriot,* one of the boarders at the Maison Vauquer crows like a rooster at the communal dinner table in the pandemonium that greets Eugene's donning his new suit (140). The meaning (that he is the cock of the roost) has no connection to Peter's betrayal of Jesus, but the setting of the rooster reference is the same as in *Crime and Punishment* where the Last Supper associations give it biblical meaning.

113. Kasatkina, "Voskreshenie Lazaria," 204.

114. Johae discusses this meaning of porfiry and Porfiry Petrovich as the "rock of the church" as a contrasting pair with Piotr Petrovich Luzhin ("Towards an Iconography," 178, 181–84).

115. After his first interview with Pilate, Pilate's soldiers dress Jesus in a purple robe and place a crown of thorns on his head, mocking his alleged pretensions to being King of the Jews (19:2–5). Dostoevsky underscores the ambiguity of man's judiciary power by giving the police inspector the purple that points to the contradiction between earthly and spiritual power.

116. Thus, it is puzzling why A. Boyce Gibson calls Porfiry's position "pure analytical psychology, depending on no religious assumptions" (*The Religion of Dostoevsky,* 91).

117. See Rosenshield, "Western Law vs. Russian Justice," 117–35. Dostoevsky rejected the "rationalistic and legalistic system" of jury trial that was introduced in Russia in 1864 as part of the reorganization of the entire judicial system (118). Porfiry embodies the compassion that Western European jurisprudence lacks.

118. Terras, *Reading Dostoevsky,* 59.

119. Ibid., 65.

120. Kirillova, "Dostoevsky's Markings," 46. She notes that Dostoevsky stopped taking communion during his Petrashevsky period in the mid-1840s and resumed in Siberia.

121. Al'tman, *Dostoevskii po vekham imen,* 55–57. I am grateful to Susanne Fusso for the reference.

122. Kasatkina discusses this in detail ("Voskreshenie Lazaria").

123. Ibid., 177–78.

124. In his *Notebooks for Crime and Punishment* Dostoevsky wrote about Raskolnikov's climbing the stairs: "(NB: Golgotha)" (235).

125. Frank, *Dostoevsky: The Miraculous Years,* 143.

126. Frequently cited are Simmons, *Dostoevsky;* and Mochulsky, *Dostoevsky,* 312. For a list of other Western critics who reject the epilogue, see Rosenshield, *Crime and Punishment,* 112n5.

127. Frank, *Dostoevsky: The Miraculous Years,* 146–47.

128. Rosenshield, *Crime and Punishment,* 99–131; Matual, "In Defense of the Epilogue of *Crime and Punishment,*" 26–34. As Ralph Savarese points out, however, artistic unity does not itself obviate the charge that the epilogue is artificial

or less credible than the rest of the novel (private correspondence). See Belknap, "The Plot of *Crime and Punishment*," pt. 1, 285.

129. Rosenshield, *Crime and Punishment*, 112.

130. Ibid., 116. As will be clear, I agree with Rosenshield's rejection of Bakhtin's view of the dialogicity of *Crime and Punishment* (127). The characters are not independent and the author's position is clear: Raskolnikov's position is indefensible and he must be resurrected from spiritual death. The open-endedness of the novel is more determined than, for example, that of Pushkin's *Onegin*. Ruth Coates must be correct in her judgment that "if an author may only be a participant in the dialogue . . . the novelist who 'invented' polyphony cannot exist as a novelist" (*Christianity in Bakhtin*, 92).

131. Another religious novelist also ends his novel using the epilogue to John. See C. S. Lewis, *The Voyage of the "Dawn Treader"* (New York: Collier, 1970), 214–16. I am grateful to Rachel Trousdale for pointing out the "Come and have breakfast" passage.

132. The epilogue of *The Brothers Karamazov* also echoes chapter 21 of John: Iliusha's stone will be the touchstone of faith in the goodness the boys have learned from Iliusha's death. After Aliosha's speech by the stone to "about twelve" boys, he affirms eternal life and urges them to come and eat *bliny*.

133. Rosenshield, *Crime and Punishment*, 105–11.

134. Ibid., 106.

135. This suggests more than the "sidelong approach to a Christian interpretation of man" in *Crime and Punishment* that is proposed by A. Boyce Gibson (*The Religion of Dostoevsky*, 102). On the other hand, "the Epilogue could be said to be artificial precisely because of its heavy-handed allegiance to the Gospel of John. One might also say that the reader can sense in the Epilogue Dostoevsky's own anxiety about redemption . . . that the Epilogue projects a kind of wish fulfillment onto an otherwise desperate situation" (Ralph Savarese, private correspondence). The recognition of Dostoevsky's explicit, if not implicit, intentions reveals that tension.

136. Brooks, *The Melodramatic Imagination*, 22.

137. Ibid., 16.

138. Dudkin, "Dostoevskii i evangeliia ot Ioanna," 340. Vittorio Strada objects that this version is oversimplified; he sees the nineteenth-century Russian tradition as "part of a process of secularization of Christianity. . . . [Its] tradition is the interweaving of traditions, its Christianity consists not only of its having adopted Christianity, but of thinking about Christianity. No other literature problematizes Christianity" ("Problemy sekuliarizatsii v russkoi literature," 302).

139. Thompson, "Problems of the Biblical Word," 94. There is a vast literature on Christianity in Dostoevsky's work. Important here is Malcolm V. Jones's article on the importance of Orthodoxy as an intertext for Dostoevsky's work. He mentions the Gospel of John's relevance to *The Brothers Karamazov*. See "The Death and Resurrection of Orthodoxy," 161.

140. This is the opposite reading of Belknap's "The Plot of *Crime and Punishment*," 286. He suggests that Dostoevsky sought to temper the non-dialogic closure of the epilogue by introducing the open-ended story of Raskolnikov's future resurrection.

Chapter 4. Tolstoy, *Anna Karenina*

1. Eikhenbaum, *Tolstoy*, 125.
2. Armstrong, *The Novel of Adultery*, 121–37.
3. Tanner, *Adultery and the Novel*, 15–17.
4. Ibid., 14.
5. Gudzii, "Istoriia pisaniia," in Tolstoi, *Pss*, 20:577.
6. Eikhenbaum, *Tolstoy*, 111.
7. Liza Knapp has shown that Victor Hugo's *Dernier jour d'un condamné* is also an important French source for *Anna Karenina* in her "'Tue-la! Tue-le!'" 4–7.
8. Tolstoy, *Tolstoy Remembered*, 57.
9. Barran, *Russia Reads Rousseau*, xv–xvi.
10. Boyer, "Chez Tolstoi," *Le Temps*, 27 August 1901.
11. Tolstoi, letter of 25 October 1891, *Pss*, 66–67:68.
12. Letter to T. A. Ergol'skaia (18 May 1857), in Tolstoi, *Pss*, 60:189.
13. Quoted in Markovitch, *Jean-Jacques Rousseau et Tolstoi*, 5.
14. Barran, *Russia Reads Rousseau*, xx, 42, 152. He cites Lotman's opinion that Catherine banned *Emile* for its criticism of religion but believes it was instead Rousseau's words in the "Notes of a Savoyard Vicar": "we are on the edge of a revolution" (42).
15. *Les Solitaires* was normally published in Rousseau's *Oeuvres Complètes*. Although Rousseau was translated into Russian voluminously from 1762 on, Russian translations of *Emile et Sophie* began to appear only seventeen years later: *Emil' i Sofiia, ili khorosho vospitannye liubovniki iz sochinenii g. Russo*, Moscow, 1779, 1820; *Emilii i Sofiia*, 2 vols. (St. Petersburg, 1799–1800); *Emil,' ili o vospitanii, sochineniia Zhan Zhaka Russo*, Moscow, 1807.
16. Rousseau, *Emile et Sophie*, 3:287–356, 365n.Citations in the text refer to this volume.
17. Book 2, part 8; 2, 30; 3, 13; 4, 4; 4, 17; 4, 19; 4, 23; 5, 21; 5, 25. This is another example of the way Tolstoy embeds his response to a non-novelistic genre in *Anna Karenina*. W. Gareth Jones finds a similarly embedded response to the society tale in "Tolstoi's Alternative Society Tales," 99–113.
18. Tolstoy, *Anna Karenina*, trans. Louise and Aylmer Maude (131). The following citations noted in the text are taken from the 1970 Norton edition of this translation.
19. See Milivojevic, *Leo Tolstoy*, 51–52.
20. Eikhenbaum, *Tolstoy*, 100–105, 137.
21. Tolstoi, letter to Tatyana Kuzminskaya, *Pss*, 62:11.
22. Eikhenbaum, *Tolstoy*, 104, 105.
23. Ibid., 137.
24. Quoted in Taylor, *The Theatre of Alexandre Dumas*, 3. Information about Dumas's biography is taken principally from this book.
25. Ibid., 69.
26. Ibid., 24.
27. Quoted in Rayfield, "Dumas and Dostoevsky: Deflowering the Camellia," 71.
28. *Le Soir*, 6 July 1872. Republished in d'Ideville, *L'Homme qui tue*, 1872.

29. Price, *A Social History of Nineteenth-Century France,* 78.

30. Dumas fils, *L'Homme-femme,* 33.

31. Eikhenbaum, *Tolstoy,* 134.

32. Sergey Tolstoy, *Tolstoy Remembered,* 60. Tony Tanner discusses the categories city-field-temple in novels of adultery, but defines "temple" as a "disturbed consciousness" rather than a divine force (*Adultery and the Novel,* 23).

33. Eikhenbaum, *Tolstoy,* 143.

34. The British Library contains nine such responses: those of Mlle. Stella Oristorio di Franca; Mme. Hermance Lesguillon; Comte Jeneseki (pseud.), "Les petites filles d'Eve"; Jules Girard; Maria Deraismes, "Eve contre M. Dumas fils"; A. de Cool, "La Femme et l'homme"; Marquis Ernst Charles Guy de Charnace; Auvergnat, "Ni Homme ni femme"; Alexandre, "Tue-la! Ou elle te tuera! Ou la femme-homme! Ou ni homme ni femme! Ou Alexandre embêté par Emile, ou Emile embeté par Alexandre. Scènes de la vie conjugale par XXX" (a play in prose and verse).

35. Girardin, L'*Homme et la femme.*

36. Dumas, *La Femme de Claude,* 74.

37. Gudzii, "Istoriia pisaniia," in Tolstoi, *Pss,* 20:595.

38. Dumas, *La Femme de Claude,* 3. Further references to this work are cited parenthetically in the text.

39. Gudzii, "Istoriia pisaniia," in Tolstoi, *Pss,* 20:597.

40. See Frank, *Dostoevsky,* 146, 290. I am grateful to Susanne Fusso for pointing this out.

41. Gudzii, "Istoriia pisaniia," in Tolstoi, *Pss,* 20:583.

42. See Eikhenbaum, *Tolstoy,* 111.

43. Steiner, *Tolstoy or Dostoevsky,* 48.

44. Other critics have rejected this possibility. Several French opinions are collected in Anisimov, *Tolstoi i zarubezhnyi mir.* For example, Romain Rolland: "The effect of Tolstoy's art does not depend on stylistic contrivance as does Flaubert's" (189); André Maurois: "What does Tolstoy owe to Balzac, Flaubert? He read them, but it does not seem to us that he learned writing technique from them. His realism does not resemble that of our naturalists . . . Elegant literary devices in the spirit of Flaubert are foreign to him" (219–20); and Jean Jaurès: "Tolstoy is most concerned with moral problems. You cannot compare him in this respect with Balzac, Sand, Flaubert, Zola. . . . Flaubert cares most about artistic form, but feels a scornful pity for the unhappy and grey human race!" (580).

45. Lottman, *Flaubert,* 137.

46. Ibid., 139.

47. Tolstoi, diary, 21 February 1857 N.S., *Pss,* 47:113.

48. Lottman, *Flaubert,* 140.

49. Steegmuller, *Flaubert and Madame Bovary,* 286.

50. Michel Cadot points out that Tolstoy wrote to his wife in 1892: "*Madame Bovary* has great qualities and is not for nothing highly regarded by the French" (Tolstoi, letter of 19 April 1892, *Pss,* 84:138). See Cadot, "La Mort comme événement social et comme destin personnel," 31–40.

51. Quoted in Gusev, *Letopis' zhizni,* 561. Tolstoy did, however, comment on reading Turgenev's translation of Flaubert's *The Legend of Saint Julian the*

Hospitaller in *Vestnik Evropy*: in a letter to Strakhov (22 April 1877), Tolstoy called the tale "an abomination" (*merzost'*) and "disgusting filth" (*vozmutitel'naia gadost'* [472]). But in a later letter to Strakhov (1881), he called *Anna Karenina* "merzost'" as well (Tolstoi, letter of 1 [?] April 1881, *Pss*, 63:61).

52. George Henri Bourdon, "En écoutant Tolstoy," *Le Figaro*, 15 March 1904. Quoted in Anisimov, *Tolstoi i zarubezhnyi mir*, 2:21.

53. Giustav Flober, *Madam Bovari*, *Biblioteka dlia chteniia* 8 (1858): 1–222.

54. Bulgakov, *Biblioteka L'va Nikolaevicha Tolstogo v Iasnoi poliane*, vol. 2 (*M-Ia*), no. 3558. See Eikhenbaum, *Tolstoy*, 100–106.

55. See Armstrong, *The Novel of Adultery*, 111–12.

56. Steiner, *Tolstoy or Dostoevsky*, 67.

57. *Madame Bovary*, 143, 120. Further references to this work are cited parenthetically in the text.

58. Anna's squint has also been used to suggest a source for *Anna Karenina* in George Eliot's *Middlemarch*. See Blumberg, "Tolstoy and the English Novel," 591–99. Blumberg draws parallels in plot and characterization. Eliot's Maggie Tulliver (*Mill on the Floss*) as well as George Sand's eponymous Indiana are unhappy black-haired married women tempted to adultery. Interestingly, none of the motifs discussed in the present chapter are thematized in these novels.

59. Steiner compares the two ball scenes too, contrasting Flaubert's ironic distance, which he finds artificial, to Tolstoy's using no single point of view (*Tolstoy or Dostoevsky*, 65–66).

60. In his *Dictionary of Accepted Ideas*, Flaubert facetiously calls the waltz "[a] lascivious impure dance" (84).

61. Flaubert also uses a blue haze in *A Simple Heart*. The story is a kind of complement to *Madame Bovary*, as Tolstoy's later stories "The Kreuzer Sonata" and "The Devil" are to *Anna Karenina*. Flaubert wanted to answer the charge that he was inhuman in his novel by writing the touching tale of Félicité's truly ideal loves. Her religious fervor is associated with a blue cloud of incense when, on her deathbed, she achieves the religious exaltation that Emma had only imitated. Félicité associates cigar smoke with her nephew because she learns he is in Havana. The motifs that had denoted corrupt, empty sensuality in *Madame Bovary* connote ideal love in *A Simple Heart*. Tanner traces the motif of mist, fog, and vapors, connecting it to the "fog in Emma's head" (*Adultery and the Novel*, 312–14).

62. Like Gary Saul Morson ("Prosaics and *Anna Karenina*," 8), I think that the book condemns Anna, but rather for her breach of the sacrament of marriage than for the self-indulgence for which Richard Gustafson berates her. See Gustafson, *Leo Tolstoy, Resident and Stranger*, especially 118–32.

63. Judith Armstrong says that Vronsky is not a seducer "of the Rodolphe type" (*The Novel of Adultery*, 84).

64. See, for example, Schulze, *The Structure of Anna Karenina*, 117–22; Stenbock-Fermor, *The Architecture of Anna Karenina*, especially 66–71.

65. Tanner traces the iron motif, connecting the whirring of Binet's lathe and a passing cart "loaded with iron rods" to the Hirondelle (*Adultery and the Novel*, 316–17, 303).

66. I am indebted to Anuj Desai for his observations on the uncanny dimension of the beggar.

67. Riffaterre, "Flaubert's Presuppositions," 10–11.

68. Tolstoy's development of "*podmostok*" is discussed in Eikhenbaum, *Tolstoy*, 119–26.

69. Letter of 12 April 1869. Quoted in Gusev, *L. N. Tolstoy, materialy k biografii*, 253.

70. See Markovitch, *Jean-Jacques Rousseau et Tolstoi*, 48–50, for further parallels.

71. Flaubert said of *Madame Bovary*: "It was in hatred of realism that I undertook this book. But I equally despise that false brand of idealism which is such a hollow mockery in the present age" (letter to Madame Roger des Genettes, October or November 1856, *Correspondance*, 4:134).

72. As Flaubert says he should be, "present everywhere, and visible nowhere" (*présent partout, et visible nulle part*). Flaubert to Louise Colet, 9 December 1852, *Correspondance*, 3:61–62.

73. Here Flaubert (unkindly) refers to the jeweled and inscribed cigar holder Louise Colet gave him. Steegmuller, *Flaubert and Madame Bovary*, 300.

74. In *The Lady of the Camellias* the motifs connote opposites: (corrupt) Paris in the distance is "in the mist," while the cottage in Bougival where Marguerite returns to rural innocence has "a green lawn, smooth as velvet" (110, 112). Alexandre Dumas fils, translator Edmund Gosse, Sainte-Beuve, and other reviewers saw Emma Bovary as a version of Marguerite Gautier (Steegmuller, *Flaubert and Madame Bovary*, 297).

75. Tolstoi, Varianty "Anny Kareninoi," *Pss*, 20:214, 217. In the draft for the long paragraph about spring (part 2, chapter 12), mist (*tuman*) is mentioned once. In the final version, it appears three times in a way that emphasizes the miraculous aspect of nature's rebirth. The draft uses both green and velvet, separated by two sentences, whereas the final version breaks the paragraph into two sections, each of which combines them. *Anna Karenina*, ed. Zhdanov and Zaidenshnur, 133, 136.

76. Tolstoi, Varianty "Anny Kareninoi," *Pss*, 20:217.

77. The correction was made in Tolstoy's handwriting. I am grateful to Tatiana Georgievna Nikiforova of the Tolstoy museum archive in Moscow for her help in discovering this.

78. Tolstoi, Varianty "Anny Kareninoi," *Pss*, 20:505–6.

79. Merejkowsky, *Tolstoy as Man and Artist*, 64.

80. Tolstoy uses the motif again later in "The Devil," assigning it the opposite meaning: the phosphates that Irtenev has been fertilizing the fields with are associated with his peasant mistress, who has borne him a child (a point Elliott Mossman made in "Plus s'accuse, plus s'excuse: Confession in Tolstoy," paper delivered at the annual AATSEEL convention, December 1992, New York). The motif thus carries the opposition between ideal wedded love and the lust that undermines it. This suggests that in Tolstoy's creative process, Anna's adultery becomes the necessary complement to Levin's wedded bliss, serving to purge it of the illicit passion that destroys her.

81. Tolstoi, Varianty "Anny Kareninoi," *Pss,* 20:52–57.

82. Morson agrees: "Stiva is the villain of the book, its representative of what evil is," as does Dostoevsky, whom he cites ("Prosaics and *Anna Karenina,*" 6).

83. *Refleksy golovnogo mozga* is the title of a book by Sechenov, who carried on a polemic with another scientist in the periodicals Oblonsky would have read. See Louise Maude and Aylmer Maude's 1939 translation of *Anna Karenina,* 1:495: "*Bylo chto-to, fizicheski deistvovavshee druzheliubno i veselo na liudei, vstrechavshikhsia s nim*" (part 1, chapter 5). Rosemary Edmonds translates this as "acts like a tonic" (27); the Maudes have "had a physical effect on" (*Anna Karenina,* 1970 edition, 13).

84. I am indebted to Rachel Trousdale for pointing out this parallel.

85. This is Pushkin's translation of Anacreon's fifty-fifth ode.

86. The insight regarding Chateaubriand's René belongs to Rachel Trousdale.

87. Eikhenbaum, *Tolstoy,* 111–12.

88. As Stenbock-Fermor puts it, Anna is "entrapped by mistaken culture with its machinery, dances, provocative dresses, and all the artificial comforts and social conventions" (70).

89. Rousseau, *Emile,* 163.

90. "A tempest in the cranium is a sublime spectacle; a tempest in the loins is a vile spectacle."

91. Ulbach, "La littérature putride," n.p.

92. "C'est un colosse qui a les pieds malpropres, mais c'est un colosse." Flaubert, letter to Madame Roger des Genettes, 18 April 1880, *Correspondance,* 9:22.

93. Tolstoi, letter to N. S. Leskov, *Pss,* 66:406.

94. Tolstoi, "Chto takoe iskusstvo?" *Pss,* 30:145.

95. Tolstoi, "Chto takoe iskusstvo?" Variants, *Pss,* 30:380.

96. Emile Zola, *Les Oeuvres complètes: Thérèse Raquin; Madeleine Férat,* Notes [vol. 34], 297. Page numbers in the text for *Thérèse Raquin* and *Madeleine Férat* refer to this edition.

97. Ulbach, "La littérature putride."

98. Ibid.

99. For discussion of the paired dreams, see Gary Browning, "Peasant Dreams in *Anna Karenina,*" 525–36 (the peasant as Anna's vision of Karenin and Vronsky); Barbara Lønnqvist, "Simvolika zheleza v romane *Anna Karenina,*" 97–107 (the peasant as symbol of Anna's death); Sydney Schulze, *The Structure of Anna Karenina* (the peasant as a symbol of Anna's degradation).

100. N. V. Gorbachev, "Kommentarii," in Tolstoi, *Pss,* 30:493.

101. Bulgakov, *Biblioteka L'va Nikolaevicha Tolstogo v Iasnoi poliane*: no. 1240, *Chelovek-zhivotnoe;* no. 1241, *Chelovek-zver'* (1890). Tolstoy also had no. 1238, *Bol'nye liudi* (1890) (uncut); and no. 1239, *Krov' (iz skazok)* (1895).

102. Tolstoi, "O Shekspire i o drame," Variants, *Pss,* 35:569.

103. Thomas Barran convincingly discusses the influence of Rousseau's "Confession of a Savoyard Vicar" on Levin's quest for the meaning of life (book 8) in "Dinamika sovesti v romane *Anna Karenina.*"

104. Gusev, Commentary, in Tolstoi, *Pss,* 24:973.

105. McLean, "Tolstoy and Jesus," 103.

106. N. N. Gusev, "*Soedinenie i perevod chetyrekh Evangelii,* Istoriia pechataniia," 984–993, in Tolstoi, *Pss,* 24:987–89.

107. See, for example, Richard Gustafson, who devotes considerable space to the argument in *Leo Tolstoy, Resident and Stranger.*

108. Tolstoi, diary, 4 March 1855, *Pss,* 47:37.

109. Tolstoi, letter of end of April–3 May 1859, *Pss,* 60:293.

110. McLean, "Rousseau's God and Tolstoy's," 27; Florovsky, "Three Masters," 175.

111. Wachtel, "Death and Resurrection in *Anna Karenina,*" 113n4.

112. Ibid., 103–4; Kujundzic, "Pardoning Woman in *Anna Karenina,*" 81n18.

113. For example, Kujundzic discusses Anna in the role of Christ, as a deconstruction of the Gospel and Levin as "writing the message of the Gospel" when he proposes to Kitty ("Pardoning Woman in *Anna Karenina,*" 81n17). See also Morson, "Work and the Authentic Life in Tolstoy," 36–48; Galagan, *L. N. Tolstoy*; Wachtel, "Death and Resurrection in *Anna Karenina,*" 100–114; Lønnqvist, "*Anna Karenina,*" 80–95.

114. Tolstoi, diary, 1894, *Pss,* 52:110.

115. Wachtel, "Death and Resurrection in *Anna Karenina,*" 100–101. He quotes the passage cited here to make this point.

116. Ibid., 26. Kujundzic agrees ("Pardoning Woman in *Anna Karenina,*" 77n11). Wachtel discusses Kitty in the context of what he interprets as her death and resurrection in childbirth.

117. McLean, "Tolstoy and Jesus," 112. Tolstoy's view is well founded. There is a discrepancy within the four gospels about the annunciation, which comes to Joseph in Matthew 1:20–23 and to Mary in Luke 1:26–33. See Helms, *Gospel Fictions,* 48–51; and Smith, *Jesus the Magician,* 24–28. I am grateful to Gary Kern for identifying these sources.

118. Jessica Frank, "*Anna Karenina,* The Gospels Revisited," unpublished undergraduate paper, Wesleyan University, 1998.

119. Greenwood, "Tolstoy and Religion," 158.

120. I am grateful to the Rev. John C. Hall for pointing out this connection to me.

121. *The New Oxford Annotated Bible,* edited by Herbert G. May and Bruce M. Metzger, 1211.

122. Lønnqvist, "*Anna Karenina,*" 93.

123. This is the resolution of Levin's discussion of electricity with Vronsky in the Shcherbatskys' drawing room. Levin criticizes the Spiritualists for wanting to put a spiritual force to a material test (49).

124. Quoted in Greenwood, "Tolstoy and Religion," 155.

125. Tolstoi's Vvedenie (introduction) to *Soedinenie i perevod chetyrekh Evangelii, Pss,* 24:21.

126. Tolstoi, *Soedinenie i perevod chetyrekh Evangelii, Pss,* 24:170–73.

127. Ibid., *Pss,* 24:22.

128. Galagan, *L. N. Tolstoi,* 131. She identifies the motifs of the sower, the

door, doubling and the abyss, and analyzes the door and doubling in *Anna Karenina*, 131–47.

129. Tolstoi, *Soedinenie, Pss*, 24:177.

Conclusion

1. Jenny, "The Strategy of Form," 39.

2. I thank Jeff Hush for this insight.

3. Perlina, *Varieties of Poetic Utterance*, 13.

4. Dostoevskii, "Pushkin," *Pss*, 26:144.

5. Perlina, *Varieties of Poetic Utterance*, 5.

6. Gudzii, "Istoria pisaniia," in Tolstoi, *Pss*, 20:578.

7. Quoted in Evdokimova, "The Wedding Bell, the Death Knell," 141.

8. Andrei Bitov describes his novel, *Uletaiushchii Monakhov* (in *Zhizn' v vetrenuiu pogodu*), as a *roman-punktir*, a "novel with ellipses."

9. Orwin, "Tolstoy's Antiphilosophical Philosophy in *Anna Karenina*," 95–103; Evdokimova, "The Wedding Bell, the Death Knell," 142.

10. Erich Auerbach, *Mimesis*, quoted in Perlina, *Varieties of Poetic Utterance*, 13.

11. Perlina, *Varieties of Poetic Utterance*, 88.

12. Dostoevskii, "Dnevnik pisatelia," July–August 1877, *Pss*, 25:199.

13. Vladimir Alexandrov discusses the "plurality of contradictory or simply divergent interpretations that the novel can sustain simultaneously" (*Limits to Interpretation*, 9). Gary Saul Morson ("Tolstoy's Absolute Language") discusses Tolstoy's use of forms of "absolute" language (proverbs, biblical commands, etc.) but does not read Tolstoy's work as monologic.

14. Emerson, "Tolstoy Versus Dostoevsky," 113.

15. As Thomas Barran writes, "Dostoevsky saw Rousseau as 'the carrier of the European sepsis'" (*Russia Reads Rousseau*, xv–xvi).

Bibliography

Aizelwood, Robin. "*Geroi nashego vremeni* as Emblematic Prose Text." In *From Pushkin to Palisandriia*, ed. Arnold McMillin, 39–51. London: Macmillan, 1990.

Akhmatova, Anna. "Pushkin i nevskoe vzmore." In her *Sochineniia*, 2:119–26. Moscow: Khudozhestvennaia literatura, 1986.

Al'tman, M. O. *Dostoevskii po vekham imen*. Saratov: Izdatel'stvo Saratovskogo universiteta, 1975.

Anderson, Benedict. *Imagined Communities: Reflections on the Origin and Spread of Nationalism*. London: Verso, 1991.

Anisimov, I. I., ed. *Tolstoi i zarubezhnyi mir*. Literaturnoe nasledstvo 75. 2 vols. Moscow: Akademiia nauk SSSR, 1965.

Arian, I. "Some Aspects of Lermontov's *A Hero of Our Time*." *Forum for Modern Language Studies* 6, no. 1 (January 1968): 22–32.

Arkhangel'skii, A. N. *Stikhotvornaia povest' A. S. Pushkina "Mednyi vsadnik."* Moscow: Vysshaia shkola, 1990.

Armstrong, Judith. *The Novel of Adultery*. London: Macmillan, 1976.

Atkinson, Nora. *Eugène Sue et le roman-feuilleton*. Nemours: André Lesot, 1929.

Bailbé, Joseph-Marc. *Jules Janin, 1804–1874: une sensibilité littéraire et artistique*. Paris: Lettres modernes, Minard, 1974.

Bakhtin, Mikhail. *Problems of Dostoevsky's Poetics*. Edited and translated by Caryl Emerson. Minneapolis: University of Minnesota Press, 1984.

Balzac, Honoré de. *La Comédie Humaine*. Paris: Editions Gallimard, 1976.

———. *La Femme de trente ans*. Paris: Garnier Frères, 1962.

———. *A Harlot High and Low (Splendeurs et misères des courtisanes)*. Translated by Rayner Heppenstall. London: Penguin, 1970.

———. *Oeuvres complètes*. Paris: Editions Garnier, 1962.

———. "La Transaction." *Revue étrangère* 2 (1832): 149–76, 223–41.

———. *The Wild Ass's Skin*. Translated by Herbert J. Hunt. London: Penguin, 1977.

Banville, Theodore de. *Mes souvenirs*. Paris: G. Charpentier, 1882.

Barran, Thomas. *Russia Reads Rousseau, 1762–1825*. Evanston, IL: Northwestern University Press, 2002.

———. "Dinamika sovesti v romane *Anna Karenina*." In *Iasnopolianskii sbornik 2000*, 47–56. Tula: Izdatel'skii dom "Iasnaia poliana," 2000.

Bazin, René. *Questions littéraires et sociales*. Paris: Calmann-Lévy, 1906.

Belinskii, V. G. *Polnoe sobranie sochinenii*. 13 vols. Moscow: Izdatel'stvo Akademii nauk SSSR, 1953–59.

Belknap, Robert L. *The Genesis of* The Brothers Karamazov: *The Aesthetics, Ideology, and Psychology of Making a Text*. Evanston, IL: Northwestern University Press, 1990.

———. "A Likely Story, Pushkin's *Bronze Horseman*: A Study in Verisimilitude." In *The Supernatural in Slavic and Baltic Literature: Essays in Honor of Victor Terras*, ed. Amy Mandelker and Roberta Reeder, 26–33. Columbus, OH: Slavica, 1988.

———. "The Plot of *Crime and Punishment*." In *Literature, Culture, and Society in the Modern Age*, ed. Edward J. Brown et al., Stanford Slavic Studies 4, parts 1–2. Stanford, CA: Dept. of Slavic Languages and Literatures, Stanford University, 1991.

Bem, A. L. *O Dostoevskom*. 3 vols. Prague: Sklad izd. F. Svoboda, 1929–36.

Bernard, Charles de. *Gerfaut*. Paris: C. Gosselin et W. Coquebert, 1838. Translated and edited by Mrs. [Catherine Grace Frances] Gore as *The Lover and the Husband*, 3 vols. (London: Richard Bentley, 1841).

Bernheimer, Charles. *Figures of Ill Repute: Representing Prostitution in Nineteenth-Century France*. Cambridge, MA: Harvard University Press, 1989.

Bethea, David M. *The Shape of Apocalypse in Modern Russian Fiction*. Princeton, NJ: Princeton University Press, 1989.

Bethea, David, and Sergei Davydov. "Pushkin's Saturnine Cupid: The Poetics of Parody in *The Tales of Belkin*." *Proceedings of the Modern Language Association* 96, no. 1 (Winter 1981): 8–21.

Blackmur, R. P. "Murder in Your Own Room." In *Eleven Essays in the European Novel*, ed. R. P. Blackmur, 119–40. New York: Harcourt, Brace, 1964.

Blagoi, Dmitri. *The Sacred Lyre*. Moscow: Raduga, 1982.

———. *Sotsiologiia tvorchestva Pushkina: Etiudy*. Moscow: Federatsiia, 1929.

Blinoff, Marthe. "Dostoevskii et Balzac." *Comparative Literature* 3 (1951): 342–55.

Blumberg, Edwina Jannie. "Tolstoy and the English Novel: A Note on *Middlemarch* and *Anna Karenina*." *Slavic Review* 30 (1971): 591–99.

Bocharov, S. G. "O smysle *Grobovshchika*." In *Kontekst*, ed. Aleksandr Sergeevich Miasnikov, 196–230. Moscow: Nauka, 1973.

Bory, Jean-Louis. *Eugène Sue, Dandy mais socialiste*. Paris: Hachette, 1962.

Boyer, Paul. "Chez Tolstoi." *Le Temps*, 27 August 1901.

Bourdon, George Henri. "En écoutant Tolstoi." *Le Figaro*, 15 March 1904.

Briggs, A. D. P. *A Comparative Study of Pushkin's* The Bronze Horseman, *Nekrasov's* Red-Nosed Frost, *and Blok's* The Twelve. Lewiston, NY: Edwin Mellen Press, 1990.

Brodie, Thomas L. *The Gospel According to John: A Literary and Theological Commentary*. New York: Oxford University Press, 1993.

Brooks, Peter. *The Melodramatic Imagination: Balzac, Henry James, Melodrama and the Mode of Excess*. New Haven, CT: Yale University Press, 1976.

Brown, Natalie Babel. *Hugo and Dostoevsky*. Ann Arbor, MI: Ardis, 1978.

Browning, Gary. "Peasant Dreams in Anna Karenina." *Slavic and East European Journal* 44, no. 4 (2000): 525–36.
Bulgakov, V. F., ed. *Biblioteka L'va Nikolaevicha Tolstogo v Iasnoi poliane, knigi na russkom iazyke.* 2 vols. Moscow: Kniga, 1972–75.
Cadot, Michel. "La Mort comme événement social et comme destin personnel: remarques sur *Madame Bovary* et *Anna Karenine.*" *Etudes comparatives,* Cahiers Léon Tolstoi 3 (1986): 31–40.
Cassedy, Steven. "The Formal Problem of the Epilogue in *Crime and Punishment*: The Logic of Tragic and Christian Structures." *Dostoevsky Studies* 3 (1982): 171–90.
Chapple, Richard. "Catalogue of Dostoevskii's References to French Literature." *Revue de Littérature Comparée* 3 (1992): 335–53.
Chasles, Philarète. "Eglantine." *Revue étrangère* 6 (1833): 364–83.
Chateaubriand, François René de. *Les Natchez.* 3 vols. London: Henry Colburn, 1827.
Choldin, Marianna Tax. *A Fence around the Empire: Russian Censorship of Western Ideas under the Tsars.* Durham, NC: Duke University Press, 1985.
Clark, Roger J. B. "Parody and Revolt: L'Ane mort et la femme guillotinée." *Orbis Litterarum: International Review of Literary Studies* 31 (1976): 243–62.
Coates, Ruth. *Christianity in Bakhtin: God and the Exiled Author.* Cambridge: Cambridge University Press, 1998.
Constant, Benjamin. *Adolphe.* Translated by Leonard Tancock. London: Penguin, 1964.
Cracraft, James. "Peter the Great and the Problem of Periodization." In *Architectures of Russian Identity, 1500 to the Present,* ed. James Cracraft and Daniel Rowland, 7–17. Ithaca, NY: Cornell University Press, 2003.
Diderot, Denis. *Jacques le fataliste.* Paris: Flammarion, 1970.
Dostoevsky, F. M. *Crime and Punishment.* Translated by Sidney Monas. New York: Signet, 1968.
———. *Neizdannyi Dostoevskii: zapisnye knizhki i tetradi, 1860–1881 gg.* Literaturnoe nasledstvo 83. Moscow: Akademiia nauk SSSR, 1971.
———. *The Notebooks for* Crime and Punishment. Edited by Edward Wasiolek. Chicago: University of Chicago Press, 1967.
———. *Polnoe sobranie sochinenii.* 30 vols. Leningrad: Akademiia nauk SSSR, 1972–1990.
———. *A Writer's Diary.* Translated by Kenneth Lantz. Evanston, IL: Northwestern University Press, 1993.
Drozda, Miroslav. "Povestvovatel'naia struktura *Geroia nashego vremeni.*" *Wiener Slawistischer Almanach* 15 (1985): 5–34.
Dubshan, L. S. "O khudozhestvennom reshenii i literaturnom istochnike odnogo iz epizodov povesti 'Bela.'" In *Lermontovskii sbornik,* ed. I. S. Chistova, 267–77. Leningrad: Akademiia nauk SSSR, 1985.
Duchesne, M. E. *Michel Iourievitch Lermontov: sa vie et ses oeuvres.* Paris, 1910.
Dudkin, V. V. "Dostoevskii i evangeliia ot Ioanna." In *Evangel'skii tekst v russkoi literature XVIII–XX vekov: tsitata, reministsenziia, motiv, siuzhet, zhanr,* ed. V. N. Zakharov, 337–48. Petrozavodsk: Izdatel'stvo Petrozavodskogo universiteta, 1998.

Dumas fils, Alexandre. *La Femme de Claude.* Paris: Michel Levy, 1873.
———. *L'Homme-femme. Réponse à M. Henri d'Ideville.* Paris: Michel Levy, 1872.
———. *The Lady of the Camellias.* Translated by Edmund Gosse. Guernsey: Alan Sutton, 1991.
Durylin, S. *Geroi nashego vremeni M. Iu. Lermontova.* Moscow: Gosudarstvennoe uchebno-pedagogicheskoe izdatel'stvo narkomprosa RSFSR, 1940.
Eagle, Herbert. "Lermontov's 'Play' with Romantic Genre Expectations in *A Hero of Our Time.*" *Russian Literature Triquarterly* 12 (Spring 1975): 299–313.
Eco, Umberto. "Rhetoric and Ideology in Eugène Sue's *Les Mystères de Paris.*" In his *The Role of the Reader: Explorations in the Semiotics of Texts,* 125–43. Bloomington: Indiana University Press, 1979.
Eidelman, Natan. *Pushkin: Istoriia i sovremennost' v khudozhestvennom soznanii poeta.* Moscow: Sovetskii pisatel', 1984.
———. *Pushkin i dekabristy.* Moscow: Khudozhestvennaia literatura, 1979.
Eikhenbaum, Boris. *M. Iu. Lermontov, Geroi nashego vremeni.* Moscow: Akademiia nauk SSSR, 1962.
———. *O proze.* Leningrad: Khudozhestvennaia literatura, 1969.
———. *Tolstoy in the Seventies.* Translated by Albert Kaspin. Ann Arbor, MI: Ardis, 1982.
Eliot, T. S. "Tradition and the Individual Talent." In *Selected Essays,* ed. John Hayward, 13–22. London: Faber and Faber, 1953.
Emerson, Caryl. "Tolstoy Versus Dostoevsky and Bakhtin's Ethics of the Classroom." In *Approaches to Teaching Tolstoy's* Anna Karenina, ed. Liza Knapp and Amy Mandelker, 104–16. New York: Modern Language Association, 2003.
Evdokimova, Svetlana. "The Wedding Bell, the Death Knell, and Philosophy's Spell: Tolstoy's Sense of Ending." In *Approaches to Teaching Tolstoy's* Anna Karenina, ed. Liza Knapp and Amy Mandelker, 137–43. New York: Modern Language Association, 2003.
Fanger, Donald. *Dostoevsky and Romantic Realism: A Study of Dostoevsky in Relation to Balzac, Dickens, and Gogol.* Cambridge, MA: Harvard University Press, 1967.
Fedorov, A. V. *Lermontov i literatura ego vremeni.* Leningrad: Khudozhestvennaia literatura, 1967.
"Ferragus" [pseud. Louis Ulbach]. "La littérature putride." *Le Figaro,* 23 January 1868.
Flaubert, Gustave. *Correspondance.* Expanded edition. 9 vols. Paris: Louis Conard, 1926–1933.
———. *Dictionary of Accepted Ideas.* Translated by Jacques Barzun. Norfolk, CT: New Directions, 1954.
———. *Madame Bovary.* Paris: Flammarion, 1966.
———. *Madame Bovary.* Translated by Alan Russell. Harmondsworth: Penguin, 1950.
Florovsky, Georges. "Three Masters: The Quest for Religion in Nineteenth-Century Russian Literature." In *Mansions of the Spirit,* ed. George A. Panichas, 157–79. New York: Hawthorn, 1967.

Fokht, U. R. *Lermontov: Logika tvorchestva.* Moscow: Akademiia nauk SSSR, 1975.

Fonvizin, D. I. *Sochineniia D. I. Fonvizina: polnoe socbranie original'nykh proizvedenii.* St. Petersburg: Marks, 1893.

Frank, Joseph. *Dostoevsky: The Mantle of the Prophet, 1871–1881.* Princeton, NJ: Princeton University Press, 2002.

———. *Dostoevsky: The Miraculous Years, 1865–1871.* Princeton, NJ: Princeton University Press, 1995.

———. *Dostoevsky: The Stir of Liberation, 1860–1865.* Princeton, NJ: Princeton University Press, 1986.

———. "The Genesis of *Crime and Punishment.*" In *Russianness: In Honor of Rufus Matthewson,* ed. Robert Belkap, 124–43. Ann Arbor, MI: Ardis, 1990.

Frank, Semen. "Pushkin kak politicheskii myslitel'." In *Pushkin v russkoi filosofskoi kritike,* ed. R. A. Gal'tseva, 396–422. Moscow: Kniga, 1990.

Fridlender, G. *Dostoevskii i mirovaia literatura.* Moscow: Khudozhestvennaia literatura, 1979.

Frow, John. "Intertextuality and Ontology." In *Intertextuality: Theories and Practices,* ed. Michael Worton and Judith Still. Manchester: Manchester University Press, 1990.

Fusso, Susanne. "Maidens in Childbirth: the Sistine Madonna in Dostoevskii's Devils." *Slavic Review* 54 (Summer 1995): 261–75.

Galagan, G. Ia. *L. N. Tolstoi: Khudozhestvenno-eticheskie iskaniia.* Leningrad: Akademiia Nauk SSSR, 1981.

Gershtein, Emma. *Geroi nashego vremeni M. Iu. Lermontova.* Moscow: Khudozhestvennaia literatura, 1976

Gibian, George. "Traditional Symbolism in *Crime and Punishment.*" *PMLA* 70 (1955): 979–96.

Gibson, A. Boyce. *The Religion of Dostoevsky.* Philadelphia: Westminster, 1973.

Girardin, Emile de. *L'Homme et la femme: l'homme suzerain, la femme vassale, lettre à Monsieur Dumas fils.* Paris: Levy, 1972.

Gobineau, Arthur, Comte de. *Etudes critiques (1844–1848).* 1844. Reprint, Paris: Simon Kra, 1927.

von Goethe, Johann Wilhelm. *Wilhelm Meister.* Translated by R. O. Moon. 2 vols. London: G.T. Foulis, 1947.

Gogol, Nikolai. "The Diary of a Madman," "The Nose," and "The Overcoat." In *The Diary of a Madman and Other Stories,* trans. Priscilla Meyer and Andrew R. MacAndrew, 1–23, 25–51, 67–99. New York: Signet Classics, 2005.

Gogol, Nikolai Vasilievich. *Polnoe sobranie sochinenii.* 14 vols. Moscow-Leningrad: Akademiia nauk SSSR, 1937–1952.

Golstein, Vladimir. *Lermontov's Narratives of Heroism.* Evanston, IL: Northwestern University Press, 1998.

Grand Larousse Encylopédique. 10 vols. Paris: Librairie Larousse, 1960–64.

Greenwood, E. B. "Tolstoy and Religion." In *New Essays on Tolstoy,* ed. Malcolm Jones, 149–174. Cambridge: Cambridge University Press, 1978.

Gregg, Richard A. "Balzac and the Women in *The Queen of Spades.*" *Slavic and East European Journal* 10, no. 3 (1966): 279–82.

Grossman, Leonid. *Balzac and Dostoevsky*. Translated by Lena Karpov. Ann Arbor, MI: Ardis, 1973.

———. *Dostoevskii, Zhizn' zamechatel'nykh liudei*. Moscow: Molodaia gvardiia, 1962.

———. *Seminarii po Dostoevskomu: materialy, bibliografiia, komentarii*. Moscow: Gosudarstvennoe izdatel'stvo, 1922.

———. *Sobranie sochinenii*. 5 vols. Moscow: Sorremennye problemy, 1928.

Gudzii, N. K. "Istoriia pisaniia i pechataniia *Anny Kareninoi*." In L. N. Tolstoi, *Polnoe sobranie sochinenii*, 577–643. 90 vols. Moscow: Khudozhestvennaia literatura, 1928–1964.

Gukovskii, G. A., ed. *Zhizn' i pokhozhdeniia Tikhona Trosnikova*. Moscow: Gosudarstvennoe izdatel'stvo khudozhestvennoi literatury, 1931.

Gusev, N. N. Commentary to *Soedinenie i perevod chetyrekh Evangelii*. In L. N. Tolstoi, *Pss*, 24:973–1000.

———. *L. N. Tolstoi: materialy k biografii s 1870 po 1881 god*. Moscow: Akademiia nauk SSSR, 1979.

———. *Letopis' zhizni i tvorchestva L. N. Tolstogo*. Moscow: Akademiia nauk SSSR, 1936.

Gustafson, Richard. *Leo Tolstoy, Resident and Stranger: A Study in Fiction and Theology*. Princeton, NJ: Princeton University Press, 1986.

Hackel, Sergei. "The Religious Dimension: Vision or Evasion? Zosima's Discourse in *The Brothers Karamazov*." In *New Essays on Dostoevsky*, ed. Malcolm V. Jones and Garth M. Terry. Cambridge: Cambridge University Press, 1983.

Harelle, Madame Aimée. "Inondation à Nantes." *Revue étrangère* 1 (1832): 24–41.

Harkins, William. Afterword. In Lermontov's *A Hero of Our Time*, translated by Philip Longworth, 193–206. London: New English Library, 1975.

———. "The Place of *Domik v Kolomne* in Pushkin's Creation." In *Alexander Pushkin: A Symposium on the 175th Anniversary of his Birth*, ed. Andrej Kodjak and Kiril Taranovsky, 196–205. New York: New York University Press, 1976.

Hartman, Geoffrey. "Romanticism and Anti-Self-Consciousness." In *Romanticism and Consciousness: Essays in Criticism*, ed. Harold Bloom, 46–56. New York: Norton, 1970.

Hastings, Adrian. *The Construction of Nationhood: Ethnicity, Religion, and Nationalism*. Cambridge: Cambridge University Press, 1997.

Hasty, Olga. *Pushkin's Tatiana*. Madison: University of Wisconsin Press, 1999.

Haumant, Emile. *La culture française en Russie (1700–1900)*. Paris: Librairie Hachette et Cie, 1910. Translated by B. V. Zevalina as *Poeziia M. Iu. Lermontova v eia otnoshenii k russkoi i zapadno-evropeiskim literaturam* (Kazan: Izdatel'stvo M.A. Golubeva, 1914).

Helms, Randel. *Gospel Fictions*. Buffalo, NY: Prometheus, 1988.

Hohendahl, Peter Uwe. *Building a National Literature: The Case of Germany, 1830–1870*. Translated by Renate Baron Franciscono. Ithaca, NY: Cornell University Press, 1989.

Holquist, Michael. *Dostoevsky and the Novel*. Princeton, NJ: Princeton University Press, 1977.

Hunt, Joel. "Balzac and Dostoevsky: Ethics and Eschatology." *Slavic and East European Journal* 16 (1958): 307–24.

———. "Color and Imagery in Dostoevskii and Balzac." *Slavic and East European Journal* 10, no. 4 (1966): 411–23.

d'Ideville, Henri. *L'Homme qui tue et l'homme qui pardonne, précédé d'une lettre à M. Alexandre Dumas fils.* Paris: E. Dentu, 1872.

Jackson, Robert Louis. *The Art of Dostoevsky: Deliriums and Nocturnes.* Princeton, NJ: Princeton University Press, 1981.

Jakobson, Roman. *Pushkin and His Sculptural Myth.* The Hague: Mouton, 1975.

Janin, Jules. *La Confession.* Paris: M. Levy, 1861.

———. *L'âne mort et la femme guillotinée.* Paris, Librairie des bibliophiles, 1876. Translated by Terry Hale as *The Dead Donkey and the Guillotined Woman* (Chislehurst, UK: Gothic Society, 1993).

Johae, Antony. "Towards an Iconography of Dostoevsky's *Crime and Punishment.*" In *Dostoevsky and the Christian Tradition,* ed. George Pattison and Diane Oenning Thompson, 173–88. Cambridge: Cambridge University Press, 2001.

Jones, Malcolm V. "The Death and Resurrection of Orthodoxy." In *Cultural Discontinuity and Reconstruction,* ed. Jostein Børtnes and Ingunn Lunde, 143–67. Oslo: Solum Verlag, 1997.

Jones, W. Gareth. "Tolstoi's Alternative Society Tales." In *The Society Tale in Russian Literature,* ed. Neil Cornwell, 99–113. Amsterdam: Rodopi, 1998.

Kahn, Andrew. *Pushkin's* "The Bronze Horseman." London: Bristol Classical Press, 1998.

Karamzin, Nikolai. *Letters of a Russian Traveler.* Edited by Andrew Kahn. Oxford: Voltaire Foundation, 2003.

Karpovich, Michael. "Pushkin as an Historian." In *Centennial Essays for Pushkin,* ed. S. H. Cross and E. J. Simmons, 181–200. New York: Russell and Russell, 1937.

Kasatkina, Tat'iana. "Voskreshenie Lazaria: Opyt ekzegeticheskogo prochteniia romana Dostoevskogo 'Prestuplenie i nakazanie'." *Voprosy literatury* 1 (January–February 2003): 176–208.

Kiiko, E. I. "Geroi nashego vremeni i psikhologicheskaia traditsiia vo frantsuzskoi literature." In *Lermontovskii sbornik,* ed. I. S. Chistova, 181–93. Leningrad, Akademiia Nauk SSSR, 1985.

Kirillova, Irina. "Dostoevsky's Markings in the Gospel According to St John." In *Dostoevsky and the Christian Tradition,* ed. George Pattison and Diane Oenning Thompson, 41–50. Cambridge: Cambridge University Press, 2001.

Kirpotin, V. Ia. *Razocharovanie i krushenie Rodiona Raskol'nikova.* Moscow: Sovetskii pisatel', 1972.

Kjetsaa, Geir. *Dostoevsky and His New Testament.* Oslo: Solum Verlag, 1984.

Knapp, Lisa. "'Tue-la! Tue-le!': Death Sentences, Words and Inner Monologue in Tolstoy's *Anna Karenina* and 'Three More Deaths.'" *Tolstoy Studies Journal* 9 (1999): 1–19.

Knapp, Shoshanna M. "The Dynamics of the Idea of Napoleon in *Crime and Punishment.*" In *Dostoevsky and the Human Condition after a Century,* ed. Alexej Ugrinsky et al., 31–40. Westport, CT: Greenwood, 1986.

Kujundzic, Dragan. "Pardoning Woman in *Anna Karenina.*" *Tolstoy Studies Journal* 6 (1993): 65–85.

Kuleshov, V. I. *Zhizn' i tvorchestvo A.S. Pushkina.* Moscow: Khudozhestvennaia literatura, 1987.

Lapshin, I. *Estetika Dostoevskogo.* Berlin: Obelisk, 1923.

Layton, Susan. *Russian Literature and Empire: Conquest of the Caucasus from Pushkin to Tolstoi.* Cambridge: Cambridge University Press, 1995.

Lednicki, Waclaw. *Pushkin's "Bronze Horseman."* Westport, CT: Greenwood, 1978.

Lermontov, Mikhail. *A Hero of Our Time.* Translated by Vladimir Nabokov, in collaboration with Dmitri Nabokov. Ann Arbor, MI: Ardis, 1958.

———. *A Hero of Our Time.* Translated by Neil Cornwell. New York: Everyman, 1995.

———. "Maksim Maksimych." *Otechestvennye zapiski,* section 3, 167–212.

———. *Polnoe sobranie sochinenii v 4kh tomakh.* Moskva: Gosudarstvennoe izdatel'stvo khudozhestvennoi literatury, 1948.

Levin, Vladimir. "Dostoevskii, 'podpolnyi paradoksalist' i Lermontov." *Izvestiia akademii nauk SSSR, Seriia literatury i iazyka,* 31, no. 2 (1972): 142–56.

Lichtlé, Michel. "Balzac et la *Revue étrangère.*" In *Balzac dans l'empire Russe,* ed. Roger Pierrot, 52–71. Paris: Musées, 1993.

Lindenmeyr, Adele. "Raskolnikov's City and the Napoleonic Plan." In *Dostoevsky: New Perspectives,* ed. Robert Louis Jackson, 99–110. Englewood Cliffs, NJ: Prentice-Hall, 1984.

Lønnqvist, Barbara. "*Anna Karenina.*" In *Cambridge Companion to Tolstoy,* ed. Donna Tussing Orwin, 80–95. Cambridge: Cambridge University Press, 2002.

———. "Simvolika zheleza v romane *Anna Karenina.*" In *Celebrating Creativity: Essays in Honor of Jostein Børtnes,* ed. Knut Grimstad and Ingunn Lunde, 97–107. Bergen: University of Bergen, 1977.

Lottman, Herbert. *Flaubert: A Biography.* London: Methuen, 1989.

Lotman, Iurii M. *Izbrannye stat'i.* 3 vols. Tallinn: Alexandra, 1992.

Makashin, S. A. "Literaturnye vzaimootnosheniia Rossii i Frantsii XVIII–XIX vv." In his *Russkaia kul'tura i Frantsiia: sbornik,* v–lxxvii. Literaturnoe nasledstvo 29–30. Moscow: Akademiia nauk SSSR, 1937.

Markovitch, Milan. *Jean-Jacques Rousseau et Tolstoi.* Paris: Librairie ancienne Honoré Campion, 1928.

Matual, David. "In Defense of the Epilogue of *Crime and Punishment.*" *Studies in the Novel* 24, no. 1 (Spring 1992): 26–34.

McLean, Hugh. "Rousseau's God and Tolstoy's." *Tolstoy Studies Journal* 9 (1997): 25–35.

———. "Tolstoy and Jesus." In *Christianity and the Eastern Slavs,* ed. Robert Hughes and Irina Paperno, 2:103–23. 3 vols. Berkeley: University of California Press, 1994.

Meilakh, B. S. "Pushkin i dekabristy posle 1825 goda." In *Pushkin: issledovaniia i materialy,* ed. M. P. Alekseev et al., 2:196–213. 15 vols. Moscow: Akademiia nauk SSSR, 1956–95.

Merejkowsky, Dmitri. *Tolstoi as Man and Artist.* London: Archibald Constable, 1902.

Mersereau, John Jr. *Mikhail Lermontov.* Carbondale: Southern Illinois University Press, 1962.

Meyer, Priscilla. "Gogol and Hoffmann: The Art of Recombination." In *Cold Fusion: Aspects of the German Cultural Presence in Russia,* ed. Gene Barabtarlo, 62–73. New York: Berghahn, 2000.

———. "Iz 'Zolotogo gorshka' Gofmanna: 'Shinel'' Gogolia." In *Gogol' kak iavlenie mirovoi literatury,* ed. Natalia Vinogradskaia, 336–44. Moscow: Institute of World Literature, Academy of Sciences, 2005.

Mikhailova, E. N. *Proza Lermontova.* Moscow: Gosudarstvennoe izdatel'stvo khudozhestvennoi literatury, 1957.

Milchina, Vera. "Frantsuzskaia literatura v proizvedeniiakh Pushkina 1830-x godov." *Izvestiia akademii nauk SSSR: seriia literatury i iazyka,* 65, no. 3 (1987): 244–54.

Milivojevic, Dragan. *Leo Tolstoy.* Boulder, CO: East European Monographs, 1998.

Miller, Robin Feuer. *The Brothers Karamazov: Worlds of the Novel.* New York: Twayne, 1992.

Millet-Gerard, Dominique. "Dandys et coquettes de Balzac à Lermontov." *L'Année Balzacienne* (1993): 41–63.

Mirecourt, Eugène de. *Jules Janin.* Vol. 24 of *Histoire Contemporaine: Portraits et silhouettes au XIXe siècle.* Paris: Librairie des contemporains, 1867.

Mirsky, D. S. *Pushkin.* New York: Dutton, 1963.

Mochulsky, Konstantin. *Dostoevsky: His Life and Work.* Translated by Michael Minihan. Princeton, NJ: Princeton University Press, 1967.

Modzalevskii, B. L. *Biblioteka A. S. Pushkina: bibliograficheskoe opisanie.* Moscow: Kniga, 1988.

Montifaud, Marc de. *Les Romantiques.* Paris: A. Reiff, 1878.

Morson, Gary Saul. "Prosaics and *Anna Karenina.*" *Tolstoy Studies Journal* 1 (1988): 1–12.

———. "Tolstoy's Absolute Language." In his *Bakhtin: Essays and Dialogues on his Work,* 123–43. Chicago: University of Chicago Press, 1986.

———. "Work and the Authentic Life in Tolstoy." *Tolstoy Studies Journal* 9 (1997): 36–48.

Motte-Fouqué, Friedrich de la. "Undine." In *Romantic Fairy Tales,* ed. and trans. by Caroly Tully, 55–125. New York: Penguin, 2000.

Murav, Harriet. *Holy Foolishness: Dostoevsky's Novels and the Poetics of Cultural Critique.* Stanford: Stanford University Press, 1992.

Musset, Alfred de. *La Confession d'un enfant du siècle.* Paris: Garnier frères, 1947.

Nabokov, Vladimir. *Nikolai Gogol.* New York: New Directions, 1961.

———. "Translator's Foreword." In Lermontov's *A Hero of Our Time,* trans. Vladimir Nabokov, in collaboration with Dmitri Nabokov, v–xix. Ann Arbor, MI: Ardis, 1988.

Natov, Nadine. "The Ethical and Structural Significance of the Three Temptations in *The Brothers Karamazov.*" *Dostoevsky Studies* 8 (1987): 3–44.

Nepomnyashchy, Catharine Theimer. "The Poet, History and the Supernatural: A Note on Pushkin's 'The Poet' and 'The Bronze Horseman.'" In *The Supernatural in Slavic and Baltic Literature: Essays in Honor of Victor Terras,* ed. Amy Mandelker and Roberta Reeder, 34–46. Columbus, OH: Slavica, 1988.

The New Oxford Annotated Bible. Edited by Herbert G. May and Bruce M. Metzger. New York: Oxford University Press, 1973.

Nilsson, Nils Åke. *Gogol et Pétersbourg: recherches sur les antécédents des contes pétersbourgeois.* Stockholm: Almqvist and Wiskell, 1954.

———. "On the Origins of Gogol's 'Overcoat.'" In *Gogol's "Overcoat": An Anthology of Critical Essays,* ed. Elizabeth Trahan, 61–72. Ann Arbor, MI: Ardis, 1982.

Perlina, Nina. *Varieties of Poetic Utterance: Quotation in* The Brothers Karamazov. Lanham, MD: University Press of America, 1985.

Pichot, Amédée. *Pocahontas, Histoire anglo-américaine du temps du Jacques premier. Revue de Paris* 42 (1832): 211–29; 43 (1832): 321–38.

Pickup, Ian. "Elements of Balzacian Portraiture in the Novels of Eugène Sue before *Les mystères de Paris.*" *Nottingham French Studies* 26, no. 2 (1987): 34–45.

Piedagnel, Alexandre. *Jules Janin.* Paris: Librairie de bibliophiles, 1874.

Plavil'shchikov, P. A. "Teatr." In *Khrestomatiia po russkoi literature XVIII veka,* comp. A. V. Kokorev. Moscow: Gosudarstvennoe uchebno-pedagogicheskoe izdatel'stvo, 1952.

Polonsky, Rachel. *English Literature and the Russian Aesthetic Renaissance.* Cambridge: Cambridge University Press, 1998.

Powelstock, David. *Becoming Mikhail Lermontov: The Ironies of Romantic Individualism in Russia.* Evanston, IL: Northwestern University Press, 2005.

Price, Roger. *A Social History of Nineteenth-Century France.* New York: Holmes and Meier, 1987.

Pushkin, Alexander Sergeevich. *Eugene Onegin.* Translated by Vladimir Nabokov. 4 vols. New York: Random House, 1964.

———. *The Complete Prose Tales.* Edited by Gillon R. Aitken. New York: W. W. Norton, 1966.

Rayfield, Donald. "Dumas and Dostoevsky: Deflowering the Camellia." In *From Pushkin to Palisandriia,* ed. Arnold McMillin, 70–82. London: MacMillan, 1990.

Reid, Robert. "The Society Tale Goes to the Caucasus." In *The Society Tale in Russian Literature,* ed. Neil Cornwell, 41–57. Amsterdam: Rodopi, 1998.

Reizov, V. G. "K istorii romanticheskogo urbanizma: 'Ispoved' Zhiulia Zhanena i 'Otets Gorio' Bal'zaka." In *Iz istorii russkikh literaturnykh otnoshenii XVII–XX vekov,* ed. S. V. Katorskii, 132–40. Moscow: Akademiia nauk SSSR, 1959.

———. *Bal'zak: sbornik statei.* Leningrad: Izdatel'stvo Leningradskogo universiteta, 1960.

Riffaterre, Michael. "Flaubert's Presuppositions." *Diacritics* 11, no. 4 (Winter 1981): 2–11.

———. *Semiotics of Poetry.* Bloomington: Indiana University Press, 1978.

———. "Syllepsis." *Critical Enquiry* 6 (1980): 625–38.

Robert, Paul. *Le Nouveau petit Robert.* Paris: Dictionnaires Le Robert, 1995.

Rodzevich, S. I. *Lermontov kak romanist.* Kiev: N. Ia. Ogloblin, 1914.

Rogger, Hans. *National Consciousness in Eighteenth-Century Russia.* Cambridge, MA: Harvard University Press, 1960.

Ronen, Omry. *An Approach to Mandel'shtam.* Jerusalem: Magnes, 1983.

Rosenshield, Gary. *Crime and Punishment: The Techniques of the Omniscient Narrator.* Lisse, UK: Peter de Ridder Press, 1978.

———. "Western Law vs. Russian Justice: Dostoevsky and the Jury Trial, Round One: The Kroneberg Trial." *Graven Images* 1 (1994): 117–35.

Rousseau, Jean-Jacques. *Emile*. New York: Dutton, 1974.
———. *Emile et Sophie: les solitaires*. In *Oeuvres Complètes*, ed. V. D. Musset-Pathay, 3:287–356. 18 vols. Paris: P. Dupont, 1828.
Rozenblium, L. M. "Tvorcheskaia laboratoriia Dostoevskogo-romanista." *Literaturnoe nasledstvo* 77 (1965): 7–56.
Rushdy, Ashraf H. A. *Neo-Slave Narratives: Studies in the Social Logic of a Literary Form*. New York: Oxford University Press, 1999.
Said, Edward. *Orientalism*. New York: Vintage, 1978.
Sainte-Beuve, Charles-Augustin. *Avant-propos, Atala et René*. Paris: Michel Levy, 1865.
Sand, George. "L'Orco." *Revue des deux mondes* 13 (1838): 584–99. Translated as "The Orco; A Venetian Tradition," in *The Mosaic Workers: A Tale of Venice*, 193–216 (Philadelphia: E. Ferrett, 1845).
Schelling, Friedrich. *System of Transcendental Idealism*. Translated by Peter Heath. Charlottesville: University Press of Virginia, 1978.
Scotto, Peter. "Prisoners of the Caucasus: Ideologies of Imperialism in Lermontov's 'Bela'." *PMLA* 107, no. 2 (March 1992): 246–60.
Schmidt, Wolf. "Psikhologiia *Geroia nashego vremeni*." *Russian Literature* 31, no. 5 (May 1992): 59–74.
Schulze, Sydney. *The Structure of Anna Karenina*. Ann Arbor, MI: Ardis, 1982.
Serman, I. Z. "Nekrasov i Viktor Giugo." *Russko-evropeiskie literaturnye sviazi*. Moscow: Akademiia nauk SSSR, 1966.
Seton-Watson, Hugh. *Nations and States: An Enquiry into the Origins of Nations and the Politics of Nationalism*. Boulder, CO: Westview Press, 1977.
Shcherbatov, M. M. *Neizdannye sochineniia*. Edited by P. Liubomirov. Moscow: SOTSEKGIZ, 1935.
Shishkov, A. S. *Rassuzhdenie o starom i novom sloge rosssiiskogo iazyka*. St. Petersburg: Plavil'shchikov, 1803.
Sicher, Ephraim. "The Boundaries of Space in the Modern Literary Text: Balzac, Dostoevsky, Dickens." *Proceedings of the 12th Congress of the International Comparative Literature Association* 12, no. 3 (1990): 306–9.
Smith, Morton. *Jesus the Magician*. San Francisco: Harper and Row, 1978.
Stead, Philip John. *Vidocq, Picaroon of Crime*. New York: Roy, 1954.
Steegmuller, Frances. *Flaubert and Madame Bovary: A Double Portrait*. London: Collins, 1947.
Steiner, George. *Tolstoy or Dostoevsky: An Essay in the Old Criticism*. London: Faber and Faber, 1959.
Stenbock-Fermor, Elisabeth. *The Architecture of Anna Karenina*. Lisse, UK: Peter de Ridder Press, 1975.
Stites, Richard. "Prostitution and Society in Pre-revolutionary Russia." *Jahrbucher für Geschichte Osteuropas* 31 (1983): 348–64.
Strada, Vittorio. "Problemy sekuliarizatsii v russkoi literature i kul'ture XIX veka." In *Russkaia literatura XIX veka i khristianstvo*, ed. V. I. Kuleshov, 298–303. Moscow: Moscow University Press, 1997.
Stroganova, E.N. "Otgoloski dekabristskoi temy v primechaniiakh k poeme *Mednyi vsadnik*." In *Pushkin: problemy poetiki*, ed. Iu. M. Nikisov, 110–18. Tver': Tverskoi gosudarstvennyi universitet, 1992.

Sue, Eugène. *The Mysteries of Paris.* [no translator given.] New York: Dedalus/ Hippocrene, n.d.

Tanner, Tony. *Adultery in the Novel.* Baltimore, MD: Johns Hopkins University Press, 1979.

Taranovsky, Kiril. "Concert at the Railroad Station." In his *Essays on Mandel'shtam,* 1–20. Cambridge, MA: Harvard University Press, 1976.

Taylor, F. A. *The Theatre of Alexandre Dumas fils.* Oxford: Oxford University Press, 1937.

Terras, Victor. *Reading Dostoevsky.* Madison: University of Wisconsin Press, 1998.

Thompson, Diane Oenning. "Problems of the Biblical Word in Dostoevsky's Poetics." In *Dostoevsky and the Christian Tradition,* ed. George Pattison and Diane Oenning Thompson, 69–99. Cambridge: Cambridge University Press, 2001.

Tiberge, Abbé (pseudonym of Regnier-Destourbet). *Louisa, ou les douleurs d'une fille de joie.* 1830. Reprint, Paris: Librairie centrale, 1865.

Todd, William Mills, III. *Fiction and Society in the Age of Pushkin.* Cambridge, MA: Harvard University Press, 1986.

Tolstoi, Lev. *Polnoe sobranie sochinenii.* 90 vols. Moscow: Khudozhestvennaia literatura, 1928–1964.

Tolstoy, Leo. *Anna Karenina.* Translated by Louise Maude and Aylmer Maude. 2 vols. London: Oxford University Press, 1939.

———. *Anna Karenina.* Edited by V. Zhdanov and E. Zaidenshnur. Moscow: Nauka, 1970.

———. *Anna Karenina.* Translated by Louise Maude and Aylmer Maude and edited by George Gibian. New York: Norton, 1970.

———. *Anna Karenina.* Translated by Rosemary Edmonds. Harmondsworth, UK: Penguin, 1971.

Tolstoy, Sergei. *Tolstoy Remembered, by his Son.* Translated by Moura Budberg. London: Weidenfeld and Nicolson, 1949.

Tomashevskii, B. "Proza Lermontova i zapadno-evropeiskaia traditsiia." *Literaturnoe nasledstvo* 43–44 (1941): 469–517.

———. "Pushkin i frantsuzskaia literatura." *Literaturnoe nasledstvo* 31–32 (1937–39): 1–76.

———. "Frantsuzskaia literatura v pis'makh Pushkina k E. M. Khitrovo." In his *Pushkin i Frantsiia,* 65–174. Leningrad: Sovetskii pisatel', 1960.

Toporov, V. N. "O Strukture romana Dostoevskogo v sviazi s arkhaichnymi skhemami mifologicheskogo myshleniia." In *Structure of Texts and Semiotics of Culture,* ed. Jan van der Eng, 225–302. The Hague: Mouton, 1973.

Tseidler, M. Untitled. *Russkii vestnik* 9 (1888): 135–36.

Turbin, V. *Pushkin, Lermontov, Gogol': ob izuchenii literaturnykh zhanrov.* Moscow: Prosveshchenie, 1978.

Tynianov, Iurii. "Arkhaisty i Pushkin." In his *Arkhaisty i novatory,* 87–227. Munich: Fink Verlag, 1967.

———. "Dostoevsky and Gogol (Towards a Theory of Parody)." In *Dostoevsky and Gogol: Texts and Criticism,* ed. Priscilla Meyer and Stephen Rudy, 101–17. Ann Arbor, MI: Ardis, 1979.

Ulbach, Louis ["Ferragus"]. "La littèrature putride." *Le Figaro,* 23 January 1868.
Vernadsky, George. "Pushkin and the Decembrists." In *Centennial Essays for Pushkin,* ed. Samuel H. Cross and Ernest J. Simmons, 45–76. New York: Russell and Russell, 1937.
Vigny, Alfred de. *Servitude and Grandeur of Arms.* Translated by Roger Gard. Harmondsworth: Penguin, 1996.
Vinogradov, V. V. *Evoliutsiia russkogo naturalizma.* Leningrad: Academia, 1929.
———. "Stil' prozy Lermontova." *Literaturnoe nasledstvo* 43–44 (1941): 517–628.
Wachtel, Andrew. "Death and Resurrection in *Anna Karenina.*" In *In the Shade of the Giant,* ed. Hugh McLean, 100–114. Berkeley: University of California Press, 1989.
Walker, Janet A. "The Cramped Room in the City: A Setting for the Nineteenth-Century Individualist." *Proceedings of the 12th Congress of the International Comparative Literature Association* 12, no. 3 (1990): 288–93.
Wellek, René. "Bakhtin's View of Dostoevsky: 'Polyphony' and 'Carnivalesque.'" In *Russian Formalism: A Retrospective Glance,* ed. Robert Louis Jackson and Stephen Rudy, 231–41. Columbus, OH: Slavica, 1985.
Woronzoff, Alexander. "The Pattern of Discovery in Lermontov's *A Hero of Our Time* and Vigny's *Servitude et grandeur militaires.*" *Zapiski russkoi akademicheskoi gruppy v S. Sh. A / Transactions of the Association of Russian-American Slavists* 23 (1990): 51–61.
Zhekulin, Gleb. "On Rereading the *Bronze Horseman.*" *Canadian Slavonic Papers* 29 (1987): 228–40.
Zhukovsky, V. A. *Sobranie sochinenii v chetyrekh tomakh.* Moscow: Gosudarstvennoe izdatel'stvo khudozhestvennoi literatury, 1959.
Zola, Emile. *Correspondance.* Edited by B. H. Bakker. 10 vols. Montreal: Les Presses de l'Université; Paris: Editions du CNRS, 1978–95.
———. *Oeuvres complètes.* Edited by Maurice le Blond. 53 vols. Paris: F. Bernouard, 1928.
Zurov, Leonid F. "'Taman' Lermontova i 'L'Orco' Zhorzh Sand." *Novyi zhurnal* 66 (1961): 278–81.

Index

Note: Italicized page numbers indicate illustrations.